VOCATIC

A

BUSINESS OPTIONS

J Evans-Pritchard
B Jewell
E Z Mayer

Edinburgh Gate
Harlow, Essex

Pearson Education Limited
Edinburgh Gate
Harlow
Essex
CM20 2JE
England

First published 2002
Second impression 2003
ISBN 0 582 453089

Illustrated by Oxford Designers and Illustrators

Printed in China
SWTC/02

The publishers' policy is to use paper manufactured from sustainable forests.

CONTENTS

UNIT 1

Marketing and Promotional Strategy

CHAPTER 1

Looking at Marketing

KEY TERMS

Advertising
Marketing
Marketing mix
Personal selling
Product life cycle
Promotion
Promotional mix
Sales promotion
Segmentation
Targeting

In this chapter, you will review the basic concepts of marketing. You will then learn about the promotional mix which can be seen as a subset of the better known term 'marketing mix'.

What is marketing?

The AVCE unit in Marketing and Promotional Strategy builds on knowledge already gained in the compulsory unit on marketing. Before looking at this unit in detail, it is necessary to review our understanding of '**marketing**'.

Marketing
'The management process responsible for identifying, anticipating and satisfying customer requirements profitably.'
The Chartered Institute of Marketing (CIM)

This much quoted definition emphasises that the marketing function includes:

- market research to identify customer needs
- forecasting to identify future needs
- product development to provide customers with the goods and services required
- distribution of goods to locations convenient to customers.

It should also be understood that the marketing function includes the need for **promotion**, to let customers know what is on offer.

Promotion covers all forms of communication with customers.

Before leaving the CIM definition of marketing, the inclusion of the word 'profitably' reminds us that the reason business organisations strive to satisfy customers is that this enables each organisation to achieve its own profit (or other) objectives.

Marketing mix

From your study of the compulsory unit, you will remember that one key idea in marketing is the '**marketing mix**'.

Marketing mix – the many variables that can be adjusted and blended to achieve the organisation's marketing objectives

This mix is often remembered as the **4Ps** (**product**, **price**, **place** and **promotion** as shown in Figure 1.1.1), although the elements of the mix can be subdivided and/or added to. For instance, **packaging** can be seen as a '**fifth P**' or, alternatively, can be included as part of promotion. If the business is failing to achieve its objectives, one or more of the elements of the mix need to be adjusted. For instance, product redesign can be used to revive a mature product. A change in pricing strategy might also achieve the same result. Alternatively, the organisation might prefer to change its method of distribution, e.g. from traditional stores to on-line sales.

One other point to remember is that the mixture will vary, both from product to product and over the product life cycle.

Figure 1.1.1 The 4 Ps of the marketing mix

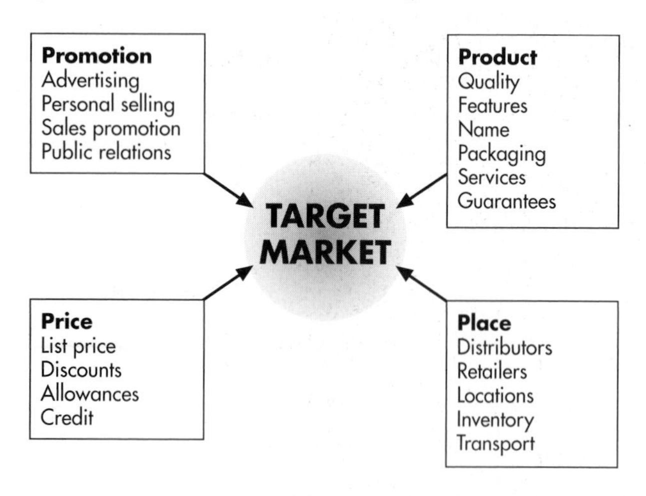

Product life cycle

The **product life cycle** (Figure 1.1.2) refers to the stages through which a typical product passes, from the **pre-launch** (or product development) stage to eventual decline and elimination. The intermediate stages are **launch** (introduction to the market), **growth** (the period of rapidly rising sales), **maturity** (slow growth of sales) and **saturation** (zero growth in sales).

The exact shape of a product's life cycle graph varies, with some products experiencing a short sales life and others enjoying a long life with no apparent decline. The classic products – e.g. Coca Cola, Kellogg's Corn Flakes – with a very long life have all experienced extensions of their life cycle in which a change in promotional strategy probably played a part. The other key point to remember from the marketing unit is that the nature of the promotion strategy will change as a product moves through its life cycle.

Segmentation

In a **segmentation** strategy, the market is not seen as a uniform whole but is divided into a large number of segments. Each segment contains people with at least one common characteristic and this is reflected in their purchasing behaviour.

Business organisations can pursue one of three strategies in relation to segments:

1. **Ignore the differences**
   Known as an **undifferentiated strategy**, this treats everyone the same, despite obvious differences in attitude and behaviour.
2. **Target a single segment**
   Small firms are advised to focus on a single segment of the market. This is **concentrated marketing.**
3. **Target a number of segments**
   This is only possible for larger firms and involves the construction of distinctive marketing mixes for each of the firm's products. This is **differentiated marketing.**

If a firm chooses a strategy based on **targeting** segments, this will have major implications for its promotional activity.

Targeting – concentrating on one segment of the market

The major methods of segmenting the market are summarised below:

Geographic

- Area of a country
- Predominant make-up of the area, e.g. urban, rural
- Climate, e.g. hot and dry, hot and wet, mild, cold, etc.

Demographic

- Age, e.g. under 15, 15–24, etc.
- Gender
- Family size
- Income, e.g. under £6000, £6000–10,000, etc.
- Occupation, e.g. skilled workers, executives, retired people, etc.
- Education, e.g. secondary school, sixth-form college, FE college, college of HE, university
- Religion, e.g. Muslin, Hindu, Christian, etc.
- Race, e.g. Afro-Caribbean, Asian, European, etc.
- Nationality

Figure 1.1.2 Product life cycle

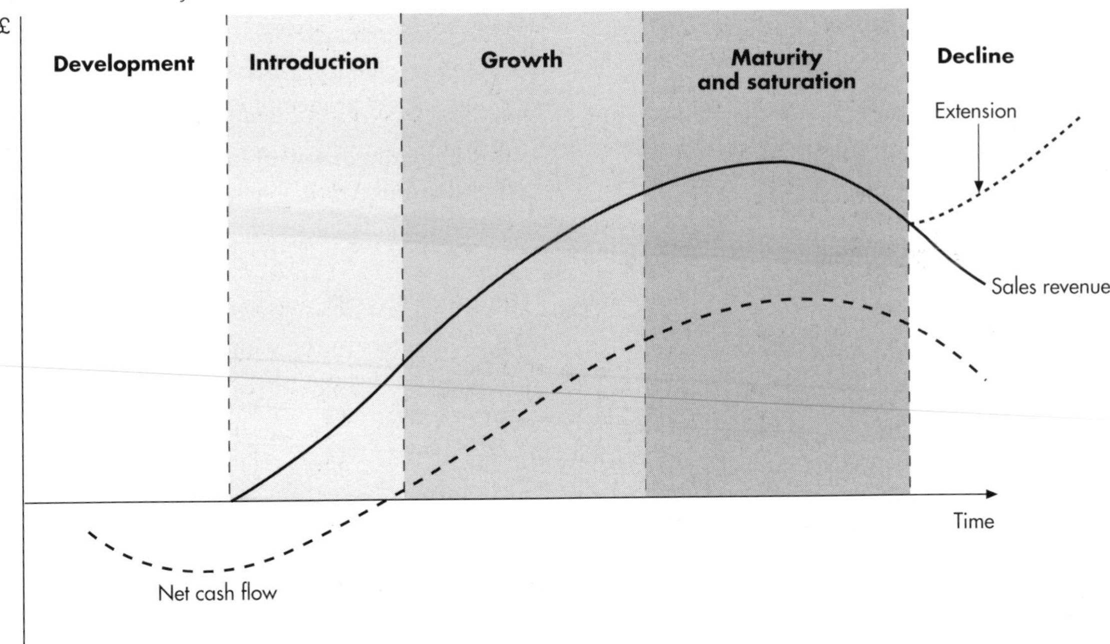

Psychographic

- Social class, e.g. A, B, C1, C2, D, E
- Lifestyle, e.g. outdoor type, party-goer, etc.
- Personality, e.g. ambitious, retiring, etc.

Behavioural

- Occasions, e.g. regular or special purchase
- Benefits sought, e.g. quality, service, economy, etc.
- User status, e.g. non-user, ex-user, potential user, first timer, regular
- Usage rate, e.g. light, medium, heavy, etc.
- Loyalty status, e.g. none, medium, strong
- Readiness stage, e.g. unaware, aware, informed
- Attitude toward product, e.g. hostile, negative, indifferent, positive, enthusiastic.

The promotional mix

Promotional mix – the mixture of promotional activities selected for use by a company at any one time

The promotional mix is a subset of the marketing mix and, like the latter concept, it will vary from product to product and over the life cycle of the product. At the end of this unit, we will look in detail at factors affecting the choice of promotional activities but, before we do this, we should be clear about the meaning of each term.

Personal selling

Personal selling – the process of making an oral presentation and engaging in two-way persuasive communication to advance a sale

The distinctive feature of personal selling is that it offers two-way (usually face-to-face) communication with prospective customers, which makes it a very powerful instrument. Personal selling involving two-way communication is a feature of industrial (business-to-business) marketing and can often be found in the marketing of complex, expensive consumer items. It should be clear from the definition that retail selling of low value goods does not constitute personal selling. The unit specification excludes personal selling and so we will focus on other forms of promotion.

Advertising (see Chapter 3)

Advertising is a paid form of non-personal presentation by an identified sponsor, transmitted to a target audience through a mass medium.

The advertising message is carried by one or more of the media: newspapers, magazines, TV, radio, the internet, cinema, public transport and outdoor posters.

Traditionally, personal selling and advertising have been seen as the key promotional activities, with the others being accorded a supportive role. However, just as in other aspects of business, promotion is subject to rapid change, with new forms of promotional activity playing an increasingly more prominent role.

Sales promotion (see Chapter 4)

Sales promotion involves the use of short-term incentives used to increase sales.

Typical **sales promotion** tactics include coupons, competitions, gifts, price discounts and 'two for the price of one' offers.

Merchandising

Merchandising refers to attempts to influence customers at the point of sale, e.g. through shop layout and posters.

Public relations (PR)

PR seeks to manage relations with different 'publics': consumers, creditors, investors, suppliers, pressure groups, society and employees.

PR is not a direct way of increasing sales and produces a somewhat unquantifiable benefit which can only be assessed in the long run.

Branding

Branding refers to the name or design which identifies a product and distinguishes it from the products of rival firms.

Packaging

Packaging plays a key role in promoting both the product and the organisation. The organisation will seek to develop a favourable image for the brand and to make it distinctive from the rival brands.

Having reviewed marketing, we now need to look at communication theory to understand the process involved.

Revision Questions

1 Explain the difference between marketing and selling. (1 mark)

2 What do you understand by a market-orientated firm? (1 mark)

3 Suggest appropriate:

a) corporate

b) marketing objectives for a large private sector business. (2 marks)

4 Comment on the value of the product life cycle. (1 mark)

5 Suggest five products which seem to have defied the decline phase of the life cycle. (5 marks)

6 Using real-life examples, explain different strategies designed to extend the product life cycle. (2 marks)

7 At what stages in the life cycle is promotion likely to focus on:

a) information?

b) persuasion?

Explain your answer. (2 marks)

8 Explain the terms:

a) marketing mix

b) promotional mix. (2 marks)

9 What is the distinctive feature of advertising as a promotional weapon? (1 mark)

10 Contrast personal selling with supermarket selling. (2 marks)

11 Suggest five types of sales promotion (5 marks)

12 What is the difference between advertising and publicity? (2 marks)

CHAPTER 2

Marketing Communications

KEY TERMS

AIDA
ATR
Communications
DAGMAR
Decode
Encode
Exchange
Feedback
Noise
Product adoption

In this chapter, you will be introduced to the theory of communication. Advertising and other forms of promotion are ways in which business organisations seek to communicate with their customers and potential customers. Hence an understanding of the communication process gives you an understanding of what makes for successful communication. You will also learn about AIDA and other models which explain how promotion influences customer behaviour.

What is communication?

The purpose of any communication is to deliver a message from a sender to a receiver. The process is complete and successful when the message is understood by the receiver in the manner intended by the sender. Communication can be delivered in a variety of forms:

- The spoken word
- Non-verbal communications by means of body language
- A letter
- A poster
- A recorded tape
- By telephone
- A broadcasted message
- A symbol
- Computer link

Irrespective of the form in which it is delivered, all communication processes can be analysed in the same way.

Marketing **communication** involves communication between the organisation and its customers or potential customers.

Marketing communication is central to the **exchange process** which forms the basis of a market system.

An **exchange** requires the participation of two or more parties, each of whom offers something of value to the other – the business organisation offers a good or service in return for money.

The role of communication within the exchange process is to:

- **make potential customers aware** of an organisation's offering
  At the same time, the response (or lack of response) from customers makes the organisation aware of the needs and values of customers
- **persuade** current and potential customers of the desirability of entering into an exchange relationship
- **remind** customers of the benefits of past transactions and so convince them that they should enter into a similar, new exchange
- **differentiate** between competing offerings, thus helping consumers to decide which exchanges to make, thereby helping to prevent monopolies from developing and forcing prices down, encouraging lower prices.

Communication theory

Communication is the process of establishing a commonness or 'oneness' of thought between a sender and a receiver (Figure 1.2.1). The sender will transmit a communication which is received and interpreted by the receiver. Only when there is shared meaning can we say that communication has been successful.

The sender will **encode** the message in words, pictures, symbols, numbers or sounds. Remember that not all communication uses words but, whatever the method of encoding the message, it is essential that it is understood by the receiver in the manner intended.

Encode – a message will be transmitted by the use of pictures, sounds, words or symbols which can be decoded by the receiver to make sense

The message is then transmitted by a communication channel: printed paper, telephone, radio, television or computer link. The transmitted message is received and **decoded** (or interpreted). However, accurate decoding depends entirely on the receiver's perceptions and is therefore affected by such factors as personality, mood, how the receiver feels about the sender of the message, and their own wants and needs.

Feedback

Personal selling provides scope for **feedback** in which the receiver can ask questions, seek clarification, ask for variation or put forward his or her view. Where feedback is provided, communication becomes a two-way process. Many promotional techniques do not provide feedback facilities.

Feedback – response from someone who has received a message

Advertising is a purely one-way form of communications, with no direct feedback. The absence of feedback increases the need for advertising to be combined with other activities in the communication or promotional mix.

Noise

Noise – any factor that interferes with any aspect of the communication process between sender and receiver

Noise includes:

- extraneous real noise
- channel hopping
- misunderstanding
- the clutter of advertising messages
- breakdown in the chosen media
- outside distraction.

All these factors (and many more) will prevent the promotional message being understood in the way

Figure 1.2.1 A model of communication

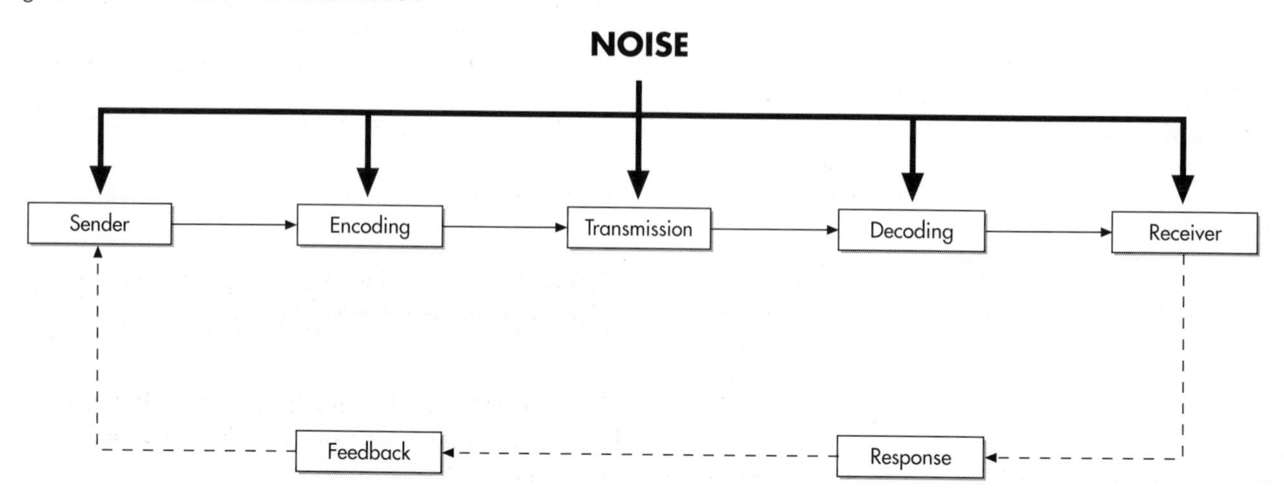

intended. This reminds us that an advertisement should not be judged in terms of its artistic merit, but in terms of its effectiveness – does it achieve its objectives?

The communication model

The elements of the model can be summarised, as in Table 1.2.1.

Table 1.2.1 The communication model

Element	Comment
Parties	
• Sender	Sends the message to the other party; source; communicator
• Receiver	Receives message; audience; destination
Communication tools	
• Message	Content of communication
• Media	Communication channels
Communication functions	
• Encoding	Meaning is given in symbolic form (words, etc.) by sender
• Decoding	Receiver translates and interprets message
• Response	Receiver reacts to message
• Feedback	Part of receiver's response is communicated back to sender
Problems	
• 'Noise'	Any interference in communication

AIDA

AIDA – Attention, Interest, Desire, Action

AIDA is one way to analyse how advertising and other promotional techniques work. It represents a model of the marketing communication process in which the potential buyer progresses from a state of unawareness of the product to its eventual purchase.

The first letter, A, (**attention**) refers to the cognitive stage of the process. The attention of the potential buyer has to be gained before attempting anything else. The second and third letters, I and D, (**interest** and **desire**) represent the stages in which the communicator seeks to develop a positive attitude towards the product, and later a preference for it. The last letter, A, represents the final or **conative** stage, involving **action** in the form of a purchase.

The AIDA model can be used to analyse the role of marketing communications in moving the potential buyer through the stages towards eventual purchase.

Each element of the communication mix can be employed to move the customer from A to I to D to A. Advertising (e.g. on TV) is especially useful in moving people from a state of unawareness of the product to awareness. This can be followed up with print-based advertising to create interest. Sales promotion, in the form of samples, coupons or discounts, can be used to develop a desire to purchase. The process can be completed by merchandising at the point of sale. This will move the customer to the action stage of buying.

AIDA has been seen as a forceful model of advertising and other promotional techniques. It suggests that promotion is sufficient to increase people's knowledge, to change attitudes and to persuade people who had not previously purchased a product to buy it. AIDA is therefore a **conversion theory** – converting non-buyers into buyers.

ATR

ATR – Awareness, Trial, Reinforcement

An alternative theory builds in **trial** and **reinforcement**. Take the case of inexpensive items, such as a chocolate bar. It is likely that we will all try a new product. The main role of advertising is not to arouse interest but, instead, to reinforce or reassure the customer. Hence, the role of promotion is not to bring in new buyers but to retain existing customers and to increase the frequency with which they continue to buy the brand.

The two contrasting models are shown in Figure 1.2.2.

DAGMAR

DAGMAR – Defining Advertising Goals for Measurable Advertising Results

The DAGMAR model dates back to the 1960s and links the communication process with advertising objectives.

Figure 1.2.2 AIDA and ATR

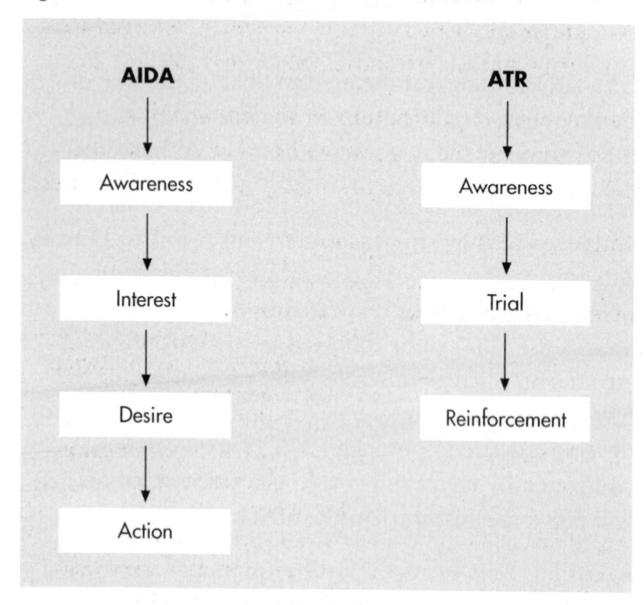

It can be used to measure the effectiveness of advertising (and other promotional activities) in moving the customer through the following stages:

1. **Unawareness** of the product or service
2. **Awareness** of the product
   Awareness implies that the customer has heard of the product but has little inclination to buy it at present.
3. **Comprehension**
   At this point, the potential customer has an understanding of the product.
4. **Conviction**
   At this stage, the potential customer is convinced that the product meets his or her requirement.
5. **Action**
   This takes the form of purchasing the product.

Advertising objectives can be identified in terms of the movement of opinion through the stages of the DAGMAR spectrum. The type of advertising (e.g. informative or persuasive) changes as we move through the spectrum. Moreover, many other promotional techniques can be employed in a supportive role at each of the stages.

A variation of these models is the **Lavidge and Steiner** model. Here the receiver of the promotional message passes through six stages:

1. Awareness
2. Knowledge
3. Liking
4. Preference
5. Conviction
6. Purchase

Product adoption

Product adoption – decision by a significant group of people to buy a new product

The promotion of a revolutionary new product (such as DVD recorders, digital television, etc. in the 1990s) should be targeted at particular groups within the community. **Product adoption** starts with a small group of innovators or trend setters. These people tend to be younger, more affluent and more adventurous than the rest of the community. Once the product has been adopted by the trend setters, the focus can be shifted to other groups in the community.

One analysis of this process is shown by a bell-shaped curve of normal distribution in which the various groups of people are classified as follows:

- **Innovators** or opinion leaders are seen to be important in beginning the process because unless they purchase, the launch will fail. This groups is motivated by status and recognition and must have the very latest in new products. They are willing to purchase if these needs are satisfied.
- **Early adopters** have similar needs to innovators but they are a little more wary. They wait to see if there is an initial take-up by the innovators or opinion leaders they respect and they will not buy products that they feel will have a short life. They will also wait for 'new product bugs' to be ironed out.
- **Early majority:** For a mass market product, purchase by the early majority is crucial as they account for 34 per cent of the population. Only if this group enters the market can economies of scale be gained and prices reduced to bring in the whole of this group as well as enticing the late majority.

The early majority are a little more cautious and will buy when a product is seen to be well established and they are convinced of its quality and value for money.

- **Late majority:** The late majority are conservative. They will reflect and compare the product with similar products offered by competitors and need heavy persuasion to purchase. Price is an important factor for this group. However, once again, it is important to persuade this group to purchase as it accounts for 34 per cent of the population.
- **Laggards:** This group is the last to enter the market and will purchase when the price has reached its lowest point. They look for bargains and 'end-of-product line' discounts. Although accounting for 16 per cent of the target population, this is a relatively unimportant group insofar as its members tend to purchase at rock-bottom prices when the product is in decline.

Leading American marketing expert, Philip Kotler, says that adopters of new products have been observed to move through the five stages shown in Table 1.2.2.

Having reviewed the nature of marketing and the communication process, we will now investigate the techniques employed to promote products and services.

Table 1.2.2 Stages of adoption

Stage of adoption	Comment
1: **Awareness**	The consumer becomes aware of the innovation but lacks information about it.
2: **Interest**	The consumer is stimulated to seek information about the innovation.
3: **Evaluation**	The consumer considers whether to try the innovation.
4: **Trial**	The consumer tries the innovation to improve his or her estimate of its value.
5: **Adoption**	The consumer decides to make full and regular use of the innovation.

Revision Questions

1 Define communication. When is communication said to be effective? (2 marks)

2 Outline the model of communication. (1 mark)

3 Which form or forms of promotion are:

a) one way?

b) two way? (2 marks)

4 What forms does encoding take in the case of advertising? (2 marks)

5 Identify sources of 'noise' which interfere with advertising messages. (1 mark)

6 Explain the AIDA model. (1 mark)

7 With reference to the DAGMAR model, how would you measure the effectiveness of advertising? (1 mark)

8 Why does advertising have to be complemented by other forms of sales promotion? (1 mark)

CHAPTER 3

Advertising

KEY TERMS

Above the line
Advertising agency
Advertising (ASA) code of practice
Below the line
Media
Media selection
Reach

In this chapter, you will learn about advertising which is seen as the form of promotion with the highest profile, although it is a mistake to equate promotion exclusively with advertising. After exploring the meaning of advertising, we will investigate the role of advertising, the different types of media used in advertising and, finally, legal and ethical issues connected with advertising.

What is advertising?

Advertising is a major form of marketing communication which is used not only by commercial profit-seeking organisations, but also by public sector bodies, charities and religious organisations. Historically, advertising (using print and other **media**) played a leading role in terms of communications activity, although that position is now being eroded by the rapid development of other forms of promotion (covered in Chapter 4).

Media – any of the broadcasting or communications outlets, such as print, TV, internet, radio, billboards

Ray Wright lists the characteristics of advertising as follows:

- It is communicating benefit messages to target audiences.
- It is used by profit and non-profit organisations in both private and public sectors.

Advertising is defined by the American Marketing Association as: 'any paid form of non-personal presentation and promotion of ideas, goods or services by an identifiable sponsor'.

The UK *Chartered Institute of Marketing Dictionary* (Norman Hart, Butterworth-Heineman, 1996) defines advertising as the: 'use of paid-for space, in a publication, for instance, or time on television, radio or cinema, usually as a means of persuading people to take a particular course of action, or to reach a point of view. [It] may be taken to include posters and other outdoor advertising.'

- Most advertising is paid for and takes place through TV, print, outdoor, radio, cinema and direct mail channels owned by companies other than the advertisers.
- Although anything can be advertised, most advertising is used for corporate and product brand advertising.
- It is an intricate part of an organisation's promotional mix and complements sales promotion, PR, publicity and personal selling.

Source: Wright, R., *Advertising* (FT Prentice Hall, 2000, P5)

Above and below the line

Advertising can be classified as **above** or **below the line** or even through the line.

Above the line advertising is main media advertising (press, TV, radio, etc.) for which commission is paid to an advertising agency.

Below the line advertising includes all other forms of advertising: direct mail, sponsorship advertising, the internet, merchandising and any other area where advertising can be seen, other than those areas classified as 'above the line'.

A combination of above and below the line is known as '**through the line**', e.g. a promotional give-away linked to a TV advertisement.

The uses of advertising

Advertising can serve a number of uses.

Promotion of products, organisation and causes

Note that advertising can be used to promote causes as well as products. For instance, advertising can be used to promote religion or a social message ('Just say No to drugs'; 'Smoking kills'; 'Eat healthy foods'). It can be used to promote an organisation without making any explicit reference to its products. The aim of institutional or corporate advertising is to:

- increase customer awareness of the organisation
- establish 'credibility and legitimacy in the eyes of the buyer' (Wright, *Advertising*, P15)
- improve or reinforce the organisation's image.

This type of advertising is especially important in the financial service sector where trust and confidence are essential. Organisations selling 'big ticket' (i.e. very expensive) items also need to establish customer confidence if they are to attract people to buy their products. Product advertising promotes a particular product or service.

The stimulation of demand

Advertising of newly launched products conveys information so as to raise customer awareness of the product, stimulate primary demand and gain acceptance of the product. Informative advertising is especially common in the early stages of the product life cycle. People require knowledge about the product before they will buy it.

Offsetting competitors' advertising

Defensive advertising is conducted to offset the impact of competitive advertising. It is used by supermarket chains and other firms operating in a very competitive market.

Persuasion

In a mature market with many competitors, the emphasis shifts from information to persuasion. Here the concern is to create a desire for the brand of a particular firm and to stimulate actual purchase. Competitive advertisements are aimed at persuading people to buy one company's products instead of those of a competing company. In some cases, the aim is **defensive** – that is, to offset the impact of advertising conducted by rival organisations. In other cases, it is **offensive** in terms of creating an 'edge' over rivals.

Other aims of advertising in the mature stage of a product's life cycle are to assist sales personnel, to complement other forms of promotion, to increase product usage (e.g. breakfast cereal as a TV snack in the evening) and to reduce sales fluctuation. For organisations with distinct seasonal fluctuations in sales, it is useful to encourage off-peak purchase.

Reminding people

The aim of reminder advertising is to prevent loss of sales or market share. It is used to let customers know that the brands are still available and to encourage people to try the product again after a long gap in consumption. This was certainly the purpose behind Kellogg's Corn Flake advertisements in which people were offered the product after a prolonged gap. After initial resistance, the characters (played by actors) rediscovered their liking for corn flakes.

Corporate identity and corporate image

Corporate identity is the outward manifestation of the organisation, a visual means of identification.

Source: Blythe, *Marketing Communications*

Corporate identity 'is the "message sources" by which an organisation develops and enhances the way it is perceived by its various publics'.

Source: Hart, *CIM Marketing Dictionary*

Outward manifestations of corporate identity include:

- the housestyle of letterheads
- design of premises
- staff uniforms
- vehicle livery
- packaging
- corporate logo.

An effective logo will aid recognition and recall, thus increasing the possibility of sales.

Promotional techniques can be used to enhance **corporate image** but, obviously, they must be backed up by substance. Hence, if an organisation wishes to project the image of being caring or responsive to customer needs, it is essential that it delivers products and services in this manner. This is the main purpose of the **public relations** activity. In this task, PR can be supported by other promotional weapons but most especially by advertising – not product advertising, but **corporate advertising**, any form of advertising which has as its objective the building up of a company's reputation.

These are the key features of corporate advertising:

- It is intended to build the company's reputation in the long run and not to increase sales in the short run.
- It rarely mentions products, brands, their features or their benefits.
- It does not seek an immediate response from the recipient.
- It is designed to promote a favourable understanding of the company's activities.
- It helps to shape attitudes and behaviour.

The great problem with corporate advertising is that the results are difficult to quantify and therefore expenditure on this type of advertising might be difficult to justify to senior managers.

Eddie Stobart Ltd is one of Britain's leading road hauliers. Its trucks are painted in a distinctive green and so familiar is the Stobart name on Britain's motorways that this firm has its own fan club and store in Carlisle, selling a range of Stobart souvenirs. Another distinctive feature of the Stobart identity is the requirement that its drivers wear green shirts and ties. Drivers who are well turned out and professional in their approach enhance the image of the Stobart name. This takes us into the related concept of corporate image, defined by Hart as 'the image which is conjured up by mention of a company's name. This can be positive or negative, weak or strong …'

Activity

Describe the corporate logo of these organisations:

- McDonald's
- Shell Oil
- The Disney Corporation
- Longman (Pearson Education)
- Granada Television
- Heinz

Activity

1 Over the space of a week, identify ten examples of corporate advertising on television.

2 In each case, justify their inclusion in your list of corporate advertisement.

3 In each case, describe the message contained in the advertisement.

4 Offer suggested objectives for each of the advertisements and analyse why you think the company concerned undertook this activity.

Objectives

The objective of an advertising campaign is to move people through the AIDA spectrum. In the first instance, the objective is to gain customer attention. Thereafter, it is to develop an interest in the product and a desire to purchase. Finally, a campaign seeks to influence customers into action to buy the product. The DAGMAR model involves movement from unawareness to awareness, to comprehension, conviction and action.

Advertising seeks to move people to the next stage. Hence the objectives of an advertising campaign are of crucial importance and the success of the campaign can be evaluated in terms of the objectives.

It should be remembered that DAGMAR stands for **D**efining **A**dvertising **G**oals for **M**easured **A**dvertising **R**esults. We also know that objectives should be SMART – **S**pecific, **M**easurable, **A**greed, **R**ealistic and **T**ime related. In all cases, there should be a reference to time, e.g. by a particular date or during a particular year. The objective should be agreed with relevant personnel, including those in other functional areas of the organisation. An objective is only valid if it is achievable. In most cases, the results can be measured in some way.

Look at Table 1.3.1 which lists the possible objectives of an advertising campaign and consider how the results should be measured and evaluated.

Table 1.3.1 Objectives of an advertising campaign

Objective
To inform potential customers
To create awareness
To create a favourable image
To increase the frequency of use
To increase quantity purchased
To remind customers
To increase market share
To improve relationships with dealers
To stimulate enquiries
To develop a new market segment
To persuade or convince people
To increase off-peak sales

Advertising media

An advertiser uses one or more media to carry advertisements. Where a combination of media is used, it is common for one of the media to be used in a primary role, with other media in a secondary or support role. For instance, the main thrust of a campaign might be through television advertising with the print media in a supportive role.

In 1998, total **advertising spend** (the industry expression for expenditure) was divided among the various media as shown in Table 1.3.2 (US figures in brackets for comparison):

Table 1.3.2 Total advertising spend

Commercial TV	31.8%	(39%)
National press	15.9%	(36%)
Magazines and directories	23.3%	(12.9%)
Regional and local press	20%	–
Outdoor	4.4%	(1.7%)
Radio	3.7%	(10.3%)
Cinema	0.7%	(not available)
(*Source*: Wright, *Advertising; Advertising Age*)		

It should be noted that the print media dominate advertising despite the appeal of TV advertisements.

Radio advertising is relatively unimportant although it is a growth area. Cinema advertising plays a minor role in total advertising, but note that outdoor advertising still plays a role in total advertising expenditure.

Television

Advertisements are carried by three terrestrial broadcasting channels (ITV, C4, C5) and by a growing number of cable, satellite and digital channels. Of the £4 billion spent annually on media advertising, around 55 per cent goes to the ITV companies, with 17 per cent to C4, 6 per cent to C5 and a total of 21.7 per cent to cable and satellite channels. The spread of channels creates new media outlets for advertising but also means that audiences for any one programme tend to be smaller than in the days of a simple BBC–ITV duopoly. Advertising rates are related to the channel and also vary with the popularity of programmes. We can contrast the advantages and disadvantages of television advertising in Table 1.3.3.

National newspapers

These can be divided into three groups, based on circulation:

- Low-circulation, upmarket broadsheets, e.g. *The Times, Daily Telegraph, The Guardian*
- Medium-circulation, mid-readership tabloids such as the *Express* and *Daily Mail*
- The high-circulation tabloids such as the *Sun* and the *Daily Mirror.*

The existence of a variety of newspapers facilitates the targeting of particular segments.

The advantages and disadvantages of newspaper advertising are shown in Table 1.3.4.

Local/regional newspapers

The UK has over 1300 regional and local newspapers – some purchased and others distributed free. Around 90 per cent of the adult population regularly read a local newspaper so this medium is invaluable for the advertiser (see Table 1.3.5). Advertisements can be set in both display (block advertisement) and classified forms.

Magazines

Over 6000 magazines are published regularly in the UK. Some are aimed at consumers, whereas others are aimed at business or people in a particular trade. Many magazines are special interest publications and, as a result, magazines are often a more selective medium than newspapers. Although most magazines have a much smaller readership than national newspapers, the TV listing guides have a circulation in excess of 1 million. A growing trend in magazine publication is magazines published by retail chains (Marks and Spencer, Sainsbury, etc.) and linked to store loyalty

Table 1.3.3 Advantages and disadvantages of television advertising

Advantages	Disadvantages
• Creative advertisements can attract attention and have a great impact. • Advertisements can demonstrate the product in use. • Can reach a vast audience • Increased scope for targeting the audience, e.g. Channel 4, Sky • The message can be reinforced by continuous advertisements. • It is valuable for developing an image.	• Relatively expensive initial cost • The message is short lived. • Consumers may not watch commercials. • Technical information is difficult to explain. • There may be a delay between seeing the ad and visiting the shops. • There is a lack of permanence in the advert.

Table 1.3.4 Advantages and disadvantages of national newspaper advertising

Advantages	Disadvantages
• National coverage • Reader can refer back. • Relatively cheap • Detail of the product can be provided. • It facilitates targeting.	• No movement or sound • Usually limited to black and white • Individual ad may be lost among large quantities of other advertisements.

cards. Table 1.3.6 contrasts the advantages and disadvantages of this form of advertising.

Radio

There are around 140 commercial radio stations in the UK. Most are local (covering a town or part of a county), although Britain now has three national stations – Classic FM, Virgin and Talk Radio. As stations concentrate on a particular type of broadcasting (usually a particular type of music), radio aids the targeting of particular segments of the market. For example, Classic FM is listened to by a different segment of the population than that listening to Virgin Radio. Although it is of minor significance in overall advertising, radio advertising is seen as a growth area and is especially important in advertising mobile phones; the two major radio advertisers in 1998 were Carphone Warehouse and Vodaphone. Table 1.3.7 contrasts the advantages and disadvantages of radio advertising.

Cinema

The rise of television, especially commercial television, saw a late twentieth-century decline in the importance of cinema as an advertising medium. However, as cinema audiences tend to be young, it does offer the opportunity to target the young age group and to advertise in an innovative way which might not be acceptable on television. Table 1.3.8 contrasts the advantages and disadvantages of cinema advertising.

Outdoor

This term covers all advertising seen in an outdoor situation:

- Roadside advertising
- Offroad advertising, e.g. in shopping centres
- Transport advertising, e.g. on buses and trains and in stations

Table 1.3.5 Advantages and disadvantages of local/regional newspaper advertising

Advantages	Disadvantages
• Good for regional campaigns and test marketing • Can be linked to local conditions	• Cost per reader is higher than in national newspapers. • Reproduction, layout, etc. may be poor. • Classified ads are only read by people seeking the product. • Free newspapers are often unread.

Table 1.3.6 Advantages and disadvantages of magazine advertising

Advantages	Disadvantages
• Colour advertisements possible • Targeting is possible with specialist magazines. • Advertising can be linked to features. • Magazines may be referred to at a later date. • Greater permanence than newspapers	• A long time exists between advertisements being placed and the magazine being printed. • Competitors' products are also being advertised. • No movement or sound • Small readership for some magazines

Table 1.3.7 Advantages and disadvantages of radio advertising

Advantages	Disadvantages
• Enables the use of sound • Most consumer groups are covered. • Minority programmes can target audiences. • Produced cheaply • Younger audience targeted • Reaches a local audience	• Not visual • There is no copy of the material to refer to. • Interruptions of the music by commercials may prove irritating. • May not capture the audience's attention since radio is a 'background' medium

Table 1.3.8 Advantages and disadvantages of cinema advertising

Advantages	Disadvantages
• Colour, sound and movement can be used. • Advertisements can be highly localised. • A 'captive' audience for advertisements. • Great impact on the consumer. • Age groups can be targeted.	• Limited audience. • The message is short lived. • The message may be seen only once.

Outdoor advertising 'has often been seen in the past as somewhat down-market, unorganised and amateur, often being associated with images of illegal flyposting. Outdoor advertising on billboards, poster sites and transport has got its act together and come of age in the 1990s, and is now a major competitor to all other media.' (Wright, *Advertising*, FT Prentice Hall).

The advantages and disadvantages of outdoor advertising are listed in Table 1.3.9.

Criteria in media selection

The choice of media depends on the product, the target audience and the available budget. The criteria for selection are as follows:

- Cost of the media and the budget available
- The reach: the number of people reached by the media
- The selectivity of the reach
  For instance, advertising in a low-circulation specialist magazine might be more appropriate than in a high-circulation general magazine.
- The impact of the media
  Clearly, media with colour, movement and sound have a greater impact than the print media.
- Permanence
  Advertisements on the television and in newspapers disappear very quickly, whereas an advertisement in a trade directory or telephone directory will last a year or more.
- The message
  Television is not very useful for conveying information. Its strength lies in impact and image. If the advertiser wishes to convey a great deal of technical information then the print media are preferred.

Advertising agencies

Although some companies organise all advertising activity in-house, it is usual for most businesses to

Table 1.3.9 Advantages and disadvantages of outdoor advertising

Advantages	Disadvantages
• National campaigns possible. • Most groups covered. • May encourage impulse buying through location close to shops. • Seen repeatedly. • Excellent for short, sharp messages, e.g. election 'promises'.	• Limited amount of information. • Difficult to measure effectiveness. • Weather and graffiti can ruin the poster.

Activity

Study one advertisement from each of the five main media. Analyse why the organisation concerned used the medium for that particular advertisement. Report any findings to the class in the form of a short presentation.

employ the services of an advertising agency such as Abbott Mead Vickers, BBDO, Ogilvy and Mather, Saatchi and Saatchi or J. Walter Thompson. The agency will undertake a range of services:

- Market research
- Message construction
- Media planning and placing
- Public relations
- Sales promotion
- Legal advice

The agency will charge a fee for its services but the advantage is that it does have the technical and creative staff who are essential for a successful campaign.

Advertising and the public interest

Advertising is a legitimate business activity and can be defended on the following basis:

- It provides information about products.
- It encourages competition.
- If it increases sales, firms will benefit from economies of scale and this can be passed on in the form of lower prices.
- It breaks down barriers to entry to markets (although there is a counter argument that it also erects barriers).

Despite these advantages, advertising is frequently criticised on the following grounds:

- It raises costs and therefore prices.
- It can be used to block entry to markets.
- It increases materialism.
- It is used to create wants.
- It can be misleading.
- It reinforces harmful stereotypes (e.g. 'a woman's place is in the home').
- It encourages addictive, obsessive and acquisitive behaviour.
- It is used to manipulate people.
- It encourages consumers (especially children) to want products that they cannot afford, causing feelings of inadequacy when the products are not obtained.
- It encourages unnecessary production and consumption.

Given the general public concern over advertising, it is natural that some form of regulation is imposed. Apart from controls present in consumer law, the advertising industry is subject to regulation by the **Advertising Standards Authority** (ASA).

The **ASA** seeks to ensure that advertisements carried by media other than broadcastors are 'legal, decent, honest and truthful'.

The ASA is funded by a levy on display advertisements and one of its functions is to ensure that all ads conform to its code of practice.

An advertising code of practice

- Advertisements should contain nothing which is in breach of the law.
- No advertisement should contain any matter that is likely to cause offence.
- No advertisement should seek to take improper advantage of any characteristic or circumstance which may make consumers vulnerable.
- No advertisement, whether by inaccuracy, ambiguity, exaggeration, omission or otherwise, should mislead consumers.
- No advertisement should play on fear or excite distress.
- Advertisements should neither condone nor incite to violence or anti-social behaviour.
- Advertisements should contain nothing which is likely to result in harm to children, or to exploit their credulity, lack of experience or sense of loyalty.
- Advertisers should not seek to discredit the products of competitors.
- No advertisement should so closely resemble another advertisement as to be likely to mislead or confuse.

Source: adapted from *The British Code of Advertising Practice*, Committee of Advertising Practice.

The Independent Television Commission and the Radio Authority perform a similar role in relation to the broadcast media.

Revision Questions

1. Distinguish between product and corporate advertising. (2 marks)
2. Why do firms which already enjoy a monopoly position in the market feel the need to advertise? (1 mark)
3. What is the purpose of advertising in the not-for-profit sector? (1 mark)
4. Explain the difference between informative and persuasive advertising. (2 marks)
5. How does the nature of the advertising message change as a product progresses through its life cycle? (1 mark)
6. What are SMART objectives? (1 mark)
7. Distinguish between a marketing and an advertising objective. (2 marks)
8. Why is the print medium dominant in advertising? (1 mark)
9. Why are advertising rates higher on ITV than on Channel 5? (1 mark)
10. At what times of the day and evening are advertising rates highest on ITV? (1 mark)
11. Why is a TV listing magazine an essential tool in advertising? (1 mark)
12. What explanations can you forward for the rise in the importance of radio as an advertising medium? (1 mark)
13. What advantages do magazines have over newspapers as an advertising medium? (1 mark)
14. Using examples, explain what you understand by the reach and the selectivity of advertising media? (1 mark)
15. Evaluate *Yellow Pages* as an advertising medium. (1 mark)
16. What are the advantages of using an advertising agency? (1 mark)
17. How do tobacco companies defend their continued use of advertising? (1 mark)
18. What do you understand by barriers to market entry? Do you think advertising is a barrier to entry or does it assist entry? (2 marks)
19. What is the Advertising Standards Authority? Is it a government body? (2 marks)
20. Suggest two ways in which market research can be used in devising an advertising campaign. (2 marks)
21. Study the advertisement for Saga home insurance and answer the questions that follow.

The Guardian, 31 October 2000

a) At which segment of the market is the advertisement targeted? Suggest reasons why Saga target this segment?

b) With reference to this advertisement and to the AIDA model, analyse the roles of advertising and personal selling in the insurance market.

c) The advertisement includes a reference number, GU0003. What is the likely purpose of including this reference number?

d) Analyse the benefits of using:

i) the print media in general

ii) the *Guardian* in particular for this advertisement.

e) Identify and explain the role of:

i) sales promotion in the promotional mix

ii) the unique selling proposition for this particular product.

22 Study the advertisement for olive oil and answer the questions that follow.

a) Which organisation placed the advertisement and what would you suggest to be the purpose of such an organisation?

b) What do you suggest is the objective of the advertisement?

c) Why did the European Community offer financial support for the advertising campaign?

d) Comment on the choice of the *Sunday Times* colour magazine as the advertising medium.

e) What is the message in this advertisement?

Sunday Times, October 2000. © European Communities, 1995–2001

After 40 days of the flood, Noah saw an olive branch in the beak of a dove. The olive tree, ever since, has been a symbol of peace and rebirth. Olive oil and home cooking, in the sunny South, are inseparable. It is the quintessence of Mediterranean delicacies. Fish fresh from the sea simply grilled with a splash of olive oil. Spanish omelette made authentic and special. The pungency of pesto with pasta. And olive oil is naturally rich in Vitamin E and high-grade mono-unsaturated fatty acids. Comforting, isn't it, to know that something you like is something that likes you?

You can pick up more from the Olive Oil Information Bureau, 67-69 Whitfield Street, London W1P 5RL, infobureau@cook-oliveoil.com or 020 7468 3642. More delicious recipes, more healthy facts, more enjoyable meals.

Olive oil has soul.

23 Study the 'BP' communication below and answer the questions that follow.

a) Is this an advertisement or merely publicity? Explain your answer.

b) What is the likely purpose of the communication?

c) What message or messages is BP seeking to communicate?

d) Comment on the design of the new BP logo.

e) Comment on the difficulties of evaluating the effectiveness of this advertisement.

BP, Amoco, ARCO, Castrol.
What does it add up to?

It means a new company able to offer global energy solutions.

It means the retail presence to serve 10 million customers a day.

It means a company that makes petrol and diesel that produce lower emissions.

It means the world's leading producer of solar power.

It means the talent and resources to go beyond what people expect.

Today, 100,000 employees in 100 countries join together to form a new company called BP. Tomorrow, we begin building a new brand of progress for the world.

beyond petroleum

www.bp.com

The Economist, October 2000

CHAPTER 4

Other Forms of Promotion

KEY TERMS

Branding
Consumer
Direct marketing
E-commerce
Merchandising
Packaging
Press release
Public relations
Publicity
Sales promotion
Sponsorship

In this chapter, you will read about the other forms of promotion. These alternative techniques are sometimes employed in a supportive role and almost always in conjunction with other elements of the promotional mix. You will also read about new and changing methods of promotion. It should be realised that not only does the promotional mix change from product to product, but it is also changing as technology opens up new opportunities.

Other Marketing Techniques

After looking at advertising in detail, we now switch our attention to other forms of promotion. Some of the techniques covered in this chapter should be seen as playing a support role in the marketing effort. Others are relatively recent additions to the armoury of promotional weapons and are expected to grow in importance in the years to come.

Branding

'A **brand** is a name, term, sign, symbol, or combination of them, intended to identify the good or services of one seller or group of sellers and to differentiate them from those of the competitors.' American marketing guru Philip Kotler, (*Marketing Management Analysis, Planning, Implementation and Control*, Prentice Hall)

This definition emphasises that a brand can take the form of words, letters, numbers, a symbol or design. Words, letters and numbers form a **brand name** whereas symbols and designs form a **brand mark**. When an organisation has the legal right to exclusive use of a brand we can refer to this as a **trade mark**.

The other important aspect of the Kotler definition is that branding is used to create product differentiation by establishing an identity for the organisation's product that distinguishes it from the products of rivals. Consequently, branding is not a feature of the economists' model of perfect competition where each firm produces a uniform or homogeneous product. In the real world, businesses seek to differentiate their products by the use of a brand. This gives the organisation an element of exclusivity, with the expectation of gaining customer preference, building up customer loyalty and increasing the firm's market share.

We can identify four types of brands: company brands, family brands, individual brands and retailer's own brands.

- **With company brands** the corporate name is used in the product name, e.g. Heinz, Sony, British Airways, American Express.
- **With family brands** a range (or family) of products are marketed under the same brand name, e.g. Fairy soap and liquid. The use of family brands is especially common in the cosmetics business.
- **With individual brands** the product is separately branded, e.g. Quality Street chocolates.

- **Retailer's own brand** products are made under contract for a large retail chain. It is usually, but not always, the case that the own brand is a cheaper version of a famous name brand. It is made to the retailer's own recipe or design and represents an attempt by the retailer to exert some control over the manufacturing process while not actually engaging in manufacturing itself. The process of own-branding was taken to its logical conclusion by Marks and Spencer in whose stores all products were sold under the M&S own brand, St Michael. This total reliance on own-branded products was a possible cause of the disappointing performance of M&S in the late 1990s and in 2000/01.

The strategic functions of branding

These are:

- to differentiate the product
- to build up customer loyalty
- to provide the product with an identity
- to facilitate customer recall and self-selection
- to provide a vehicle for advertising and promotion
- to make it easier to obtain both distribution and shelf space
- to facilitate segmentation
- to provide quality certification
- to obtain legal protection for product features.

A successful brand has a **goodwill value** (known as **brand equity**) and can be accorded status as an intangible asset if the business is sold. For instance, when Rupert Murdoch's News International purchased *The Times*, the newspaper's tangible assets could easily be replaced but the brand name of *The Times* could not be obtained by any other means.

A successful brand can also be applied to a new product. In other words, the brand is extended. For instance, many premium brands of ice-creams share a brand name with well-established chocolate bars such as Mars, Bounty and Kitkat. Brand extension aids the introduction of new products as customers are more likely to try this new product because of the familiar old name. Not surprisingly, this activity is known as 'piggy-backing'.

Activity

In *Framework for Marketing*, Kotler argues that the 'branding challenge is to develop a set of positive associations for a brand'. This can be analysed in terms of levels of brand meaning. Use Table 1.4.1 to suggest examples of what each of the following brands means:

- Mercedes cars
- Nike sportswear
- Rolex watches
- St Michael clothes
- Microsoft

Table 1.4.1 Levels of brand meaning

Meaning	Description	Examples
Attributes	Attributes of the product	
Benefits	Functional and emotional benefits of the product	
Values	What it says about the producer's values	
Culture	The brand represents a certain culture	
Personality	The brand projects a certain personality	
User	What it tells us about the user	
(*Source*: adapted from Kotler, P., *Framework for Marketing Management*, Prentice Hall, 2001)		

Packaging

Packaging can be seen both as part of the product and also as a promotional tool.

The utilitarian function of packaging is to protect and contain the product. Consequently, packaging should be evaluated in terms of durability, ease of transport and storage, convenience, weight and impact on the environment.

Packaging is also an important promotional tool:

- It informs customers.
- It aids the use of the product (e.g. ring-pull cans).
- It adds value to the product.
- It enhances the brand image.
- It differentiates the product from other brands.

The design features in packaging include choice of colour, labelling and the use of graphics. Table 1.4.2 illustrates characteristics commonly associated with different **colours**.

The **labelling** used is important in terms of:

- product identification
- providing instructions
- promoting alternative uses for the product
- promoting other products in the range
- providing information about sales promotion
- providing information about contents
- encouraging first-time purchase.

'**Graphics**' refers to the visual image conveyed by the pack: the logo, print font and illustration used on the package. Graphics can attract attention, add to the aesthetic quality of the product and reinforce brand image.

The **packaging** of goods and services enhances the overall benefit to the customer and, as a result, can rightly be seen as a 'silent salesperson'.

Table 1.4.2 Characteristics commonly associated with different colours

Colour	Association
Yellow	summer, sunrise
Red	warmth, passion, a premium product
Purple	upmarket
Blue	coolness and cleanliness
Green	nature, the environment or Irishness
Pink	femininity
White	purity and cleanliness
Brown	strong flavour
Black	exclusivity

Activity

Analyse the nature and role of packaging used for the following products:

- Pepsi Cola
- A compact disc
- Nescafé Gold Blend coffee
- Toblerone chocolate
- A blockbuster paperback novel, e.g. a 'Harry Potter' book, a Catherine Cookson novel, a Tom Clancy novel, or a Stephen King novel

Public relations (PR)

Public relations can be defined as a conscious effort to improve and maintain an organisation's relations with its stakeholders (the community at large, employees, customers, suppliers, distributors, creditors, opinion leaders and pressure groups) with a view to strengthening its reputation.

The purpose of public relations is to influence opinion, develop a positive image for the organisation and raise its profile in the market place. It is important to remember that PR is about image building, not making sales. It is a long-term activity with a pay off only in the long run.

Large organisations will employ PR specialists to undertake this role, whereas smaller organisations will employ PR consultants when required.

We can make a distinction between **reactive** (defensive) PR and **proactive** PR. The former is a response to outside threats to the organisation's reputation as they arise. This might mean 'damage limitation' after an oil spillage or publicity about defective goods. Proactive PR, on the other hand, involves planning for, anticipating and meeting threats before they arise. It involves creating a favourable image, publicising progress and achievements and emphasising the organisation's contribution to community life. Like many other organisations The Body Shop seeks publicity for its charitable activities and its promotion of good causes. It is well known for its opposition to testing cosmetic products on animals and for its support of progress in the developing world.

Organisations seek good publicity by the use of in-house journals, seminars, visits, sponsorship of events, community activities and press releases.

A **press release** is a statement issued to the print and broadcasting media concerning the activities of an organisation.

For instance, press releases might be used to announce a technological breakthrough or the use of a new waste recycling process. It is hoped that the media will report the story in a manner favourable to the organisation.

The advantage of press releases (compared with paid-for advertising) are as follows:

- Press coverage is free.
- The message carries greater credibility because it is included in the editorial part of the newspaper.
- People are more likely to read a news item than an advertisement.

However for a press release to be successful it must:

- be newsworthy
- fit the editorial style of the medium
- not be a thinly disguised advertisement.

In summary, good PR:

- helps to build up a positive image
- counters bad publicity
- improves employee motivation
- increases the effectiveness of advertising and the sales force.

However, PR will not:

- directly increase sales
- cover up something that is detrimental to the company's image
- replace other promotional activities.

Sponsorship

Sponsorship – when a business organisations provides funds for a sporting or artistic event

Business organisations sponsor sporting, artistic, community and other activities so as to gain coverage and prestige from association with a socially desirable activity. This is known as the 'halo effect' – it creates good publicity, public goodwill and, at the same time, gains extensive coverage of the organisation and its products.

The WIIFM ('What's in it for me?') factor should always be remembered in sponsorship deals. This means that it is no use providing sponsorship unless the public is made aware of the firm's activities. Consequently, sponsorship has to be accompanied by advertising and other promotional activities to draw public attention to the link. Sponsors of the Millennium Dome at Greenwich (e.g. Tesco) included a reference to its sponsorship in advertising and, at the same time, sold dome merchandise in their stores. Kellogg's was one of the official sponsors of Team GB at the 2000 Olympic Games in Sydney. Again, they included this fact in advertising and sold a range of related goods (e.g. Team GB cereal bowls).

Other sponsorship-linked promotional activities include corporate hospitality, corporate logos on sportspersons' clothing and public appearances by famous beneficiaries of sponsorship. Television interviews with players and managers are also conducted against the background of the corporate logo (e.g. the England football team and the Nationwide Building Society). As a general rule, each pound spent on sponsorship should be matched by a further pound spent on other promotional activities linked to sponsorship. The advantages of sponsorship are as follows.

- It provides scope for wide coverage, reaching large numbers of potential customers, especially if the sponsored event or team is televised.
- It can be targeted at particular groups of people.
- It has provided a way of bypassing advertising bans (e.g. a ban on advertising tobacco products) and of securing coverage on the BBC.
- It enhances the organisation's prestige by association with socially desirable and beneficial activities.

Against these advantages, there are a number of disadvantages and potential problems.

- The effectiveness of sponsorship is difficult to assess.
- In some cases, the event or personality overshadows the sponsor.
- Association with an unsuccessful activity (the Millennium Dome) or unsuccessful sporting team does not enhance the organisation's image.
- Scandals (e.g. drugs, sex, financial) associated with star names produce negative publicity. The sponsor will need to be assured that the beneficiary of sponsorship will not let them down. It is common to include a 'morality clause', giving the sponsor the right to withdraw sponsorship if there is misbehaviour by the sponsored person. Glenn Hoddle's resignation as the England Football Team coach was not the result of misbehaviour but did follow an infamous comment about reincarnation and disability. The sponsors of the England team were unhappy about association with a comment that alienated disabled people.

Sales promotion

The term 'sales promotion' refers to any non face-to-face activity concerned with the promotion of sales, other than advertising. It takes the form of short-term incentives that seek to increase sales. Promotions are usually designed to accompany other elements of the promotional mix (such as advertising). They give a boost to sales, although the benefits might be short lived (see Figure 1.4.2). Once the promotional incentive is withdrawn, there is a danger of sales falling back to the previous level. On the other hand, if the primary objective of the promotion is to encourage people to try a new product, it is possible that the benefit might be longer lasting.

Promotions aimed at distributors

We should make a distinction between promotions aimed at the distributor and promotions aimed at the

Activity

Produce a list of five examples of sporting sponsorship, five examples of sponsorship of the arts and five examples of sponsorship of community action. In each case, analyse what you consider to be the WIIFM factor ('What's in it for me?').

Figure 1.4.1 Consumer and trade promotions

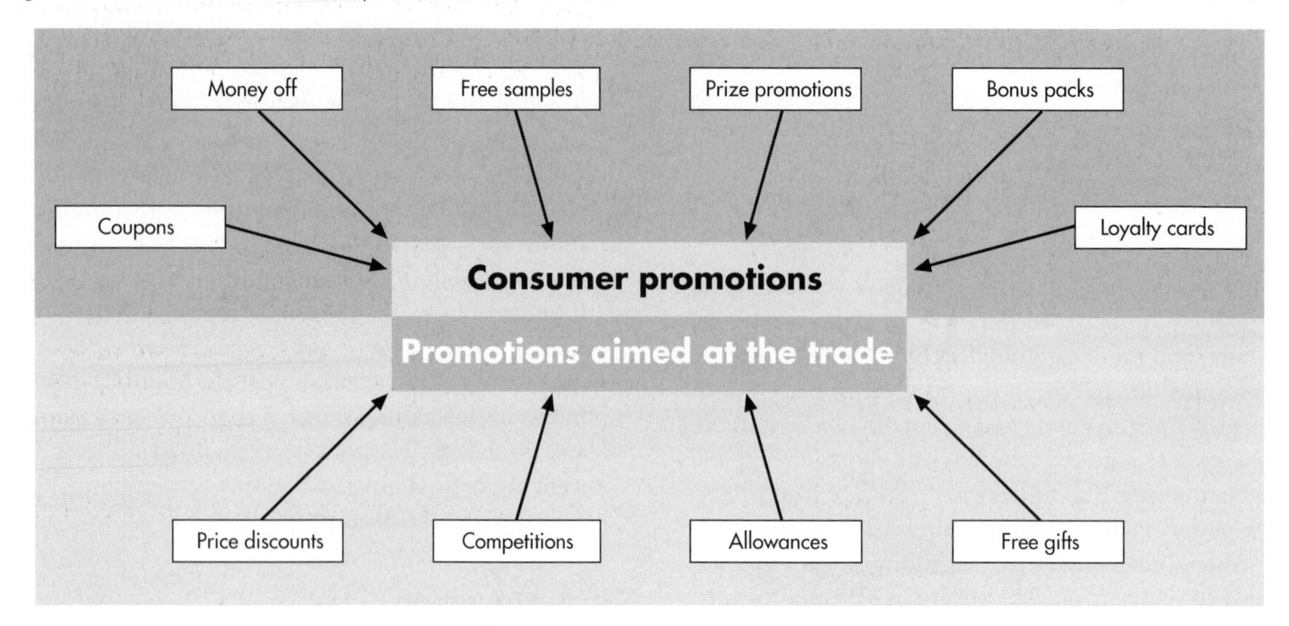

consumer. Promotions aimed at distributors or intermediaries are designed to:

- increase stock levels held by the distributor
- gain increased or superior shelf space
- even out fluctuating sales
- counter competition
- assist a product launch.

Promotions aimed at distributors are part of a 'push' strategy intended to provide incentives to encourage the intermediary to push the product actively. Major forms of promotions aimed at distributions are:

- sales volume bonuses (discounts)
- packaging
- merchandising
- point of sale materials
- competitions with prizes for successful distributors
- trade gifts.

Promotions aimed at consumers

Manufacturers will also use sales promotions aimed directly at consumers. Here the aim is to encourage the consumer to pull the product through the channel of distribution. More specifically the objective is:

Figure 1.4.2 Sales promotion produces a short-term rise in sales

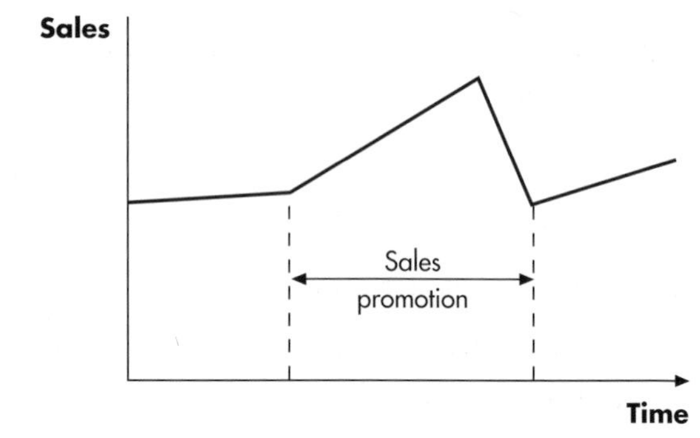

Figure 1.4.3 Sales promotion aimed at different targets

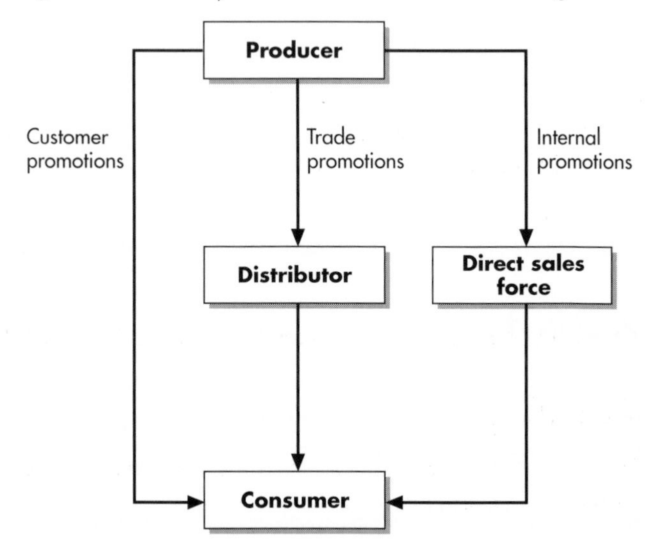

- to encourage trial
- to increase usage
- to attract new customers
- to encourage trading up (buying bigger packs)
- to encourage loading up (stockpiling to block out competitors)
- to develop customer loyalty
- to penetrate new market segments
- to offset the activities of rival manufacturers.

The retailer will also engage in promotional activity:

- to increase store traffic
- to increase the frequency and amount of purchase
- to increase store loyalty
- to increase own-brand sales
- to even out fluctuating sales
- to stimulate impulse buying
- to penetrate new market segments
- to reduce stock levels so as to improve cash flow or clear shelves for new products
- to offset the activities of rival stores.

The main forms of customer-targeted promotions are:

- competitions and prize draws
- free gifts, free samples and free trials or trial packs
- on-pack offers ('piggy backing')
- loyalty cards, trading stamps and air miles
- tokens
- coupon inducements
- price offers, including discounts, 'buy now, pay later', 'beat price rises', 'two for the price of one', and BOGOF ('buy one, get one free')
- self-liquidating offers.

A **self-liquidating offer** is a promotion where the cost of provision is covered by payment made to customers who respond.

Merchandising

The key feature of merchandising is that it is promotional activity at the point of sale. It is concerned with the way products are displayed at retail outlets. As up to 75 per cent of purchasing decisions are made inside the shop, it is not surprising that manufacturers and retailers co-operate over the layout and appearance of the shop.

The major **point of purchase** (POP) promotional tools are:

- stickers directing customers to the product being promoted
- window displays
- posters, cutouts and show cards
- branded displays linking a range of products of the same brand
- in-store sampling
- injection-moulded, three-dimensional plastic images
- video-walls
- interactive systems such as expert advice via a keyboard system.

Shelf position is especially important in influencing the buyer. Premium locations are near the entrance door and the checkouts (although not too near). This is especially important in the encouraging of impulse purchases. Research shows that supermarket customers scan the shelves at the rate of four feet per second. Consequently, to avoid being overlooked a product requires a reasonable minimum amount of space. To increase customer awareness of the products on shelves, manufacturers design eye-catching patterns to allow a range of goods to be seen as a block on the shelf.

Activity

Produce a list of 25 sales promotions, each associated with a different product. For each promotion, suggest specific objectives.

Activity

Produce a list of ten sales promotions currently found at a particular retail store of your choice. Suggest the objectives of each promotion.

Direct marketing

The American Direct Marketing Association defines **direct marketing** as 'an interactive system of marketing which uses one or more advertising media to effect a measurable response and/or transaction at any location'.

An alternative definition, used by the UK Direct Marketing Association, is that it is 'a cybernetic process which uses direct response advertising in prospecting, conversion and maintenance'. **Prospecting** is searching for possible buyers. **Conversion** implies converting potential buyers into actual buyers. **Maintenance** refers to repeat purchases and customer loyalty.

Both of the definitions quoted above distinguish direct marketing from old-style mail order systems and mail shots. Direct marketing communicates with individuals rather than the population as a whole. It is interactive in that customers respond directly (and measurably) to direct communications which are targeted only at those individuals who are likely to be interested in the product or service on offer.

Direct marketing usually involves the use of computer databases and hence is sometimes known as **database marketing**. There is, however, a key distinction.

'Database marketing is only that part of direct marketing that is handled by computers; other forms of direct marketing exist that are not computer driven, although it should be said that these are becoming rarer, as the advantages of using computers mean that they are becoming ever more ubiquitous.'

Source: Blythe, J., *Marketing Communications*

The use of a computer database produces benefits in terms of targeting individuals, measuring response, appealing to each customer in different ways, the production of highly customised and high quality material and the storing of data about individuals. Computer-driven direct marketing avoids the 'scatter gun' approach of the unaddressed mail drop. Consequently, it has the potential of reducing the amount of much criticised junk-mail. However, this also assumes that databases are accurate and kept up to date! The other requirement of successful database marketing is security and confidentiality of computer records. Material held on computer is subject to the **Data Protection Act.**

Included in direct marketing is **direct response TV advertising** (DRTV). Unlike traditional TV advertising, DRTV includes a telephone number, address, fax number or web site address which viewers can contact to place orders. Around one quarter of TV advertising is now DRTV (according to the Direct Marketing Association Census) and this is likely to increase with the proliferation of TV channels, with audiences being more accurately targeted and defined. DRTV advertising is associated with the shopping channel QVC (Quality, Value and Convenience) but such advertisements are also carried by other channels, including the terrestrial channels of ITV and C4. In addition to targeting particular segments, DRTV has the advantage of aiding the measurement of response.

Some direct marketing does not require the use of computers, e.g. party plans, door-to-door canvassing.

E-commerce

E-commerce means selling products and services on-line via the internet.

E-commerce is seen as a growth area for marketing both in terms of transactions with other business organisations (**B2B** transactions) and with consumers (**B2C** transactions).

E-commerce has advantages and disadvantages for both the supplier and the customer as shown in Table 1.4.3.

'**Internet-based marketing** usually revolves around a firm's web site. This is a page on the web which can be accessed by web subscribers, and contains information and directions to other pages of interest. A web site contains a sales pitch, solid information about a product or company, an e-mail address to ask questions or buy the product using a credit card.'

Source: Blythe, J., *Marketing Communications*

Table 1.4.3 Advantages and disadvantages of e-commerce

	Advantages	**Disadvantages**
Supplier	Global market Additional revenue stream Reduced reliance on traditional methods 24-hour business Low promotion costs Assists small firms to compete Reduces barriers to market entry	Cost of development, site maintanence, marketing of the site Requires specialist skills Need for updating Dependence on internet service Inability to cope with increased demand
Customer	Access to extensive information On-line documentation is available at all times Facilitates price comparisons Mass customisation – increased variety at lower prices Customers can search using search engines	Purchases made on the basis of a picture Lack of personal contact Dependence on 'low-tech' transportation Dependent on the technology available Issues related to security

Activity

Provide five examples of products marketed by means of:

- DRTV
- the internet
- computer-driven mail shots.

In each case, suggest reasons why the product is especially suitable for this type of marketing.

Revision Questions

1 Why do firms seek to differentiate their products? (1 mark)

2 Without using examples quoted in the text, name two examples of company brands, family brands, individual brands and own brands. (4 marks)

3 What is piggy backing? (1 mark)

4 Why is packaging an important marketing tool? (1 mark)

5 Why do large firms employ public relations specialists? (1 mark)

6 What are the disadvantages and risks associated with sponsorship? (2 marks)

7 Why are loyalty cards such an important feature of retailing? (1 mark)

8 Distinguish between trade and consumer sales promotion. (2 marks)

9 What do you understand by merchandising? (1 mark)

10 Why is the location of shelf space considered so important? (1 mark)

11 Outline the role of databases in direct marketing. (1 mark)

12 Explain the difference between direct response TV advertising and traditional TV advertising. (2 marks)

13 Outline five ways in which developments in technology are changing promotional activities. (5 marks)

14 With reference to the AIDA model, comment on the role of packaging, public relations, sales promotions and merchandising. (4 marks)

15 Explain the terms 'impulse buying' and 'trading up'. (2 marks)

16 Suggests three sales promotions for use in marketing a new product. For each technique, explain why it is appropriate. (3 marks)

17 Study the CTP advertisement overleaf and answer the questions that follow.

a) Analyse the differences between promotion in business-to-business (B2B) markets compared with business-to-consumer (B2C). (5 marks)

b) What are the likely objectives of this advertisement? (5 marks)

c) Explain what you understand by e-business. (2 marks)

d) Comment on the advertisement in relation to the AIDA model and suggest the role of other elements of the promotional mix. (3 marks)

e) In what ways does the advertisement criticise CTP's competitors? (2 marks)

f) What is the significance of the word 'partner' in this advertisement? (3 marks)

Choosing an e-business partner is no simple task. Organizations that pride themselves on strategy too often leave you with a stack of papers, no closer to realizing your goals than you were when you began. Pure plays, which focus only on the Internet, don't have the business knowledge to transform your entire organization. Cambridge Technology Partners is uniquely qualified to turn a sound strategy into a business reality. In working with some of the world's most innovative companies, we've uncovered e-business opportunities our clients never imagined at the start. Together, we've developed and implemented digital strategies that transformed their businesses. We can do the same for you. Stop by our Web site or contact us in one of our 53 offices around the world. See how much further our complete e-business solutions can take you.

© 2000 Cambridge Technology Partners

18 The following article appeared in *The Guardian* during the 2000 Olympic Games.

a) Analyse the benefits to Coca-Cola of sponsoring the Olympic Games. (4 marks)

b) Why are sponsors taking such a tough line on the products of non-sponsors? (3 marks)

c) Explain what you understand by 'ambush marketing'. (3 marks)

d) One rule of sponsorship is that each pound spent directly on sponsorship should be matched by a further pound spent on related activities. Explain why it is important to match the spending and suggest complementary activities in which sponsors engage. (3 marks)

e) The Sydney Olympics were regarded as an outstanding success. How would sponsors evaluate the success of the event? (4 marks)

f) Why do you think Ansett was willing to bid more than its rivals to be the airline of the games? (3 marks)

Any bombs, knives, Pepsi? Security gets tough at the Olympics

Vivek Chaudhary in Sydney

Pepsi has been classified alongside bombs, knives and other dangerous weapons by officials at the main Olympic Park venue in Sydney.

Security guards checking for dangerous items have been asking visitors attending sports events at the Olympic complex if they are carrying "knives, weapons or cans of Pepsi" in an attempt to appease official sponsors Coca-Cola. Those who refuse to give up their cans or bottles of Pepsi are told that they will be refused entry.

The move, which also involves clamping down on other non-official products, is an attempt by Olympic officials to preserve the exclusivity of companies which, according to some estimates, have paid almost £1bn to become official sponsors of the games.

Olympic officials have been scouring the games venues to ensure only products of official sponsors are visible. Logos on computers and televisions that are not IBM or Panasonic respectively have been covered up with black tape, while a café inside the Olympic complex was told to remove a bacon and egg roll, known locally as a "damper", from its menu because it resembled the Egg McMuffin, sold by McDonald's, another official sponsor.

Visitors to the Olympic complex are prevented from entering with alcohol, although it is on sale inside. The choice is limited as only one company has the right to sell beer while another has paid for the right to sell the only brand of wine.

There is also a limit on the amount of food visitors can take in. A spokesman for the organising committee said: "People are allowed to bring reasonable quantities of food but there are dozens of restaurants in the complex where they can eat.

"Non-game sponsor products are not allowed. That's why sponsors pay huge amounts of money. Coca-Cola is the official sponsor and only their drinks are allowed."

The Sydney Olympics has sparked a fierce brand war off the track as non-sponsors attempt to attach themselves to the Olympics in a strategy known as "ambush marketing".

The strategy has led to a number of legal rows between rival companies in Australia. Carlton & United, the official beer supplier, is to sue rival Lion Nathan following claims that it is unofficially using Olympic imagery in its advertising.

Qantas, which is not an official sponsor, was accused by New Zealand airline Ansett, which has paid to become the airline of the games, of using the Olympics in its advertising. The row led to a legal challenge which was settled out of court.

The International Olympic Committee was criticised by a number of sponsor companies after the 1996 Atlanta games when non-sponsors brought up advertising around the city and used Olympic imagery.

Special laws have been introduced in Sydney to prevent non-sponsor companies from using advertising hoarding outside Olympic venues.

Australian authorities have the right to remove them and take legal action against companies using the words "Sydney 2000" or the Olympic rings.

The Guardian 18 September 2000.

CHAPTER 5

Promotional Strategy

KEY TERMS

Effective	Positioning	Pushing
Efficient	Promotional budget	SMART
Message	Promotional research	Strategy
Objective	Pulling	Unique selling proposition

In this chapter, you will learn about the development of a strategy to produce a firm's products and services. Successful strategy-making requires the clarification of objectives prior to making decisions about the combination of techniques to be used, the role assigned to each technique, the message to be delivered and the audience to be targeted. The strategy should be planned and a budget should be allocated.

What is strategy?

In a chapter called promotional strategy, it is essential to explore the meaning of the word **strategy**. A strategy is the course that is to be followed so as to achieve certain objectives.

Strategy is a course of action designed to achieve a specific objective.

An **objective** is something a person or organisation seeks to achieve.

A fuller definition is that strategy is a comprehensive plan which sets directions and guides the allocation of resources to achieve long-term objectives. This second definition places strategy in the context of the planning process. From your knowledge of the Business Planning unit you will be aware that planning can be thought of in terms of four questions:

- Where are we now? (an audit of the present situation)
- What do we want to do? (objectives)
- How are we to get there? (strategy)
- How will we monitor our progress towards the destination? (control and evaluation)

This definition focuses on long-term goals and the setting out of the general direction. In this way, strategy can be distinguished from **tactics** which are concerned with achieving short-term objectives and with a detailed plan of action. The differences between strategic and tactical decisions are listed in Table 1.5.1.

Table 1.5.1 The difference between strategic and tactical decisions

	Strategic	**Tactical**
Decision maker	Senior management	Middle management
Importance	Very	Medium
Resource requirement	High	Medium
Time-scale	Long term	Short–medium term
Amount of detail	Only general statements	Very detailed

Promotional strategy

Promotional strategy is concerned with the choice of promotional techniques used to achieve promotional objectives. As with all statements of strategy, we are concerned here with general principles rather than detailed implementation. We are concerned with the balance of techniques within the chosen promotional mix and with the message that the organisation is seeking to communicate.

Like all business strategies, the promotional strategy should be planned. The features of the plan are as follows:

- **Promotional objectives** – what the organisation seeks to achieve through the use of promotional techniques
- **Promotional strategy** – the promotional mix
- **The target audience**
  The organisation needs to be clear about the audience at which it is going to aim its message.
- **The message**
  Content and presentation should be in line with the product positioning strategy.
- **Promotional tactics** – the detailed implementation of strategy
- **Budget** – the allocation of money for the promotion
- The **timing** of the campaign
- **Responsibilities**
  Who is responsible for what?
- **Control mechanism** – the evaluation of results
- **Integration**
  It is essential that all methods used are integrated in a consistent and logical manner to meet customer needs.

Promotional objectives

Objectives are crucially important in business. They are:

- a means of communication within the organisation
- a means of co-ordinating action
- a guide for decision making
- a constraint
- a benchmark for evaluating progress.

Promotional objectives fit into a hierarchy of objectives. The highest point of this hierarchy is **corporate objectives**, usually expressed in terms of profits or return on capital. Below the corporate objectives lie **marketing objectives**, expressed in terms of sales or market share. **Promotional objectives** are subsidiary to marketing objectives and might be expressed in terms of customer awareness or customer 'reach' (the number of people reached in the campaign).

If corporate objectives are to be met, it is necessary to achieve the marketing objective which, in turn, requires successful achievement of the promotional objective. As you know objectives should be expressed in **SMART** terms: specific, measurable, agreed, realistic and time-related.

Deciding the promotional mix

The promotional mix refers to the combination of promotional techniques used to sell a particular product or service. There is no ideal mix for all products – it will vary between products and over time. A number of factors must be taken into account when deciding the mix:

- **The nature of the market**
  Advertising plays a major role in the consumer market but is less significant in industrial or business-to-business markets. In 'B2B' markets, personal selling is of greater importance in view of the large size of the orders placed and the relatively small number of customers.
- **The type of product**
  Inexpensive, fast-moving consumer goods are subject to heavy advertising, whereas, for more expensive and complex products, there is a greater role for sales promotion and personal selling (see Figure 1.5.1).
- **Promotional message**
  The message which has been chosen will influence the medium to be used. If a demonstration of the product is required then television or, better still, face-to-face selling is preferred. Where a substantial information content is included, a print-based medium will be preferred.
- **The buyer-readiness state**
  Advertising and public relations play a key role in creating awareness of the product but personal selling and sales promotion will play a greater role when customers are moving from comprehension to action. (See AIDA, page 9, DAGMAR, page 9–10, and Figure 1.5.2.)

SMART is an acronym which reminds us that objectives should be specific, measurable, agreed, realistic and time-related.

S – specific rather than vague – capable of communicating to a target audience (*who*) a distinct message (*what*) over a specified time frame (*when*). Promotional objectives must therefore include:

- identification of the target audience
- a clear message
- expected outcome in terms of trial purchase, awareness and so on
- a measurement of results
- mechanisms for monitoring and control.

M – measurable and quantifiable so as to check progress. Statements such as 'increase consumer awareness' are vague, whereas 'increase awareness of the 55–65 year age group from 40 per cent to 80 per cent' is more precise and capable of measurement.

A – agreed with relevant personnel, e.g. the other functional areas of management. 'A' could also be used to mean aspirational, to remind us that objectives serve to motivate.

R – realistic or achievable. Purely from an internal company perspective, if sales are targeted to increase by 25 per cent over a designated time period, then manufacturing capacity will have to be secured to meet this target. Likewise, attempting to gain additional shelf space within a retail outlet will require additional resources to be devoted to the sales force, to sales promotion and to advertising.

Objectives need to be set with a degree of realism rather than on the basis of wild imagination. Otherwise, a company would be better off having no targets at all. An unrealistic target would tend to ignore the competitive and environmental forces affecting the company, the available resources at the company's disposal and the time frame in which the objectives have to be achieved. Unrealistic objectives are not only of little use, they also serve to demotivate employees.

T – time related – a time limit should be set to enable measurement criteria to be established. The time element might be expressed as a year but then subdivided into quarters or months for detailed monitoring of progress.

Figure 1.5.1 Advertising versus personal selling

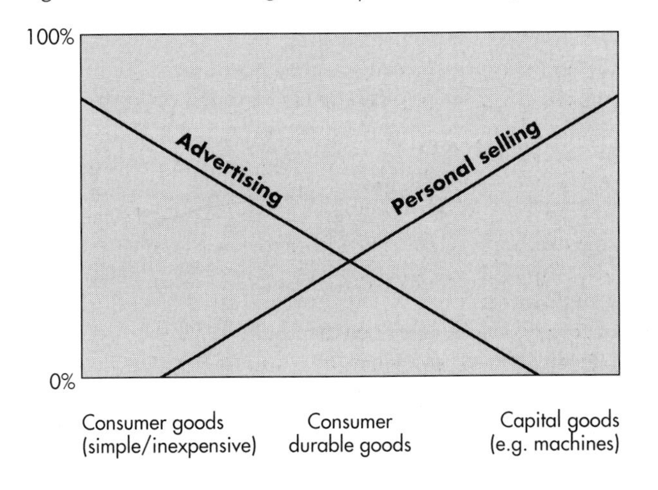

Figure 1.5.2 AIDA and promotional techniques

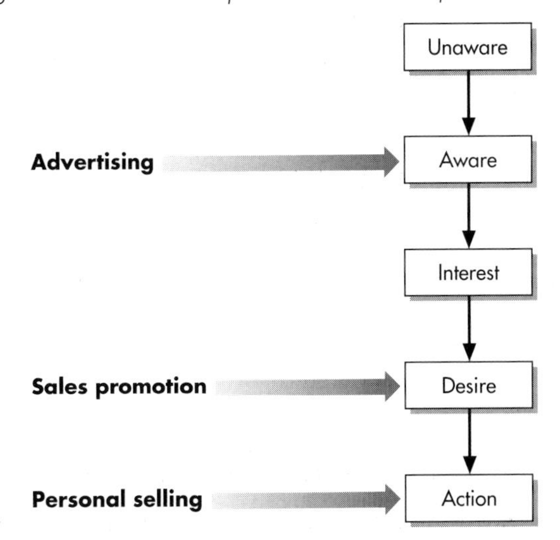

- **Product life-cycle stage**
  The effects of different promotion tools also vary at different stages of the product life cycle. In the introduction stage, advertising and public relations will produce high awareness, and sales promotion is useful in promoting early trial. Personal selling must be used to persuade the trade to carry the product. In the growth stage, advertising and public relations continue to be powerful influences, whereas sales promotion can now be reduced because fewer incentives are needed. In the mature stage, sales promotion again becomes important relative to advertising. Buyers already know the brands and advertising is needed only to remind them about the product. In the decline stage, advertising is kept at a reminder level, public relations are dropped and salespeople give the product scant attention. Sales promotion, however, might continue at a high level to stimulate trade and customers.
- **Competition**
  The choice of promotional techniques will be made after considering the mix adopted by rivals.
- **Distribution**
  As shall be seen, a 'push strategy' requires personal selling and sales promotion directed at intermediaries. A 'pull strategy', on the other hand, requires advertising and sales promotion directed at consumers.
- **The budget available**
  Those in charge of the promotional campaign will be constrained by the budget available but will seek to spend the money in the most cost-effective way. The strengths and weaknesses of each method are summarised in Table 1.5.2.

Promotion and the product life cycle

The promotional mix will change as the product moves through its life cycle. Advertising is used most extensively in the early phases (especially if a pull strategy is pursued). In later stages, the other forms of promotion play a more significant role although, as the product moves into the decline phase, it is likely that there will be a reduction in the use of each of the techniques (see Table 1.5.3).

The nature of the promotional message also changes. In the early days, the emphasis will be on **information**. In the growth and mature phase there is a switch towards **persuasion**. This is because, at this point, there will be numerous competitors and, consequently, a battle over market shares. Finally, in the late mature phase, the emphasis will be on **reminding** people about the product.

Promotion and buyer readiness

In Chapter 2 we met the AIDA model of buyer readiness for the product. Advertising is very useful in

Table 1.5.2 Summary of strengths and weaknesses

Advertising • Good for awareness building because it can reach a wide audience quickly. • Repetition means that a brand positioning concept can be effectively communicated. • Can be used to aid the sales effort and legitimise a company and its products. • Impersonal: lacks flexibility and questions cannot be answered. One-way communication. • Limited capability to close the sale. • Used as part of a pull strategy.	**Direct marketing** • Individual targeting of consumers most likely to respond to an appeal. • Communication can be personalised. • Short-term effectiveness can easily be measured. • A continuous relationship can be built through periodic contact. • Activities are less visible to competitors. • Response rates are often low. • Poorly targeted direct marketing activities cause consumer annoyance.
Publicity • Highly credible as the message comes from a third party. • Wider readership than advertisements in trade and technical publications. • Lost control – a press release may or may not be used and its content can be distorted. • Benefits are difficult to quantify.	**Sales promotion** • Incentives provide a quick boost to sales. • Effects may be only short term. • Excessive use of some incentives (e.g. money off) may weaken a brand image. • Used as part of a push strategy.

creating awareness and stimulating interest, so advertising dominates the mix at these stages. As the buyer is moved to the action of buying the product, sales promotion (especially at the point of purchase) and personal selling assume a more important role (see Table 1.5.4).

Push and pull effects

The term '**channel of distribution**' refers to the combination of institutions and organisations located between the manufacturer and the end-customer (known as a **consumer**). Typically, wholesalers and retailers act as intermediaries in the channel of distribution for consumer products. There are exceptions in which manufacturers sell direct to consumers (factory shops, mail order, selling on-line) but intermediaries are more typical.

One issue for the manufacturer to consider is how to move goods through the channel: how to encourage the intermediaries to stock the good and actively sell it on to customers. The problem is all the greater when we remember that both wholesalers and retailers also carry the products of rival organisations. To move the goods through the channel, organisations use one (or a combination) of two strategies: **pushing** and **pulling**.

A **push effect** is used to move the organisation's goods into the distribution network. The aim is to encourage the various distribution outlets to stock and sell the product. The manufacturer directs the bulk of promotional effort towards selling the product into the channel so as to persuade the members of that channel to push the product forward until it reaches the final consumer. Sales promotion is used to push the product to wholesalers who, in turn, push it to retailers. The retailer will then employ sales promotion at the point of sale to push it to the consumer.

Pushing is a technique favoured by organisations without strong brands, which are involved in price competition.

With **pulling**, the manufacturer focuses the promotional effort on the consumer in the belief that he or she will be motivated to 'pull' the product through the channel. For instance, a consumer responding to an advertisement might place an order for the product or merely ask for it in a retail store. The retailer will then place orders for the product with wholesalers and the manufacturer. Advertising is the key technique used in a pulling strategy. This is a technique favoured by owners of strong brands.

In practice, many organisations will use a combination of pushing and pulling as part of an overall promotional campaign. Table 1.5.5 lists advantages and disadvantages of both pushing and pulling techniques.

Table 1.5.3 Phases of the life cycle: Use of promotional techniques

	Pre-introduction	**Introduction**	**Growth**	**Maturity**	**Decline**
Advertising	Selected	Extensive	Extensive	Moderate	Limited
Sales promotion	None	Extensive	Extensive	Moderate	None
Public relations	Some	Extensive	Moderate	None	None
Personal selling	Selected	Extensive	Extensive	Moderate	Limited

Table 1.5.4 Buyer readiness: Use of promotional techniques

	Awareness	**Interest**	**Desire**	**Action**
Advertising	Extensive	Extensive	Declining	Declining
Sales promotion	Minimal	Minimal	Growing	Extensive
Personal selling	Minimal	Minimal	Growing	Extensive
Public relations	A minor but unchanging role			

Figure 1.5.3 Push and pull strategies

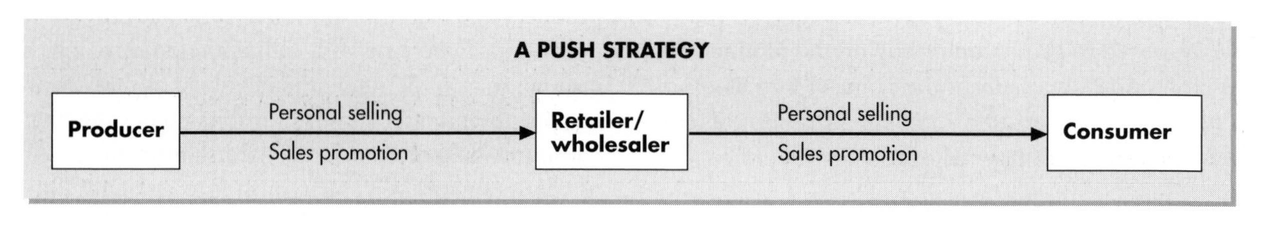

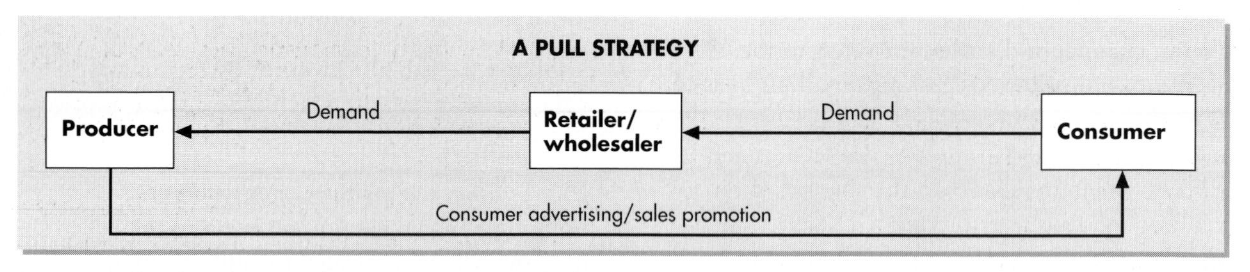

Table 1.5.5 Advantages and disadvantages of pushing and pulling techniques

	Advantages	**Disadvantages**
Pushing Techniques		
Distributor	They gain shelf space	No contact with the consumer
Incentives	They gain distributor support	The cost involved reduces profit margins
Trade advertising	They educate distributors	The need to differentiate from competitive promotions
POP display material	They build relationships with distributors	The power of distributors to control distribution
	They offset competitor activity	Their effects are only short term
Sales force incentives	They improve profitability through increased sales volume	
Pulling Techniques		
Advertising	Build brand image	High cost of media
	Develop relationship between brand and consumer	Fragmenting audiences
Consumer incentives	Create rapid brand awareness	More 'canny' consumers
	Differentiate product	Power of distributor
Packaging	Maintain loyalty	No trade support
	Can be used tactically	

B2B or B2C?

There is an importantant distinction between marketing to other business organisations (known traditionally as industrial marketing but in the internet age increasingly referred to as business-to-business, B2B) and marketing in consumer markets (business-to-consumer or B2C).

In general, the buyer in B2B markets is likely to be more knowledgeable, more rational and less moved by emotion. Moreover, as an industrial buyer is placing large orders, it is likely that the decision to buy will be taken by a group of people (known as the decision-making unit).

In contrast, in B2C markets, the average consumer is less knowledgeable and more likely to be moved by emotion. In most cases, the decision to purchase is taken by an individual but, for larger items, it is likely to be a family decision in which even young children may play a role. Table 1.5.6 identifies the main differences between the two markets in terms of promotional strategy.

Table 1.5.6 Differences between B2B and B2C marketing

B2B	B2C
Group decision Personal selling dominates Use of rational, logical information-based messages	A single person or small group makes the decision Advertising and sales promotion dominate Use of emotion and imagery

Positioning

Positioning is defined as 'the place the product occupies in the consumer's perceptual map' (J. Blythe, *Marketing Communications*). Notice that we are concerned here with the customer's subjective view of the product in relation to rival products on the market. An effective marketing strategy requires the product to have a clear position in the market in terms of both:

- a target market – where the organisation wishes to compete, and
- a differential advantage – how it wishes to compete.

The basic principle behind positioning is that companies must differentiate their products or risk being seen as a provider of generic products sold at the lowest price. Positioning entails the placement of a company and its products (within the minds of potential and actual customers) in terms of:

- quality
- service
- capabilities
- price.

Positioning seeks to place a company's products or services in the minds of people so as to influence their behaviour. Products and services created to solve customer problems or satisfy their wants must use their position:

- to promise the benefit the customer will receive
- to create the expectation that the product will solve the customer's problems
- to offer a solution to customer problems that is different from, and superior to, that of competitors.

Promotion places a key role in positioning a product and company. Lucozade has now been positioned as a drink providing energy for those engaged in sport (in earlier decades, it was seen as a drink to give energy to those recovering from illness). Volvo positions itself on the safety features of its cars, while BMW stresses luxury and engine performance. Avis car rental uses an interesting slogan: 'We're number 2 (to Hertz), so we try harder.' Avis admits that it is a market follower but makes a virtue of this by emphasising that it makes them try even harder.

The objective of **positioning** is to create and maintain a distinctive place in the market for a business organisation and its products.

There are four keys to successful positioning:

1. A clear message in terms of both target market and differential advantage, e.g. 'A Mars a day helps you to work, rest and play'
2. A consistent message
3. Credibility – the differential advantage must be credible in the mind of the target customer.
4. Competitiveness – the differential advantage should have a competitive edge.

Figure 1.5.4 shows a position or perceptual map relating to supermarkets. The two dimensions used are price and range of products. The plot points are based on customer perception of rival supermarkets in terms of these two attributes. There are four stages in drawing up the map:

1. Identifying a set of competing brands
2. Identifying important attributes that consumers use when choosing between brands
3. Conducting market research in which consumers are asked to score each brand on the key attributes
4. Plotting brands on a two-dimensional map.

The perceptual map has a number of functions. In the case of new product development, it can be used to identify gaps in the market and to develop positioning strategies for the product. For an existing product, it can be used to **reposition** the product. Repositioning occurs when sales are poor or when a change in customer taste threatens future sales. It involves changing the target market and/or the differential advantage, as shown in Figure 1.5.5:

- **Image reposition**
  No change in the product or target market but promotion is used to change the image of the product.
- **Product repositioning**
  This involves a modification of the product.
- **Intangible repositioning**
  This involves targeting a different market segment with the same product.
- **Tangible repositioning**
  This requires a change in both product and target market.

Advertising and positioning

Advertising plays a major role in positioning brands in the mind of the target audience. Creative positioning develops or reinforces an image for the brand. This is achieved in seven ways.

1. **Product characteristics**
   This focuses on the quality of the product and the benefit to consumers, e.g. BMW – 'the ultimate driving experience'.
2. **Price quality**
   This focuses on value for money, e.g. 'Good food costs less at Sainsbury's'.
3. **Product use**
   This involves associating the product with a particular use.
4. **Product user**
   Here the product is associated with a particular user or type of user.
5. **Product class**
   'I Can't Believe it's Not Butter' was positioned within the butter range by a carefully constructed name.
6. **Symbols**
   Symbols position the product and aid recognition. The Andrex puppy positions the product in terms of softness.
7. **Competition**
   The organisation seeks to position itself by reference to a competitor, e.g. 'Volvo has built a reputation for surviving accidents. Subaru has built a reputation for avoiding them.'

Figure 1.5.4 A position map for supermarkets

Figure 1.5.5 Repositioning strategies

Target market \ Product	Same	Different
Same	**Image repositioning**	**Product repositioning**
Different	**Intangible repositioning**	**Tangible repositioning**

Unique selling proposition (USP)

This is the product benefit which can be regarded as unique in a primary selling argument. It is the product feature which stands out as different from the competition. In some cases, the USP represents a unique feature of the product, e.g. Dyson vacuum cleaners uniquely do not require a bag. In other cases, USP can be identified in terms of packaging (Toblerone chocolate or Mateus Rosé wine bottles) or distribution. Whatever the source of the USP, it will play a major role in advertising the product.

Activity

Classify the following in terms of the repositioning grid:

- Repositioning Lucozade as a drink for sportsmen and women
- A change in the formulation of Castlemaine XXXX
- Nike's reinvention of trainers as a 'rebellious statement'

Choosing the message

The purpose of advertising and other forms of promotion is to move people through the AIDA framework. To achieve this task, it is necessary to construct a message. This is defined as 'the propositions to be put to a target audience as part of the marketing communications plan' (*Source*: Hart, *CIM Marketing Dictionary*). The message is likely to arise out of the attributes of the product but will then be converted into benefits that the customer will derive from the product. Hence the *Financial Times* message, 'No FT, no comment', tells us that only by reading the *Financial Times* will we be able to talk in an informed way and to make judgements on the major issues of the day. In *Principles of Marketing*, Kotler states that the message is composed of three features: message content, message structure and message format.

Message content is about 'what to say'. The communicator has to identify an appeal or theme that will produce a desired response. There are three types of appeal:

- **Rational** in relation to self-interest
  This type of message is designed to show that the product will produce desired benefits in terms of quality, economy, value and performance.
- **Emotional** appeals
  These messages are designed to stir up negative or positive emotions. BT's 'it's good to talk' campaign was an example of appeal to positive emotions, but a campaign based on messages such as, 'There are some things you can't afford to gamble with …' play on people's fears and negative emotions. Great care is needed with the latter message since it can be counterproductive and, moreover, contrary to advertising regulations.
- **Moral** appeals
  These are directed at people's sense of what is right and proper. This type of appeal is widely used by charities.

Message structure refers to what is to be said and how it is said. There are several issues to consider here:

- Choice of language
- The amount of background knowledge required by the audience
- Whether to draw a conclusion or leave it to the audience
- Whether to present a one-sided or two-sided argument
- Whether to present arguments in ascending or descending order of strength

Message format: Issues to consider in print-based advertising include the headline, illustration, colour and font size and type. In the case of the broadcast media, the choice of voices is of crucial importance. Whereas young announcers and actors are essential when selling products to the younger age groups, selling to the elderly is most effective when older actors are used. The makers of stairlifts, walk-in baths and similar products for older people make extensive use of older actors such as Thora Hird, Frank Windsor and June Whitfield. The choice of actor or celebrity to endorse the product is also crucial. The effectiveness of the message source depends on its credibility and attractiveness. Carol Vorderman is widely used in advertising because of her mathematical talents. This lends credibility to the message as she is seen as an 'expert'. However, problems can arise:

- if a scandal is associated with the celebrity endorser of the product (e.g. Michael Jackson, OJ Simpson, Gary Glitter)
- if people perceive that the celebrity is only 'doing it for the money'
- if claims are shown to be false.

Celebrity claims for sports equipment were undermined when it was demonstrated that the endorser did not actually use the golfball, tennis racket, etc. that they were endorsing.

Kotler concludes that the message must:

- be of practical value to the target audience
- communicate new information about the product
- reinforce or help to justify the buyer's recent purchase decisions
- be 'impactful'.

Promotional budget

The **promotional budget** is the sum of money set aside for spending on a promotional campaign.

The budget holder must decide how this money is to be spent in the most cost-effective manner. He or she is required to use the budget to provide maximum impact so as to achieve the organisation's marketing objectives. The budget system is seen as combining control (since it imposes a limit on spending) with freedom of action (decisions on how and when to spend are delegated to the budget holder).

The budget can be expressed as a spreadsheet with promotional techniques shown horizontally and divisions of time shown vertically. The relative importance of each promotional weapon is shown in terms of share of promotional spending, and decisions about timing can be shown in the distribution of spending ove the year. As with all budgets, the time period ends with a comparison of the budgeted figure with the actual figure. Deviations from the plan are known as **variances** and they will need to be studied and explained.

The size of the budget will be set with reference to one of the following:

- Percentage of sales
- Affordability
- Matching competion
- Objective and task method

The chosen **percentage of sales** may be based on company or industry tradition and, clearly, this has its appeal. However, it suffers from grave deficiencies.

- As sales decline, promotional spending declines, thus compounding the decline.
- It ignores market opportunities which might suggest the need to spend more on promotion.
- It fails to provide a means of determining the correct percentage.

The problem with **affordability** is that it neglects the objectives set for the product and any marketing opportunities that arise.

Matching competition is a defensive and cautionary method. Not only does it suffer the problems noted above but it also leads to a solidifying of market share.

The **objective and task method** has three stages:

1 Define objective.
2 Determine strategy.
3 Finally estimate the cost of executing that strategy.

Activity

Identify five advertisements shown on television and five printed in newspapers. In each case make comments on their message content, message structure and message format. Suggest reasons for the choice of message each time.

Activity

You are the Marketing Director of a large electrical goods manufacturer. Construct and justify a promotional budget in each of the following cases.

1 £100 million budget for promotional spending on a revolutionary new consumer product to be introduced three months into the year.

2 £30 million budget for promotional spending on an existing product which has recently entered the mature phase of its life cycle.

Kotler argues that 'The main advantage of this method is that it forces managers to define their communication objective, to determine the extent to which each objective will be met using selected promotion tools, and the financial implications of alternative communication programmes.'

Source: Kotler *et al.*, *Principles of Marketing*

Promotional effectiveness and efficiency

The two words 'effectiveness' and 'efficiency' are sometimes confused.

Effectiveness is about achieving results.

A promotional campaign is effective if it achieves the objectives set for the campaign.

Efficiency refers to the relationship between the result and the use of financial and other resources.

The campaign is efficient if it achieves a result with the minimum use of resources. The evaluation of any promotional campaign should be in terms of both effectiveness and efficiency.

Promotion is both **efficient and effective** if the right message is transmitted to the right audience so that objectives are achieved at the lowest promotional cost. This means that the campaign has been cost-effective. However, some campaigns are inefficient and/or ineffective, as illustrated in Table 1.5.7 which shows a promotional effectiveness grid.

Promotional research

This branch of marketing research is concerned with the effectiveness and efficiency of the advertising campaign. The research takes place before the campaign (**pre-testing**) and after the campaign (**post-testing**).

Pre-testing of promotional techniques is designed to assess whether the campaign is likely to be effective. The aim is to reduce the risk of producing an ineffective campaign since it is better to identify potential failures before the organisation is committed to substantial expenditure. It is certainly better to test reaction before an inappropriate and harmful message is sent out. Unfortunately, no amount of pre-testing can eliminate failure. A classic case of failure occurred in the early days of television advertising when Strand cigarette advertisements featured a single individual walking the rain-drenched streets in a raincoat. Instead of the individual being perceived as a self-assured private detective of film noir, he was perceived as a 'loner in a

Table 1.5.7 Promotional effectiveness grid

	Effective	Ineffective
Efficient	The right message to the right audience at the lowest promotional cost.	Low promotional budget, but the message was not received by the right people.
Inefficient	The right messages received by the right people, but at an unnecessarily high promotional cost.	High spend and the wrong message!

raincoat'. The advertisement was a major factor in the demise of the brand. More recently, Sainsbury's used a campaign featuring John Cleese as a hectoring branch manager in the mould of Basil Fawlty. Again this was seen as a failure since it irritated many viewers. The campaign was replaced by one that stressed a softer, more caring image. The most common technique for pre-testing is a **focus group** in which people are brought together for a frank discussion.

Another aspect of pre-testing is **media research**. This research concentrates on the audience in terms of both quality and quantity. TV ratings provide figures for viewers of television programmes while the Audit Bureau of Circulation (ABC) publishes circulation figures for newspapers. However, as well as finding out how many people watch, listen or read, we should also be concerned with the type of person in terms of age, social class, occupation and other methods of segmenting the market.

Post-testing research occurs during and after the campaign. In the case of coupons (and similar techniques in which potential customers communicate to gain more information), effectiveness can be measured in terms of the number of enquiries received. By including an identifying code on the coupons, it is possible to judge which media are working.

Surveys can be used to measure the impact of an advertisement. These consist of:

- **recognition tests** in which people are shown the advertisement and asked if they recognise it
- **recall tests** in which people are asked if they can remember seeing it.

Ultimately, the campaign should be judged in terms of the extent to which it achieves its objectives (and in a cost-effective manner). Consequently, if the aim was to raise sales by a certain amount, success should be judged in terms of sales figures. One problem, however, is that it is difficult to prove that a campaign caused a rise in sales rather than the two events being coincidental.

Efficiency (or cost effectiveness) can be measured in terms of the relationship between results and the input, e.g.

- advertising costs per thousand target buyers reached by the media vehicle
- cost per enquiry.

Activity

1 Research:

   a) circulation figures for a major national newspaper

   b) advertising rates on one local and one national newspaper.

2 Construct your own recognition and recall test for five advertisements carried by TV and newspapers.

3 Engage in a focus-group discussion about two advertisements.

Revision Questions

1. What is meant by the word 'strategy'? (1 mark)
2. What is the role of objectives in devising a strategy? (1 mark)
3. What is meant by a logo and what is its purpose? (2 marks)
4. With illustrations, explain the factors influencing the promotional mix for a particular product? (1 mark)
5. What is a budget and what is its role in promotional strategy? (2 marks)
6. Explain the difference between pushing and pulling strategies. (2 marks)
7. Explain how the promotional mix is different for a pushing strategy compared with a pulling strategy. (2 marks)
8. What is meant by positioning? (1 mark)
9. Why is it beneficial to develop a unique selling proposition? (1 mark)
10. What factors influence the size of the promotional budget? (1 mark)
11. Explain the difference between the word 'efficient' and the word 'effective'. (2 marks)
12. What is promotional research? (1 mark)
13. Explain the difference between pre- and post-testing of advertisements. (2 marks)
14. Why is it important to develop a positive corporate image? (1 mark)
15. Using real life examples, explain what is meant by the advertising message. (1 mark)
16. Study the advertisement opposite and answer the questions that follow.
    - **a)** Comment on this product in terms of the product life cycle.
    - **b)** Comment on the message in relation to the product life cycle.
    - **c)** Why do you think this advertisement carries a list of stockists?
    - **d)** Comment on this advertisement in relation to the AIDA model.
    - **e)** How would you evaluate the effectiveness of this advertisement?
    - **f)** Suggest roles for other elements of the promotional mix for this product.

Time Times Oct 2000

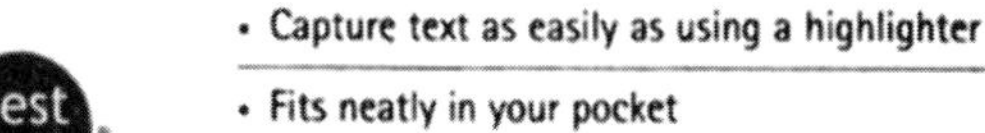

- Capture text as easily as using a highlighter
- Fits neatly in your pocket
- Collect information anytime... anywhere!
- Download to your PC, Laptop, PDA or Mobile Phone (via IrDA/Serial cable)
- Comes with handy QuickLink applications
- Enter data instantly into any application
- Stores a massive 1,000 pages of text

best buy

Compatible with:
- PALM/VISOR/ WINDOWS CE*
- MOBILE PHONES
- PCs
- LAPTOPS

* requires download

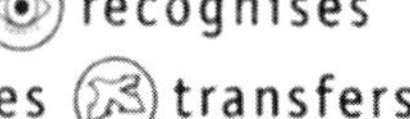

Why type it, when you can QuickLink it!

Wizcom QuickLink PEN

For more information visit: www.wizcomtech.com

available from all good electronics retailers

PC WORLD electronics boutique JOHN LEWIS Department Stores Micro Anvika Dixons WHSmith easyscan.com 21store.com jungle

17 Read the article below and answer the questions that follow.

a) Why have Kellogg used Tony the Tiger for advertising?

b) Why did Exxon/Esso develop the 'tiger in your tank' slogan?

c) Outline ways in which Kellogg combines advertisements featuring Tony the Tiger with other sales promotion techniques

d) Outline ways in which Exxon combines its cartoon tiger advertisements with other sales promotions

e) Why has Kellogg objected to the Exxon promotional strategy?

CEREAL KILLER: THERE'S A BIG CAT IN COURT AS KELLOGG SUES EXXON

A BITTER cat-fight that has been rumbling on for years is about to end with a legal showdown between two of America's best-known companies, **writes Leo Lewis**.

The US Supreme Court has finally cleared the way for breakfast-cereal maker Kellogg to proceed with a lawsuit against Exxon Mobil, the US parent of Esso. It argues that the oil giant's tiger-in-your-tank character is invading Tony the Tiger's territory.

Kellogg contends that as long as Exxon's tiger was only being used to promote the fuel itself, there was probably no confusion.

But more recently, the company has started using the image to advertise the chain of TigerMart convenience stores at its petrol stations.

The big-cat battle began in 1996 when Kellogg sued in a Memphis federal court, saying Exxon had crossed the line by using "Cartoon Tiger", as it is uninspiringly known, to sell food. The case was thrown out two years later and referred to the Supreme Court – which has now ruled that the case can be heard back in Memphis.

Both characters have been used in advertising campaigns since the mid-1960s. "During that time", said an Exxon spokesman, "the Cartoon Tiger has peacefully co-existed with a number of Tiger trademarks, including Tony."

The Independent on Sunday 22 October 2000

References

Blythe, J. *Marketing Communication*, FT Prentice Hall, 2000

Fill, C. *Marketing Communications*, Butterworth and Heineman for CIM, 1998

Kotler *et al.*, *Principles of Marketing*, FT Prentice Hall, 1999

Smith, P. R., *Marketing Communications: An integrated approach*, Kogan-Page, 1999

Wright, R., *Advertising*, FT Prentice Hall, 2000

Web sites

Advertising Association	www.adassoc.org.uk
Advertising Standards Authority	www.asa.org.uk
Audit Bureau of Circulations Ltd (ABC)	www.abc.org.uk
Chartered Institute of Marketing	www.cim.co.uk
Department of Trade and Industry (DTI)	www.dti.gov.uk
Market Research Society	www.marketresearch.org.uk
Marketing Society	www.marketing-society.org.uk

UNIT 1

End of Unit Assignment

This assignment is in two parts.

1 'A comparison and evaluation of two competitor organisations' strategies for the promotional aspects of marketing similar products'

You should note that two organisations in direct competition should be used for this assignment. These might be:

- rival firms in the mobile phone business
- rival car manufacturers
- rival brands of soft drink
- rival supermarkets

or any other pair of competitors for whom information is available.

The study should identify and explain similarities and differences in

- the use of different elements of the promotional mix
- the nature of the promotional strategy
- the choice of advertising media
- the nature of the message
- product positioning and the targeting of segments.

To access high marks, it is necessary to go beyond description and explanation to an analysis of the promotional mix, for instance the use or non-use of particular elements of the mix and possible reasons for the choice of advertising message. Reference should be made to promotional objectives and to the models of marketing communications.

2 'A marketing promotional plan for a selected organisation's product or service'

Your promotional plan should contain:

- a review of the current position based on market research
- an analysis of the external environment including analysis of the competition
- a clear statement of marketing objectives (e.g. targets for sales revenue, market share, introduction of new products and entry into new markets)
- a clear statement of promotional objectives including objectives for each element of the promotional mix, with reference made to AIDA and DAGMAR
- an outline of marketing strategy with particular reference to positioning, targeting and the unique selling proposition
- an outline of promotional strategy with reference to the elements of the promotional mix and the blending of elements into an integrated strategy
- a promotional budget
- choice of advertising media
- the evolution of a message
- a statement of how the strategy is to be evaluated, with reference made to both effectiveness and cost effectiveness in achieving objectives.

In addition to description, your account should include a clear explanation and rationale for your promotional strategy. Your plan should be reasoned and based on referenced research.

UNIT 2

Marketing Research

CHAPTER 1

The Purposes of Marketing Research

KEY TERMS

Elasticity	Marketing mix	Qualitative data
Forecasting	Marketing research	Quantitative data
Loss leaders	Marketing research plan	Target population
Market orientated	Pricing policies	Trends
Market research	Product orientated	

In this chapter, you will learn what marketing research is and why it is so important to businesses. We will look at:

- the difference between 'product orientated' products and 'market orientated' products
- what the term 'marketing research' means and how this differs from the term 'market research'
- why marketing research is so important to businesses
- examples of how wide marketing research can be
- examples of the different types of data which can be collected.

Product-orientated and market-orientated products

Before any new product is manufactured and made available for sale, some kind of research must be carried out. This may be research into the nature of the market, e.g. finding out what prices people are prepared to pay. It may be research into how the product should be made, e.g. is it possible to make it out of plastic? It may be research into how the new project can best be financed, e.g. would the issue of additional shares be better for the business than borrowing from a bank?

When a new product is manufactured all of these research aspects are important, but this unit is only concerned with elements of marketing and the research that is necessary for businesses to make the right decisions about marketing their products.

Businesses can take one of two approaches to marketing research.

1 They can assume that their products will automatically sell and make high profits for the business. This is known as **product orientation**.

2 They can carry out research to check whether the market wants their products and adjust the **marketing mix** to meet this demand. This is known as **market orientation**.

Marketing mix – all the factors involved in successful sales – price, promotion, place of sale, etc.

Some products do not need very much marketing research; other products do.

Product orientation

Product orientation – when a business simply produces its goods and believes they will sell without checking to see what the market wants

Product-orientated goods and services are those products which do not need any significant amount of marketing research. There are various reasons for this.

- The product may be in very short supply, but there is a high demand for it.
- The product is so good that people will want to buy it with a minimum of marketing.
- The product is a necessity and people must buy it.
- The supplier is a monopoly and if people want the product they must buy from this one supplier.
- The marketing is done for the business (as with Pet Rocks, see opposite).

Truly product-orientated goods and services need no significant marketing because they 'sell themselves'. This means that only limited marketing research is required such as where to sell the product and what would be the most profitable price to charge. Some products become product orientated because they have become necessities. Once the first three Harry Potter novels had been produced and sold, the subsequent books had a vast captured market. As long as the writing remained as good as in the first three, J. K. Rowling and the publishers (Bloomsbury) needed to do little more than tell the eagerly waiting public when the next book would be on sale. Harry Potter had become a product-orientated good.

Market orientation

Market orientation – when a business conducts marketing research to find out what products the market wishes to buy

Most goods and services are produced and sold into competitive markets and require significant marketing research. If careful marketing research is not carried out, it is quite likely that the products will not sell as well as they could. In some cases (see the Sinclair C5 opposite), lack of marketing research can be disastrous.

Market-orientated products require extensive marketing research for the following reasons.

- The producers may not know who their target population is and what features these people consider important.
- There may be a very competitive market. If their product does not *exactly* match what the customers want, they will find it very difficult to sell.
- Many products need a high level of persuasive marketing to make people buy them.
- Tastes and fashions change rapidly in some markets and research is therefore necessary if new products are to meet the new demand.

Pet Rocks make a $ million

In 1975, Gary Dahl from California was joking with friends about not having a real pet because he had a pet rock which took no real looking after. He pointed out that it needed no feeding, was house trained and could be taught tricks such as rolling down a slope.

When he returned home, he thought more about his joke and spent two weeks writing the *Pet Rock Training Manual* with instructions on how to care for your pet rock and teach it tricks like playing dead. He then bought some medium sized grey pebbles from a local builder's merchant and placed each in a gift box with the training manual. They were first offered for sale at a gift show in San Francisco and, because the idea was so way out, many newspapers and television programmes reported his idea and interviewed him. Soon people were buying pet rocks all over the USA. Within six months, Gary Dahl had sold more than a million Pet Rocks and had become a millionaire, all with a minimum of marketing research.

Sinclair C5

Clive Sinclair produced the first pocket calculator in 1972 and the first real home computer, the Spectrum, in 1982. Both made him a fortune. Then, in 1985, he produced the Sinclair C5 electric car which he sold for £399. It required no driving licence, no tax and no insurance and could be driven by underage drivers. It was also environmentally friendly.

Sinclair, convinced that he was on a winner, carried out very little marketing research. The general public did not share his view. Worried about safety aspects, the downmarket look of the C5 and the fact that the heavy batteries had to be recharged every 20 miles, very few people bought a C5. Within a year, Sinclair Vehicles was closed.

With more careful marketing research, Sinclair would not have tried to sell this as a road car. Instead, he could probably have found a highly prosperous market in the USA where some C5s were bought as expensive toys for rich American kids.

For many products, extensive marketing research is normal and a considerable amount of money is spent on perfecting the product. Cars, pet food, holidays, breakfast cereals, shampoo and many other standard products are mainly market orientated; whenever a new product is brought out in these markets, it is carefully researched beforehand.

Marketing research and market research

The term 'marketing research' covers a much wider area than just **market research.** It relates to all the elements of the marketing mix, including market research.

Figure 2.1.1 The elements of the marketing mix

In **market research**, the business carries out research about its customers, about the competition, and about any factors that might affect the market into which it is putting its products.

Here are some questions that market research may answer:

- Where does the **target population** live?

Target population – the segment of the market that the product is aimed at and who are expected to show most interest in it

- What price are potential customers prepared to pay?
- How often do they buy the products and where do they buy them?
- What qualities do they think are most important in these kind of products?
- What similar products are they buying and why?

- What age, gender, etc., are they?
- What lifestyle, interests, etc., do they have?
- Who are the competitors, what prices do they charge, etc?
- Is the market expanding or contracting?

In **marketing research**, all the elements of marketing are consider before a product is produced and sold.

In addition to the kind of questions that are being asked in market research, marketing research asks these questions:

- How should the product be designed so that it will appeal to the target population?
- What channels of distribution would be best for the consumer and the producer?
- What pricing strategy will ensure entry into the market and good profits?
- What mix of advertising and public relations would be best?
- What after sales services should be provided to the customer?
- How does a new product fit in with the current product portfolio of the business?

All elements of marketing require research so that the right marketing decisions can be made. That is the purpose of marketing research.

Why is marketing research so important?

The problems that Sir Clive Sinclair experienced with the C5 demonstrate very clearly the importance of marketing research. That was an extreme case, in which the product failed completely, but there are many other products on sale that are selling far fewer units than they could and their manufacturers are losing profits simply due to insufficient marketing research.

Every aspect of marketing is important, even for product-orientated goods and services, and careful research into a new or existing product should ensure that the right marketing decisions are made. Table 2.1.1 shows some of the stages that should be carried out during the marketing research for a new product. At each stage the table gives a brief explanation of what kind of research would be carried out and why it is important.

In each of the chapters in this unit, there are examples of marketing research and an explanation of why they are important to businesses. Below are some general examples of pricing information that businesses collect and an explanation of how this helps businesses to make the right pricing decisions.

Pricing decisions

How do supermarkets work out which products to use as loss leaders?

A **loss leader** is a product that is sold at a reduced price to attract customers who may then buy other products at the full price.

When supermarkets use products as loss leaders, they are trying to attract customers into their stores. The supermarkets reduce the price of one or more products. This attracts customers into the store and, while they are there, they may buy lots of normally priced products. The more people attracted into the store the better, but the stores must also consider the fact that lowering the price of the original product is losing them profits. Choosing the right product to reduce is therefore very important and marketing research helps them to do this.

What supermarkets are looking for when they choose their loss leaders is a product that has a high **price elasticity of demand**. This will be a product for which a relatively small drop in price will make a large percentage of customers want to buy the product.

High price elasticity means that a drop in price will encourage higher sales.

To find out which products behave in this way, supermarkets use market research data:

- Records of how customers have reacted to price cuts in the past
  Supermarkets' own sales records should provide this information.

Table 2.1.1 Stages in a marketing research plan

The Marzipan Pigs is a local Newcastle band which has recently completed a tour of the UK, playing in various pubs and nightclubs. The band has a small, but growing, loyal fan base. The music is similar to that of groups such as Travis, Radio Head and Cold Play. They have produced demo tapes and have approached some record companies. The members of the band are now considering setting up their own record label and producing and marketing their CDs themselves. Below is some of the marketing research that they are considering.

Stages in marketing research	Type of marketing research	Why this is important
1 Identification of the target population	**a)** Observing the type of people who come to their live gigs **b)** Inviting a wide range of people to listen to their taped music and to fill out a simple questionnaire about what they thought of the music and about themselves	Establishing who the target population is allows the band to target all their marketing efforts at people who they know will be interested in buying their music.
2 Confirming who their competitors are	**a)** Carried out by listening to a wide range of CDs and talking to informed friends **b)** Checking price lists of other artists in major retail outlets and on the internet	This will tell them which market segment they are in. Finding out details about similar bands will allow them to price their product correctly.
3 Deciding on the channel of distribution	**a)** Asking fans, through their web site, where they currently buy CDs and if they would buy CDs directly from the hand via the internet or at gigs **b)** Checking the relative costs and profit level of direct and indirect selling	Access to consumers is vital. They need to know if major retail stores will take their CDs and, if not, what other methods of selling are available.
4 Deciding on the design for the CD case and the content of the inset	**a)** Checking other CD details **b)** Approaching professional designers to check costs and ideas	Although the band wants its own individual approach for the CD design and the inset, the members recognise that it must look professional and be properly costed.
5 Deciding on the price	**a)** Checking the prices of competitors **b)** Checking all the costs of producing, marketing and distributing the CDs	The price must allow them to be competitive but, at the same time, they must ensure that they are making enough profit to justify carrying out much of the work themselves.
6 Deciding on the best method of promotion	**a)** Checking details of all the main radio stations and music journals **b)** Checking the costs of advertising through magazines, radio, internet sites, point of sale materials and merchandising	Raising awareness among potential consumers is vital but the promotion needs to be carefully targeted so that it is not wasted. The use of press releases and reviews helps to add an element of independence but the band needs to know that music stations and magazines will respond positively.
7 Ensuring good after sales service	**a)** Checking how other bands keep in contact with fans after the sale, and what services they offer, such as a web site, pre-release brochures and details of future live performances **b)** Checking the cost of producing a fanzine publication	The band is aware of the importance of building up a solid fan base but it wants to make certain that it is doing this is a way that will appeal to the fans themselves.

- How many close substitutes there are
  Elastic products tend to have many close substitutes.
- What the other supermarkets are doing and what their loss leaders are
  The closest substitute for, say, fresh pork prime shoulder sold by Tesco will be fresh pork prime shoulder sold by Sainsbury, Asda, Waitrose or Somerfield.

Tesco Fresh Pork Prime Shoulder (small and medium) Was £3.29/kg (£1.49/lb)
Now £1.64/kg (£0.74/lb)
Offer Ends 03/0601

Details of weekly offers for Tesco can be found at **www.tesco.com/whatsinstore/**

- The results of customer surveys where the supermarket has asked the customer, either directly or indirectly, how they would react to the price being cut for a range of specific items

How marketing research helps other pricing decisions

Data about the market as a whole and how customers and competitors are likely to react is also vital for all decisions about pricing.

These examples show a range of different pricing strategies and how these have been influenced by marketing research:

- Book publishers know that they can use a **skimming** pricing policy by having a high introductory price for their hardback books and then, after a reasonable time delay, a lower price for the paperback edition. Marketing research tells the publishers very clearly that this is common practice for the industry.
- Publishers of new magazines frequently use **penetration pricing** to launch their new product onto the market. Again, this is common practice for the industry and marketing research tells the publishers that this is the case. It should also tell them that if they continue to sell their magazines at a price below the general market price, the bigger, move established, magazines will cut their prices and drive the new magazine out of the market.
- Marketing research will tell any greengrocer setting up in business that the normal pricing policy for the industry is to add a 33% mark up on the cost of the fruit and vegetables and that, if the new business does not follow this practice of **competitive pricing,** it is likely to be competed out of business by other local greengrocers.

What types of data are collected through marketing research?

Many different forms of data can be collected through marketing research, from tables of figures and recorded interviews, to samples of television adverting and the opinions of people on consumer panels. The data collected records different characteristics, some of which are examined here.

Quantitative and qualitative data

Quantitative data measures the quantity of something, e.g. the number of people in the market, the incomes of the customers, how often they shop, the costs of advertising in a newspaper.

When quantitative data is collected, it is recorded numerically. Where a number of different answers are being taken, the data is normally displayed in a table or as a graph. Data shown in a table and on pie diagrams would be useful to businesses such as plumbers and electricians; it would tell them which sector they should be trying to sell their services to.

Advantages of quantitative data

- It is easy to work out the relative importance of different parts. It can, for example, be turned into percentages.
- It can be converted into graphs and diagrams which are easy to interpret.
- It is often easier to collect because it usually comes from short questions or observations.
- It can, in some cases, be collected automatically, as with data from EPOS systems.

Table 2.1.2 The number of houses produced by the public and private sectors of industry (1989 and 1999)

Year	Private enterprise	Social landlords	Local authorities	All houses
1989	162 182	19 342	16 550	198 074
1999	160 128	22 684	361	183 173

Figure 2.1.2 The proportion of houses produced by the public and private sectors of industry (1989 and 1999)

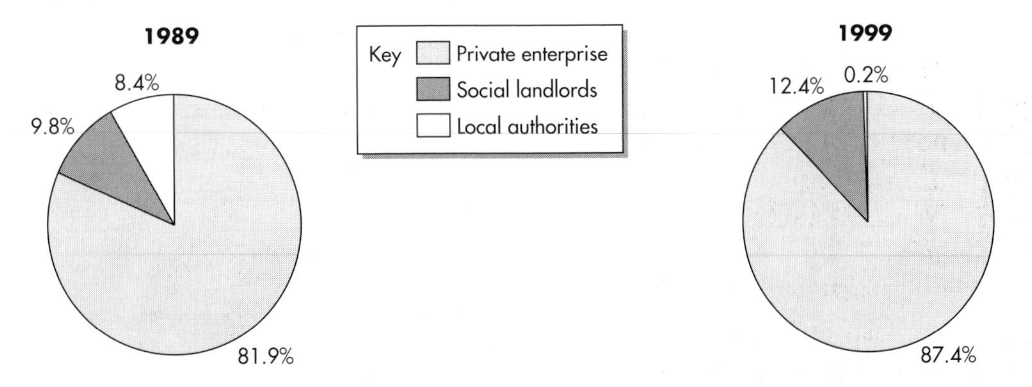

Qualitative data records what people think about something.

Questions that are looking for qualitative answers tend to be opened ended so that answers can be developed. Examples of questions and the qualitative data that they might collect are given in Table 2.1.3.

Quantitative data is the most common type of data collected by marketing departments. In many cases, qualitative data is turned into quantitative data by adding up particular responses. The answers to question 1) in Table 2.1.3 could all be matched against a set of likely answers and the number of people giving each answer added up. Any people giving answers which are not on the list would be recorded as 'others'.

Advantages of qualitative data

- It can explain why people behave and think in the way that they do.
- It allows people to express their feelings.
- It often gives more detail than quantitative data.
- It allows people to make value judgements which tell businesses how important certain factors are to their customers.

Trends

Trends show if a market is expanding or contracting. Trends can be used to predict future sales.

Most data can be recorded again and again for different periods of time. If the data is then compared from one time period to another, it may be possible to identify a trend, e.g. the number of households with modems and internet links is rising. Identifying trends is very important for business for many reasons:

- **Trends** show if a market is expanding or contracting.
  If the market is contracting, the businesses should
  - move into a different market
  - lower prices to attract more customers
  - re-launch the product with an up-dated image.

  If the market is expanding, the businesses should
  - plan for increased demand
  - possibly consider raising prices
  - monitor carefully what competitors are doing.
- Trends can be projected into the future to give some indication of what is going to happen.

Table 2.1.3 Qualitative marketing research data

Questions	Examples of qualitative data given in typical answers
1) What aspect of the hotel where you spent your last holiday did you find most enjoyable?	**a)** The fact that we had half board and did not need to worry about buying breakfast and dinner. **b)** The views from the balcony were stunning. **c)** A licensed bar 24 hours a day.
2) Why do you think the Budweiser 'Wasssaaa' advertisements were so successful?	**a)** It was entertaining and made me laugh. **b)** It was simple and appealed to people even if they didn't drink Bud. **c)** A lot of money was spent on making sure that it worked.
3) How do you feel about charges?	**a)** It's a good idea because you always know what you have to pay each month. **b)** I liked it at first but when the interest rates fell I felt I was losing out. **c)** I wouldn't touch it with a barge pole.
4) In what circumstances would you consider buying private health insurance?	**a)** If I felt that the National Health Service could not give my children proper care. **b)** If I had a higher income. **c)** Never. I think that health care should be provided free by the state to all who need it.

- Trends can be compared. For example, a business can compare its own sales figures against the changing national demand. This allows businesses to work out if they are doing better, worse or the same as the national trend.

The trend in birth rate in Northern Ireland over the period 1988 to 1998 shows a fairly clear downward movement. This would be important for businesses that produce baby food, baby clothes, nappies, rattles, etc. It would also be important for businesses producing products for older children because it shows that they there will be fewer children in the future to buy bicycles, computer games, etc., and eventually teen magazines, mobile phones, etc.

Forecasts

Forecasting predicts what may happen in the future.

A major part of marketing research involves trying to forecast what may happen in the future so that the right decisions about future production and marketing can be made now. Where trends have been identified, the business may then work out what the future data may look like. Usually, a business will consider a range of possible changes. For the number of births in Northern Ireland, for example, the *trend* is clearly moving

Figure 2.1.3 Number of births in Northern Ireland 1988–98

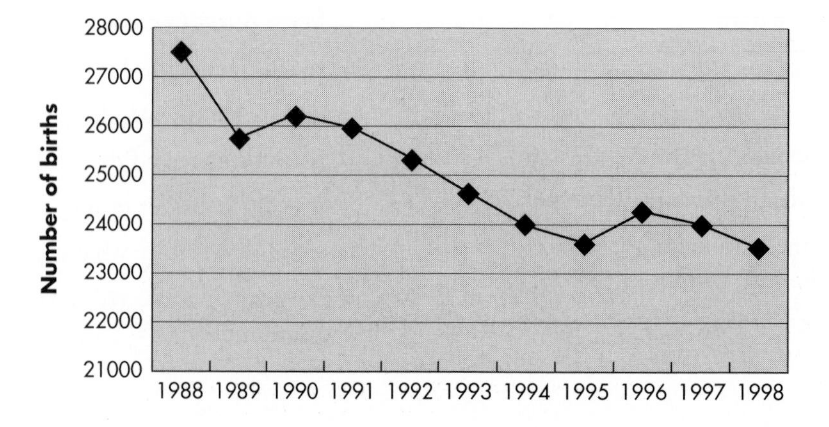

Figure 2.1.4 Forecast number of births for Northern Ireland (1999–2005) showing likely extremes

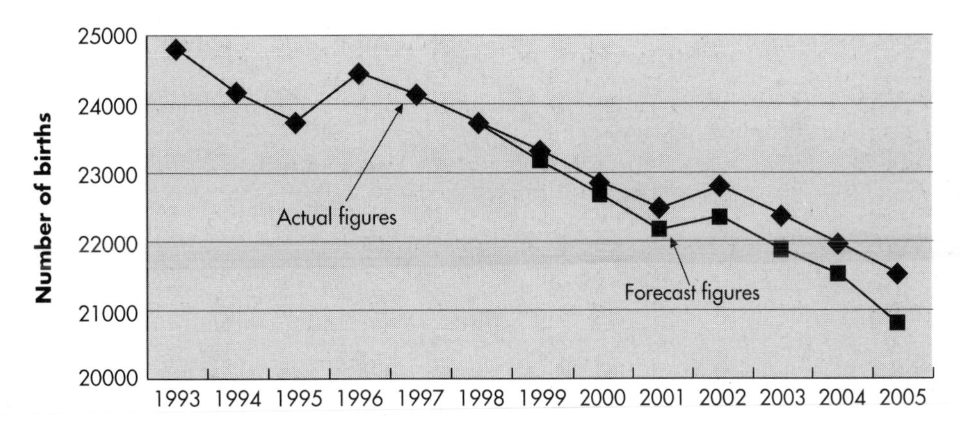

downwards, but the number of births actually rose in the years 1990 and 1996.

On average, the drop in births might accelerate or slow down. Figure 2.1.4 gives the figures for the next seven years, with two separate trends showing these two extremes. The actual figures are likely to be somewhere in between. Both extremes show a falling trend but, over the seven years, the difference between the top of the forecast and the bottom of the forecast has risen to 700 births or about 3.5%. This difference can be very important when firms are deciding on future plans.

Forecasting is not just about working out what is likely to happen to trends. It is also about predicting what will happen in the future for all aspects of marketing.

These examples show some events that might change how businesses market their products in the twenty-first century.

- Indirect taxes in the EU may be harmonised so that all businesses pay roughly the same indirect tax. With alcoholic products, this would mean very much lower prices for beers, wines and spirits sold in the UK, and UK wine merchants, supermarkets, etc., could expect very much higher demand for these products.
- Laws may be introduced to prevent certain types of advertisements being shown on television, especially ones that encourage young children to buy (or badger their parents to buy) products.
- Consumers (or the government) may insist that packaging is made from recyclable or biodegradable materials and businesses will need to work out how they can change their packaging to meet this demand.
- Competitors may be planning a price cut so as to capture market share. Other businesses must be prepared to react quickly to prevent this.

Revision Questions

1 **a)** For each of these products, state whether they are 'product orientated' or 'market orientated'. (5 marks)

- **i)** Table salt
- **ii)** Virgin cola
- **iii)** McDonald's Indian range of burgers
- **iv)** Life assurance
- **v)** Adventure holidays

b) Explain why you have decided that this is the right category to put each product into. (5 marks)

2 Taking one product that you have studied, or have first hand knowledge about, describe the product, state if it is product or market orientated and justify your answer. (6 marks)

3 For each of these pieces of research, state if they are simply 'market research' or if they are *another* part of 'marketing research'. Justify your answers.

a) A business contacts various magazines to find out the cost of a full-page advertisement.

b) A producer of thermal underwear uses government statistics to find out if the number of people over the age of 70 in the UK is increasing.

c) A producer of cola drinks checks the prices of its competitors before it set its own prices for drinks.

d) A supermarket calculates the price elasticity of supply for a number of its products so as to choose the best loss leader. (8 marks)

4 Create a table to outline the major stages of a marketing research plan for one of these new products:

- **i)** A supermarket introducing a range of organic ice cream products
- **ii)** Sega preparing to launch a new games console to compete with the PlayStation 2 and the X Box
- **iii)** A business planning to sell a new version of pet rocks as novelty gifts for next Christmas.

(Use the headings shown on Table 2.1.3.) (15 marks)

5 **a)** Explain the difference between qualitative and quantitative data. (2 marks)

b) For each of these examples of data, state if they are quantitative or qualitative data.

- **i)** Details of the prices of competitors' products
- **ii)** Details from suggestion slips which customers in fast food restaurants are invited to fill in, giving their ideas on how the service could be improved
- **iii)** A record of the average amount spent by each customer visiting a shop
- **iv)** A record of customers' opinions on a new layout for a shop (4 marks)

c) What are the advantages of **i)** quantitative data, and **ii)** qualitative data? (6 marks)

6 This table shows the changing pattern of UK trade with EU countries, expressed as a percentage of our total trade.

Percentage of UK trade with EU countries

Year	1962	1973	1999
Exports	37.7	44.8	58.1
Imports	29.7	42.4	54.0

a) On the basis of what the table shows, forecast the likely percentages for the year 2001, showing clearly why you have chosen these percentage figures. (4 marks)

b) Explain why the actual figures for 2001 might be different from those you have forecast. (6 marks)

CHAPTER 2

Market Segmentation

KEY TERMS

Benefits sought	Green market	Psychological pricing
Business customers	Grey market	Segmentation
Consumers	Niche marketing	SINKs
Demographic	Price discrimination	Socio-economic groups
DINKs	Product differentiation	Target population
Geographic	Psychographic	Yuppies

In this chapter, you will learn what market segmentation is and why it is so important for businesses:

- The meaning and importance of market segmentation
- The major forms of segmentation, including geographic, demographic and psychographic segmentation
- Examples of how segmentation benefits businesses
- The role of marketing research in establishing the nature and importance of market segments

What is market segmentation?

Segmentation – dividing the market up into sections based on customer characteristics

Market segmentation is the process of dividing a market on the basis of the different characteristics that customers have. The main reason for doing this is that people with different characteristics frequently have different needs and wants. It is important that businesses recognise these differences and tailor their products to meet them.

Figure 2.2.1 (overleaf) shows how the UK population was split up in terms of its age in 1998. People in different age categories have different needs, wants and interests. Children under the age of ten will want different toys, read different books, listen to different music, etc., than teenagers. People over 70 may need more heating and medical care but they also have more leisure time than 30–39-year-olds who are mostly working. If they are going to provide the right products and make good profits, businesses need to know how many people are in each segment and what the main characteristics are for that segment.

Segmentation can take place wherever there are distinct differences in the market or between one customer and the next. Sometimes these differences are already present, e.g. gender, race, religion, language, income, location and political opinions. Sometimes governments create the differences, e.g. the age categories for films. Sometimes businesses create their own differences, e.g. when they use persuasive advertising to convince consumers that they want a particular type of product. Many people did not know that they were environmentally conscious until The Body Shop told them that they were.

Why market segmentation is important

Market segmentation is important for businesses because it allows them to meet the needs and wants of customers and, through this, to sell products and make profits. In some cases, as with charities, the final objective may not be making a profit, but segmentation will still help the business to meet its objectives.

Figure 2.2.1 Age distribution in the UK (1998)

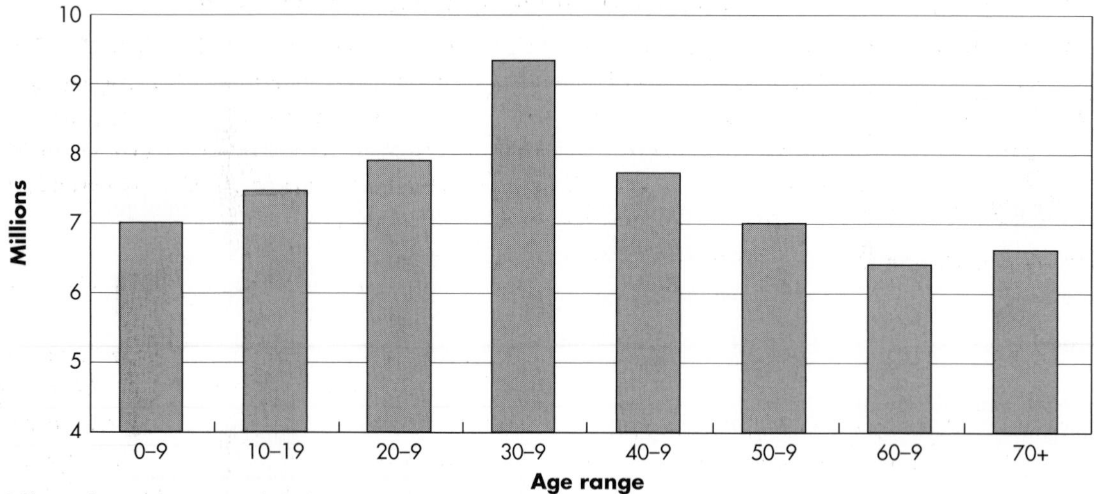

Source: Office of Population and Census Surveys

The Body Shop

'We will use environmentally sustainable resources wherever technically and economically viable. Our purchasing will be based on a system of screening and investigation of the ecological credentials of our finished products, ingredients, packaging and suppliers.'

Details of The Body Shop's activities can be found at **www.bodyshop.com**

Market segmentation takes place for many reasons.

- It helps to define the characteristics of the market and the target population and this helps the business to produce the right products.
- It allows product differentiation. The business can split up its markets and produce slightly different products for each segment.
- It can identify new markets, which allows the business to expand or to specialise in niche markets.

In niche marketing, a business concentrates on one specific segment of a market.

- It allows the business to treat different customers differently, e.g. by price discrimination, and, through this, to increase its revenue and profits.
- It helps to identify which segments competitors are concentrating on and that helps the business to decide how it should react.
- Regular measurement of the size of the segments helps to identify changes taking place and helps to create accurate forecasts of the importance of specific segments in the future. This allows the business to make the right planning decisions for the future.

Niche marketing

In the ice-cream market, Haagen-Das concentrates on the luxury, quality end of the market. In the clothes market, bridal shops concentrate on selling clothes that are generally likely to be worn only once. Many farmers now produce only organic meat, fruit and vegetables for the expanding organic market in supermarkets.

Benefits of **niche marketing**

- Small firms can afford to set up in a niche market because they are relatively small and often do not need high levels of start-up capital.
- Many niche markets are exclusive and businesses can therefore charge high prices for their products.
- For large firms, frequently, these segments are too small and may not give the economies of scale required, so there may be less competition for those firms that do produce in niche markets.
- Small firms can build up a reputation in niche markets and this may allow them to move into larger markets in the future.

Niche marketing for the demographic segment of pregnant mothers

In the competitive world of clothes manufacturing and retailing, *Room For Two Maternity Wear* has found a niche market for mothers-to-be. Originally set up to provide quality maternity wear from a home-based showroom and through independent retailers across the UK, the business has now expanded to provide a web site and mail-order facilities. A wide choice of fabrics and designs is available and individual requirements are made to order. Details can be found on **www.room42maternity.co.uk.**

Product differentiation

With product differentiation, products are changed in some way so that they can be targeted at different segments of the market.

Products may be differentiated to meet different customer needs, as with shoes. Most shoe companies, like Clarks, will produce shoes in a variety of sizes, colours and styles. This will target many segments of the shoe markets, e.g. men and women, adults and children, work and fashion shoes.

With some products, such as soap powders, cat food and cola there is essentially only one type so producers then tend to create what are mainly artificial differences. Most cat food is made from the same raw materials, but flavourings are added to convince the cat owners that the products are different. Some are packaged in small cans and marketed as superior products.

Benefits of product differentiation

- Providing customers with the products that meet their particular needs and wants
- Being able to charge different customers different prices for what are essentially the same products
- Offering existing customers slightly different products in order to keep their interest
- Changing existing products slightly to allow the business to enter new markets.

Price discrimination

With price discrimination, businesses charge different prices for essentially the same product.

The reason why businesses can do this is because different segments of the market have different price elasticities of demand. Where the product has few substitutes, is a necessity and is not too expensive, the business can put up the price without losing customers. This is shown for commuters in Figure 2.2.2 (on page 66) which also shows the benefit to the business of putting up the price of rail tickets. For commuters travelling to London there are no acceptable alternatives. It is also a necessity for them to travel as their jobs are in London and, generally, the cost of travel is low compared to their incomes.

Where there are many substitutes, the product is a luxury or it represents a relatively high proportion of a person's income, then demand will be elastic. In such circumstances, if the price is put down, as for day trippers in Figure 2.2.2, the business can attract a great many additional customers.

It is, however, vital that the business can keep the customers separate, otherwise the commuters would simply buy day tripper tickets at the lower price. In the case of the railways, the train-operating companies keep the two segments separate by only offering off-peak tickets after a certain time of day, too late for commuters to reach work on time.

Table 2.2.1 shows three examples of price discrimination and the different segments for which different prices are charged.

Major types of market segmentation

Business customers and consumers

Businesses sell products to both **consumers** and to other businesses. The needs of the two groups can be very different and it is important that businesses respond to these different needs. In some cases, the products and

Figure 2.2.2 The benefits of price discrimination for the business

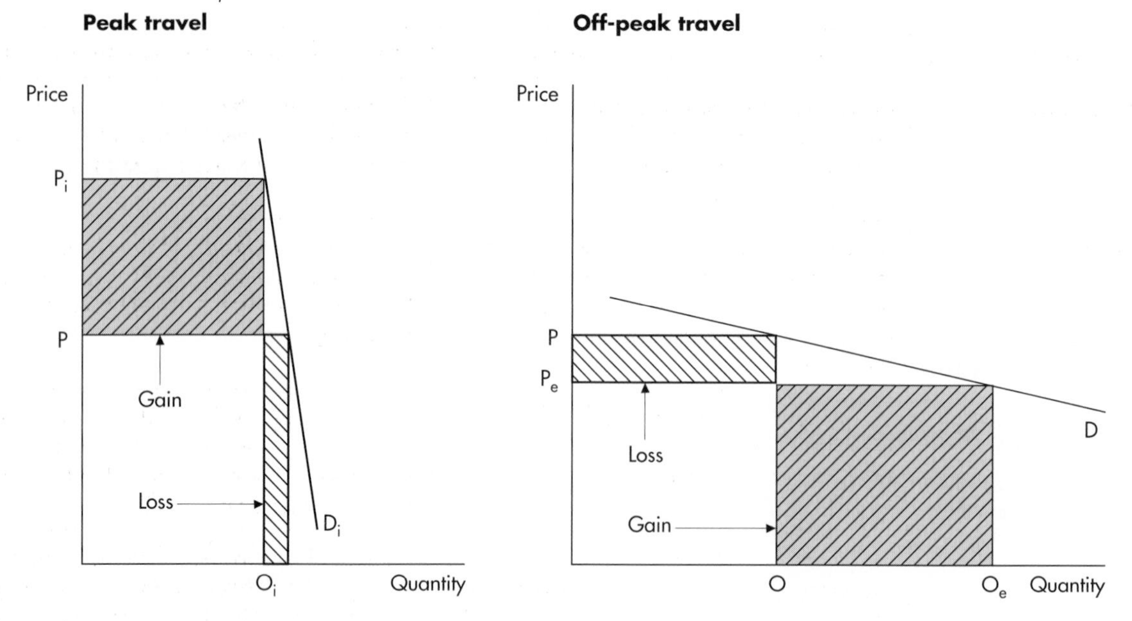

Table 2.2.1 Examples of segments which allow price discrimination

The market	How price discrimination is used
Electricity	• Different prices for consumers and for businesses • Different rates at different times of day • Different rates if bills are paid early • Different rates if you buy other services, like gas supply, from the same provider
Cinemas	• Different rates for adults and children • Different rates at different times of day • Special rates for season ticket holders
Cross channel ferries	• Different rates for car passengers and foot passengers • Different rates at different times of the year • Different rates for customers who have loyalty cards • Different rates for people who book and for people who turn up on stand-by

uses are very similar. A small business buying a potted plant to put in its reception area might well go to a garden centre in the same way that a private individual buying a plant to keep at home does. In other cases, the products and uses can be quite different. A household needing to keep food chilled might have a stand-up refrigerator and a deep freeze. A butcher who needs to keep his meat frozen is likely to have a walk-in refrigerator which has to be specially built by the manufacturer.

Customers buy products which they may use themselves.
Consumers always use the products themselves.

Business **customers** may use the products themselves, as with food delivered to a works canteen or a telephone service, or they may resell the goods, as retailers of clothes, food and electrical goods do. Consumers will always use the products for themselves, their families, their friends, etc. The differences between these markets affect the way in which businesses carry out their marketing and therefore the detail they need to find out when in their marketing research. Examples of the differences in marketing are given in Table 2.2.2.

Table 2.2.2 Differences in marketing to consumers and to business customers

Element of marketing	Approach taken for consumers	Approach taken for business customers
Marketing research	Many consumer markets are very large and therefore some kind of sampling is necessary (e.g. family cars).	Business markets tend to be smaller and it may be possible to survey all businesses in the market (e.g. there are relatively few car showrooms).
Channels of distribution	The channel chosen should be the one that is most convenient for the customer and provides the producer with most profit (e.g. selling baked beans direct to supermarkets then to consumers.)	The most likely connections will be either direct or through distributors, agents or wholesalers (e.g. using distributors to sell baked beans into other countries).
Pricing	Various strategies may be used, including skimming, penetrations pricing and competitive pricing (e.g. skimming for books).	Other businesses will expect competitive prices, discounts on large orders, credit facilities, etc. (e.g. discount for more than 10 of the same textbook order by a school).
Promotion	Frequently through the media as this targets consumers (e.g. TV, magazines) and direct promotions such as point-of-sale, leaflets, etc. (e.g. advertising a new washing machine in a women's weekly).	Details will tend to come through representatives calling, sales literature, price lists, etc. (e.g. providing sales literature to electrical goods stores, showing all the main features of the new washing machine and its cost and recommended sales price).
Product	Frequently mass produced, with standard features (e.g. home computers).	May be specially made so that it will do the specific job that the business needs it to do (e.g. computer-aided manufacturing).
Packaging	Individual items up to family size, sizes to fit normal cupboards, refrigerators, etc. (e.g. wine glasses sold separately or in packs of six).	Cases, bulk packaging, reinforced for safe transport (e.g. thick cardboard boxes with 36 glasses in each, delivered by van to the kitchenware shop).

When businesses use marketing research to acquire consumer details, it is likely to be carried out using published data from general sources, such as government statistics, and surveys using questionnaires, interviews, consumer panels, etc. When businesses use marketing research to find out details about business customers, it is likely to be done by using published details about the businesses, such as their annual reports. Primary data may also be obtained from representatives who visit the firms, and from market specialists.

Demographic segmentation

Demographic segmentation means dividing markets on the basis of the different characteristics found in the population.

Demography is the study of population. Demographic segmentation divides the market on the basis of different characteristics:

- **Physical differences**, such as total populations sizes, age, gender, race, size of family, native language and even hearing and eyesight
- **Differences in status**, such as, married or single, divorced, widowed, retired, employed or unemployed, religion, level of education and level of income

Table 2.2.3 shows typical examples of markets segmented on the basis of demographic features.

Nearly all products can be segmented on the basis of one demographic feature or another. Many markets can be segmented on a range of different demographic features. This is shown for food in Figure 2.2.3.

Table 2.2.3 Demographic segmentation of markets

Demographic feature	Products segmented on this basis	Examples of how products are segmented
Age	Clothes Bus travel Cinema	Children, teens, adults Children, adults, OAPs Any age, over 12, over 15, over 18
Size of family	Hotels Holidays Cars	Single, double, family rooms Singles, couples, families, couples whose children have left home Two seaters, family saloons, people carriers
Income	Accommodation Whisky Toilet paper	Flats, terraced houses, semi-detached, detached, mansions, estates Blended, single malt, 10 to 50 year old malts Economy, own brand, major brands

Figure 2.2.3 Different demographic segments in the food market

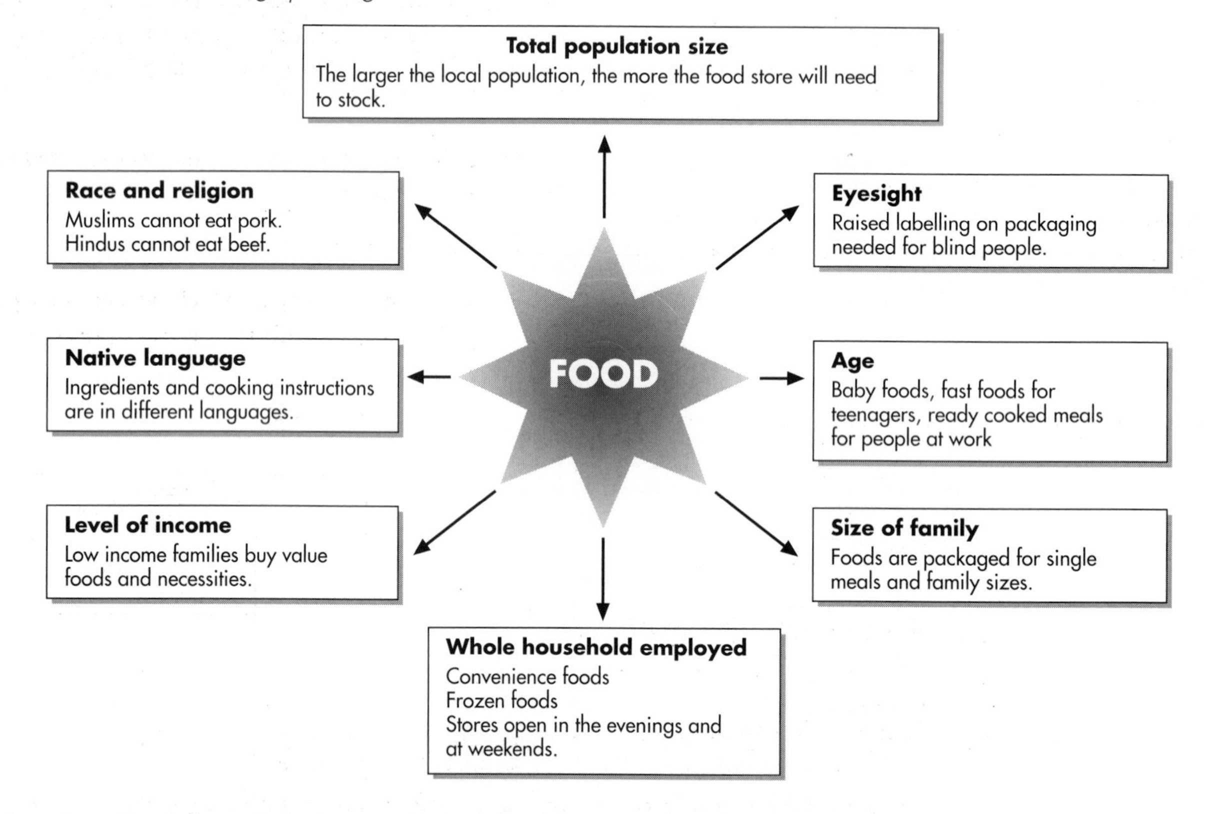

Age has always been a major factor on which markets have been segmented. In the twenty-first century, a growing percentage of the UK population is over retirement age and this has become an important segment in many markets (see the grey market on page 75).

Another major factor is income because this, with savings, determines how much money customers have available for buying good and services. Income is usually related to the kind of job one has and a common way of dividing up potential customers is to do this on the basic of their jobs. This is known as **socio-economic grouping**. Professional people tend to have higher paid jobs than skilled manual and skilled non-manual workers. The lowest pay comes with unskilled jobs.

Socio-economic grouping differentiates between people according to income.

It is important for businesses to know how the employed population is split in terms of these socio-economic groups. Figure 2.2.4 shows the size of these segments for men and for women in 2000. As well as showing that there are relatively few high paid professional or low paid unskilled workers, it also shows that there are three times as many men in high paid jobs as there are women (about 1.37 million men to 0.36 million women).

The demographic features of a particular market will have a major effect on the way that marketing research is carried out. Some of these are obvious; some of them less so:

- The larger the total population in the market, the greater will be the need for some form of sampling.
- Collecting data from children will require more straightforward questions than collecting data from adults.
- Many people are reluctant to give data about the incomes they earn, so this may have to come from other sources, e.g. the average wage/salary for the job that they say that they have.
- Many older people do not like to fill out long questionnaires or to be rung up or visited at home. This is not so much of a problem for younger adults.
- A great deal of general demographic data is published in national and regional data tables Primary research is likely to be used mainly to collect data about a particular customer base that the business has, e.g. from its own customers.

Psychographic segmentation

Psychology is the study of the mind and the way in which we think.

With **psychographic segmentation**, markets are divided on the basis of what people think and, because of that, how they want to live their lives.

Psychographic segmentation is sometimes referred to as **lifestyle segmentation**.

Psychographic characteristics

- **Personality** and the way in which we behave, e.g. caring, outgoing, optimistic, aggressive, self-centred

Figure 2.2.4 Percentage of the UK labour force employed in each socio-economic group (2000)

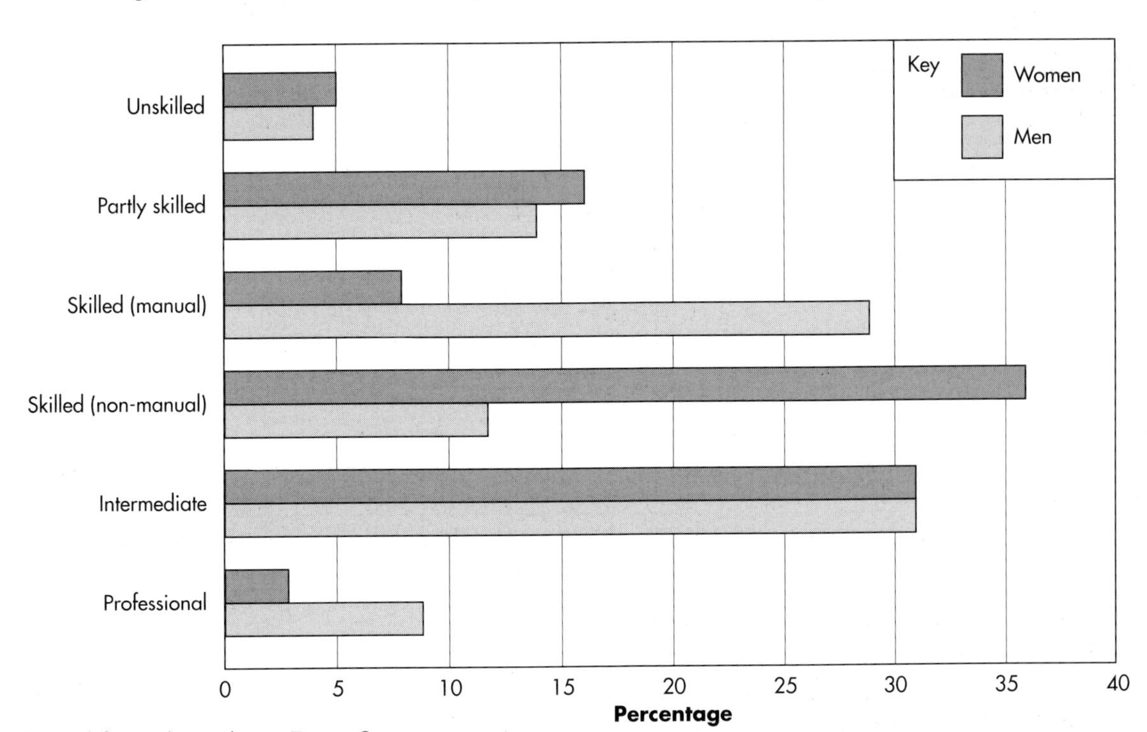

Source: Adapted from the *Labour Force Survey*

- **Interests**, e.g. tastes in music, sport, the opposite sex, hobbies
- **Beliefs**, e.g. religious faith, environmental concerns, animal welfare
- **Opinions**, e.g. political persuasions, class differences, peer pressure
- **Aims** and **ambitions**, e.g. being the best, improving one's image, getting married and having a family

In many cases, successful marketing is about finding out what makes people tick and appealing to that. People who are passionate about a clean, healthy and sustainable environment do not want to be sold products that deplete the ozone layer or create mounds of unsightly rubbish. It may, however, be possible to attract them by using recycled packaging or offering them an organic alternative in food products.

For a firm selling sports equipment, it is usually fairly obvious what the customers' interests are but, even here, the way that a product is presented, priced, promoted, etc., is likely to depend on other psychographic factors.

Panther Tennis Racquets
Original price £35.99
Now only £32.99
Save a massive £3

Customers like to think that they are buying a bargain, which is why many goods are priced at, say, £4.99 rather than £5, and why sale prices emphasise in large bold letters what you are saving rather than what you are spending. These pricing strategies are known as **psychological pricing**. However, many customers also imagine that they could be just as good as the professional sports players and so they want to buy the same kind of tennis racquet as that used by Tim Henman or Martina Hingis, or to play golf with the same clubs as those used by Tiger Woods or Laura Davies. This is why companies which produce sports equipment pay the top sports professionals so much to endorse their products.

Some markets have a large number of segments, as is shown by the huge number of magazines on sale, many dealing with very specialist segments. Table 2.2.4 shows the categories offered for sale by W H Smith stores.

In each of these categories, there are often a number of subsections showing specific interests and uses. Figure 2.2.5 shows how computer magazines are further subdivided.

Figure 2.2.5 Subsegments in the computer magazines market

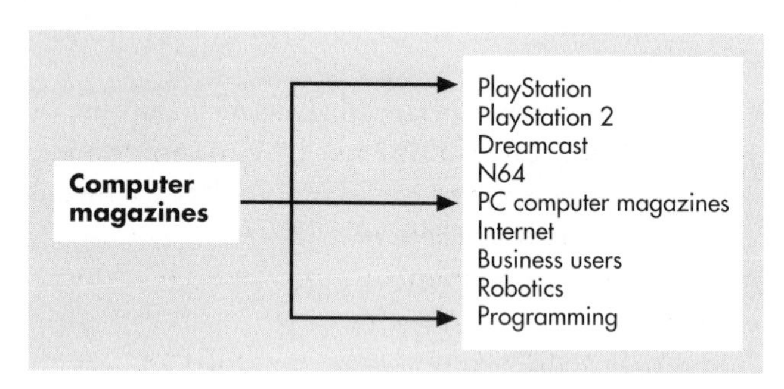

In the past, social class and upbringing had a major effect on the way in which we thought, how we lived our lives and what we bought. It is now much easier for someone from a lower class background to have a good job and a high income and to move into a different class. A person's job and level of income have become much more important than the traditional differences of working, middle and upper class. Today, class tends to be defined by the job that people have, as in socio-economic classification. In 2001, a new classification was created by the National Statistics Office (Table 2.2.5).

Table 2.2.4 Major magazine segmentation categories offered by WH Smith

• Boating and water sports	• General interest	• Photography
• Business	• Health	• Puzzle magazines
• Comics	• Hobbies	• Railways
• Computing	• Lifestyle	• Sport
• Crafts and needlecraft	• Men and style	• Teenage
• Culture and media	• Motoring	• Transport
• Films and TV	• Music and hi-fi	• TV and satellite
• Football and rugby	• Pets and wildlife	• Women's weeklies

Table 2.2.5 The National Statistics Socio-economic Classification (NS – SEC)

Class		Occupational Categories
1.1	L1	Employers in large organisations
	L2	Higher managerial occupations
1.2	L3	Higher professional occupations
2	L4	Lower professional and higher technical occupations
	L5	Lower managerial occupations
	L6	Higher supervisory occupations
3	L7	Intermediate occupations
4	L8	Employers in small organisations
	L9	Own account workers
5	L10	Lower supervisory occupations
	L11	Lower technical occupations
6	L12	Semi-routine occupations
7	L13	Routine occupations
8	L14	Never worked and long-term unemployed
	L15	Full-time students

Recognising the different psychographic segments is very important for businesses because it helps to explain the ways that people behave and can help to explain why different types of promotion work with different customers, why people are repeat buyers, even why some people will buy products in gold or green packaging but not in brown or red.

Collecting data on psychographic factors is more complicated that collecting other marketing research data. Because this is about how people behave and think, and about their opinions, data is likely to be collected in different ways:

- Using questionnaires which have more detailed questions on them and ranges of answers
- Using interviews where people can be asked qualitative questions and where answers can be discussed
- Studying people's buying habits to see how they react to different prices, promotions, packaging, etc.
- Using consumer panels where consumers are free to discuss their personal views about products
- Using market research agencies – experts who understand why people behave in particular ways

Geographic segmentation

With **geographic segmentation**, markets are divided on the basis of characteristics that change because of where the market is located.

Geographic characteristics

- **Geographical features**, e.g. climate, weather conditions and mainland or island
- **Physical location**, e.g. distance from factory or shop, number of people in each area and country, region and area
- **Urban or rural**, e.g. population density, transport links and main types of jobs
- **Local tastes and fashions**, e.g. what people generally eat, how they spend their incomes and what times shops normally open
- **Different local facilities**, e.g. regional media such as television and newspapers, public transport networks and government aid
- **Local demographic features**, e.g. differences in employment, incomes, age distributions and marital status

People living in the South East and London tend to be much better off than people living in the North West, Wales and Northern Ireland. This is reflected in the kinds of products that they are able to buy. Figure 2.2.6 shows the percentage of households in different regions that have a home computer.

Producers of computers may use this data to decide to target those areas with the highest percentages because these show that households are already interested. More ambitious businesses may see the areas with low percentages as good potential markets because many households do not yet have home computers. First, however, they should conduct market research in these regions to find out why they do not have computers.

Even in areas where the levels of income are fairly similar, households may choose to spend their incomes in quite different ways. In 1999, the average expenditure for people in Yorkshire and the Humber was £134.50 per person per week. In the South West region, the expenditure was almost identical at £135.80 per person per week, but the pattern of expenditure was quite different (Figure 2.2.7).

Figure 2.2.6 Percentage of UK households with a home computer (1999), by region

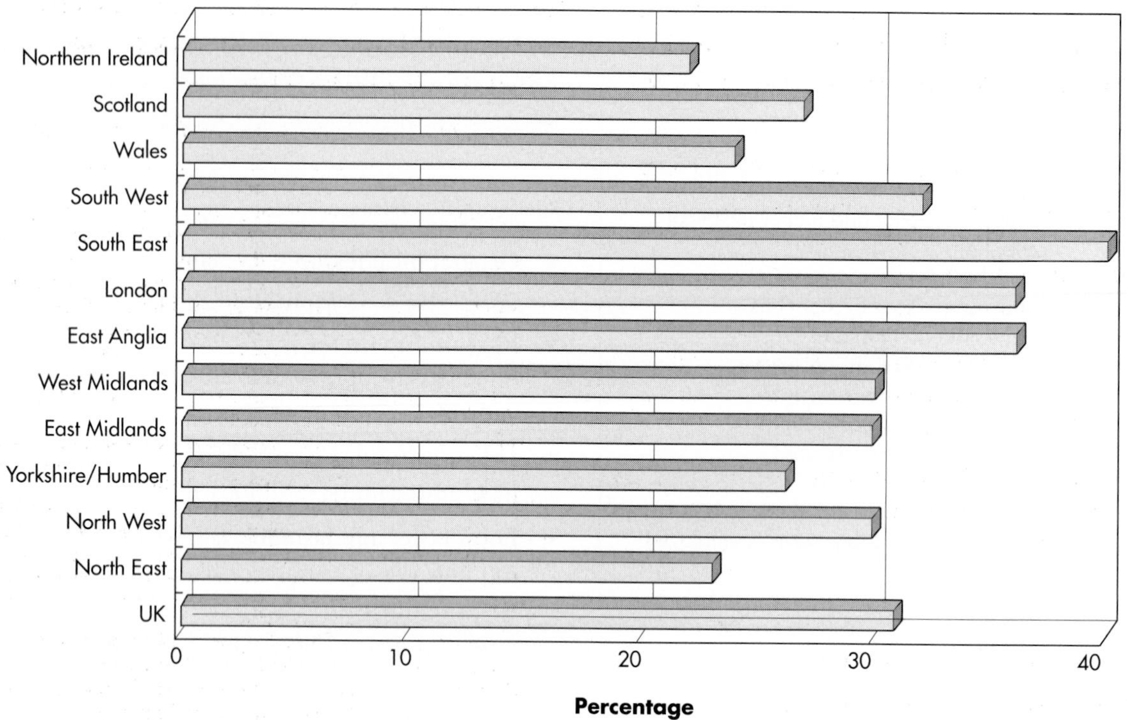

Source: Adapted from *Regional Trends* (2000 edition)

Figure 2.2.7 Household expenditure by commodity and service, selected regions (1999)

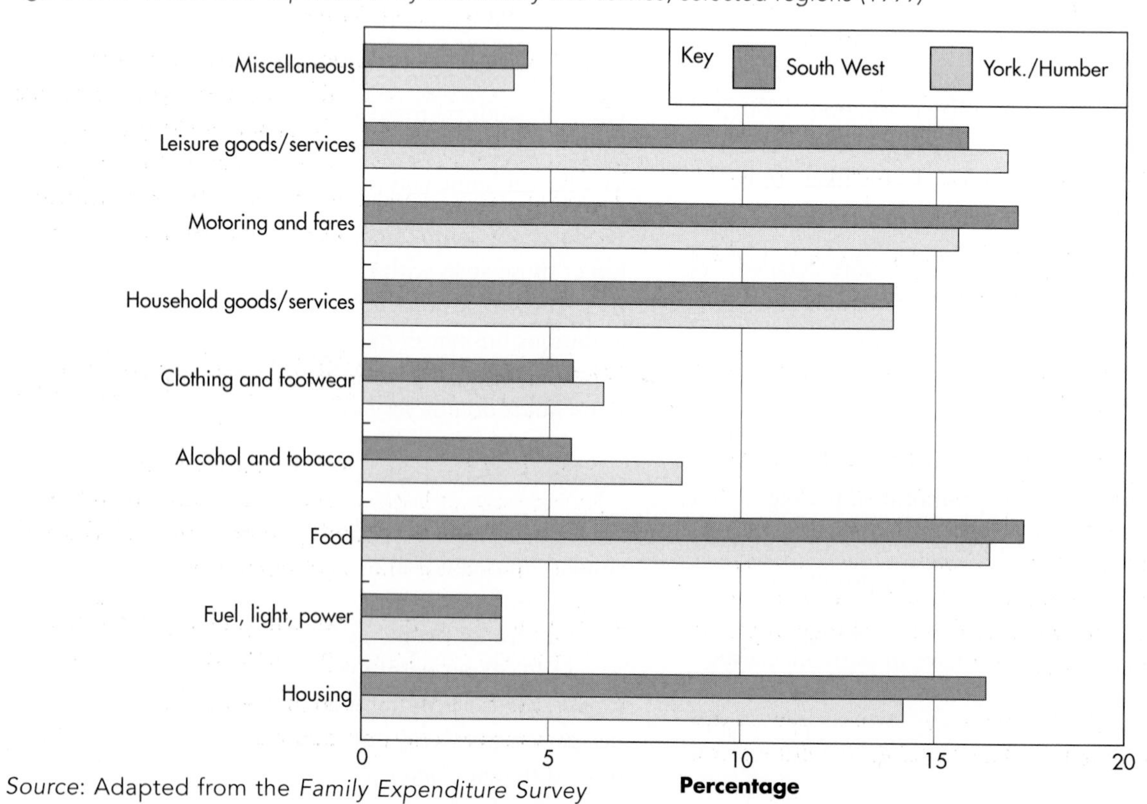

Source: Adapted from the *Family Expenditure Survey*

The comparatively high expenditure on housing and low expenditure on alcohol and tobacco in the South West could be explained by the fact that this area has a high percentage of retired people (see the grey market on page 75).

The way that the population is divided geographically obviously affects the marketing research process. Where original primary research is being carried out, there will be significant costs differences in local, regional, national and international surveys.

- With international surveys, the business may have to rely on secondary data or on employing a market research firm with access to the other countries.
- National surveys will require some form of sampling, which reduces the reliability of the data. It may also prove more difficult to reach the people you want to contact.
- Regional surveys are more manageable but may still be expensive and difficult for small firms.
- Local surveys can be carried out by the business itself fairly easily.

Segmentation by benefit sought

Some businesses consider it important to segment specific markets on the basis of the different **benefits** that consumers expect from particular products:

- **Value for money**, e.g. bargains, sale items and multi-buys
- **Convenience**, e.g. ease of use, different methods of payment and where products are offered for sale
- **Quality**, e.g. reliability, durability, doing what the product is expected to do and facilities such as guarantees
- **Improving image**, e.g. being popular, looking smart and being up to date

Customers are always seeking some benefit from the products they buy. Good marketing research will be able to identify what this is and then guide the marketing strategy to meet it. Sometimes it will be necessary to make changes to the product itself but, for many products, all that is needed is a change in the way that the product is promoted.

The benefits sought may be fairly obvious, as with the example of toothpaste in Figure 2.2.8. Sometimes, it is less obvious. In the past, soap powder was sold on the basic of class differences. Today, many products are sold on the basis of sex appeal, from perfumes and deodorants to cars and jeans.

Figure 2.2.8 Major benefits sought from toothpaste

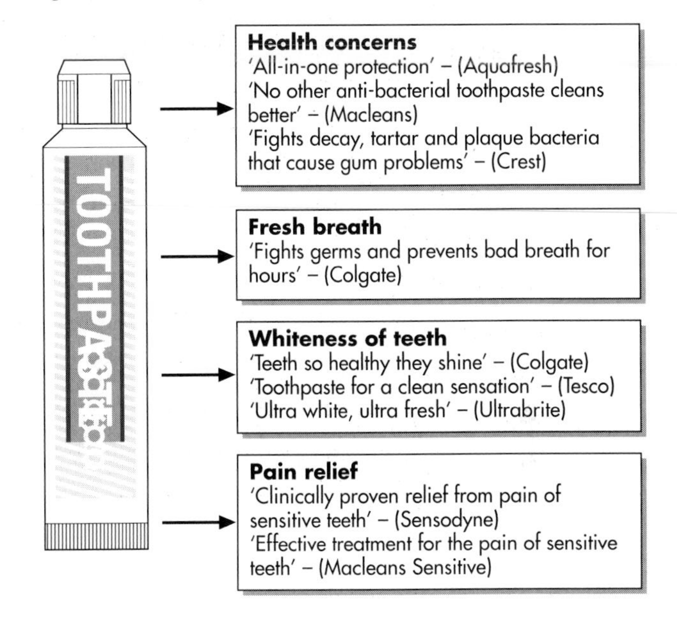

Specific market segments – DINKs, SINKs, Yuppies, Greens and Greys

Marketing firms and marketing departments within businesses are keen to identify particular types of people with similar characteristics. This allows them to target a large group of people with one marketing campaign, thus saving costs. Various groups have been identified: DINKs, SINKs, Yuppies, Greens and Greys.

DINKs

DINKs – dual income no kids

DINKs refers to couples, either married or living together, who are both earning. They have no children and currently are not planning to have any. DINKs are likely to have the following characteristics:

- High joint incomes – can afford luxury products, more than one holiday per year, etc.
- Tend to be committed to jobs – will buy convenience foods, eat out, etc.

- Mostly are aged between 18 and 35 – go out at weekends, leisure activities include entertainment, may be into keep fit, skiing, etc.
- Tend to have other DINKs as friends – shared interests, may take holidays as a group, etc.

Lifestyle shopping profile

DINKs are young trend-setting couples enjoying life to its fullest. You can usually find DINKs at happy hour, enjoying a restaurant dinner or in the airport waiting to go on a great vacation.

SINKs

SINKs – single income no kids

SINKs are people who have not yet formed a lasting relationship with a partner – young singles, rather than older spinsters, bachelors, widowers or widows – likely to have these characteristics:

- Generally fairly young, 16–25, not committed to future planning, may live at home, spend most of their income, like instant gratification products
- Fairly independent, may rent shared accommodation or flat, want to make their own decisions, live for the moment
- Income as a major factor, likely to change jobs, limited commitment to brands, follow fads

Businesses targeting SINKs need to provide products that are in fashion or create a new fashion. They should expect limited repeat purchases and limited long-term commitment to any particular brand.

Yuppies

Yuppies – young upwardly mobile people

'Yuppies' was an American term used to describe young urban professionals. That remains the basic meaning but, in the UK, it was changed to refer to young upwardly mobile people: people who are very ambitious and have the primary objective of improving both their status and their income. They have these characteristics:

- Very ambitious – want products that enhance their image, fast cars, designer clothes
- Relatively high incomes – want other people to know that they have good incomes, tend to spend ostentatiously, luxury products, state-of-the-art products, expensive holidays
- Very keen on being seen as 'with-it' – will read fashion magazines, follow current fashion trends, go to wine bars

Filofax, the personal organiser, was the must-have accessory for Yuppies for much of the 1980s and 1990s, but now it has been replaced by handheld computers such as Psion and Palm. As a result, Filoxfax is in serious trouble and is now up for sale for the second time in three years as personal organiser sales plummet.

Jan. 2001

The green market

The **green market** customers are concerned about environmental issues and to the businesses and products that meet these concerns.

This is a growing market. More and more people are becoming aware of the problems of global warming, the depleted ozone layer, pollution, dangerous pesticides and herbicides, etc., and they are demanding products that do not cause these problems. People in the green market have these characteristics:

- Concerned with the environment – looking for eco-friendly products, recyclable packaging, products from sustainable sources
- Tend to be fairly well educated – likely to read broadsheet newspapers and watch current affairs programmes
- Will generally have goods jobs and incomes – prepared to pay more for green products and may buy organic food products

- Are usually older – house owners, likely to be into gardening and DIY
- Often married with families – high weekly shopping bills, expect safe products for their children

Sainsbury's position on GM food …

In response to overwhelming customer concern we have eliminated GM ingredients from all our own brand food, pet food and dietary supplements.

This was a considerable task, involving over 4000 products and was achieved by replacing soya and maize ingredients with alternatives or using validated non-GM sources.

Sainsbury's position on GM in animal feed

Sainsbury's already offers an extensive choice for customers wishing to avoid meat from animals fed a diet which may contain GM crops. In addition, we currently offer a wide range of organic poultry, fish and dairy products.

Source: **http://www.sainsbury.co.uk/gm/**

The grey market

The **grey market** are older people, sometimes taken as being over 50 years old, or sometimes people over retirement age (60 for women, 65 for men).

As health and medical treatment improve and people live longer, the **grey market** is rapidly growing. Many greys now have relatively high incomes and spending power because of good company pensions and the capital released when they have sold large family homes and moved into smaller retirement properties. These richer greys have these characteristics:

- Fairly high spending power – tend to buy more up-market products, grocery shopping at Waitrose or Marks & Spencer.
- Plenty of time – take more than one holiday, spend time in the garden and/or watching TV.
- Old – tend to have fairly conservative tastes, often buy traditional products, higher demand for comfort products, heating, medicines, etc.
- Concern for their own old age – savings, ISAs, putting money aside for possible long-term medical care

Cruise to magnificent St Petersburg with ports-of-call in enchanting Baltic capitals; discover the lands of fire and ice and dramatic fjords in Iceland; or, for the ultimate travel adventure, join us on an epic 100-night around-the-world cruise – all aboard the comfort and luxury of our very own cruise ship, the *Saga Rose*!

The role of marketing research in market segmentation

It is vital that a business knows what the market segments are for its products, and the characteristics of the customers in those segments. Without this information, the business will find it very difficult to produce products that are exactly what the customers want and can be sold with the most effective marketing.

The existence of different market segments affects the business because it has to match its marketing to these segments, e.g. low prices for people with low incomes; direct sales to people who find it difficult to visit the shops; recyclable packaging for the green market. At the same time, marketing research plays a major role in identifying the segments in the first place. By studying the needs and characteristics of its customers, a business can build up profiles of different markets and customers and tailor its products to meet these differences.

Marketing research can also be used to create general profiles such as DINKs or greens. These are often created by specialist market research agencies which survey hundreds of thousands of consumers to build up profiles. Table 2.2.6 shows the general profiles created by the Meat and Livestock Commission and by Taylor Nelson.

The existence of segments is very important in terms of marketing research planning. The stages in planning were considered in Chapter 1 and will be considered again in Chapter 3 when we look at sampling. The existence of segments is likely to add these stages to any marketing planning:

- Establishing if the market is segmented
- Deciding for which segments marketing research is required
- Deciding how any survey should be effectively divided if more than one segment is being researched
- Checking collected data across segments to see if there are any similarities and differences
- Analysing how important these similarities and difference are and how that should affect future marketing plans.

There are a great many ways in which businesses, governments and academics segment markets, and readers are adviser to check out other sources:

- **www.statistics.gov.uk/nsbase/methods_qualityns_sec/**
- **www.caci.co.uk/cp-acorn-neighbourhood-class.htm** This latter web site provides access to the CACI Ltd Acorn consumer targeting classification. A brochure with full details is available for downloading.

Table 2.2.6 Profiles of general consumers and of purchasers and users of meat

Taylor Nelson's general profile of consumers	The Meat & Livestock Commission's profile of purchasers and users of meat
Self-explorers – interested in new things and finding out about themselves; very tolerant	**Mrs Good and wholesome** – looking for quality and healthy products, but not exotic products; middle aged
Social resistors – interested in fairness and good social values; caring, but may force their opinions on others	**Takeaway Tracey/Kevin** – tend to eat 'junk food', easy to prepare; single
Experimentalists – interested in new things, personal enjoyment and rather materialistic	**Old Mother Hubbard** – looking for bargains that can be stored away; pensioner with limited budget
Conspicuous consumers – interested in possessions and showing others what they can spend	**Moussaka and muesli mum** – health conscious but also ready to experiment
Belongers – interested in the quiet family life and tend to be conservative in their views	**TV diners** – after convenience foods, easy and quick to prepare, likely to be out at work during the day; no children
Survivors – interested in keeping things as they are and surviving; tend to be concerned about others	**Takeaway gourmets** – looking for food that is easy to prepare but are interested in the more exotic menus
Aimless – their circumstances mean they tend to live from day to day with few, if any, long-term plans	**Chips and things mum** – preparing cooked meals but they are fairly traditional and downmarket
	Completely competent – accomplished cooks; seeks out specific ingredients and cooks gourmet meals

Activity

Find out what the 'Acorn consumer targeting classification' is and, for each section of the classification, provide a list of products that you feel would meet that segment.

Revision Questions

1 For each of these products, list four different segments that exist in the market.

i) Cars
ii) Holidays
iii) Insurance
iv) CDs (8 marks)

2 The teenage market is different in many respects from markets with either younger or older consumers.

a) Choose one product that you consider to be a typical teenager product. Give details of how it is marketed in terms of:

i) pricing
ii) promotion
iii) where and how it is sold. (4 marks)

b) Explain why the products are marketed as you have described above, and explain why that is important because this is a teenager product. (6 marks)

3 Describe a niche market in one of these general markets and explain the benefits that a business would have in producing products for that niche market.

i) The music industry
ii) Education
iii) The leisure industry (10 marks)

4 Price discrimination is possible because markets can be segmented. At the same time, the basic product is the same.

Cinemas charge a range of different prices. Give details of the different prices that they charge (e.g. afternoon and evening) and explain why the prices are different and how this relates to the targeted segment. (10 marks)

5 A computer manufacturer specialises in making PCs for use in the home and by small businesses.

a) Take two elements of the marketing mix and explain the likely differences in the way that the business would market to the two segments. (4 marks)

b) For each element of the marketing mix you have taken, outline the likely marketing research that would have to be done in order to find out data from

i) the householders, and
ii) the small business. (8 marks)

6 **a)** Outline the likely demographic segments for the alcoholic drinks market. (6 marks)

b) Selecting two of the segments you have given, explain how this will affect the way in which marketing data will be collected. (6 marks)

7 Below are some of the psychographic profiles for women identified by McCann Erickson market research agency.

- Lively ladies
- New unromantics
- Blinkered
- Down-trodden

a) For each of these categories, write a short profile of the kind of person that you feel would fit this category – how they think, behave, etc. (8 marks)

b) For each category, list two products that you think would be suitable and explain why they would be suitable. (8 marks)

c) Outline any differences that might exist in the way that marketing research should be carried out to gain information about each of these categories. (8 marks)

8 Explain, giving examples, why businesses use both demographic and psychographic segmentation. (10 marks)

9 For each of these categories of people select on product they are likely to buy and explain what characteristics they have that make them an obvious target market for the producers.

i) DINKs **ii)** SINKs **iii)** Yuppies
iv) Greens **v)** Greys (10 marks)

CHAPTER 3

Marketing Research Methods

KEY TERMS

Ad hoc surveys
Consumer panels
Continuous surveys
Custom-designed research
Desk research
Electronic monitoring
Field research
Focus groups
Footfall counts
Internal and external data
Interviews
Observation
Omnibus surveys
Primary research
Questionnaires
Secondary research
Surveys

In this chapter, you will learn about the marketing research methods that are used to collect data:

- The most appropriate method for particular kinds of data
- The difference between primary and secondary research, and field and desk research
- Examples of primary and secondary research methods

How data is collected

Different methods are suitable for different types of data, and depend on who and what the data is being collected for and where the data is being collected from. Each method can be evaluated to consider its suitability against these following criteria.

- **Cost** of collection
- **Ease of access**
  Is the data readily available?
  Can people be contacted easily?
- **Time/speed**
  How long does it take to collect the data?
  How urgently is it needed?
- **Likely response** by person being surveyed
  Is the survey intrusive?
  Is it inconvenient?
  Does it affect the way they behave or answer?
- **Accuracy** and **reliability**

Primary and secondary research; field and desk research

There can be some confusion over these terms. Generally, primary research and field research are the same; and secondary and desk research are the same. There can be differences, as shown below, but many businesses and commentators take each pair to be alternative names for the same methods of research.

Primary research collects data not collected before.

Examples of **primary research** include conducting a survey using a questionnaire, and observing how customers move around a store. This is data that is being collected for the first time.

Secondary research finds and uses data that has been collected already.

Field research is collected by researchers going out of the business premises.

Desk research is found by someone inside the business looking at data collected already.

Secondary research may involve data that the business already has, such as past sales records, or data that someone else has collected, such as government statistics on household expenditure.

In many cases, primary data is collected by researchers going out from the business to gather new data. When this happens this is called **field research**. With secondary data, the data is frequently gathered by someone sitting at a desk and looking at published data. This is why secondary research is often referred to as **desk research**.

Unfortunately, it is possible for a researcher to 'sit at a desk' and conduct a telephone questionnaire with customers. This would be **primary desk research**. It is also possible for a researcher to go out to all of the competitors and collect copies of their price lists, which are published secondary data. This would be an example of **field research gathering secondary data**.

The rest of this section will refer only to primary and secondary research. Generally that will be the same as field and desk research, but occasionally the terms will not match.

The basic difference between primary and secondary data is whether or not it has been collected as new data. These and other differences are shown in Table 2.3.1.

When businesses decide to carry out marketing research, and they know what data they need, one of their first considerations will be whether primary or secondary research would be better.

Here are four examples of situations in which a business would need to carry out marketing research:

1 A greengrocer has noticed that some of his customers, who used to buy their fruit and vegetables in the store every week, now only visit the store occasionally.

Solution The reasons for this change may be very specific to this one greengrocer. The greengrocer also needs to find out what the customers feel about his products. It is fairly unlikely that any secondary data will be able to provide the business with the reasons. Here the best approach would be to talk to the customers, or give them a questionnaire – both primary research.

2 A local bakery is thinking about producing a loaf of bread that is half white bread and half brown bread. It wants to test the viability of this product in the local market.

Solution Very little secondary data exists for this product. The best way to find out what customers think would be to produce white/brown loaves, see how they sell and question customers on what they thinks about them – all primary research.

Table 2.3.1 Characteristics of primary and secondary data

Feature	Primary	Secondary
Originality	All primary data is new and therefore original.	All secondary data is at least second hand.
Up to date	Primary data is collected when it is needed so it is up to date.	Secondary data has been collected in the past, then published, so it tends to be out of date.
Relevant	Primary data is collected for a specific purpose so it should be relevant.	Secondary data has often been collected for a different purpose, so it may not provide the exact information that the business needs.
Time-consuming	Primary data needs to be collected from scratch and then analysed and this takes time.	Secondary data has already been collected and published so it should be available immediately or with little time delay.
Cost	This will vary. Big surveys are expensive, but some data may already be in the process of being collected, e.g. EPOS data.	This will vary. Some secondary data is free, in libraries or on the internet. Other data can be very expensive, as with Mintel reports.
Access	Some primary data is readily available because it is collected directly from the business's customers. Collecting data from non-customers is more difficult.	Some secondary data is readily available in libraries, on the internet and through trade magazines. Other data, especially about competitors, is more difficult to obtain.

3 A garden centre wants to find out which of its products have had increasing sales and which have been declining in sales. It then plans to concentrate on only the best lines.

Solution This data is about trends and past sales records. This data must have been collected in the past and must therefore be secondary data. Primary data would require people to remember what the sales were and that would be inaccurate. Secondary research would be best.

4 A small national business is planning to expand its sales by exporting to foreign countries and it wants to find out which countries have customer profiles similar to those of its British customers.

Solution This would require data about many countries and about large parts of their population. For the business to collect this data itself, or to pay a market research firm to do this, would be very expensive and time-consuming. It would be best to find and use existing data, which would be secondary research.

Marketing research is carried out for different reasons and this will determine the type of research that is needed. This will also determine which of primary or secondary research is most appropriate. Sometimes both will be required. A business that wants to find the trends in its sales will check its sales records but it may also wish to find out why trends have changed by checking customers' opinions through interviews or questionnaires – both primary research.

Other basic types of marketing research may be used depending on why the data is being collected. These are briefly outlined here.

Ad hoc research

***Ad hoc* marketing research** is carried out to deal with one particular situation that the business is considering.

If the business is thinking about launching a new product, it will want to find out in advance if the product is likely to be well received by potential customers. If a sports shop has run an advertisement on television during Wimbledon week, it may want to check if this has had an effect on its sales of tennis clothes and equipment. This is a specific piece of research that is not planned to be repeated.

Some of the benefits of ad hoc *research*

- Very specific so it should provide the business with the information it needs
- Only dealing with one specific objective so it should be relatively cheap
- Fairly limited research required so it may be worth employing expert marketing research agencies who will carry out the work professionally and this should increase the accuracy of the results

Some of the drawbacks of ad hoc *research*

- Because it only relates to one specific situation it is unlikely to be of much use when the business is considering other situations, e.g. will positive results for the advertising during Wimbledon week also apply to advertising during the Ryder Cup golf competition?

It takes the biscuit

As part of their market research, biscuit manufacturers sometime use hall tests to see if potential customers would like new products. In the hall tests, customers sample the biscuits and are then asked if they like them and if they would buy them.

Even with positive replies, manufacturers often find that when they come to produce and sell the biscuits, the sale are very much lower than the research suggested. The reason is that this kind of *ad hoc* research is too limited. Most people who are given something free are likely to say that it is good. When it comes to having to buy it they will consider more important factors, such as it price and how it compares with their usual purchases.

- Can be too specific, e.g. only looking at what existing customers think about a new product when, many non-customers might be more likely buyers

Continuous research

Continuous research is carried out all the time.

This would include data being collected through the EPOS system. It is being collected every time goods are scanned at a supermarket till. Continuous research would also include recording customer complaints or the collection of weekly data on prices and employment by the government.

Some of the benefits of continuous research

- Trends are easy to discover because the data is being collected continuously over time. This will also make it easier to forecast what will happen in the future.
- Once the collection process has been set up, it is easy to continue collecting data in the same way.
- Marketing research is going on all the time so any changes can be rapidly identified and reacted on.

Some of the drawbacks of continuous research

- The costs of setting up the collection system, e.g. EPOS, can be high.
- If the collection system involves repeating questionnaires or interviews, this can be expensive.
- Continuous research always looks at the same data, so it is frequently of limited use where special or new situations arise.

Wade Pottery keep weekly records of their sales figures. This allows them to forecast their sales for April. Overall they are likely to rise, but they are also likely to peak in the first week, fall back in weeks 2 and 3, then rise again in week 4 (Figure 2.3.1).

Custom-designed research

Custom-designed research is specially designed to meet the needs of a specific piece of research.

Sometimes custom-designed research is created in-house by the business itself; sometime, it is created by expert market research agencies. It may be designed for one particular piece of research, in which case, it will also be *ad hoc*, but it can also be designed for ongoing or continuous research. What makes it distinct is the time and effort taken to design the way the research is carried out so that it will be the most appropriate research for the needs of the business. If a business wants to launch a new product which it has already made, custom-design research will check all the relevant information that will tell the business who wants the product, where it should be sold, how it should be advertised, what price would be acceptable for the customers and the competition, etc.

Some benefits of custom-designed research

- The research is tailor-made and should therefore provide the business with all the details it needs to make the right marketing decisions.

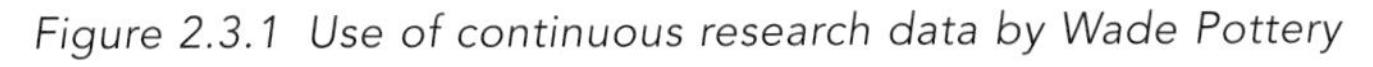

Figure 2.3.1 Use of continuous research data by Wade Pottery

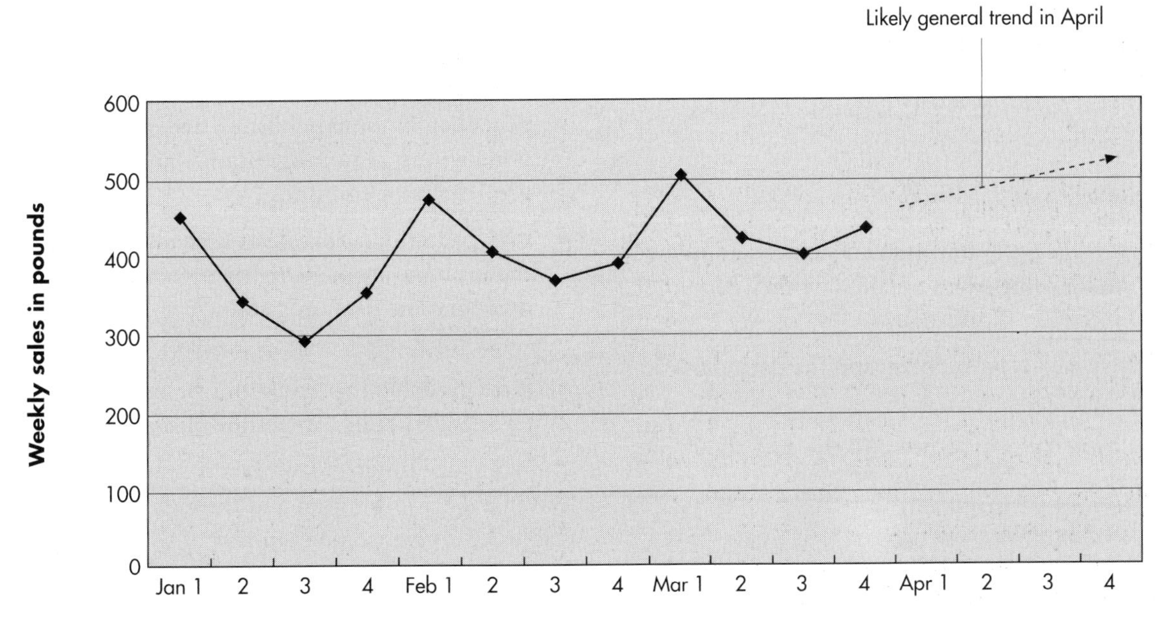

- All of the research data should be relevant so less time is wasted in analysing it to remove irrelevant data.
- The process of carrying out this kind of in-depth research helps the business to see the benefits of marketing research.

Some drawbacks of custom-designed research

- It takes more planning and thought and is therefore slower to set up and to conduct.
- It is also likely to be more expensive because of the planning.
- Small firms may not have the expertise to design such research for themselves so they will have to use marketing research firms, which will be expensive.

Omnibus research

Omnibus research is carried out for different businesses.

There are different types of **omnibus research**:

- A group of businesses, together, create a joint survey. The survey will include all the questions that the separate businesses want answered.
- One business is planning a survey and agrees to include questions from another business or businesses.
- A market research firm is planning to conduct a general survey and offers individual businesses the opportunity of having their questions included.

This is quite a common method of research for small firms which could not afford a full research of their own. It is also common where firms are looking for specific data from other countries.

Some benefits of omnibus research

- Low costs for small businesses which can combine with other businesses to obtain data they could not afford to collect individually
- Relatively easy way to obtain specific data about foreign markets
- Often carried out by experts, so the data should be reliable

Some drawbacks of omnibus research

- Often takes time to bring all of the businesses together and to incorporate all of the separate questions so it is not a good way of obtaining data quickly
- Confusion for the people being interviewed or answering the questionnaire due to the different questions, about different products and markets, possibly leading to inaccurate answers or sections not covered
- Where one major business is included in the survey, possibility of less care being taken about the details that smaller businesses want collected

Secondary marketing research sources

All secondary marketing research comes from published sources. The data, collected for other purposes, is presented in a form that other people can use: written, kept on video, stored electronically or presented in diagrams, graphs, etc.

Secondary data maybe taken from a business's own records (**internal**) or from other published records (**external**).

Some advantages of internal data

- Applies directly to the business itself, whereas external data may not be totally relevant
- Data already collected and within the business, so should be readily available and at no, or very low, cost
- Data usually obtained very quickly

Some advantages of external data

- A much wider range and higher volume of data to be gathered, some published free, e.g. size of populations, percentage of men and women, the age breakdown of countries
- Can collect data that deals with situations in which the business is not currently involved, e.g. demographic data on a country that the business is thinking about selling its product to
- Data available that could not be found internally, e.g. details about competitor businesses

A huge range of secondary data is available, especially external data, in libraries and through the internet. Table 2.3.2 gives some examples of sources of internal and external secondary data available to firms.

Table 2.3.2 Examples of internal and external secondary data

Internal sources	**Examples**
Sales records	• EPOS record of every item sold in a supermarket • Profit and loss accounts
Customer complaints	• Filed complaint cards with details of what customers feel is wrong, and sometimes valuable suggestions • Record of refunds
Customer records	• Providing name, address, possibly age, details of products purchased, how products were paid for • If additional services were used, such as credit, insurance, extended warrantees, and delivery
Supplier records	• Providing details of what products are available, cost, delivery times, etc. • Details of what has been purchased, how much, when, what credit facilities are available, etc.
External sources	**Examples**
Government publications	• *Social Trends*, *Regional Trends*, *Annual/Monthly Abstract of Statistics*, census data and many others • Details on legislation that affects how products can be advertised, priced, what age groups are allowed to buy them, etc.
Publications from international organisations	• *EUROSTAT*, *Portrait of the Regions*, from the EU • *Main Economic Indicators* from the OECD • *The Demographic Year Book* from the UN
Marketing research businesses	• Mintel, Keynote and Euromonitor all produce market research reports available for purchase by interested businesses
Trade directories	• The *Yellow Pages*, *Thomson.* • *Kelly's*, *Kompass*
Specialist trade magazines	• *Farmer's Weekly*, *The Grocer*, *The Investor's Chronicle*, *Autotrader*, *Computer Weekly*, *The Radio Times*
General magazines, papers, consumer affairs publications	• *PC Plus* • *The Telegraph*, *The Financial Time*, *The Sporting Chronicle*, *Metro* • *Which?*
Competitor details	• Companies' annual reports • Published price lists • Published product details
The internet	• Data from many of the above sources can be accessed through the internet • Data from competitors' web sites • Articles, reviews and analysis covering a huge range of business topics, references and situations

Primary marketing research methods

Primary marketing research may be carried out on a structured or an unstructured basis. Most primary research is **structured** research: the objectives and methods of gaining the data are carefully planned and a full **survey** is carried out.

Unstructured research is not part of a survey and tends to be collected almost incidentally. Sales staff serving customers in, say, a record store, may notice that customers prefer to browse rather than be asked if they need help the moment they enter the store. Staff will use this information to change the way in which they approach customers and market the goods. They may use feedback from customers to change the lay-out of the store, provide headphones and stations so that customers can listen to samples of the music, etc. – all from unplanned and unstructured market research.

Observation

Observation – watching people

Observation is far more common than people imagine. It can be a very useful method of finding out how people buy products, where they shop, what appears to interest them, etc. It is frequently used to find out what customers actually do, but it will also be used in wider marketing research as these examples show.

- Observing how customers move around a store so that the business can decide where to place its goods, customer services desks, checkouts, etc.
- Observing how customers use products such as toothbrushes, potato peelers and portable CD players so that more user-friendly products can be designed
- Observing competitors' advertisements on TV to decide how to change the business's own advertising approach
- Observing the number of people who use certain parts of a town centre with a **footfall count** to decide on the best location for a new retail shop
- A stall holder in a large competitive market sending an assistant round to the other stalls to check on their prices so that the stall holder can set competitive prices
- A business looking for a location for a new outlet driving around to find a site that is well placed in the market

Some benefits of observation

- It shows what people actually do rather than what they say they do.
- It can be carried out without the customers' knowledge, so the conducting of the survey does not affect them or change the way they behave.
- Many stores already have closed circuit television (CCTV) and security cameras so it may not be difficult or costly to gather the information.
- Where competitors' behaviour, adverts, prices, etc., are being observed, this can be done without the competitors knowing or being able to object.

Some important drawbacks and limitations of observation

- It cannot be used if the business does not have access to the customers, adverts, etc., e.g. if the customers buy by mail order or if the new advert of a competitor has not yet been released.
- It can be time-consuming and costly. Someone needs to do the observing, or check through videos, etc.
- Observation in new or large markets can be difficult and costly.
- It may show how, where and when people buy products but not usually *why* they buy them.
- If people know they are being observed, they may object to it as an invasion of privacy.
- It may only give partial information, e.g. where a good site for a shop might be but not about the price, planning restrictions, etc.

Figure 2.3.2 shows a fairly typical layout for a supermarket store. This kind of layout did not come about by chance. The businesses observed the way that people moved about normal stores – frequently in a rather haphazard fashion. They decided that it would be better to make people go up and down all the shelves so that they could pick up the goods that they wanted but would also make other, impulse, purchases of goods which attracted them as they passed. Alcoholic drinks tend to be put as far away from the entrance as possible so that customers only coming in for these will still be tempted to buy other products as they pass them.

Figure 2.3.2 Typical layout of a supermarket

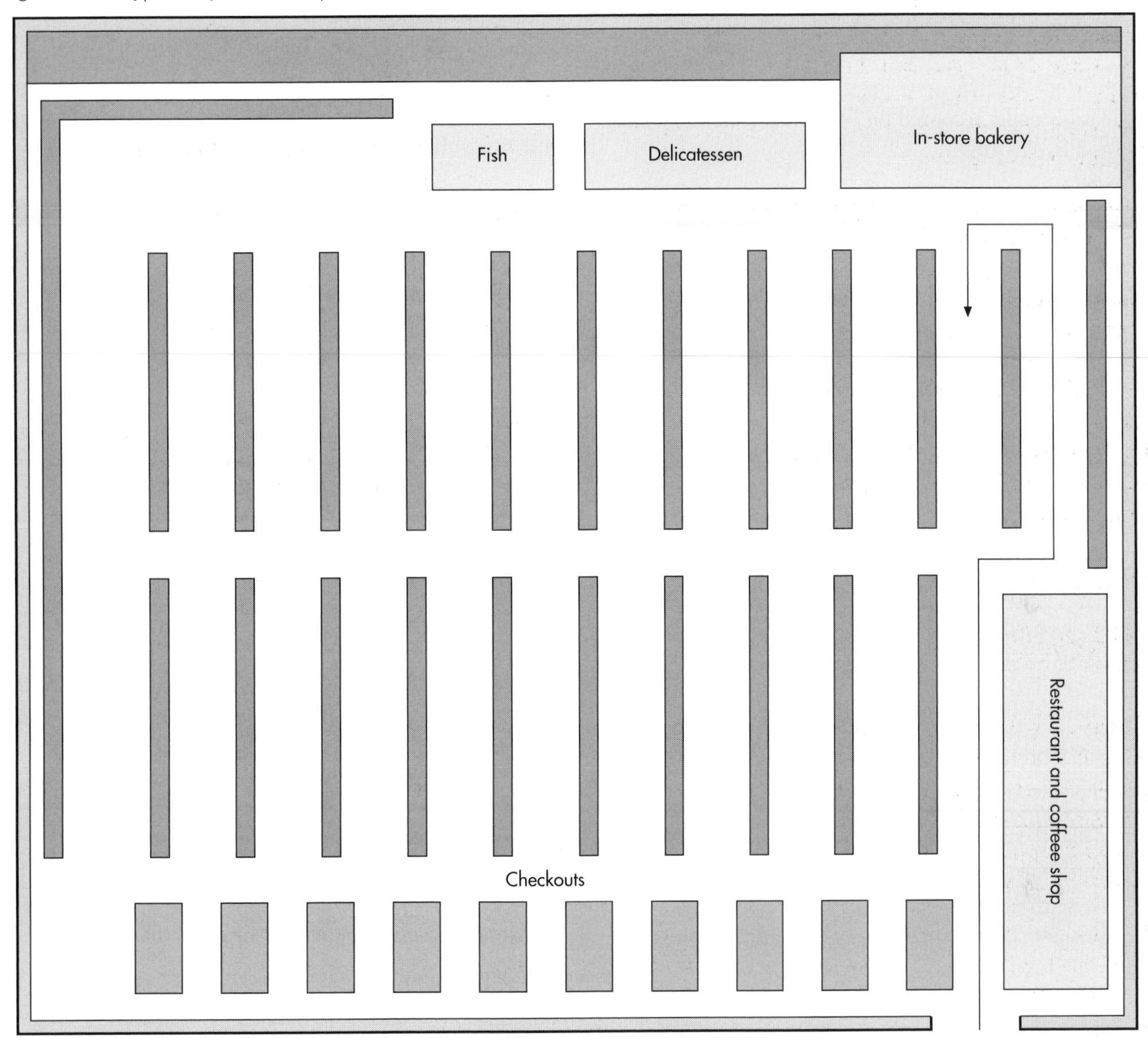

Today, most people shopping in supermarkets walk obediently up and down the rows one at a time. Supermarkets have also observed that customers soon learn where the products they want are situated and, even though they go up and down most rows, they ignore the other products. This is why supermarkets periodically change where particular products are kept, making customers look for them, notice the other goods, and buy more than they really want.

Electronic data collection

Nowadays, a great deal of data is collected electronically, e.g. the data collected from the EPOS system, **electronic monitoring** of the number of people entering and leaving a shop, recording telephone messages and CCTV.

Electronic monitoring – collecting data via computers

Some advantages of electronic monitoring

- Once it is set up, it is usually automatic.
- It is very quick.
- It is generally recorded on file, video etc., and can be used in the future.
- When connected to the facilities of a computer and the right software, it can provide analysed data in a form that is immediately useful.

Some drawbacks of electronic monitoring

- Initial costs of the equipment are fairly high, although cheaper and cheaper versions are being offered all the time.
- Sometimes the data is presented in a complex form and requires trained staff to interpret it.
- Electronic data does not usually explain why people behave in the way that they do.

The data collected through electronic systems such as EPOS can provide businesses with a huge amount of important marketing research data:

- What was bought and how much was bought
- How buying changed as prices were changed
- Which stores sold most of which products
- Which day of the week and time of the day is best for sales
- Where these systems can identify individual customers (as with loyalty cards), who bought what

Electronic data collection also includes such techniques as pressure pads or light beams that record the number of people entering and leaving a shop – a kind of footfall count. If this is compared to the till receipts, it will tell the business how many people entered the shop and left without purchasing anything.

Questionnaires

A **questionnaire** collects data using a set of questions that require fairly simple and short answers.

The questions for a questionnaire will have been decided in advance and written down with spaces provided for the answers. The usual method for **telephone** and **street** surveys, is for the person doing the market research to ask the questions and write down all the answers. With **postal** surveys, ones placed in **magazines**, on the **internet** or left in stores, etc., the customers will fill in the answers.

Questionnaires can provide businesses with a great deal of data in a relatively short time. The questions tend to be short and easy to answer and most people are fairly happy to take part in a questionnaire survey. They can be constructed and carried out fairly quickly and they remain a popular way of collecting data.

Some benefits of well-constructed questionnaires

- Most people are prepared to answer them.
- They can provide data in a form that is easy to analyse and draw valuable conclusions from.
- Much cheaper and can be carried out more quickly than interviews
- No particular skills required to carry out a questionnaire survey

Many small businesses choose to use questionnaires as their primary method of research for any new products. This is because they do not have the skills to use the other main methods. They can, however, create a clear set of questions that they need to know the answers to. They are also aware that if the questionnaire is kept fairly simple they will obtain the answers that matter.

Some problems with questionnaires

- They do not allow customers to give detailed answers and that may mean the business does not find out the real reasons behind customers' choices.
- Many questionnaires are completed with inaccurate information because the person filling them in is not really interested. Frequently, the businesses cannot distinguish between genuine answers and bogus answers.

Each main method of conducting questionnaires also has particular problems that need to be thought about before choosing them.

Street surveys need to be conducted so that they do not annoy people who are shopping, trying to catch a train, etc. It is also difficult to ensure that the right people are being selected, especially when the person carrying out the survey must select on such features as whether people are married, have certain incomes, or have life insurance.

Postal surveys tend to have very low rates of response. Many people simply throw postal questionnaires into the bin. To encourage people to return questionnaires, businesses may offer incentives such as a chance to win a money prize. A further problem is that if any of the questions are not understood, there is no one readily available to help.

Telephone surveys can be the most difficult. Most people do not want to have their privacy invaded by a telephone call. They often simply say 'no' and hang up. Where they do agree to answer questions, they may give any response simply to answer as quickly as possible. If surveys are conducted by poorly trained interviewers/questioners, this can annoy the person being asked the questions.

Magazine and **internet surveys** will only be completed by those who read the magazine or access the internet site; all other potential customers are ignored.

Each method of surveying customers also has advantages, such as knowing that the right customer base is being surveyed in a magazine questionnaire.

Constructing a good questionnaire

Constructing a good questionnaire is often more difficult than people think, but it is important if the data collected is to be accurate and useful. Certain general rules should be applied:

- There should not be too many questions. Otherwise, people will ignore them, refuse to complete them or make up answers to speed things up.
- Questions should be short and, where there are alternative answers, not too many answers.
- Questions should be asked that have short answers, otherwise people will not answer them and where they are answered they will be difficult to analyse.
- Questions must be clear and unambiguous. This is especially important with postal, magazine and internet questionnaires, because there is no one available to explain any points that may cause confusion.
- Personal questions need to be asked very carefully, otherwise people will not answer. Normally, for example, people will be presented with ranges of incomes to choose from rather than being asked, 'What is your income?'
- The order of the questions should be logical so that the person being asked the questions can see the point of the survey.

Typical types of questions are dealt with on pages 102–5.

Interviews

In an **interview**, the interviewer asks a series of questions and can ask follow up questions that depend on the answers given.

There is much more discussion in an **interview** than with a questionnaire.

Interviews may take place in the street or on the telephone, but this is not often convenient because the interviewees may have more important things to do. The best interviews are pre-arranged and held face to face so that the interviewee has put time aside to consider the questions and is able to answer in depth.

Figure 2.3.3 Example questionnaire

NEWHAVEN SHOPPING CENTRE QUESTIONNAIRE

4 On which day(s) do you normally do your shopping?

Monday	Tuesday	Wednesday	Thursday	Friday	Saturday	Sunday

5 Do you usually visit the same shops each week?

Yes	No

6 Which of these specialist shops do you tend to visit on a regular basis?

Clothes shop	Newsagent	Chemist
Shoe shop	Sports shop	Florist

7 On average, how often would you visit clothes shops/stores each month?

Once per week	
Once per fortnight	
Once per month	
Once every three months	

Some benefits of interviews

- Answers can be discussed and developed so that it is easier to find out exactly what people really think.
- They tend to be longer than questionnaires, so more information can be gathered.
- When they are face to face, the interviewer may be able to gain additional information from the way that people answer the questions and from their body language. Good interviews can provide information that the interviewees do not even realise they are giving.

Some drawbacks to interviews

- Trained interviewers are needed, and interviews usually take longer than questionnaires, so it is costly.
- Interviews also take longer to set up, complete and analyse than questionnaires.
- There is a danger of **interviewer bias;** interviewers may interpret answers in the way that they want to, rather than by what was actually said or meant.
- Many people are not prepared to put the time aside for an interview, so access to the people who are really important may not be possible.

For business-to-business communications, market research interviews are particularly useful because they allow the two businesses to discuss the vital elements of the marketing that they will be working on together:

- When a retailer visits a producer to discuss the best way to promote products at point of sale
- When a business needs to discuss the launch of a new product with its advertising agency so that effective promotion can be created
- When a business is deciding to expand its sales into new international markets and wants to find out which distributor can offer the best services

Focus groups and consumer panels

Focus groups are people brought together to consider specific marketing research situations.

Where focus groups comprise consumers (or potential consumers) of a product, they are known as **consumer panels**.

Focus groups may be internal groups working on a particular project within a business. **Quality circles** and **project groups** within the marketing department will operate in this way when they are carrying out their research. In many situations, the focus groups may involve people from both within and outside the business, all working on a particular marketing issue (Figure 2.3.4).

Where market research is dealing only with customers, the focus group may be made up of customers from different segments of the market or from just one segment. Where different segments are represented, this will ensure that all the important views of customers are taken into account. Where the views of just one group of people are wanted, all panel members will be selected from that one group.

The selection of the people to take part in these panels is very important; otherwise it may be difficult to obtain reliable data.

- Panels should include representatives from all of the segments of the market that the business wants to find out about.
- Between 5 and 12 people is ideal. Any fewer and views will be limited. Any more and some people may not want to speak out, or too much discussion and argument may take place and few decisions will be made.
- A chairperson is needed to start the discussion and to control the panel without dominating it. This may be the interviewer.

Figure 2.3.4 Focus groups with internal and external members

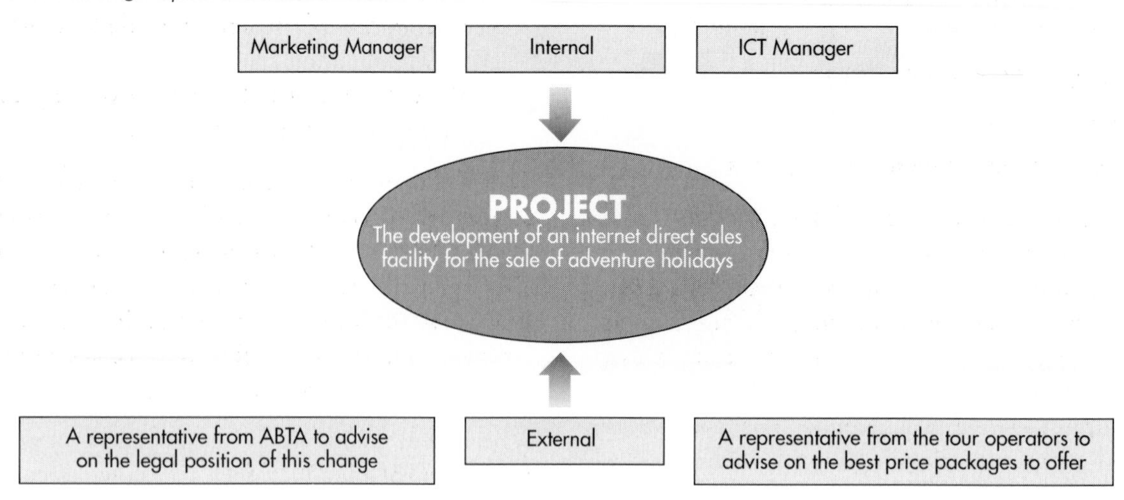

- Often, people who have been on panels before are best because they know what is expected and can communicate ideas in a way that can be easily understood by the market research team.

Consumer panels are fairly common when new products are being launched, such as a new range of yoghurts.

Some benefits of consumer panels and focus groups

- They allow discussion and more developed answers.
- They can use experts and special interest groups who know about the product and the market.
- Samples of the product, advertisements, etc., can be provided so that the panel can try, see, etc., what the marketing is about.

Some disadvantages of focus groups

- They can be dominated by one or two people so all the views are not heard.
- They are usually fairly small so only a small part of the market is being tested.
- As with interviews, the data may be difficult, and take time, to analyse.

The term **consumer panels** is also used to describe panels of consumers who collect data for businesses by recording details about their purchases, television viewing habits, etc. Businesses and market research agencies use groups of consumers, often spread around the country, to record details of some activity each day or each week over a period of time. Sometimes, this is continuous; the consumers keep a diary of their activities:

- What they spend their money on each day
- What television or radio programmes they watch or listen to each day
- Their reactions to particular products, tried over a period of days
- How often they take part in leisure and recreation activities and for how long

Where this data is collected by a great many people, it is very useful for finding out how people behave, and this helps businesses to target their marketing more effectively. Specialist market research organisations frequently have these kind of consumer panels through which they gather general information about consumer behaviour. They then sell this data to interested businesses.

Other methods of primary market research

Hall tests

Hall tests provide potential customers with the opportunity of sampling products. Originally, they took place in halls (hence the name) to which potential customers were invited. Today, this kind of research is found in many situations:

- Actual hall tests to sample products, to make comments on proposed advertising campaigns, etc.
- Sampling of new products in supermarkets
- Test-driving cars
- Free weeks in new timeshare complexes

Many of these are used as part of the promotion of products, but where records are kept of consumer reactions and opinions, they form a valuable marketing research resource. The main advantage of this kind of research is that the customers are trying out the actual products. The major drawback is that when people receive something free they do not usually make negative comments about it.

Field trials

Field trials take place when a business tries its products out by offering them for sale to a small part of the market. Often this is done on a regional basis, where one part of the country is selected and the product is sold there first, to test whether there is a market for it. This may be combined with other forms of market research, such as a questionnaires or interviews with customers in the selected area.

This kind of trial should provide vital information to the business about the likely success of a full-scale national launch:

- From the sales records,
  - The likely national sales
  - How quickly consumers started to buy the product and whether the sales then grew as expected
  - Which outlets sold most and therefore the best channel of distribution.
- From customer questionnaires or interviews
  - The best price to maximise profits
  - Where customers want the products to be sold
  - What forms of promotion would be most attractive
  - What changes need to be made to the product (if any) to make it more attractive.

Field trial are very valuable because they show what customers will actually do and not what they say they will do. The major drawback with them is that the trial area may not reflect how people will react to the product in the whole market. Choosing a truly representative trial area is therefore the key to how successful this kind of market research will be.

Post sales market research

All businesses should carry out post sales research to ensure that customers were satisfied with the product and to find out if the customers want, need or expect any changes or improvements. Businesses which do this can change their products to meet customer expectations and keep their customers on board.

The methods of carrying out post sales research include most of the methods mentioned above such as questionnaires, interviews and observation:

- Comment cards found in many stores, restaurants, etc., where customers are invited to comment on the service they have received – see Figure 2.3.5
- Customer complaint records, which should record details of what customers found unsatisfactory
- Returns records which show how many, and which, products customers found unsatisfactory
- Records from help lines, enquiry desks, etc., which should indicate whether customers experienced problems with the product

Figure 2.3.5 Customer comment card

Customer Comments

We would like to hear your comments so that we can continually improve our services for you.
You can call us on **01793 695195** (Monday to Friday 9am – 7pm, Saturday 9am – 5.30pm) or write to us completing the details below. E mail: customer.relations@whsmith.co.uk

Name: .... Date: ....

Address: .... Telephone: ....

.... WHSmith Store: ....

Your comments: ....

....

....

....

....

....

....

EAN 00403030

Thank you for taking the time to complete this card.

WHSmith

www.whsmith.co.uk

Revision Questions

1 For each of these statements about marketing research methods, indicate whether it is true or false, and justify your answer.

a) All primary research is also field research.

b) Primary research will always be more up to date than secondary research.

c) Secondary research is more reliable than primary research.

d) *Ad hoc* surveys cannot be continuous.

e) Omnibus surveys are only used by small businesses.

f) Businesses using external sources for secondary data will always be charged for this data.

g) Observation can only be carried out if a business has CCTV.

h) Electronic monitoring is always a costly method of marketing research.

i) Postal questionnaires will be more successful if return postage is paid.

j) Field trials cannot be used when businesses sell services rather than goods. (20 marks)

2 When many businesses are thinking about producing and selling new products, they choose to use questionnaires as their main form of primary market research. Trends Ltd, a small local clothes store, is thinking about a new range of imported Italian leather clothes. Trends is considering using a questionnaire to find out if its regular customers would be interested in this new line.

a) List five pieces of information, or questions, that you expect Trends to include in the questionnaire. For each of these, explain why it would be important for this business. (10 marks)

b) Explain the benefits and drawbacks of using a street survey to carry out the research. (10 marks)

3 A college has decided that it could make more money out of its canteen if it sold the types of meals that students really wanted. It has therefore decided to carry out a questionnaire in the college. The questionnaire will be written on A4 paper and left in the canteen so that students can fill in their replies.

a) Outline the benefits and drawbacks of this method of research in this situation. (6 marks)

b) What alternative, better, method of research could have been used? Justify your answer. (6 marks)

4 A farmer on the Scilly Isles, who specialises in growing flowers for the cut flower market, has for many years used a distributor in Britain to find suitable buyers. He is now planning to sell direct to florists in the UK so that he can gain a higher profit margin.

a) Advise him on whether he should use primary or secondary research to find suitable florists. Back up your decision with reasons based on access, time, cost and reliability. (10 marks)

b) If he decided to use primary research, advise him on which would be the best method of primary research in this situation. Justify your answer. (10 marks)

5 A games company is about to launch a series of games for the X Box games console, but first the company wishes to carry out market research to ensure that it will be able to promote the games in the right way and to supply the games to the most appropriate retail outlets. It has decided to use focus groups for this marketing research and it wants to include all likely segments of the target market in each group.

a) Outline the benefits of using focus groups for *this type of product.* (6 marks)

b) Advise the company on which segments should be included in each focus group. (6 marks)

c) What problems might occur because these different segments are all together in the focus group? (4 marks)

6 Explain why:

a) an *ad hoc* survey would be used by a company planning to sell hotel accommodation in Beijing to people in the UK who want to attend the 2008 Olympic Games (6 marks)

b) a custom-designed survey would be used by a market research agency working for a small business which has just invented a laser-operated cooling device and does not know who to sell it to (6 marks)

c) an omnibus survey would be used by a group of independent high street shops selling a wide range of different products. (6 marks)

CHAPTER 4

Marketing Research Techniques

KEY TERMS

Analytical techniques
Averages
Cluster sample
Convenience sample
Correlation
Dispersion
Distribution
Elasticity
Judgement sample
Quota sample
Random sample
Random walk
Sampling frame
Sampling size
Snowballing
Stratified sample
Systematic sample
Target population
Time series

In this chapter, you will learn about the marketing research techniques that are required for the collection, analysis and evaluation of marketing research data:

- Sampling methods used in data collection
- The stages involved in good marketing research
- How good marketing research questions are constructed
- How marketing research data is analysed and evaluated to produce clear and valuable results

Research techniques

For data to be collected accurately, careful planning is required; otherwise the data may be unreliable and any decisions based on it could lead the business into serious trouble. This section looks at three features of marketing research:

- Planning the research
- Choosing the right sampling method
- Constructing good research questions

First, however, it is important to recognise why most marketing research is carried out using **sampling** rather than a full census.

Sampling

In the UK, there are more than 58 million people. In the Basingstoke and North Hampshire telephone region, over 120 000 households have telephones. There are 10 000 people who bought copies of the last edition of Margaret Thornby's *Guide to Tea Rooms of Britain.* For most businesses carrying out market research with their customers, and potential customers, it would be very difficult, time consuming and costly to survey *everyone* in a target population, i.e. a **census**. It is therefore necessary to take only a **sample** of the target population and use that to draw general conclusions about the whole market.

A **census** collects data from every single member of a target population.

A **sample** collects data from only some of the target population.

Before a survey can be carried out the business needs to

- identify the customers and potential customers, i.e. identify the **target population**
- select the **sampling frame**
- decide the **sample size**
- decide what method of sampling to use.

Identifying the target population

It is important to identify the target population when conducting a survey; these are the people whose opinions and details matter.

Example
A local garden centre has about 3000 customers recorded on its customer database. It believes that at least twice this number of customers actually visit the centre but it has no details of the other 50%. It also believes that other residents in the local towns might become customers if they could be persuaded to visit the centre. In total, the marketing manager (Clare Bracher) believes that the target population is about 9000 people.

Selecting the sampling frame
Clare wants to find out how many of her customers would like to be offered a delivery service. This may appeal to customers who are visiting the centre or those ordering over the phone or internet. Clare decides to contact customers directly and ask them how they feel about the new service and how they would like it to operate. She also decides that the easiest and quickest way to conduct the survey would be to approach existing customers already on the customer database. The **sampling frame** is therefore the 3000 customers listed on the customer database.

Deciding the sample size

Clare knows it is important that as many customers as possible are interviewed, but she also knows that this will take time and cost money. She therefore, decides to select 10% of the customers in the sample frame for her survey, so her **sample size** will be 300 people.

Deciding what method of sampling to use

Clare then needs to decide how the 300 people will be selected. She will need to choose one of the sampling methods given on pages 96–102.

This basic process of sampling is shown in Figure 2.4.1, where each dot represents 10 people.

Planning marketing research

Marketing research covers research into any aspect of the marketing process. This chapter deals mainly with the research carried out to identify consumers' behaviour and interests, but marketing research is much wider than this.

The **target population** is the group of people, companies, etc., at which the marketing effort is being directed.

A **sampling frame** shows the number of people who could be included within a sample after certain conditions have been set.

A **sampling size** is the number of people actually sampled.

Careful planning, reflecting the type of marketing research that is being carried out, will ensure the collection of accurate and valuable data. The planning for finding out which competitors are most likely to affect the business will be very different from that needed to find out how consumers are likely to react to a new product, but there will be some common parts to the planning. The likely stages involved in these two pieces of research are shown in Table 2.4.1 (page 96).

Many types of marketing research survey might be carried out:

- **Advertising and promotion tests** – measuring how effective advertising is
- **Awareness tests** – carried out to find out if people in the target market have heard of the product, know of any changes, have seen advertisements, special offers, etc.
- **Audits** – looking at sales of goods or services to see which are selling well and which are selling poorly
- **Pack testing** – evaluating the design and suitability of the packaging of goods
- **Pilots** – selling the products in limited areas to test the effectiveness of the pricing strategies, channels of distribution, etc.
- **Product tests** – testing the attitudes of customers to a business's products
- **Usage surveys** – aiming to establish why people buy products

Figure 2.4.1 The target population, sampling frame and sample size

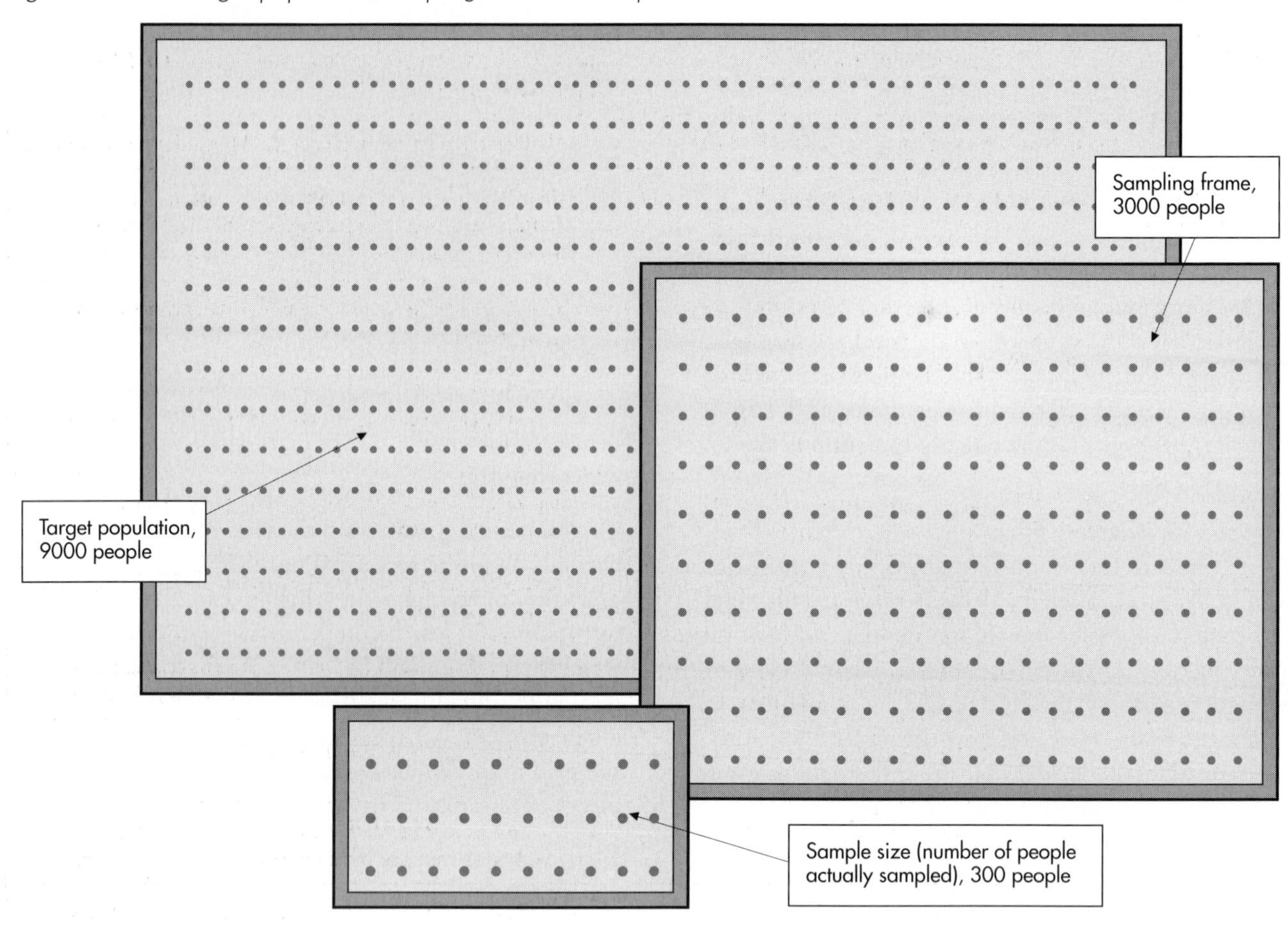

Sampling methods

Once the sampling frame and the sample size have been chosen, one of the various sampling methods must be chosen. First, however, the researcher will need to decide if the sampling will be **random** or **non-random**, or a mixture of the two.

In **random** (or probability) **sampling**, all of the actual people being sampled are selected at random so they all have exactly the same chance of being selected.

A **non-random** (or non-probability) **sample** is one where the people in the sampling frame do not have an equal chance of being chosen because specific conditions have been introduced.

Random and non-random sampling

Figure 2.4.2 shows a random selection for a sampling frame of 1200 people. One hundred people have been selected at random by putting all of their names in a hat and pulling out the first 100. The 'x' shows the people actually selected. This type of sample is known as a **simple random sample**.

The benefit of a random sample is that everyone is treated exactly the same so it removes any possible bias in the selection of the people. The major problem is that it may not reflect the actual profile of the target population. For example, where there are 600 men and 600 women in the sampling frame, it is possible that the 100 people selected might all be women or all be men.

The business may want to interview people of different ages because that is how their market is segmented. The researcher therefore chooses a set number of people from each age group. Once that number of people in the age group, say, teenagers, have been surveyed, all the rest of the teenagers are excluded.

Table 2.4.1 The stages involved in planning marketing research

Which competitors will affect the business the most?	**How will the business's customers react to their new product?**
1 Decide on the main purpose of the marketing research.	**1** Decide on the main purpose of the marketing research.
2 Identify which businesses are in competition with our business.	**2** Assess which aspects of the new product should be researched, e.g. price, design, usefulness, the best place to sell it, etc.
3 Decide which parts of the marketing mix are most likely to affect our sales: price, advertising, special offers, the quality of the product, etc.	**3** Identify who the target population is and how it is segmented.
4 Decide if a census or a sample should be used for	**4** Choose the sampling frame and decide on an effective sample size.
5 Identify where all of the competitors are located and where the information required can be found.	**5** Choose the most appropriate sampling method, e.g. cluster, quota.
6 Decide how the data will be collected and recorded.	**6** Choose the most appropriate method of collecting the data, e.g. questionnaire, interview.
7 Carry out the marketing research.	**7** Construct the questions so that the customers being sampled will give clear, accurate and useful answers.
8 Analyse the data to establish the relative importance of the marketing elements being used by the competitors.	**8** Carry out the marketing research.
9 Evaluate the effects of the competitors' marketing on our business.	**9** Analyse the data and identify which elements of the marketing mix are most important to the customers.
10 Alter our marketing strategies to effectively counter any negative effects from the competitors.	**10** Choose the marketing mix that will most effectively launch the new product into the market.

This kind of sampling does tie the research more closely to the known characteristics of the market. At the same time, it prevents a truly random survey which might provide important unexpected answers.

Of the main types of sampling – convenience, snowballing, cluster, judgement, quota, stratified, systematic, random walk – some are fairly random; others are very structured. Each is now considered, and diagrams are used to show how the sampling works.

Convenience sampling

With **convenience sampling** people are selected for the sample simply on the basis of convenience.

People may be chosen because they are passing by, as in a street survey. They may be chosen because they are the customers whose names happen to be on the customer database. One extreme convenience sample included all the houses that happened to be between the researcher's home (H) and the office (O) (see Figure 2.4.3).

Some benefits of convenience sampling

- There are quick and easy to set up.
- They are relatively cheap.
- They are based on specific knowledge which may be important for the situation being studied, e.g. the price of competitors' products in shops in the same street as the business.
- Conducting the survey again should be fairly simple.

Figure 2.4.2 Simple random sample

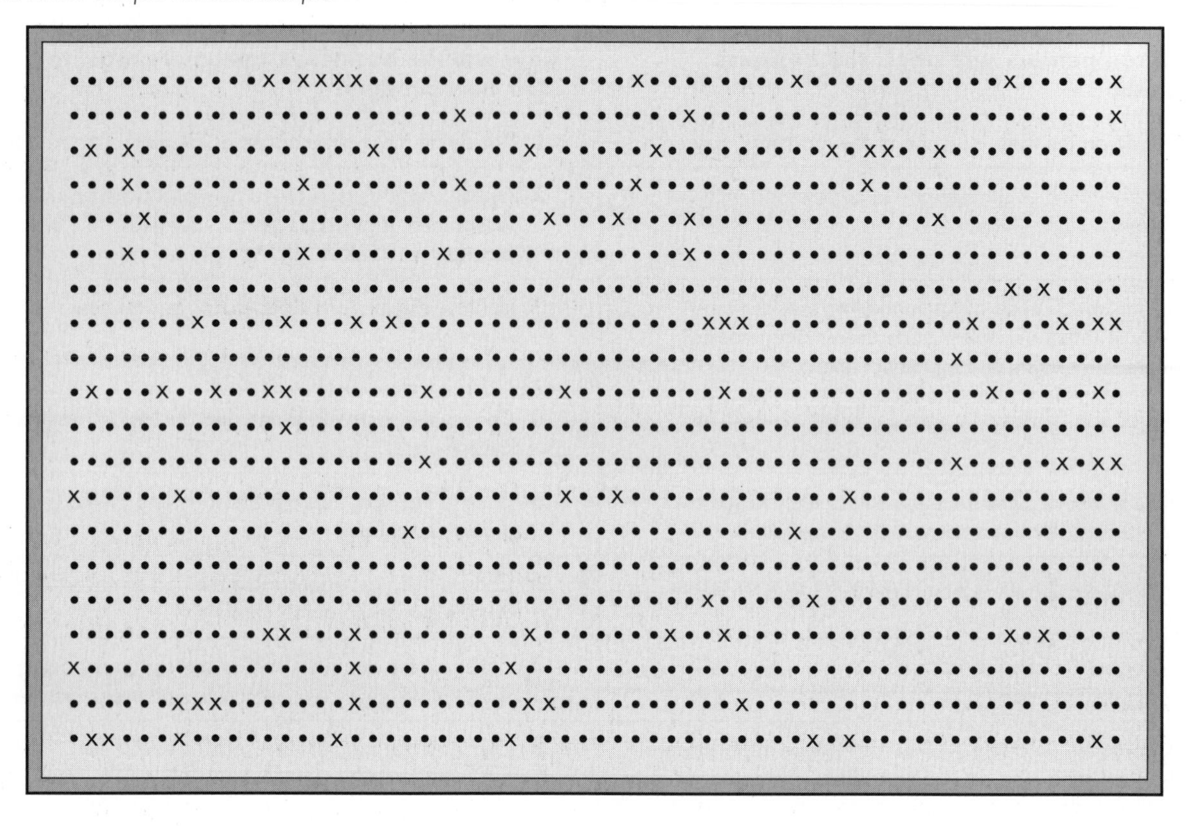

Figure 2.4.3 One pattern for a convenience sample

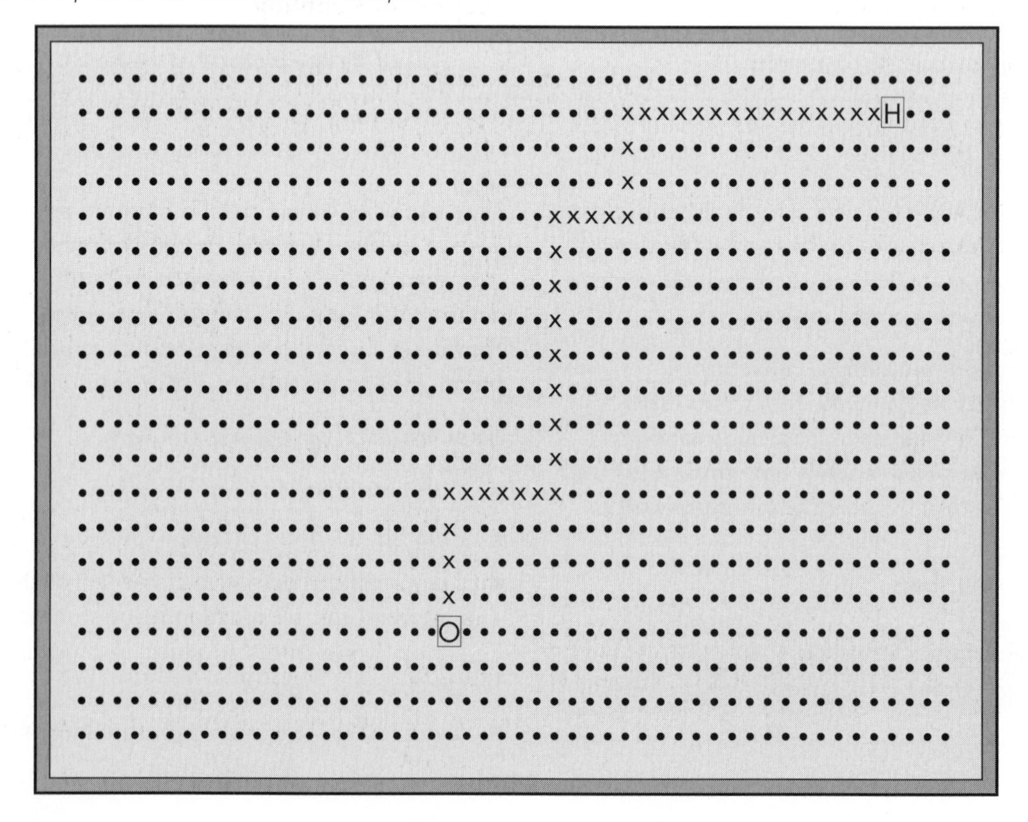

Some drawbacks of convenience sampling

- The data collected may not be representative.
- Any people who cannot conveniently be surveyed will be ignored and this may well include potential new customers.

Snowballing

In **snowballing**, the people to be surveyed are chosen on the basis of who has already been surveyed.

Snowballing is a type of convenience sampling.

For example, the owners of an historic house may want to know if it can attract foreign visitors. The owners have noticed that some Japanese people do occasionally visit the stately home. The Japanese clearly enjoy the visit and buy many souvenirs. The owners have no way of carrying out a survey in Japan so they ask the Japanese visitors to fill out a questionnaire and to provide the names and addresses of any other people in Japan who might be willing to fill out a questionnaire. Each time someone is contacted in Japan, additional names are asked for, so the survey snowballs.

The main benefit of snowballing

- It allows the business to contact people it does not know at a fairly low cost.

The main drawback of snowballing

- The additional people are likely to be friends or family and therefore a fairly narrow group of types of people is likely to be contacted.

Cluster sampling

For many businesses, marketing research is expensive. This is especially true for a small local business which is planning to become a national, or even international, business. Businesses in this situation often use **cluster sampling.**

In **cluster sampling** the business chooses one or more areas (or clusters) where the sample will be carried out.

This area or areas chosen in cluster sampling are then taken to represent the whole market. It is therefore very important that the right clusters are selected.
Figure 2.4.4 shows how this might work. The total area here represents the whole of the UK, but it could represent all of the segments or the whole of a customer database.

Some benefits of cluster sampling

- It reduces the cost of the marketing research.
- It is much quicker to carry out than a full national (international) survey.
- It can identify regional variations.

Major drawbacks of cluster sampling

- The possibility that the chosen cluster does not represent the whole national (international) market.
- The need to plan very carefully which clusters will be used.

Where the clusters are broken down into different layers, e.g. country, regions, town, district and street, this is know as **multi-stage sampling** and is similar to the stratified sampling explained on page 101.

Judgement sampling

Judgement sampling relies on the judgement of the researcher.

If, for example, the researcher carrying out a survey for a toy store believes that most toys for under five year olds are bought by mothers then a decision may be made to ask proportionally more mothers than other groups. This is shown on Figure 2.4.5, where it was decided to survey four groups on the basis of 50% of the sample being mothers, 20% being fathers, 20% being other adults (such as uncles, aunts and friends) and 10% being other children (brother, sisters, friends). No children under five were surveyed because they would not actually purchase the toys themselves. Inside each group, the sample was carried out randomly and a total of 60 people were surveyed.

Benefits of judgement sampling

- If the judgment is correct, it avoids unnecessary sampling.

Figure 2.4.4 Cluster sampling

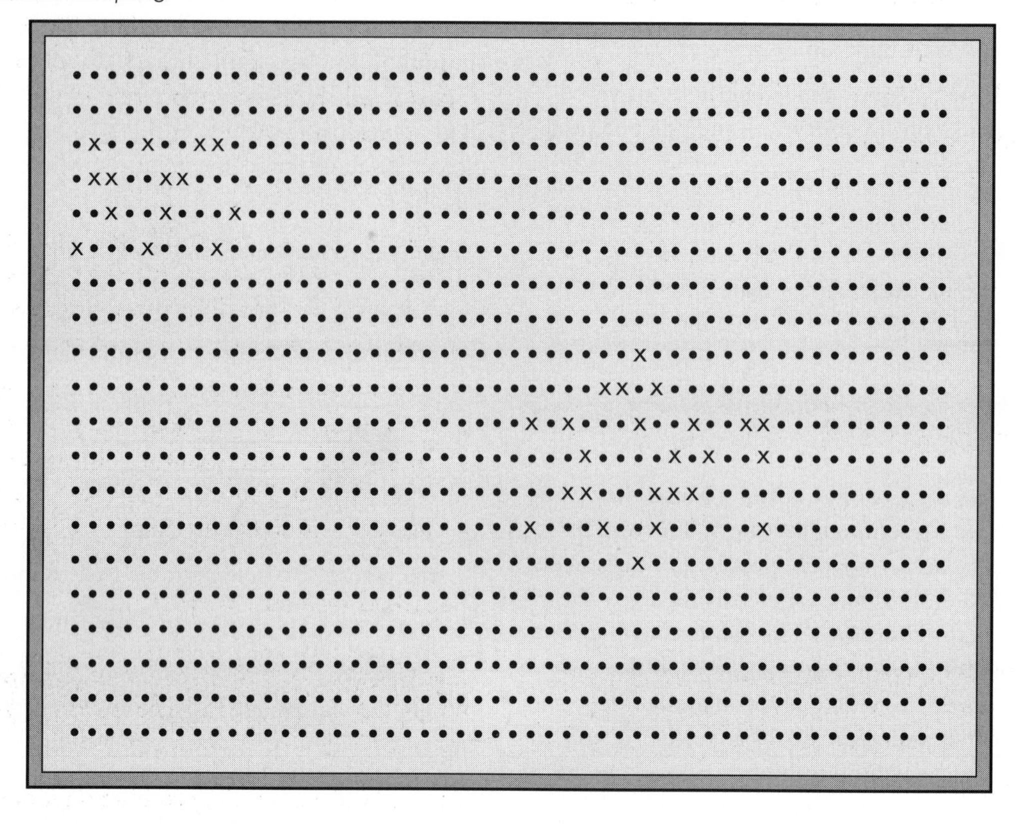

Figure 2.4.5 Judgement sampling in a toy store survey

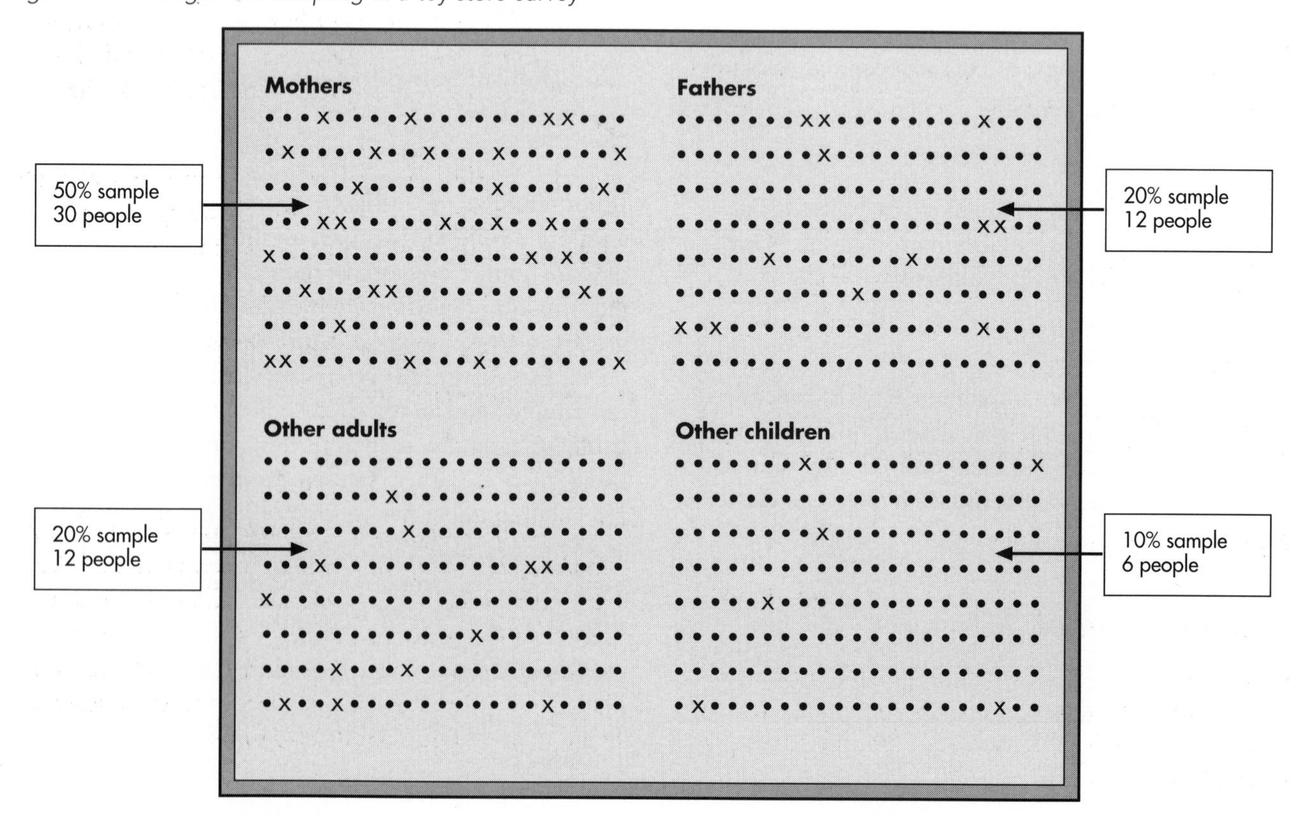

- It tries to identify which are the most important segments: the ones that need to be sampled.

Major drawbacks of judgement sampling

- It depends very heavily on the people making the judgement and they may be wrong.
- Where whole groups of people are excluded, the researcher will never know if they could have provided valuable answers.

Quota sampling

Quota sampling splits the market into segments.

Similar to judgement sampling, quota sampling involves splitting the market into segments that have already been decided.

Example
A business knows that 70% of its customers are men and only 30% are women. For a general customer survey, it makes sense to keep the same proportions when selecting the sample.

Businesses or researchers using quota sampling use these sources to decide on the quotas to be used:

- Past sales records, customers' databases, etc.
  These need to be used to identify which segment the customers are in and how important each segment is to the business.
- Published records
  These can give details of percentages of people in different segments, e.g. how many people are in each age group and are particularly useful when businesses are entering new markets for which they have no data of their own.

Quota sampling is a common method of sampling. If well conducted and the right quotas are chosen, it has certain benefits.

Some benefits of quota sampling

- The sample will accurately represent the customer profile of the business.
- The splitting down of the survey into different segments will allow the business to determine the different reactions of each segment and plan separate marketing strategies for each.
- If the quotas and the people within them can be easily identified, this will allow the firm to reach the people that it wants to contact much more easily. This will reduce costs and the time needed to conduct the survey.

Some drawbacks of quota sampling

- New businesses will find it very hard to decide what quotas are appropriate for them because they have no actual data for this. Relying on general data may cause them to make the wrong quota choices.
- Firms that have been established for a long time often research their exiting customers when it may be better for them to survey potential new customers. If the quotas have been taken from a customer database, this will not be possible.

Stratified random sampling

In **stratified sampling**, different characteristics are broken down into different layers or strata.

This method of sampling combines random sampling and quota sampling. It recognises that, for certain markets, the way that the target population is segmented is very important but, at the same time, it recognises the benefits of random sampling and allows anyone within a certain group to be chosen for the survey.

Figure 2.4.6 show how a market for cinema goers might be broken down ready for a survey. The figures are based on ticket sales for the last month.

- Males 56%　　Females 44%
- Adults 62%　　Children 38%
- Where they have come from:
  Downley: 20%　　Popley: 16%
  Ireton: 15%　　Swaith: 24%

The final line of Figure 2.4.6 shows how many of each group should be in a survey with a sample size of 150. Of the 150 people being sampled, 14 should be adult men from Downley, 11 should be adult men from Popley, etc. If the cinema found that, say, 58 adult men visited from Downley, the 14 people would be selected by random sample from those 58 men.

Figure 2.4.6 Stratified random sample for a cinema

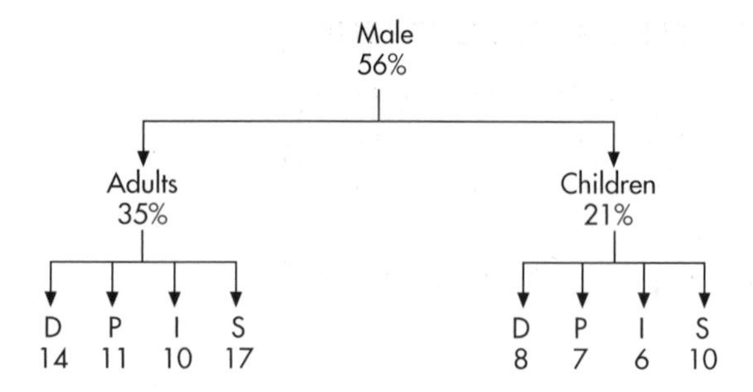

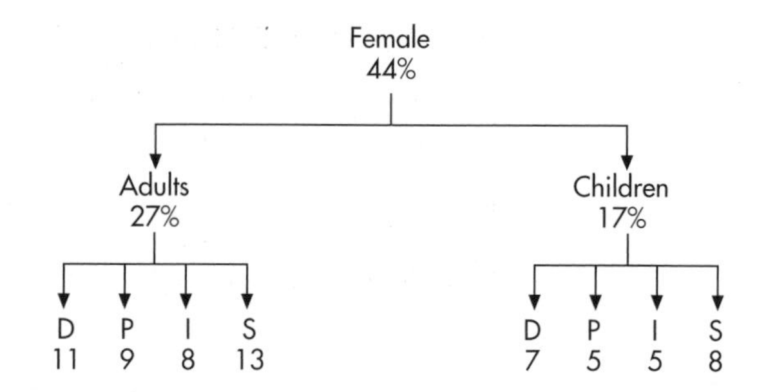

Other sampling methods

The specific sampling methods given above are the most commonly used of a huge range but they may well combine features of other methods. Below is a very brief outline of some of these other methods.

Systematic random sampling

A simple random sample gives every person in the sample frame the same chance of being selected. Today, with sophisticated computer programmes that is fairly easy to do, but many businesses still choose to use other methods of randomly selecting the people to be surveyed. Many of the methods that they choose are based on specific **systematic** ways of trying to ensure that the sample is random:

- Using the electoral register, which lists every voter in a certain area, and choosing every 50th person on the list
- Taking the customer database and interviewing everyone whose telephone number ends with a '1'
- Standing in the street and asking every 20th person to carry out a street interview
- For a company that has a customer help line, recording every 10th telephone call so that customer service can be assessed and improved

Another example is shown in Figure 2.4.7.

Random walk sampling

In this method of sampling, the sample frame is decided and then the people to be surveyed are chosen almost as if the researcher was taking a random walk around the dots in the sample frame (Figure 2.4.8). Each of these are random walk surveys:

- Selecting a housing area, walking randomly around it knocking on people's doors and asking questions
- Choosing people at random as they pass by in a shopping precinct
- Starting at a random name in the telephone directory and then ringing up the next 100 listed people

At first, they may appear to be totally random but there are drawbacks:

- People in the same housing area may have similar incomes, interests, etc.
- People out shopping may exclude people who work full time
- Taking the same names may mean you are ringing up people who are related

Where the random walk survey takes place in a particular location, on the ground, or in a telephone area, etc., this is also known as **location sampling**.

Different types of questions

When conducting interviews or questionnaires, there are various ways in which the questions can be asked. For the answers to be accurate, effective and reliable, it is important that the right types of questions are used.

Open and closed questions

An **open question** has no set number of answers and invites the person being questioned to answer in the way that they wish to.

Figure 2.4.7 A systematic random household survey with the researcher going to every tenth house

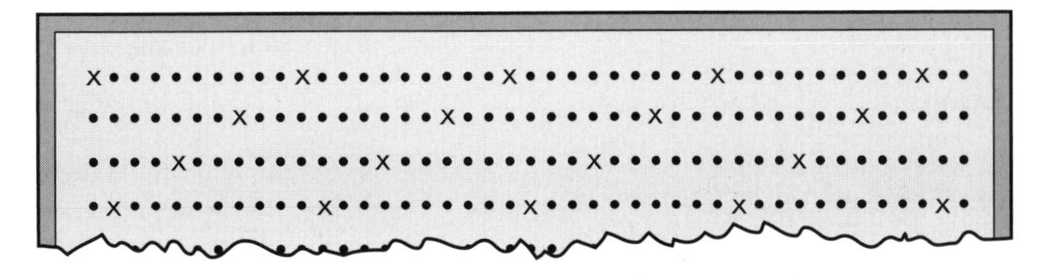

Figure 2.4.8 Random walk sampling

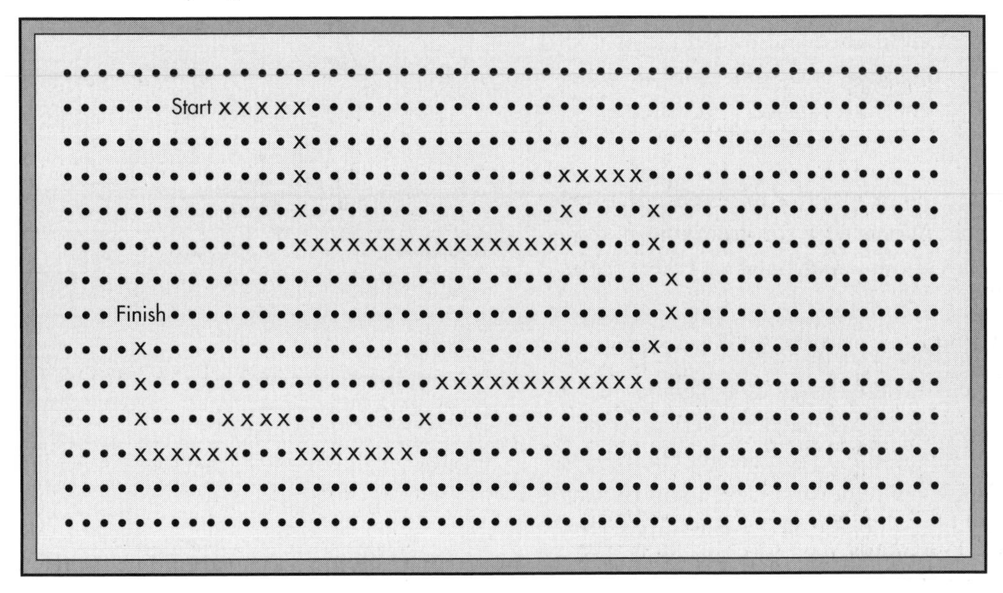

Open questions, also known as **open-ended** or **unstructured** questions, are particularly useful when there is likely to be a wide range of answers and where you want to find out how people think, why they buy products, etc. Here are some examples of open questions:

- Why do you use an out of town supermarket?
- How do you think we could improve our customer services?
- What aspects of television advertising do you find most appealing?

A **closed question** has a set number of answers and the person being questioned is limited to those answers.

Closed questions, also known as **structured** or **direct** questions, are used when clear, direct answers are required and when there are only very limited answers. The questions are clear and therefore quick and easy to ask and easy to analyse. Here are some examples of closed questions:

- On which day of the week do you do your main family shop?
- Do you smoke?
- Which age bracket are you in? 16–25; 26–50; 51–70; over 70

A **dichotomous question** is a closed question, with only two answers.

Dichotomous questions are usually asked on a questionnaire with tick boxes (Figure 2.4.9).

Multiple-choice questions

Multiple-choice questions are closed questions which give the person being surveyed a set number of possible answers.

Using multiple-choice questions allows the researcher to collect answers that are needed and to exclude ones that are not thought to be important. Sometimes an 'other' answer is offered to cover any answers not listed (Figure 2.4.10).

Some multi-choice questions offer the choice of a **scale** of possible answers. Where they run from one extreme to another they are known as **bi-polar** or **Likert scales** (Figure 2.4.11).

The multiple choice answers in Figure 2.4.10 give the person no choice about the degree of agreement or disagreement. One of the five listed answers must be chosen. A way of giving the person greater choice is to provide only the two extremes and leave them to decide what is in the middle. This is called a **semantic scale** (Figure 2.4.12).

Sometimes lists are provided so that people can give more than one of the answers, or people are asked to scale the answers in term of what is considered to be the most important, best value, most convenient, etc. Scaling is often done by being asked to award marks out of, say, 10. These questions provide the researcher with useful additional information but are still basically multiple choice question (Figure 2.4.13).

Most questionnaires and interviews use a variety of questions so that basic and more complex answers can be collected. Varying the types of questions also makes the collection of data more interesting for the people being questioned.

Figure 2.4.9 Dichotomous questions

Please place a **tick** in the appropriate box below.

Male		Female	
Over 18		Under 18	
Married		Single	

Have you taken more than one holiday in the last year?	
Yes	
No	

Figure 2.4.10 Multiple choice questions

Which Cola drink do you purchase most often?	
Coke	
Pepsi	
Virgin	
Supermarket own brands	
Value/economy cola	
Other	

Figure 2.4.11 Bi-polar or Likert scale

All cars should be fitted with roll bars
(please indicate your opinion with a tick)

Strongly disagree	Disagree	Neither agree or disagree	Agree	Strongly agree

Figure 2.4.12 Semantic scale

On the scale shown below indicate with a cross how you find your normal journey using our rail service.

Crowded — — — — — — — — Uncrowded

Clean — — — — — — — — Dirty

Figure 2.4.13 Multiple choice questions with multiple answers

Which of the following newspapers do you read regularly?	
Times	
Telegraph	
Guardian	
Express	
Sun	
Mail	

Place in order (1 to 6) which features of the park you enjoyed most.	
The rides	
The shows	
The swimming area	
The restaurants	
The free park transport	
The zoo	

Research analysis and evaluation

If the data collection stage of the marketing research is well planned and properly conducted, it should provide relevant and valuable data, but before any decision can be made it needs to be analysed and evaluated.

Analysing data is the process of changing the data into a form that can be easily understood.

Analysing data is done by turning the raw data into a usable format:

- Using statistical techniques such as working out trends, averages, probabilities, etc.
- Displaying the data so that it is easy to understand and interpret, e.g. in tables, as graphs and ratios.

Evaluating data is the process of matching the data against the original objective(s) of the marketing research, assessing its importance and making decisions about future marketing.

The case study overleaf shows the object, then the analysis and, finally, the evaluation and conclusion of a simple piece of marketing research.

Some basic statistical techniques that can be used in the analysis of marketing research data are now considered.

Price elasticity of demand

The Dorsan Pottery data – see Case Study on page 106 – could have been just as easily analysed by using the formula for price elasticity of demand:

% change in demand ÷ % change in price

For the wedding plates a rise in price from £5 to £6 (20%) would have caused demand to fall by only about 11%, giving a price elasticity of demand of –0.54. More importantly, if Clive had decided to increase the price to £7, a 40% increase from £5, the percentage fall in demand (from 92 to 80 people) would only have been 13%. This would give a price elasticity of demand of $\frac{13}{40}$ or –0.31. This shows that he should have put the price up further.

Averages

By looking at its till receipts, a business has found that customers have spent the amounts of money shown in Table 2.4.2.

The average amount that each person has spent, the **mean**, is calculated by adding up all of the expenditure and dividing this total by the number of people:

Table 2.4.2 Amount spent by customers on single visits

Person	1	2	3	4	5	6	7	8	9	10
Spent (£)	7.54	12.90	4.86	32.56	8.98	13.78	34.65	11.34	11.70	22.34
Person	11	12	13	14	15	16	17	18	19	20
Spent (£)	17.43	18.40	32.00	13.12	19.02	42.50	17.65	11.70	6.20	9.56

CASE STUDY

Objective

Dorsan Pottery is a part of a small craft complex. The owner, Clive Dorsan, noticed that the other units in the complex were selling their products at very much higher prices than his. He carried out research with his customers to find out what they would be willing to pay for his products.

Clive sets the objective of the research – to find if he should change his pricing policy.

Survey results: how many of 400 people questioned were willing to buy the product for a stated price or less

	£4.00	£4.30	£4.60	£5.00	£5.50	£6.00	£7.00
Wedding plate	136	120	101	92	86	82	80
21st beer tankard	50	35	17	10	2	0	0

The analysis

The data displayed in graphical form (Figure 2.4.14) shows very clearly the difference between the demand for commemorative wedding plates and beer tankards. For the wedding plates, the demand continues to be fairly strong, even though the price is rising. It is very inelastic. The demand for the tankards, though, is very elastic and a small rise in price will cause a large fall in demand.

Clive changes the data into a form that is easy to understand, to help him to draw conclusions.

Figure 2.4.14 Demand curves

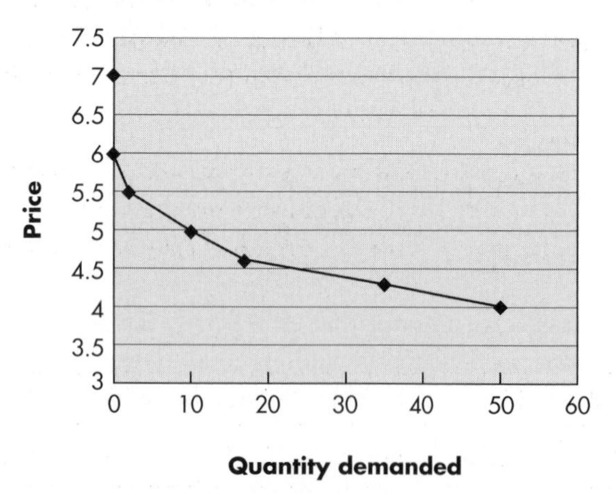

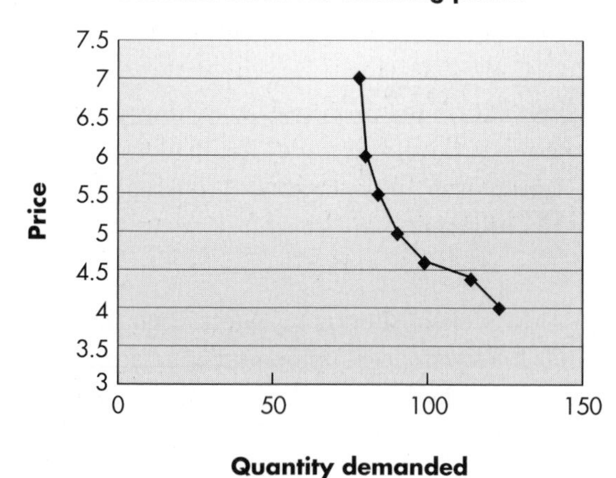

The evaluation and conclusion

Currently it costs Clive £3 to make the tankards and £4 to make the plates. He sells both for £5 each. The data suggests that he can increase the price of the plates to £6 or £7 without losing many customers. Putting the price down to, say, £4 for the tankards could increase his sales of tankards by 400%. The conclusion was to put the price of the plates up to £6 initially and the price of the tankards down to £4.

Clive considers the importance of the data and makes decisions about the future pricing for the two products.

mean = £348.23/20 = £17.41

This is a useful figure for the business to know because if it can increase the number of people using the shop, it would be reasonable to assume that each additional customer would, on average, spend this amount. It could therefore balance the costs of attracting extra customers against the profit that each additional customer is likely to bring.

Unfortunately, the mean only indicates the overall average. When the table is re-written to show how the amount spent was distributed, it shows that some people spent a great deal more than other people (Table 2.4.3).

The **range** of spending went from £4.86 to £42.50. There were also four people spending more than £30, which distorts the average. If the amount being spent by the person in the middle of this ranking is taken, the **median**, this would be between £13.12 and £13.78.

The median here would be £13.45 compared to the mean of £17.41. If there is any doubt about how representative the high spenders are, it might be safer for the business to consider the median as a better average to use than the mean. Alternatively, they could find out what most people spend by measuring the **mode**. To do this the business might see how many people spend in £5 ranges (Table 2.4.4).

The mode here shows six people spending between £10 and £14.99. It also shows that no one spent £25 to £29.99 or £35 to £39. This suggests very strongly that the top figures are not representative and should perhaps be ignored. Both the mode and the median suggest an average expenditure of around £12 or £13.

The mean, median and mode each have advantages.

The mean

- The mean is easy to understand.
- It is easy to calculate.
- It takes every item into account, so it shows the full data.
- If the mean and the number of people are known, the total can be worked out fairly accurately, e.g. from a mean spend of £17.41 by 20 people, the total spent will be £348.20.

The median

- The median is easy to understand.
- It is not affected by extreme data at either end of the list of data.
- It is easy to calculate once the data is ranked.

The mode

- The mode is easy to understand.
- It is not affected by small, extreme results.
- It gives the biggest group, which is important in marketing.

The actual average chosen will depend on what the data is being used for. For a supermarket planning how many people to have on the checkouts, and working out when people shop, the **mode** will be most important. This will tell them when the peak periods are.

A business wanting to price its products competitively is likely to take the **mean** of its competitors' prices as this is what people buying the products are likely to look for.

Table 2.4.3 Data ranked by how much was spent

Spent (£)	4.86	6.20	7.54	8.98	9.56	11.34	11.70	11.70	12.90	13.12
Spent (£)	13.78	17.43	17.65	18.40	19.02	22.34	32.00	32.56	34.65	42.50

Table 2.4.4 Working out the mode

Spent (£) between	0.00 4.99	5.00 9.99	10.00 14.99	15.00 19.99	20.00 24.99	25.00 29.99	30.00 34.99	35.00 39.99	40.00 44.99
People	1	4	6	4	1	0	3	0	1

A business offering a discount to customers who spend more than a certain amount may take the **median** as this would tell the firm exactly how many people would gain the discount on current spending patterns.

Dispersion

Dispersion is how data is distributed across the range of date.

There are problems with using any of the averages because they do not tell us how the data is distributed across the range of data. For a business making decisions about marketing, that can lead to decisions that will damage the business. For the data in Table 2.4.3, the data ranges from £4.86 to £42.50, a range of £37.64. Unfortunately, the spending is not equally distributed across this range. As we saw above, the mean, median and mode were all different.

One way of seeing how the data is distributed is to divide it into sections as we did with the mode, but into four sections, or **quartiles**. The lower quartile occurs 25% up the range and the upper quartile occurs 75% up the range. The middle quartile at 50% up the range, is also the median. For the data on Table 2.4.3, the quartiles are:

	Lower quartile	Middle quartile	Upper quartile
Ranked item:	5th and 6th	10th and 11th	15th and 16th
Averaged at:	£10.45	£13.45	£20.68

- 25% of the customers spent less than £10.45
- 50% of the customers spent less than £13.45
- 75% of the customers spent less than £20.68

It is also allows the researcher to see how **skewed** the data is. If the data is evenly distributed, the average of the upper and lower quartiles would give the median – in this case (£10.45 + £20.68)/2 = £15.56 which is considerably above the median. This shows that the figures above the median are uncharacteristically high and may be unreliable.

Dispersion is most commonly measured by finding the **standard deviation** of the data. This relatively complex process, important for assessing the reliablility of marketing research data, is calculated by working out how far away from the mean each figure is. Each difference is then squared and these are then summed and divided by the total number of data items. The answer is then square rooted. The formula is:

$$\text{standard deviation} = \sqrt{\frac{\Sigma(x-\bar{x})^2}{n}}$$

For the data in Table 2.4.2, the standard deviation is 10.16. In simple terms, the standard deviation tells the researcher how far, on average, each piece of data is away from the mean figure. In this case, each figure is, on average, £10.16 away from the mean of £17.41. We would therefore expect half of the people to be spending between £7.25 and £27.57. This is a fairly big range of expenditure and will affect the marketing decisions that the business takes.

Looking at Table 2.4.3 again, it also shows us that only two people actually spent less than £7.25 whereas four people spent more than £27.57. This again shows that the average expenditure was significantly affected by a few high spenders.

Correlation

Often, it is very important for businesses to find out if two sets of data relate to each other:

- What is the relationship between the level of people's income and how many holidays they take?
- Do more people buy ice-creams as the temperature rises?
- Do people buy different newspapers as they grow older?

In each case, the question is trying to establish whether there is a correlation between two variables, income and number of holidays, etc.

Some of these correlations are very well known and understood, such as a demand curve which shows a negative correlation between price and the quantity demanded, i.e., the higher the price, the lower the demand.

Other relationships need to be confirmed through analysing the marketing research. This is frequently done with a **scatter diagram**.

A **scatter diagram** plots a set of two variables on a single graph, generally as a series of points.

Example
A business wanted to find out if the hours of sunlight affects the number of miles that retired people between the ages of 55 and 70 drive. To obtain the data, the business asked selected people in the correct age range to keep a record of the miles driven on the same day of the week for 20 weeks. The data then plotted on a graph (Figure 2.4.15).

The scatter diagram shows each record (in this case just twenty). The line of best fit is found using the least squares technique; it is the line that has the same amount of hours of sun above it as below.

The line of best fit shows the basic correlation between the amount of sun there is and how much driving this age group is likely to do. This will allow businesses in, say, garden centres, stately home, golf courses, etc., to plan their marketing to emphasise what facilities they offer for sunny days. It also shows that when there is no sun, i.e., a completely cloudy day, this age group will still travel, on average, about three miles by car.

Time series

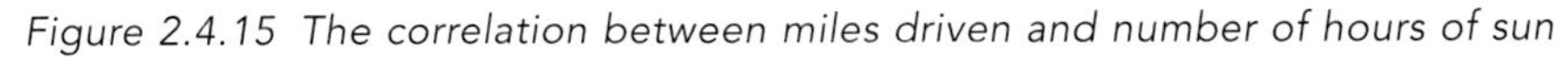
Time series show how data varies over time.

For businesses, **time series** provide vital information, allowing them to plan for the future and for any cycles that may affect their products.

Here are some examples of situations where a business would want data on how demand for its product might change over time:

- **Daily sales figures through the week**
  Where there are fluctuations, the business will need to arrange for different numbers of sales staff to be present and will try to boost sales on slack days.
- **Seasonal sales throughout the year**
  In peak periods, the business may be able to raise prices. In poor periods, it should perhaps think about other products to sell.
- **A steady decline in sales over a period of years**
  Perhaps it is time for a totally new product, an upgrade, selling into new markets abroad or simply more aggressive marketing?
- **Sales and profits figures that show the product life cycle**
  When will each stage of the cycles of research and development, introduction, growth, maturity and decline occur? This will affect advertising, pricing and placing decisions.

Simple time series are usually shown graphically with a line graph (Figure 2.4.16) or a bar chart. These show very quickly what is happening.

A business, currently operating across the southern half of England, wants to set up a regional branch in the north of England. The business offers personal fitness

Figure 2.4.15 The correlation between miles driven and number of hours of sun

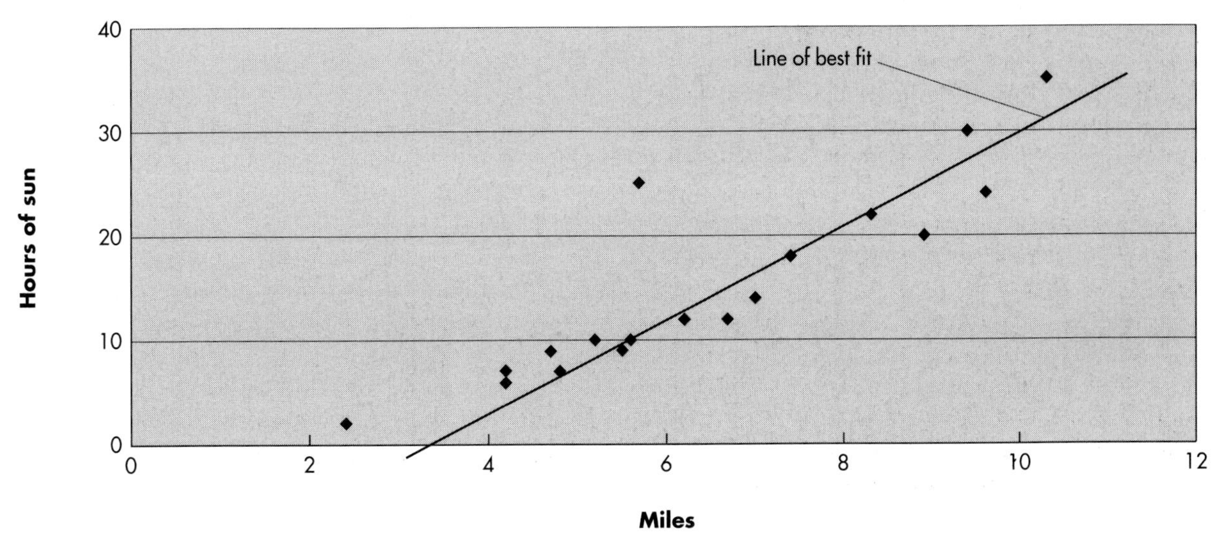

programmes. These fitness programmes can be used by any age group, but the business wants to locate its new regional head office in a part of the country where the population is expanding. Figure 2.4.16 shows that Yorkshire and the Humber region would offer the best potential expanding market.

Time series data frequently shows a cyclical fluctuation, with the units rising and falling over time.

Example

John Phillips has recently planted a vineyard and he now has his first year of bottled wine. He has been ambitious and has managed to produce a high quality sparkling wine. He wants to ensure that he brings it onto the market at the best possible time in the year. He has therefore checked the national statistics to find out when most sparkling wine is offered for sale. Figure 2.4.17 shows the **seasonal** fluctuations.

Figure 2.4.16 Percentage growth in selected regions 1981–1997 (1981 = 100)

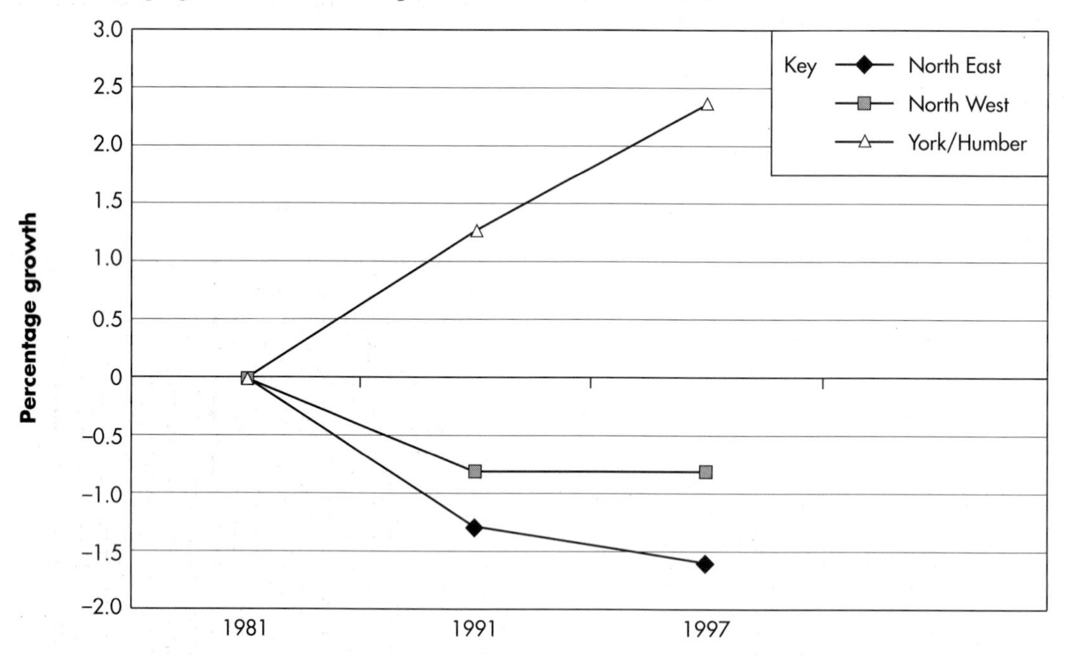

Figure 2.4.17 The amount of sparkling wine released for home consumption per month in the UK ('000 hectolitres) Jan 1997 to April 2001

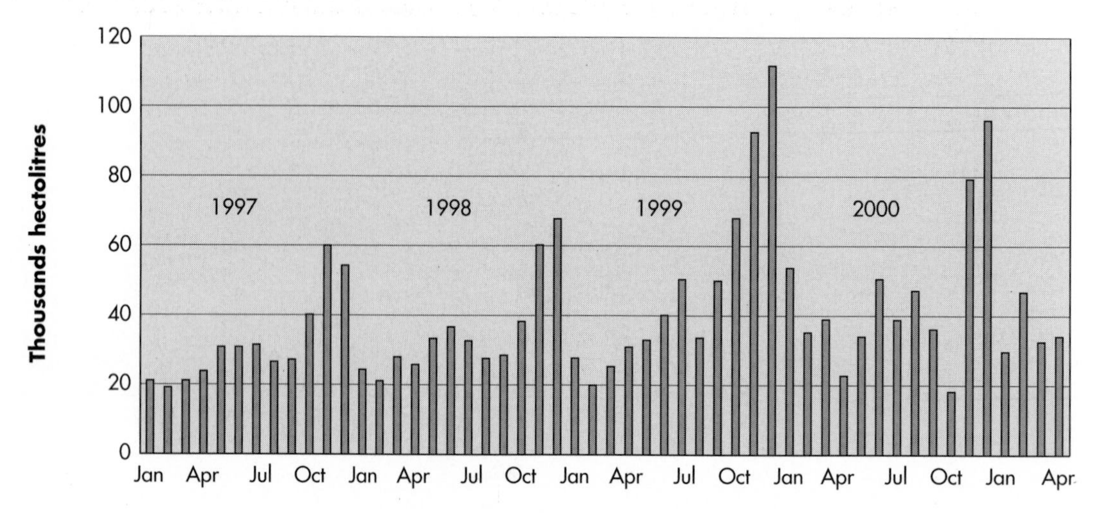

The pattern of sales through the year is very clear, with sales peaking in November and December as Christmas approaches, and then dropping dramatically in January and February. There is also some evidence of a slight rise in the summer months. John clearly needs to aim for the Christmas market to maximise sales, but he may find that that is what all the other producers are doing, so there may be some price competition.

The figures also show an upward **trend** over the years. The very high figures in the last three months of 1999 can be explained by people anticipating celebrations for the millennium. John needs to find the underlying trend so that he can make certain that the market is expanding. The most common way of doing this is to use **moving averages**. For Figure 2.4.18, this has been done by taking the average for the first 12 months and then replacing the figure for January 1997 with that for January 1998 to calculate the next average. As each new month is added, the oldest month is dropped.

Figure 2.4.18 shows how this smooths the seasonal variations and gives an overall trend. It also highlights that 1999–2000 was an exceptional period but that the overall trend is rising from 382 thousand hectolitres in 1997 to 543 thousand hectolitres in 2000.

For John, the two graphs should show him that he is in an expanding market and that he must think carefully about when, during the year, he should sell his sparkling wine.

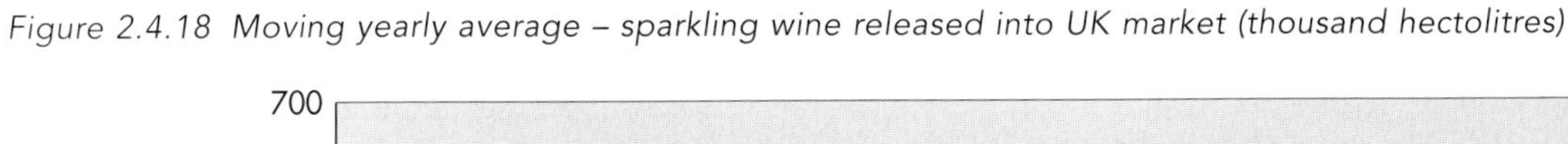

Figure 2.4.18 Moving yearly average – sparkling wine released into UK market (thousand hectolitres)

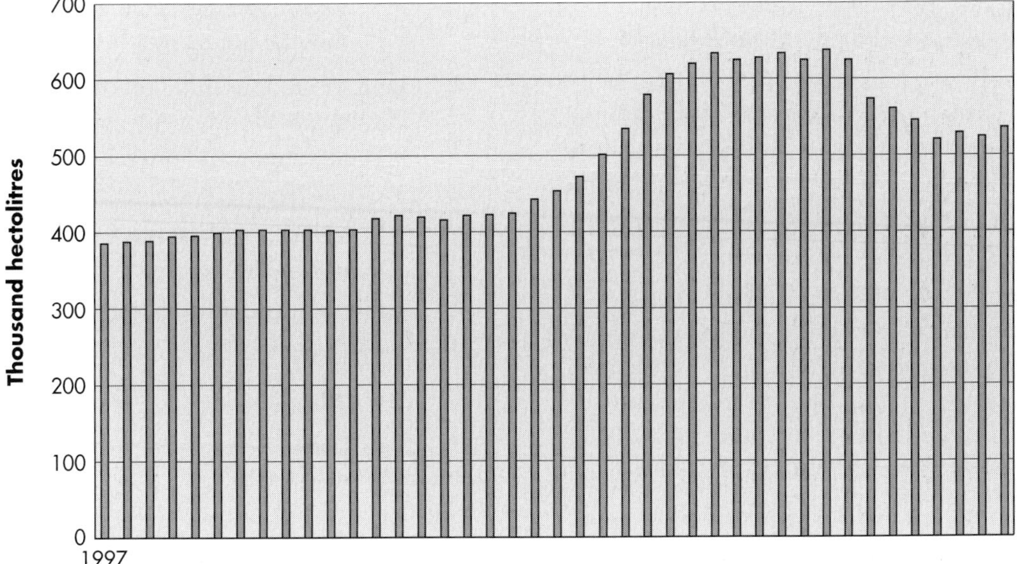

Revision Questions

1 Sangeeta Gashi has taken early retirement so that she can set up a mail-order business providing a wide range of scented cushions that are custom made for people all over the UK. She already sells some of these locally to small shops and to friends, relatives and neighbours. She now needs to carry out market research on a national basis and she has asked you for help with this. She believes the potential market for her products could be very large indeed.

   a) Explain briefly to her why she will need to use **sampling** for her research. (5 marks)

   b) Explain why **cluster sampling** is likely to be the most cost effective method of sampling for this business. (4 marks)

   c) Outline what she would need to do to decide on the **sample frame**. Who should be included and who should be excluded? (5 marks)

   d) Sangeeta would like to sample 1000 people. Explain how she could make certain that the 1000 people are chosen at **random** from the cluster area. Also explain why it is important for the sample to be random. (6 marks)

2 Powders Ltd is a small travel agent located north of London, specialising in skiing holidays. As part of their expansion plans, the owners are looking into the possibility of starting a new agency in Reading. They have decided to use quota sampling for their marketing research.

   a) Explain briefly what **quota sampling** is and why it would be important for this kind of business. (6 marks)

   b) What segments of the market would be suitable for this kind of business? Justify your selection. (6 marks)

   c) What sources of information could the owners use to work out the right size for each of the quota being used in the sample? Again, justify your answer. (6 marks)

3 For each of these situations explain

   i) why the business is likely to have chosen that form of sampling and

   ii) what drawbacks this choice might cause.

   a) A market stall holder using **convenience sampling** to ask his customers what new products they would like to see on the stall (6 marks)

   b) An estate agency, which has a few foreign customers buying properties in the higher end of the UK market, using **snowballing** to find out how large the potential international market is for its services (6 marks)

   c) The owner of a small chain of car showrooms using **judgement sampling** to compare her radio advertisements with those of her competitors (6 marks)

4 Opposite are four questions used by Chessington World of Adventures in their 2000 questionnaire. For each of the questions:

   a) State what type of question it is (using the list below – each question may be more than one type).

   Possible types of question include:

   - closed
   - open
   - dichotomous
   - multiple choice
   - bi-polar
   - semantic
   - list
   - scale

   b) Explain why they asked the question in this way.

   c) Explain how easy it will be to analyse and evaluate the data collected.

Question 1: **Please give marks out of 10 for the animals you saw.**

Beaks and Bills (Birdland)		Creepy Caves	
Great Apes (Gorillas)		Hooves and Horns	
Monkey Business (Monkeys)		Meerkats	
Paws and Claws (Big Cats)		Otters	
Penguins		Sea Lions	

Question 2: **Tell us what you thought of our new attraction – Beanoland.**

Question 3: **Did you require a parent and baby changing facility?**

Yes ☐ No ☐

Question 4: **Please indicate how strongly you agree with the following statement: 'In general the rides are worth queuing for.'**

- Strongly agree ☐
- Agree ☐
- No opinion ☐
- Disagree ☐
- Strongly disagree ☐

(30 marks)

5 The table below shows the results of a survey conducted by a computer games company. It asked a random group of teenage boys to record how long they spent playing computer games in a normal week. One hundred teenagers were surveyed.

(To help you to work out the answers to the questions given below, it is advised that you enter them into a computer spreadsheet. Ranking the data will also help you to answer the questions.)

Number of whole hours spent playing computer games in one week

4	2	9	4	21	1	7	4	4	11
7	8	3	2	5	19	12	7	18	3
2	4	6	8	7	4	4	8	4	9
8	2	10	12	3	3	3	9	7	2
19	0	4	13	2	3	2	5	3	15
6	7	8	2	5	5	6	3	10	17
6	9	11	6	7	2	6	8	5	0
12	16	3	3	6	9	14	6	7	12
15	3	7	3	7	13	3	5	9	4
3	4	6	9	10	2	18	9	8	1

a) Calculate these averages for this data,
  i) the **mean**,
  ii) the **median** and
  iii) the **mode**

b) State what the **range** is. (4 marks)

c) Explain the importance of each of these measures for the computer games company. (8 marks)

d) Calculate the **quartiles** for this data and explain why the answer might affect the marketing plans of the computer games company. (For your answer, you should consider such parts of the marketing mix as promotion, special offers, etc.) (12 marks)

6 The 2000 Family Spending Survey showed that the average weekly spending on specific products depended strongly on the socio-economic group in which the person was. The table below shows how the expenditure was dived between four main types of expenditure.

Percentage of expenditure, by socio-economic grouping, spent on four selected categories (as a percentage of the four categories)

	Leisure	**Tobacco**	**Alcohol**	**Fuel & Power**
Professional	45.0	4.1	31.8	19.1
Employers/mangers	39.4	9.2	32.5	18.9
Intermediate non-manual	41.8	8.1	31.3	18.9
Junior non-manual	44.1	8.7	27.5	19.7
Skilled manual workers	33.7	14.6	33.4	18.2
Semi-skilled manual	29.3	17.4	32.8	20.5
Unskilled manual	33.7	19.1	26.6	20.7

a) **i)** Identify which product generally has a higher expenditure by manual workers than by non-manual and professional workers. (1 mark)
  ii) Explain how this might affect the way that a business might promote and price the product. (4 marks)

b) For each category of spending, compare the figures for the 'Junior non-manual' group with the other groups. Do they represent the overall average? Explain your answer. (6 marks)

UNIT 3

Customer Service

CHAPTER 1

Providing Customer Service

KEY TERMS

Demographic changes	Red tape
Passing trade	Regular customers

In this chapter, you will learn what customer service is and why it is of vital importance to business organisations. You will also learn about different types of customers and their needs, and how a business organisation can meet those needs.

What is customer service?

A business organisation must sell its goods or services at a profit in order to survive. However good these are, in today's world, competition is very strong and every business must try to stay ahead of its competitors all the time. One way to do this is to provide something extra for its customers. Customer service is that 'little extra' and, nowadays, most businesses realise how important it is.

Customer service consists of the various ways in which a business looks after its customers. Clearly, a helpful and knowledgeable shop assistant is more likely to make a sale than one who knows little and seems to care even less about the product and the person who might buy it. The importance of well-trained assistants is recognised by everyone, but customer service includes much more than the point-of-sale meeting of seller and buyer.

A business that wants to provide a comprehensive high-quality customer service must be aware of, and be able to analyse, customer needs, and also to set up systems to ensure that those needs are catered for from first enquiry to after-sale service.

Every business should remember that customers are the factors which affect demand for the product. It is of the greatest importance, therefore, for the organisation to know its customers – who they are, what they need and want – and how it can satisfy those needs and, whenever possible, ensure that the customers return.

It is also important to realise that the needs and wants of customers are subject to change. Greater or reduced spending power, new products and demographic changes can all affect demand for goods and services.

Customer service today consists of a wide range of activities. The purpose of these is to make sure that customers are happy and will return again and again. As you probably already know yourself, some business organisations are better at customer service than others.

Demographic changes are changes in the structure of population. For example, the population of the UK has been growing steadily older in recent years.

Who are the customers?

Customers can be divided into several distinct groups. A business organisation must know who its actual and potential customers are.

- **General public** – anyone who might want to buy a particular good or service. This category includes **passing trade** and **regular customers**.

Passing trade – customers who might come into a shop or call on a service provider because they happen to be in the vicinity or want to try a new supplier

Regular customers – those who use the same supplier time and time again

- **Trade** – many businesses do not sell to members of the public but trade with other businesses. For example, a manufacturer of motor parts will sell to car manufacturers, while pharmaceutical companies sell to chemists, doctors and hospitals.
- **Categories of individuals** – depending on what its products are, a business might sell mainly to adults, the elderly, children or teenagers. This last category is a very important segment, particularly for fashion and computer industries. Customers with special needs have to be considered and their particular needs catered for by suppliers.

Customer requirements

When we decide to buy something, we usually have a good idea of what it is that we are looking for. In some cases, we know exactly what we want. Consider the following items which most people buy on a regular basis:

- Bread
- Writing paper and envelopes
- Shoes
- Orange juice
- Crisps
- Potatoes

With the exception of shoes, we do not usually spend a lot of time deciding on the items listed above. Most people, for example, tend to buy a certain kind of bread only – perhaps sliced white or wholemeal. Few shoppers are likely to investigate all varieties of potatoes available before they make their choice. However, even when buying everyday items like these, the choice is there.

CASE STUDY

Know Your Customers!

Rebekah and Hannah are twins who have both completed a Vocational A Level in Business and have now decided to set up in business for themselves. They were both given £5000 when they turned 18, and intend to use the money to start up their partnership.

The girls want to open a sandwich bar in a shopping parade near their home. Rebekah, who is interested in catering, will be in charge of buying all ingredients and making filled rolls and sandwiches. Hannah, they have agreed, will deal with customers and all paperwork.

The girls' father, who is himself a businessman, has told them to try to analyse the potential market for their business. 'Unless there are enough people near your snack bar who need to buy a lunchtime snack, you are not going to do very well,' he said.

'Of course there are,' said Hannah. 'There are the office workers and the shoppers, and all sorts of people who happen to be passing through.'

Their father was not convinced. 'What you must not forget is that there are several restaurants nearby, including a Pizza Hut and a McDonald's. There is also a Chinese restaurant and takeaway and a sushi bar. Why should anybody come to your snack bar?'

The twins are still confident that there are enough people who would use their snack bar, but they have realised that they must try to analyse exactly to whom their snack bar might appeal. Rebekah has now had a good idea.

'I know what we should do,' she told her sister. 'We must find out what we could offer, in addition to the sandwiches, cakes and drinks that we are going to sell, that would be so attractive to the customers that they would come to us rather than go somewhere else!'

'It is a good idea,' said Hannah, 'but what exactly do you have in mind?'

Activity

In your local supermarket, find out how many different varieties are on sale of the following products:

- Potatoes
- Apples
- Instant coffee
- Chocolate biscuits
- Mayonnaise

Now carry out a simple survey. Ask three people who do family shopping how many of these items they buy regularly and how they decide which variety to buy.

All the items in the list can be bought in many outlets – the food in supermarkets, the shoes in chain shops. What makes the customers decide to shop in a particular supermarket or shoe shop?

When asked the question, shoppers might give different answers:

- Because the prices are lower
- Because the goods are always of good quality
- Because the assistants are helpful and willing to assist
- Because the cashiers are efficient
- Because any mistakes are put right politely and quickly

While low prices are always a priority with the majority of shoppers, the other reasons for the choice of shop or store are very important. This holds true for other businesses as well and they all want to achieve the same aims:

- To attract as many customers as possible
- To keep existing customers
- To turn passing trade into regulars

If a business does manage to achieve these aims, it will maintain or increase its turnover and make the profits it requires. However, in the cut-throat world of competition, where every business wants to achieve the same goals, it is very difficult to prove to the customers that your business is the one they should deal with. Good customer service is one of the main ways to succeed.

The everyday items that we have looked at are fairly easy for customers to decide on. The problem becomes much more difficult when the customer wants to buy something which can only be objectively assessed by an expert. How many people can tell which washing machine is the best on the market? How many can judge the relative merits of a camcorder? How can the seller help?

The first step that a seller must take is to provide a good quality product. If the products on sale are not of sufficiently high quality, customers will, after a time, stop buying.

Products on sale must be introduced to the customers. This is why marketing is nowadays such an important function of business activity. No matter how good a company's marketing strategy is, however, it will not ensure customer satisfaction if the product is not good enough, or if the service provided is not up to standard. Consumer legislation (see Chapter 3) lays down rules regarding the sale of goods and services, to which all business organisations must adhere, but more is needed to give a business an edge over its competitors. Before deciding on what service to provide, the business organisation must understand clearly the customers' expectations.

The slogan 'The customer is always right' has, for very many years, indicated that customers are of vital importance to a business and should therefore be treated well. It is only in recent years, however, that companies have recognised the need to provide staff training, and to set up systems to ensure that customers' expectations are met.

Customer Expectations

- High quality goods/services
- Quick and efficient response to enquiries
- Quick and efficient response to orders
- Informative, polite and efficient sales staff
- Efficient after-sales service
- System for following up and dealing with complaints
- Good communication systems
- Minimum of redtape and paperwork

You know already that the first priority for a business is to ensure the quality of its products. However, the other expectations must also be fulfilled to achieve customer satisfaction.

Quick and efficient response to enquiries

Any enquiry about the company's products, prices, availability, terms of payment and delivery should be responded to quickly and fully. Failure to do so is likely to result in the customer going elsewhere. It is, therefore, very important that the person receiving the enquiry is competent to give the required information, or can, without delay, pass the potential customer to someone who can help them.

Quick and efficient response to orders

The same applies to orders received. It is sound practice to ensure that all orders are processed within three working days, and most large companies have procedures that allow this to happen. If a delay is inevitable, an acknowledgement should be sent, indicating clearly when the order will be dealt with.

Informative, efficient and polite sales staff

This is an aspect of customer care which most of us tend to take for granted. We assume that sales personnel will be efficient and polite and should know enough about the products they are selling to give factual and correct information. Unfortunately, some companies assume that sales work is easy and do not provide adequate training. We have all met the surly, disinterested and bored sales assistant who can hardly be bothered to answer any questions or offer suggestions. Most business organisations realise that such sales staff are likely to lose customers, and more and more businesses now provide initial training, often followed by refresher sessions, for their sales personnel.

Efficient after-sales service

When making a purchase, both the seller and the buyer hope that when the transaction is completed nothing more will need to be done. This is true in the majority of cases, but not always. Sometimes things go wrong, and it is up to the supplier to put them right. Exchanges or refunds for faulty goods are two examples of this, and should always be dealt with courteously and quickly.

After-sales service includes prompt response to customer complaints and, when appropriate, a repair service which should be reasonably priced.

System for dealing with complaints

Dealing with complaints is part of the after-sales service but it is so important that separate procedures should be set up to deal with this aspect of customer service. Every complaint should be investigated, and the customer should be treated politely. Sometimes, this might be quite difficult if the customer is upset or irate, so this part of the service calls for tact and the ability to deal with people who might themselves not be very polite.

Good communication system

If the business organisation does not have a good communication system, customer service is unlikely to be helpful and efficient. Not very many years ago, communication both within the business and with customers was by means of personal visits, in writing or by telephone. Today, every business has e-mail facilities, and more and more have internet facilities. This means that personnel must be trained to deal with a very wide variety of communications, and be proficient in their use. There would be no point, for example, in a company inviting its customers to communicate by e-mail if incoming e-mail is not checked regularly and answered promptly.

Minimum of red tape and paper work

Everyone recognises the need for receipts, warranties and contracts. These documents form part of necessary records which safeguard both the seller and the buyer. However, too many forms and too many procedures tend to delay action, and should be avoided.

Red tape – systems for dealing with customer requirements, queries and complaints that are so complicated that they cause unnecessary delays

CASE STUDY

Is the Customer Right?

Rebekah and Hannah have now been in business for three months. Their snack bar, which they have called Snappy Snacks, is doing quite well. Last week, however, something very unpleasant happened. In the middle of the morning rush, when both the twins were very busy, a woman marched in and demanded, in a very loud voice, to see the manager. When Rebekah said that she and her sister were the owners, the woman became even angrier.

'I thought you were just the assistants,' she shouted. 'I was hoping to speak to somebody sensible who could deal with a serious complaint!'

'Oh, I see,' said Hannah. 'Please tell us what is the matter? I'm not sure what it is that has upset you.'

'Upset?' said the woman. 'I am more angry than upset. I have been buying rolls and sandwiches from you for the last six or seven weeks, and I was very pleased with them. Last week, on Monday, I telephoned and ordered two dozen prawn rolls and ten ham and pickle sandwiches for twelve o'clock. When my assistant came to collect my order, it wasn't ready. She (she pointed at Rebekah) said she didn't know anything about it. Anyway, mistakes do happen, and the order was made up quickly. Karen, my assistant, brought it back to my office where I was having a meeting and served it to the rest of the staff. That was when we found out that there were only five ham sandwiches, the rest were salami, and the prawn rolls were crab! That was bad enough, but when I looked at the receipt, I found that I was overcharged by £2!

The following day I telephoned to complain and one of you, I don't know which, promised to look into the matter and sort it out. Today is Friday of the following week and nothing has happened. Are you surprised that I am angry?'

Hannah was very embarrassed, particularly as all the other customers were listening to this conversation.

'I am so sorry,' she said. 'I didn't know anything about this. Did you, Rebekah?'

Rebekah looked very uncomfortable. 'Yes,' she said. 'I meant to tell you about it. I even wrote this lady's name and telephone number on a piece of paper, but then we were so busy I forgot, and I don't know where the piece of paper is!'

Hannah was not sure what to do, but she took the woman into the back room, apologised, returned the £2, and offered to provide free lunches for her firm for a whole week. The woman left, still mumbling about bad service and how disappointed she had been.

When the twins were alone again, after the lunchtime rush, Hannah asked Rebekah exactly what had happened. Rebekah was still shaken.

'Well, it's my fault, I suppose,' she said, 'but I don't see what all the fuss was about. I just forgot about her complaint. Anyone can make mistakes.'

Hannah is very worried. She is upset that Rebekah cannot see how bad for business this incident might be, and is determined to make sure that nothing like this will ever happen again.

In addition to the above, customers who pay personal visits to shops and stores have a right to expect a certain standard of service. Clean and well-lit premises, with clear signs, are important, as is a logical layout. Wide doors for pushchairs and ramps for wheelchair users are now installed in very many outlets. In recent years, large supermarkets with their own car parks have introduced special spaces for the disabled and for parents with small children.

Customer service in the public sector

So far we have looked at the need for business organisations in the private sector to establish and maintain high standards of customer service. Public sector organisations also need to do so, although their prime objective is not profit. There are several reasons for this.

- Some public sector organisations do have competitors – private hospitals can take patients away from the NHS.
- Schools depend on their intake of students, and a school that does not provide good service is likely to attract fewer students, so that, eventually, teachers may lose their jobs.
- Even those public sector organisations which do not have to compete with others, and where jobs are safe, are accountable to the people who help to fund them – and this means all of us who pay taxes.

It is probably true that we only think about customer service when we have just had a bad experience in a shop or store, or have been upset and annoyed by the failure of a company to provide us with information, help us with a problem or answer our telephone calls, letters or faxes promptly. We rarely think how much effort an organisation must put into establishing an efficient system of customer service and yet most of us choose to deal with those businesses which do care for their customers.

Customer safety

Another aspect of service that must be provided for customers is safety. The minimum requirements are laid down in the relevant legislation, and all business organisations are aware that they are responsible for the safety of customers on their premises. Well-lit interiors, sturdy and secure handrails on staircases, accessible and uncluttered fire escapes are some of the facilities which must be provided. In supermarkets, for instance, arrangements should be made for any spillage on the floor to be cleared immediately, eliminating the risk of slipping and injury.

Little extras

In recent years, many companies have introduced additional services, designed to make life while shopping easier and more convenient for customers. For example, some offer a packing and carryout service, while others will now deliver your shopping to your door. Many supermarkets and off-licences lend glasses free of charge to customers who buy drinks for a party. In this way, business organisations hope to persuade customers to use their services in preference to those of other organisations – in other words, they hope to create **customer loyalty**.

Activity

How do they compare?

1 Visit three local supermarkets, and compare their services. Use the following checklist.

- Is a packing service available? If there is, does the customer have to ask for it, or is it offered by the cashier?
- Is there a carryout service?
- Does the supermarket offer a delivery service? If so, how often do they deliver?
- Are there designated parking spaces for parents with small children and the disabled?
- Are the aisles wide enough for pushchairs and wheelchairs?
- Is there a wheelchair ramp?
- Are there customer toilets? Is there a toilet for the disabled? Is there a mother and baby room?
- Does the supermarket have a cafeteria?
- Are enough checkouts open, particularly at busy periods such as Friday and Saturday?
- Are staff available to direct and advise?

Present your findings in table form. Summarise your findings. Which supermarket offers the best service? Explain your conclusion.

2 Ask three people who shop regularly at supermarkets the reasons for their choice of supermarket. You might find that quality, price and distance from home are listed as some of the reasons. Try to find out what else makes a difference to your chosen shoppers. Write a brief analysis of your survey.

Revision Questions

1 Define the term 'customer service'. (1 mark)

2 Name three ways in which a business organisation provides customer service. (3 marks)

3 What is after-sales service? Give two examples. (3 marks)

4 What are demographic changes and how can they affect demand? (4 marks)

5 Why is customer service more important now than it used to be? (3 marks)

6 Give two reasons why someone might choose one supermarket in preference to another. (4 marks)

7 How can a high standard of customer service help a business to attract and keep customers? (3 marks)

8 Why do we need advice when buying? (2 marks)

9 What is red tape, and why should it be avoided? (2 marks)

10 What is the likely result of the lack of a good system to deal with complaints? (2 marks)

11 What customer service 'extras' can be provided by a supermarket? (3 marks)

12 Name two categories of shoppers, and explain how a business might provide special customer services for each. (5 marks)

13 How can businesses ensure that their staff are efficient? (2 marks)

14 Give an example of *good* customer service that you have experienced. (4 marks)

15 Give an example of *bad* customer service that you have experienced. (4 marks)

CHAPTER 2

Customer Protection Legislation

KEY TERMS

Amendment	Consolidate	Implied terms
Caveat emptor	Contract	Negligent
Caveat vendor	Criminal offence	Satisfactory quality
Civil courts	Damages	Selling by sample
Code of practice	Description	
Confidential	Ethical responsibilities	

In this chapter, you will learn about the legal and ethical responsibilities of a business organisation towards its customers, as laid down in UK and EU legislation. You will also learn how the relevant laws are implemented through the principles of fair trading.

What is customer protection?

Most business organisations are aware of the importance of good customer care; this is necessary if a business is to have an edge over its competitors. It is, however, not sufficient to say that good customer care *must* be provided. To ensure that businesses know precisely what their responsibilities are towards their customers, legislation is necessary.

In the UK, several Acts of Parliament lay down the responsibilities of the seller to the buyer. As a member of the EU, the UK must also implement legislation passed by the EU.

In addition to the government providing relevant legislation, systems must be put in place to ensure that the laws are implemented, and procedures must be established for dealing with business organisations that fail to obey the law. In the past, the principle of ***caveat emptor*** – 'let the buyer beware' – used to apply in all business transactions, and this meant that total responsibility lay with the buyer.

If you bought something and then found that it was faulty or unsuitable, or that it broke down almost immediately, there was nothing you could do. There were no laws to protect the buyer and if you took the goods back to the seller he was quite entitled to shrug his shoulders and tell you that you should have been more careful.

Caveat emptor – Let the buyer beware. It is the buyer's responsibility to check the goods and make sure he is not cheated.

At that time, there were few goods, and even fewer services, that people could buy. Food, simple tools, some clothing and building materials were available for sale and it was relatively easy for a buyer to examine the goods and be sure that what he or she bought was of good quality. However, this situation began to change during the Industrial Revolution, around the middle of the eighteenth century. New inventions and processes brought more and more goods onto the market, and soon it became impossible for any one person to be able to judge the quality of everything available in shops and markets.

This industrial development brought about the realisation that sellers must take responsibility for what they sell. Gradually, the principle of 'caveat emptor' changed into ***caveat vendor*** – 'let the seller beware', and governments realised that legislation was needed to make sure that the sellers knew what their obligations were.

Today, the legal responsibilities of the seller to the buyer are clearly laid down by the law.

Caveat vendor – Let the seller beware. It is the seller's responsibility to make sure the goods are of the quality he has promised they will be.

Contracts

A **contract** is a legally binding agreement between two parties.

All transactions between the buyer and the seller are contracts, with both sides having clearly defined responsibilities.

Briefly, the responsibility of the buyer is to pay for the goods or services purchased. The responsibilities of the seller are much more complex.

Consumer protection legislation

These are the main Acts of Parliament dealing with consumer protection:

- Sale of Goods Act (SGA) 1979
- Sale and Supply of Goods Act 1994
- Supply of Goods and Services Act 1982
- Supply of Goods (Implied Terms) Act 1973
- Consumer Protection Act 1987
- Data Protection Act 1984

Sale of Goods Act (SGA) 1979

Many people think that this Act was the first to regulate the law of sale. In fact, the first Act of Parliament to deal with this subject was passed as long ago as 1893. The SGA 1979 **consolidated** the 1893 Act and its amendments.

Consolidate – in legal terms, this means including earlier provisions and additions in a new Act of Parliament.

An **amendment** is an addition, or change, to an existing Act of Parliament.

The right of the seller to sell

In every contract, there are some **implied** conditions. An implied condition is one known so well to both the parties that it is unnecessary to include it in a particular contract. One such implied condition is that the seller has the legal right to sell. When you go into a shop, you do not ask the shopkeeper if the goods that he or she is offering for sale are legally his or hers – you assume that it is so. If, later, you discover that the seller did not have the right to sell, the SGA 1979 lays down your rights to recover the money you have spent.

Mason *v* Burningham 1949

Mason bought a typewriter from Burningham and had it repaired. He later found that it had been stolen. Mason was entitled not only to recover the price he had paid to Burningham, but also the cost of the repairs.

This Act applies to all contracts, including purely private sales between individuals

Description

Another implied condition in a contract of sale is that the goods must correspond with the **description**. 'Correspond with **description**' means that the goods must be as described. For example, a pair of gloves described as made of leather must be made of leather, not of plastic.

Selling by sample – a small part of the goods are shown to the buyer with the promise that the rest of the goods are of the same quality.

Goods such as coffee or tea are usually sold in large quantities, and the buyer cannot see the whole consignment. The seller shows prospective buyers a sample, in other words a small amount of the goods, and promises that the rest of the consignment will be of the same quality. This is known as 'selling by sample', and the law states that the whole consignment must be of the same quality as the sample that was seen by the buyer.

Section 13 of the SGA 1979 also states that the seller is responsible for the description of the goods even when the buyer examines and selects the goods himself. For example, when buying a tin of baked beans at a supermarket, we may look at the tin and make our choice ourselves, but the law requires that the list of ingredients on the label is accurate.

The responsibility of the seller for the description of the goods is a very important part of consumer protection legislation, particularly when goods are sold by mail order and, nowadays, on the internet. The law states that the components, quantity, quality and packaging of the goods must be correctly and accurately described.

Satisfactory quality

Satisfactory quality – items must be of good enough standard of manufacture to be used as they are intended to be used.

The SGA 1979 recognised that the quality of goods sold was of very great importance. It stipulated that goods had to be 'fit for the purpose' and 'of merchantable quality'. This meant that anything sold must be usable for the purpose for which it was intended – shoes could be worn, for example, or an electric iron used to press clothes – and that the quality was good enough. Over the years, however, it was found that these definitions were rather confusing and, in the Sale and Supply of Goods Act 1987, they were replaced by the requirement that goods must be of 'reasonable quality'. This phrase was inserted into the SGA.

Reasonable quality does not mean perfect, but it does mean that goods must meet the standard 'that a reasonable person would regard as satisfactory'. We can see at once that this can be interpreted differently by different individuals and organisations. To make this problem easier, the law now provides several guidelines.

This is what the amended Act says:

> For the purposes of this Act, the quality of goods includes their state and condition, and the following … aspects of the quality of the goods:
>
> a. fitness for all the purposes for which the goods of the kind in question are commonly supplied
> b. appearance and finish
> c. freedom from minor defects
> d. safety
> e. durability (SGA).

Sale and Supply of Goods Act 1994 (SSGA)

This Act is important for its substitution of the term 'satisfactory quality' for the previously used phrases 'merchantable quality' and 'fit for the purpose'. The guidelines quoted above were set out in the SSGA 1994, but are implemented through the SGA.

Supply of Goods and Services Act 1982 (SGSA)

The SGA 1979 dealt only with the legal responsibilities of sellers of goods. The Supply of Goods and Services Act 1982 added the responsibilities of providers of services. For many years the range of services available has been increasing and, today, there can be few, if any, individuals or business organisations that do not pay for a number of services.

In Part II of the SSGA, a contract for the supply of a service is defined as 'a contract under which the supplier agrees to carry out a service'. In such a contract there is another, **implied term**. This is that the supplier of a service will carry it out with 'reasonable care and skill'. All service providers are included in this, whether they are professionals, working for a local authority or a government department, or in the private or the public sector.

Implied terms are terms that are not actually stated or written down but which can be assumed or expected to apply.

The Act states that a professional person, e.g. a doctor or an architect, must act with the skill of a competent member of their profession. This does not mean that the service provided will always be perfect, only that the provider has the necessary standard of skill and exercises the duty of care.

CASE STUDY

A Treat for Toby

Toby is seven years old. He has two older brothers, Jamie and Roy, and an older sister, Janine. Two months ago, Toby had an accident, playing in the back garden. His mother had told Janine, Jamie and Roy to look after their little brother, but they had become bored and had gone indoors to watch television.

Jamie kept coming out to see what Toby was up to but when nobody was looking Toby climbed onto a ladder that his father had left leaning against the wall, lost his footing and fell. When the others heard him crying, they rushed out but it was too late. Toby had broken his leg and had to be taken to hospital. His leg was put in plaster and he had to hobble about on crutches for several weeks.

The children's parents were very upset and angry with the older ones. Jamie, Janine and Roy felt very guilty and decided to do something to cheer Toby up. They knew that their little brother wanted a new shiny steel scooter, but their parents said it was too expensive.

'We can't afford to spend £100 on a scooter for you,' his mother said when Toby kept asking her to buy him one.

Now his brothers and sister decided to pool all their pocket money and buy a scooter for Toby as a coming home from hospital present. They had only £45 between them, but Roy saw an advertisement in a magazine offering scooters at £38 each.

'This is great!' said Janine. 'It's exactly what Toby wants, and we can easily afford it.'

SCOOTERS FOR SALE

Suitable for children from the age of 6. Sturdy steel construction – very strong and well made. Fold down when not in use. A real bargain at £38, while stocks last.
Write to ...

They wrote to the company selling the scooters, enclosing a postal order for £38 plus postage and packing, and waited impatiently. The scooter arrived a few days later. They unpacked it. It looked like other scooters that they had seen but they could not make it fold so they asked their father to help. When he looked at the scooter, he shook his head.

'This scooter does not fold,' he said. 'Also, it is not made of steel – the metal is much too soft. In fact, I don't think this scooter is safe to use – I'm sorry, I know you wanted to give Toby a lovely present, but this is so badly made that he could have another accident if he started riding it!'

The children were very upset.

'This is not what it said in the advert,' said Janine.

'We have spent all our money on something that cannot be used,' added Roy.

'Is there anything we can do?' asked Jamie.

Activity

Roy, Jamie and Janine want to know what they can do now, because the company selling the scooters has refused to refund their money. Do you think the company has broken the law, as set out in the Sale of Goods Act, regarding the quality of goods?

Write a letter to the children, explaining the situation, with reference to the guidelines in the Act.

The SGSA also recognises that there are implied terms regarding reasonable time and reasonable price for services. If the price has not been agreed, or the time for the delivery of the service clearly stated in the contract, then the courts can be asked to determine what would be 'reasonable' in a particular case.

Supply of Goods (Implied Terms) Act 1973

This Act, now amended, deals with the responsibilities of the seller in relation to hire-purchase contracts.

Basically, anyone buying goods on hire purchase has the some protection under the law as a person who buys the goods outright.

The supplier must ensure that:

- he or she has legal title to the goods (in other words, has the right to sell)
- the description of the goods is accurate and not misleading
- the quality of the goods is of reasonable standard
- if selling by sample, the sample is representative of the rest of the consignment.

CASE STUDY

Who is at fault?

Five years ago, George bought a three-bedroom house on the outskirts of a large town. Last summer, George decided that the house needed painting. George's wife, Lillian, told him to call in a friend of a friend, who does painting and decorating in his spare time, but George disagreed.

'I'm not going to use someone who is not a professional,' he told Lillian. 'It can only lead to trouble, and poor quality work.'

'But it will be much cheaper,' said Lillian.

'True,' said George, 'but I want to make sure that the job is properly done. It will be cheaper in the long run, believe me.'

So George called in a local firm, Quick and Fair Decorating Ltd. Jerry Quick, one of the directors, came to see the house, and he and George agreed on the price. Jerry said that to paint the whole house, front and back, including all the doors and windows, would cost George £2200, and said that his men could start work the following week.

Sure enough, two decorators arrived on the Monday and started work. They worked through Monday and Tuesday but disappeared at lunchtime on Wednesday. Lillian was very unhappy.

'What are they playing at?' she demanded. 'They were supposed to be working all day, every day, surely?'

'Don't worry,' said George. 'I'm sure they will be back tomorrow and will make a good job of it'.

Unfortunately, George was wrong. The workmen came for a few hours each day and were gone by midday. George telephoned Jerry, only to be told that, 'Something urgent has come up, but it will all be back to normal next week.'

Next week came and went but things did not improve. George had assumed that the whole job would not take more than a week but in fact it took Quick and Fair Decorators six weeks to complete.

George was furious. He became even angrier when he discovered that the decorators had failed to scrape the window frames before painting, and had used inferior quality paint instead of the one that he and Jerry had agreed on. He went to see Jerry and told him that, in view of the length of time it had taken the workmen to complete the job, and because of the poor quality of the work, he was not prepared to pay the agreed price.

'You can't do that,' said Jerry. 'You had agreed to the price and now you must pay me in full as the job is finished!'

George is very upset especially when Lillian reminds him that she suggested he employ the friend of a friend.

What is George's legal position?

In one important respect, the buyer who enters into a hire purchase agreement is in a stronger position than one who pays for the goods outright. When buying on HP, it is still possible to reject the goods after accepting them, whereas in transactions in which the full price has been paid, once the goods are accepted, they cannot be rejected.

Consumer Protection Act 1987

This Act was the first to be introduced in the UK to bring the UK into line with other EU countries. It deals with three aspects of consumer protection:

- Product liability
- Consumer safety
- Misleading pricing

The Act was passed as a result of a European Community directive of 1985. The Product Liability section made producers liable for any damage done by defective products. Prior to the implementation of the Act, producers could claim that they had not been **negligent**, or that they did not know that the goods were defective. Neither of these claims can now be made, which should make manufacturers much more careful in the production and quality control of their goods.

Negligent – lacking a reasonable degree of care

The Act goes even further in ensuring that customers are protected from damage or injury caused by faulty goods. In addition to the manufacturers themselves, importers are also liable, as are sellers who put their own brand name on goods manufactured by someone else. Suppliers can also be liable if they do not provide, when asked, the name of the manufacturer, their own supplier, the owner of the brand or the importer.

Prior to this Act, the consumer had no redress against the manufacturer or importer as his or her contract was only with the supplier.

The second part of the Act deals with consumer safety and allows the government to regulate the design, components and construction of goods which could, if defective, cause injury or even death. Such goods include electrical appliances, oil heaters and flexes on domestic electrical goods.

It is a criminal offence to breach the regulations contained in the Act. In addition, any consumer who has suffered loss or injury because of an infringement of the Act has the right to sue for damages in the civil courts.

Criminal offence – a breach of the law
Those accused of criminal offences are dealt with in criminal courts.

Civil courts deal with disputes between two parties and their aim is to ensure that the dispute is resolved in such a way that neither party suffers a loss.

Damages is the term used for money awarded by a civil court to the person or persons who have suffered a loss or injury as a result of an action by another person or organisation.

Part Three of the Act makes it illegal to mislead consumers about the price of any good, service or facility. The provisions of this part are quite comprehensive and cover such services as banking, gas and electricity supplies, telephone services and parking, and also accommodation and all goods.

Data Protection Act (DPA) 1984

This Act protects the confidentiality of information stored in computers. As more and more organisations now hold personal information in their databases, it has become necessary for the government to regulate the ways in which such information should be stored and used. The Act requires anyone – an individual or an organisation – holding personal data on computer to register with the Data Protection Registrar. It also requires that:

- data must be acquired legally
- data must only be used for the purpose for which it is held
- data must not be disclosed to others unless this is necessary for the purpose for which it is held

CASE STUDY

What's in a name?

Eileen Brown is 30 years old and has been working as a senior accounts clerk for the last eight years. She has never taken out any loans and has always lived with her parents. When her friends asked her when she was going to 'become independent', Eileen always laughed and told them that she was perfectly happy where she was.

'I like my parents, we get on well, and also it is very convenient and much cheaper than renting a place,' she told those who asked.

Last year, Eileen met Joel, a junior executive in an export company. They began to see a lot of each other and gradually they fell in love and decided to marry. This decision led them to discuss buying a house. Although Joel was not earning much, Eileen's salary was quite substantial and they were sure that, between them, they could obtain the necessary mortgage.

However, they were in for a very nasty shock. Joel's application for a mortgage was approved, but Eileen's was refused. When she asked why, she was told that she was on a credit 'black list', there was a County Court order for non-payment of instalments on a hire-purchase contract.

'But I've never bought anything on hire purchase,' said Eileen.

'Sorry,' said the mortgage lender's clerk. 'Your name is on the list.'

When Eileen demanded to see the details, she found that the name on the list was the same as her own but the other Eileen Brown lived at a different address and was five years older.

Eileen was furious. She now wants to know:

- how such an error could occur
- what she should do to put matters right
- how such mistakes can be avoided in the future.

- data must be accurate and up to date
- people whose data is held must be allowed access to any information about them
- any incorrect information must be corrected
- every data holder must make proper security arrangements to ensure that no unauthorised person gains access to the data.

In practical terms, this means that computer users must not give unauthorised printouts of data to anyone, and must ensure that such print outs are not left lying about. Passwords and IDs should be kept confidential and not disclosed to anyone.

Ethical responsibilities

We have now seen that a whole range of legislation exists which is aimed at ensuring that providers of goods and services are aware of their legal responsibilities towards their clients and customers. It is important to remember that all providers also have **ethical responsibilities**, although these are not part of legislation.

Ethical responsibilities are not insisted on by law but are expected and followed by honest and decent people.

Although law and ethics are often connected and may overlap, it is the opinion of many people that, in a business relationship, only the legal implications of actions should be considered. Those who hold this view say that there is no room in business for the subtleties of ethical behaviour. Fortunately, in recent years, more and more organisations have come to regard ethical standards as a vital part of customer care, and many have introduced their own **codes of practice** to be followed by employees. Examples of behaviour that would be unethical include:

- giving a customer misleading information to secure a sale – this might be a temptation to someone trying to reach a sales target
- telling a customer an outright lie – this could also be against the law in some cases
- discussing any personal details given in confidence
- promising to contact a customer who needs help or has a complaint when you have no intention of doing so
- giving wrong information when you do not know the answer to a customer query.

Many people who deal directly with customers have access to information which should be kept **confidential** and not shared with anyone else, e.g. financial details relevant to a transaction and revealed by the customer, or medical details relevant to insurance policies, etc. must never be disclosed to third parties.

Confidential – private

It is the policy of most business organisations to provide private rooms in which confidential matters can be discussed. Such facilities would prove useless unless the staff concerned understand clearly the need to keep any information given strictly confidential.

CASE STUDY

What went wrong?

Leah Motambu has recently started work for a large company as a trainee receptionist. During the induction attended by all new employees, Amar Muhammed, Head of Human Resources, gave a talk on customer care. He explained that it was company policy to provide the best possible service, and emphasised that all employees were expected to be polite, courteous and helpful to all customers at all times.

Leah listened to the talk and came to the conclusion that everything Amar said was so obvious that there was no need to say it. She knew that she liked people, wanted to help them, and was confident that she had the right attitude to her new job.

After several weeks, Leah's line manager, Arturo Centi, was pleased with her progress and told her that he was going to leave her alone at the reception desk at lunchtimes as he was sure that she could cope. Leah was delighted but not really surprised.

On Monday of the following week, Leah took a call from a customer, Mrs Bhatti, who had a complaint. Mrs Bhatti said that she had written twice to the company about a faulty kitchen gadget that she had bought, but had had no reply. Leah promised to find out what had happened and ring Mrs Bhatti back that afternoon. Unfortunately, Leah was so busy for the rest of the day that she forgot all about Mrs Bhatti, who phoned again on Tuesday. Leah did not know what to say so she made the excuse that the person who would know the answer was off sick. She apologised to Mrs Bhatti and assured her that she would find out and let her know immediately. Again, however, Leah was under such pressure that she forgot to deal with the matter.

On Wednesday at one o'clock, Leah was alone at reception once again. There were several people waiting to speak to her when the phone rang. Remembering Mrs Bhatti and her own failure to deal with the problem, Leah did not answer the phone. When the woman waiting in front of her desk said, 'It's all right, do answer the phone, I'll wait;', Leah said, 'No. It's all right; it's only a customer making a nuisance of herself about some complaint or other. This is the third time that she has rung, and I can't be bothered to talk to her when I am so busy! Now, can you tell me how I can help you?'

'Certainly,' said the woman. 'I want to speak to someone in charge. My name is Mrs Bhatti.'

Now Arturo has told Leah that Amar Muhammed wants to see her urgently. Arturo himself is very upset. 'I can't understand it,' he said. 'You were doing so well and seemed to be so confident, efficient and helpful. Leah, what has gone wrong?'

Activity

Some of the situations listed below should be treated as confidential. Which ones are they, and why is confidentiality important in those cases?

- Information about the educational qualifications of a job applicant
- Medical details of someone who wants to take out an insurance policy
- A request to a building society from someone wanting to reduce the amount of her monthly mortgage repayments because she has just lost her job
- A customer's change of address
- A personal reference
- A letter from a potential customer asking for a catalogue
- A conversation between a customer and a member of staff, in the course of which the customer, who was applying for a loan, revealed that he or she had a criminal record
- Gossiping with work colleagues about a customer's family problems
- The contents of a customer's personal file
- A thank you letter from a customer

Fair trading

In 1973, the Fair Trading Act established the **Office of Fair Trading** (OFT) which operates under the supervision of the **Director General of Fair Trading**.

The duties of the Director General are far reaching and include:

- reviewing and collecting information about commercial activities in the UK so that he or she may become aware of any practices that are not in the interest of consumers
- arranging for the publication of information and advice for consumers
- encouraging trade associations and individual business organisations to prepare codes of practice
- making recommendations to the government regarding action to be taken to improve customer services in general or in particular. (For example, in 1975, the director recommended action against many kinds of 'bargain offers'.)

The **Office of Fair Trading** is responsible for overseeing all matters relating to consumer protection.

A **code of practice** is a set of guidelines issued by an industry or a business organisation, setting out procedures to be followed when dealing with consumers.

While the director can only recommend to the Government that certain action should be taken, he or she can take direct action against persistently unfair traders.

When a trader has been found to be unfair to customers, and/or to act in a manner that is detrimental to the customers' interests regarding health, safety and other matters, the OFT can demand that the trader should give a written assurance that he or she will stop acting in this manner. Unfair practices include any breach of the law, misrepresentation, misleading pricing, misleading advertising and unfair methods of salesmanship.

If the trader fails to give such written assurance, or fails to act on it, the OFT can bring proceedings against him or her either at the Restrictive Practices Court or in the County Court.

The OFT has branches throughout the UK, and individuals as well as organisations can report cases of unfair practice directly to OFT staff who will help and advise on the best action to take.

Independent consumer organisations

The OFT was established by the Government with the aim of watching over trading standards and providing customers with help and advice. There are also other, independent organisations with the same or similar aims.

In your library you are likely to find copies of *Which?* magazine, published by the Consumers' Association, a body that follows up complaints about defective products or services. The Association also makes recommendations to customers, based on independent research into quality, reliability and value for money.

Results of its research into goods and services available – from cameras to fridges to banking services – appear in the magazine. Over the years, *Which?* has established a reputation for sound and thorough reporting, based on extensive tests and comparisons. Many people will not consider buying a car or booking a holiday without first consulting the relevant issue of the magazine.

The TV programme *Watchdog* is another example of an independent consumer body. Its format includes reports on cases of malpractice which have been investigated by the team. Some of these cases have been reported by viewers unable to deal with a problem themselves, and quite frequently a favourable outcome is the result of the programme's intervention. *Watchdog* also informs and warns viewers about dubious traders and exposes notorious cases of dishonesty by providers of goods and services. These have included extortion by unscrupulous landlords and fly-by-night firms offering lucrative but non-existent home working opportunities on payment of a large one-off sum.

Due to its high profile at peak viewing time, *Watchdog* is feared by those it aims to expose, and thus achieves a high rate of success in its efforts on behalf of consumers.

Competition

Most companies, keen to stay ahead of their competitors, are eager to improve customer service. Unfortunately, the urge to do better sometimes has the opposite effect. Quite often, a business organisation decides that taking over or merging with another company is the way forward. The resulting organisation is now larger than all of its rivals and thus more likely to increase its profitability. However, such large businesses can be contrary to the interests of customers, depriving them of choice and providing a lower standard of service. To prevent this, the Government has established the **Competition Commission,** a body which reviews all proposed mergers and take-overs and can, if it deems it necessary, recommend that the amalgamation should not take place.

Sometimes, a business organisation resorts to steps that are both illegal and unethical in its quest for more customers and higher profits. An example of such behaviour was the case of *Virgin Atlantic Ltd v British Airways plc.* BA tapped into Virgin's customer database and contacted Virgin customers in an effort to persuade them to switch to BA. This action, by one of the largest and best known UK companies, illustrates the length to which businesses will go to try and increase their customer base.

Consequences of non-compliance with legislation

The purpose of consumer protection legislation is threefold:

- To ensure that providers of goods and services understand exactly the legal requirements of customer care that they must provide
- To establish procedures of redress for customers
- To establish legal procedures for dealing with sellers who are in breach of the legal requirements

The relevant Acts of Parliament contain all the information needed by sellers who want to know their legal responsibilities towards their customers. It would be no excuse for a seller to claim that he or she did not know what the law requires.

As far as customers are concerned, the legislation also includes information about the steps they can take when sellers fail to provide satisfactory customer care, whether by giving misleading or untruthful information, not dealing with enquiries or complaints, or failing to fulfil their contractual obligations. Additional information about specific cases can be obtained from the OFT or other organisations such Citizens' Advice Bureaux. If all attempts to obtain satisfaction from the seller fail, the customer can take the seller to court. This, however, does not often happen, for two main reasons. First, many people do not know what their rights as buyers are and are not aware of what redress is available to them. Second, in cases where the amounts involved are small, people think that the time, trouble, and sometimes cost, of starting legal proceedings are not worth the trouble. They are more inclined 'to vote with their feet', and simply never deal with that particular seller again. It should be noted that the Small Claims Courts, which have been set up specifically to deal with cases *not* involving large sums of money, might be the answer here, as this system is cheap and works much faster than other courts.

As far as the sellers are concerned, the consequences of non-compliance with consumer protection legislation can be significant. If a business organisation is found guilty in the courts, it can be fined or, in some cases, particularly where standards of safety, hygiene and quality of food and drink are concerned, be ordered to carry out expensive improvements, or even be closed down.

Even if customer dissatisfaction does not lead to a court case, businesses are aware that it can lead to the loss of existing and potential customers who hear about the bad experiences of others. Good customer care enhances a firm's reputation; bad customer care can ruin it.

The UK and the EU

As a member of the EU, the UK has to conform to standards set out in EU directives. This brought about the Consumer Protection Act 1987. These directives, which aim to ensure that all EU members operate to the same standards, are likely to increase in the future. Regulations regarding the safety of various appliances have already been upgraded in accordance with EU directives.

For customers themselves, UK membership of the EU means that they can now have redress to the EU judicial system if they are not satisfied with the outcome in the British courts. In practice, however, this is a complicated and costly procedure and is unlikely to be used often.

Conclusion

Customer services are many and complex. For this reason many Acts of Parliament have been implemented. These lay down the minimum requirements of customer service to be provided, and give customers the means to deal with unsatisfactory services. Independent 'watchdog' organisations are also of importance because their reports and recommendations are unbiased and do not take sides. The OFT also keeps an eye on what is going on in customer care.

As new products and services are introduced, and the consumer is faced with an ever-widening choice, the need for more and better ways of ensuring high standards in customer care is likely to increase.

Revision Questions

1. What does it mean when a business 'has an edge' over others? (1 mark)
2. How can good customer care give a business that 'edge'? (1 mark)
3. Why has the principle of *caveat emptor* now been replaced by *caveat vendor*? (4 marks)
4. How does a contract differ from other agreements? (2 marks)
5. What is an 'implied condition'? Give two examples. (5 marks)
6. What is meant by 'description'? (1 mark)
7. What is meant by 'selling by sample'? (1 mark)
8. With reference to 'A Treat for Toby' on page 127, what can his brothers and sister do? (6 marks)
9. How can 'satisfactory quality' be judged? (2 marks)
10. Why is the SSGA 1994 very important? (1 mark)
11. What are the main provisions of the Consumer Protection Act 1987? (3 marks)
12. What is an EU directive? (1 mark)
13. What is the aim of the Data Protection Act, and why is confidentiality when dealing with customers so important? (4 marks)
14. What are ethical aspects of customer care? Why are they considered to be important? (5 marks)
15. What is the OFT and what are the functions of its director? (6 marks)
16. What is a code of practice? Should all businesses have one? (3 marks)
17. Why, in your opinion, do many people rely on *Which*? magazine? (2 marks)
18. What steps can a customer take if dissatisfied with the customer care received? (2 marks)
19. What can be the outcome for a business of a legal action by a customer? (3 marks)
20. Why do few unhappy customers take legal action? (1 mark)

CHAPTER 3

Customer Service Skills and Communication

KEY TERMS

Articulation	Interpersonal skills	Projection
Communication	Non-verbal	Verbal
Energy	Pitch	Volume
Face to face	Product knowledge	

In this chapter, you will learn how an organisation establishes and implements effective communication so as to present the best image to the customer. You will also learn about the skills required to provide customer service in a variety of situations.

What is customer service?

Customer service includes a variety of tasks, some more specialised than others, but all of crucial importance if a business organisation is to keep its existing customers and gain new ones. All forms of customer service require **communication** between the provider of the goods or services and the customer or potential customer.

Communication – contact and discussion

All members of staff dealing with customers must have specific skills and understand the importance of a number of aspects of this front line activity:

- Customer behaviour
- Modes of communication
- Interpersonal skills
- Telephone manner
- Technological skills
- Product knowledge

Customer behaviour

When dealing with customers, it is important to realise that different people react differently, and that a customer's response is frequently a direct result of the attitude and behaviour of the person they are dealing with. This includes not only appreciating the reasons for an individual customer's behaviour on a particular occasion, but understanding the reactions of people in situations which are often quite stressful, as when seeking information that is difficult to obtain, asking for assistance or making a complaint.

Modes of communication

In customer service, many different modes of communication may be used: written, verbal, non-verbal face-to-face (i.e. body language).

Written communication can be by letter, fax or e-mail. It should always be remembered that letters written to customers on behalf of an organisation are formal and all the rules of formal letter writing must apply. The customer's name and address must be correct and the contents of the letter should be clearly laid out, brief and concise. If the letter is in response to a communication by the customer, care should be taken that it deals with matters raised by the customer.

While faxes and e-mails need not be quite so formal in format, they must still be well written, give all the correct information and be properly laid out.

Verbal communication can be face to face or on the telephone. While politeness and courtesy are always important when talking to a customer, when the

CASE STUDY

The Young Veterinary Surgery

Sarah Ainsworth is the senior receptionist at the Young Veterinary Surgery in West London, a very busy practice, dealing with all kinds of small animals. Sarah and her team have to deal with the patients and also their owners.

Here is what Sarah has to say about customer care at the practice. 'The work of the receptionists is often hectic and can be quite stressful. The important thing is to try and be calm, and deal with each problem as quickly and as efficiently as possible.'

The receptionist is the first person the client speaks to, so the impression that she makes is all-important. A friendly, helpful telephone manner is essential. The receptionists give information and book appointments, and can sometimes give advice. If they cannot answer a client's question, they refer him or her to the veterinary surgeon on duty. Many questions are routine and can be dealt with quickly. These include information about vaccinations and flea treatment, for example.

'Most people,' says Sarah, 'are polite and grateful, and create no problems for the busy receptionists. Sometimes, however, a client can be difficult, demanding immediate attention when this is not possible, or complaining about having to wait. The receptionists are trained to be patient, and try to diffuse the situation by talking to the person and trying to calm them down.'

It is inevitable that sometimes a sick animal does not recover from its illness or operation, and this causes great distress to the owner. Sarah says that it is most important, if the animal has been put to sleep in the surgery, to allow the owner some time with their pet. If the owner is very upset, the receptionist will take them out of the waiting room, offer tea or coffee and talk to them quietly. In no circumstances, should a bereaved owner be pressed for immediate payment.

'The best indication of successful customer care at the practice,' says Sarah, 'is the number of people who are regular clients, bringing new pets to be looked after, and always certain of a courteous and friendly service.'

The practice staff promise to look after all its patients as if they were their own and a large part of this promise is carried out because of the customer service provided by Sarah and her team of receptionists.

conversation actually takes place face to face, appearance and dress also become important.

Verbal – spoken communication by one person to another

Non-verbal face-to-face communication can convey more than is intended. Actions communicate our attitude to others and are certain to bring about certain responses. A bored-looking shop assistant, who avoids eye contact and keeps looking at his or her watch, might not say anything that could be interpreted as negative, but the impression on the customer will be negative nevertheless.

Communication via the internet is used more and more frequently and the same rules of attention, patience and helpfulness should apply.

Interpersonal skills

These skills are so important that many companies organise courses for their employees. While it is true that some people know instinctively how to listen to and talk to others and some do not, it is possible for everyone to acquire the necessary basic skills.

Interpersonal skills – the verbal and body-language skills needed for good communication between people

Appearance is important in all face-to-face situations, so many companies lay down ground rules on how their employees should dress. A clean, neat appearance is businesslike and more likely to impress than dishevelled hair, untidy clothes and down-at-heel shoes.

Activity

Is it true?

Carry out this activity working with a friend.

Make a list of ten TV advertisements that emphasise not only the product offered, but also the way in which the business organisation in question looks after its customers.

(If you watch a lot of television, you might already know some such commercials – if you do not, you will have to spend some time on research!)

When you have compiled your list, show it to six people you know, and ask them:

- if they believe the promises made in the advertisement
- whether they ever choose to buy from a particular seller because of the standard of care provided.

Write a short report on your findings.

One of the basic aims when talking to customers is to put them at ease. This will only happen if the member of staff is willing to listen to them, does not interrupt and shows polite interest in what they are saying. The right attitude to the customer has the added advantage of making it more likely that he or she will not feel slighted or threatened, thus making it easier to deal with the matter in hand.

Telephone manner

People use the telephone so often that many assume that *anyone* can talk effectively on the telephone. However, in telephone conversations, it is important to learn the principles of PPEVA:

- **Pitch**
  Nobody wants to listen to a screeching voice on the other end of the line.
- **Projection**
  The voice should carry sufficiently to be easily heard.
- **Energy**
  The speaker should ensure that he or she comes over as confident and fully in control.
- **Volume**
  Should not be so loud that it deafens the listener or so low that the listener has to strain to hear what is being said.
- **Articulation**
  Each word should be clearly pronounced, to avoid confusion and misunderstandings.

Projection – in speaking, this means making oneself heard.

Volume – loudness of a sound

Articulation – clarity of speech

These telephone skills have to be learned, and wise employers provide training for employees, either in-house or from their supervisors.

CASE STUDY

In need of advice

Serena Strong is 19 years old and has recently completed the Vocational A Level course in Business. She accepted a management trainee post at Auto Phones Ltd, a medium-sized company manufacturing and selling trendy, up-to-date mobile phones mainly for young, trendy customers.

Having spent some time in the Production and Accounts Departments, Serena is at present working for Sangeeta Patel, the head of Administration and Customer Services. Sangeeta told Serena how important customer services were, and added that their Managing Director, Charles Duval, had introduced special training days for all those working with customers. 'The next training day is on Thursday,' said Sangeeta, 'and I want you to attend.'

Serena went for the training and sat through a session on different modes of communication and on technological skills. At 5 p.m., Serena was dismayed to be told that the training day was not due to end until 7 o'clock. Sangeeta had said it would be a long day, but Serena had a date with her boyfriend at 6 o'clock and decided to leave early, thinking that no one would notice. She was also sure that the last session, on telephone manner, would be of no use to her.

The next day, Sangeeta had to attend a meeting and asked Serena to remain in the office and deal with all calls. 'If you don't know the answer to anything,' she said, 'explain that I'm out of the office, but will call back tomorrow.'

Serena enjoyed her morning in sole charge of the office, listening to her portable radio. There was little to do, so she made herself a coffee and began to paint her nails in readiness for the evening. Just then, the telephone rang.

'Oh, what a nuisance,' said Serena, trying to pick up the receiver without messing up her nails. She dropped it twice before succeeding in wedging it between her shoulder and her neck. She did not bother to turn off her portable radio. 'Yes?' she said crossly.

The male voice on the other end of the line sounded rather hesitant. 'Is that, um, Sangeeta Patel's office?' 'Of course it is,' said Serena, still concentrating on her nails. 'What do you want?'

There was a pause. 'I'd like to speak to Sangeeta, please.'
'Well, she isn't here, so you'll have to speak to me.'
'Well, could you tell me who you are?'
'I'm her assistant. What is it that you want?'
'Well, actually,' the caller continued, 'I wanted to ask her opinion about the new range of phones, and what she thinks about the advertisements in the press?'

'I'm sure', said Serena firmly, thinking that the man was not making himself very clear, 'that they are very good and customers will like them. Personally, I haven't seen the adverts, but I'm certain that they are all right, too. Is there anything else?'

'I'm interested in what after-sales service is offered to those buying the phones,' said the caller. By now Serena had noticed that two of her nails had smudged and was hardly listening to the man on the line. 'We always offer excellent after-sales service, as you would know if you read our publicity material,' she said firmly. 'Good bye.' But the caller had already rung off.

Serena thought she had handled the call rather well. Although it did occur to her that she had not asked the caller's name, nor answered his questions in any detail, she was not too worried. 'If he needs more information,' she thought to herself, 'he can always ring again.'

The rest of the day passed quietly. A few minutes before 5 o'clock, Serena was surprised to see Sangeeta storm in, her face like thunder. 'Are you all right?' she asked. 'Is anything the matter?'

'I was all right till five minutes ago,' replied Sangeeta. 'Then I ran into Charles Duval who asked which useless person was answering my phone. Someone who kept dropping the phone, had the radio playing at full volume, was barely polite and knew nothing about the company, its products or its policy regarding customer service. He was not asked his name and no mention was made of anyone calling him back. He was furious with me and I'm furious with you. You've just been to the training session on telephone manner! Didn't it teach you anything?
Serena was silent.

Technological skills

Staff working in customer services need to be trained in IT to be able to retrieve information, refer to records, handle customer accounts and personal files, set up and use customer databases and obtain feedback from internet/intranet websites.

Product knowledge

Last, but certainly not least, staff in the front line of customer services must have a good knowledge of the goods or services provided by the business. Failure to do so will result in customers losing confidence in the products offered.

While the above skills are equally important for all organisations, whatever their size, it is, of course, easier for a large company to train its employees than it is for a small business.

In recent years, many public utility providers have introduced training programmes in customer care, and provision of such care nowadays features very strongly in advertisements and publicity material.

Customer charters

Many industries and organisations have their own codes of practice which set out in detail the customer services that they aim to provide. On the basis of such codes of practice, organisations create customer charters. These contain information about customer rights and the services offered. While customer rights are statutory, in other words laid down in the various Acts of Parliament, it is the additional 'extras' that are likely to interest customers and persuade people to buy from the company. Customer charters are only worth having if the promises they contain are kept. For example:

- Tesco promises to open another checkout if there is more than one person waiting at those that are open (this promise was adhered to at all Tesco stores visited).
- Another well-known supermarket chain promises 'to provide quality customer service at all times', but fails to open enough checkouts at peak times, thus increasing waiting time at the tills.

Where would you rather shop?

Conclusion

Not all the skills described in this chapter are needed by every person dealing with customers. A receptionist does not have to be able to handle accounts, and a shop assistant does not necessarily need to know about feedback from the internet. However, all must understand the importance of treating customers with politeness and respect, and be aware of the possible consequences to the business, and indirectly to all employees, of failing to do so.

Activity

Good, bad or indifferent?

If you shop regularly at your local shopping centre, you can answer these questions yourself. If you do not, ask someone who does.

1 Which shops do you use regularly?

2 Why do you shop there?

3 How would you rate each shop's customer service standard: poor, good or excellent?

4 Give two examples of excellent service you have met, and two of poor service in any shop or store you have used in the last year.

Revision Questions

1 What are interpersonal skills?
Give two examples. (3 marks)

2 Why are interpersonal skills important when dealing with customers? (3 marks)

3 What is meant by face-to-face communication? (1 mark)

4 Why is appearance important in dealing with customers? (2 marks)

5 What is meant by 'articulation'? (1 mark)

6 You want to buy a camera but know nothing about them. You ask an assistant for advice. He tells you, 'I'm new, I don't know anything about cameras.' What would you do? (4 marks)

7 How can a business ensure that all its employees recognise the importance of customer care, and can provide it? (5 marks)

8 What is a customer charter?
Under what circumstances can it do more harm than good? (3 marks)

9 Why is product knowledge important? (2 marks)

10 Have you ever been given wrong information on the telephone, or been promised a call back which never happened? If so, what did you do? What should you have done? (5 marks)

CHAPTER 4

Improving Customer Service

KEY TERMS

Customer feedback	Mission statement	Reward schemes
Customer service policy	Mystery shopper	Suggestion schemes
Management information analysis	Panel discussions	

In this chapter, you will learn how an organisation can improve customer service, and about the techniques which can be used to carry out such improvements. You will learn how staff can be trained, and what methods of research are used to find out how well an organisation looks after its customers.

How can customer service be improved?

Customer service is important to all organisations, large and small, in the private and in the public sector. We have already looked in detail at the laws that must be obeyed by all providers of goods and services, and at the legal rights of customers. All the rules and regulations, however, are just the theory – what business organisations actually do to look after their customers is the practice, and we are now going to examine the ways in which organisations establish, monitor and constantly try to improve customer service.

As the case study opposite shows, a huge organisation like the AA can provide a wide range of customer services, and has at its disposal the financial and technological means to try and establish its edge over others. The same rules for providing quality customer service apply for all organisations, including small ones, as the Tomo Communications Limited case study shows.

All business organisations, big or small, now recognise the importance of customer services. It is obvious, however, that the ways in which a high standard of customer service can be achieved vary greatly between businesses of different sizes.

Tomo Communications has no need to set up complex communication systems to process queries, requests or complaints. The presence of the Managing Director on the premises means decisions can be reached quickly and efficiently, and provides the 'personal touch' that makes customers, actual or potential, feel valued.

The AA, however, is so large that it could not operate without communication systems in place. There must be means of contact between the separate departments and between the many employees in each department. It is also vital that customers are able to reach the correct department and, eventually, the person or persons with whom they need to deal. In a large business organisation, there is always the danger that decisions have to be referred through several channels, making for delays, and the failure of one part of the system can easily lead to customer dissatisfaction. The 'personal touch' approach is difficult, if not impossible, to achieve. The AA, like many other organisations, now ensures that its telephone operators – the first link with customers – identify themselves by name when answering the phone. This has the twofold aim of creating a more informal atmosphere during any conversation, and giving the caller a name which he or she can then refer to or ask for again.

Improving customer care

How can a business improve existing standards of customer service? Many industries and stand-alone organisations have their own **codes of practice** to provide a benchmark against which the efficiency of their customer care can be monitored and measured, and any necessary improvements made. Although a code of practice is not legally binding, the business concerned usually guarantees that the contents of the

CASE STUDY

Automobile Association (AA)

The AA is the largest organisation providing help for motorists in the UK and when travelling abroad. It calls itself 'the fourth emergency service' and is a huge business group, with 9 million members, more than 12,000 staff and 40 different business activities. AA patrols attend 4.9 million breakdowns per year and the organisation takes and receives 35 million telephone calls each year. Its members are divided into two main groups – personal and business members.

The organisation is currently divided into four major business groups:

- AA Membership and Call Handling
- AA Insurance, Financial Services and Retail (including Direct Sales)
- AA Commercial Services (including the driving school, publishing and maps, hotel approval scheme, in-car technology and multi-media)
- Cross-business support activities (including a range of important activities such as market research, public relations, print and information technology)

The group mission statement of the AA is encapsulated in a consumer statement:

'I instinctively turn to the AA – you are always there, easy to reach and ready to help. You have standards I can trust and you impress me more every time you serve me and solve my problems.'

'Trust' is a very important part of the relationship the AA has with its members. Stranded motorists are particularly vulnerable and want to know they are being cared for and looked after by an organisation which has their interests at heart. In some ways, the relationship is similar to that between a doctor and a patient.

This is what the AA says about customers and their choice of provider:

'Customers buy goods and services from one organisation rather than another because the "winning organisation" provides better value for money by providing the "benefits" that consumers want at an attractive price.

'The key to success is to provide these benefits in a competitive way. The usual route to competitive edge is through adding more value to your product than your competitor.'

In other words, to be highly successful, a business has to demonstrate to customers that the values it delivers are significantly more appealing than those offered by alternative organisations.

The reason for the success of the AA and others like Kodak and IBM is that these businesses, have clearly demonstrated the provision of 'excellent benefits' in their relevant markets.

The core benefits of personal membership of the AA are:

- roadside security
- roadside repair of more than eight out of ten vehicles or a tow to nearest garage.

Other benefits include:

- AA magazine
- member's benefit book at policy renewal
- members' handbook mailed to all personal members once every two years
- discounts for AA members in AA shops, on insurance policies and other financial services
- technical and legal advice and information
- a service setting out the best routes for journeys in the UK.

The speed of response to calls and the high level of successful roadside repairs are maintained by continuous training of AA patrols and by keeping their vehicles well equipped. The AA has the world's most comprehensive database of technical information, accessible to patrols through a telephone helpdesk, to help repair.

Source: Times 100

CASE STUDY

Tomo Communications Limited

Tomo Communications Ltd is a computer and language-training centre situated in Acton, West London. It was established three years ago and offers English courses for foreign students, both full and part-time, and computer courses, including the Microsoft suite of programs. There is an internet facility on the premises, which is open to members of the public. The language school is open from Monday to Friday, but the other facilities are available seven days a week, from 9 a.m. to 8 p.m. There are eight staff members, plus freelance trainers for the computer courses.

Read opposite what David Price, Tomo's Managing Director, has to say about customer care at Tomo Communications Limited.

David considers it vital that every person, whether an existing or a potential customer, is treated as an individual at all times, and all members of staff recognise that there are differences between individuals, their attitudes, needs and previous experiences, as well as their backgrounds. Putting people at ease is an important part of customer service at Tomo Communications. While it goes without saying that foreign students newly arrived in the UK need advice and reassurance, this can also apply to trainees who have never dealt with new technology and are lacking in confidence.

Another important part of customer service is the physical environment. Tomo's premises are comfortable, clean and welcoming. There is a students' sitting area where they can meet and talk during their breaks, and tea and coffee are provided free. On Fridays, David provides free snacks and doughnuts – a facility much appreciated by all!

All the above factors combine to make Tomo a happy place. Its small size is an advantage – everyone knows everybody else, making for accessibility and openness in personal relationships.

Front of house

The first impressions of potential clients are of greatest importance. We make sure that all calls are answered promptly and in a courteous manner. If a client asks for information which is not readily available and is promised a phone call, this must be done as soon as possible. All messages are passed on without delay.

Personal callers are dealt with quickly and efficiently, and systems are in place to ensure that clients do not have to wait to be allocated a computer space.

High quality of service must include a high standard of teaching and training. To achieve this, Tomo's teachers and trainers are carefully selected, and made fully aware of the need to treat each student or trainee as an individual.

The service offered to foreign students includes more than teaching. They are met on arrival by a member of Tomo staff, frequently the Managing Director himself, and taken to the family with whom they will stay while in London. These host families are vetted before being accepted, and the system works so well that advertising for new homes has not proved necessary – recommendation is sufficient.

There is close contact between Tomo and the host families, so any difficulties, which can sometimes arise, are dealt with quickly. At the end of their stay, the students are asked to fill in a questionnaire about their host homes, teaching received, and personal opinion about the services provided. These questionnaires allow Tomo to make any adjustments or changes if necessary.

If a host family has a complaint about a student, he or she will be relocated immediately while the complaint is looked into. Every effort is made to reconcile the two parties. This is often possible as most conflicts arise out of misunderstandings.'

code will always be adhered to. If a customer can show that the theory of the code of practice is not being translated into practice, he or she has very strong grounds for complaint.

Many organisations also have a specific **customer service policy** which includes detailed information on how staff must treat customers in a variety of situations. Although the general principles of customer care are applicable in all businesses, the nature of each business dictates how these should be implemented. The requirements of a shopper at Sainsbury's are quite different from those of a student at college or of the client of an insurance company, for example. The customer policy is a follow up of the organisation's **mission statement.**

Mission statement – a brief summary of an organisation's aims and objectives

To assess its existing standard of customer service and be able to introduce improvements, an organisation needs to know what their customers need and want, and how these needs and wants can be satisfied. A number of techniques can be used to find out.

Customer questionnaires can be very useful in providing information on customer expectations, reasons for choice of provider, and negative as well as positive views about the organisation. (The foreign students at Tomo Communications are asked to fill in such a questionnaire at the end of their stay.) Sometimes, the organisation organises such surveys itself, but more frequently it will use a market research firm to carry out the research. (See the Marketing Unit, page 1.)

Customer service policy – this sets out in detail how staff should treat customers at all times.

Interviews, especially personal interviews with customers can often provide an insight that may be lacking in a questionnaire response. Frontline staff are also often asked for their views on services provided and their experience of customer reactions.

User panel discussions also provide valuable information but are quite difficult to set up and are also expensive. If a user panel is successfully selected so that it to includes a representative cross-section of customers, the results can give the business organisation a good indication of what the customers want and need.

Management information analysis is now much easier to carry out, as the information from every area of an organisation's activities is usually stored on computer. Computerised information is only as good as the input, however, so, to be effective, management information analysis must be based on correct input, and reliable methods of analysis must be applied.

Internet websites are now in general use, and valuable feedback can be obtained from websites.

Telephone surveys can be carried out in one of two ways.

- Calls can be made using an existing customer database, to tell customers about new additional services, and/or invite their opinions on services already provided. This method is now used by a number of providers, including BT.
- The second method invites customers to phone in themselves and provides a free phone number on which to call.

While useful, both of these methods have drawbacks. Repeated phone calls at inconvenient times can be regarded by many recipients as a nuisance rather than a genuine desire by an organisation to provide a better service. The second method relies on customers making use of the facility offered and many of those who might have something constructive to say do not bother to do so.

Suggestion schemes are run by some organisations, inviting customers to suggest ways in which services could be improved. This might be a question of opening hours, store layout or information provided, or specific facilities such as access for the disabled or mother-and-baby rooms. This sort of customer **feedback** can be very useful.

Mystery shoppers are employed by some stores. These shoppers visit the stores to ascertain the standard of customer care. Their activities might include playing the part of a 'difficult' customer or lodging a complicated complaint.

Customer feedback – information from customers about what they really think about the service they have received

All the above methods are only valuable if the findings obtained are then analysed and practical conclusions drawn, which can then be incorporated in the company's customer policy.

To improve customer service, training is vital. The type, duration and frequency of training must be decided once the needs are identified. Refresher courses and the introduction of new ideas are some of the ways in which training can be delivered. The days when it was believed that receptionists, counter assistants and service engineers, to name but a few, needed no training in dealing with customers are now (fortunately for customers) long gone.

Some companies encourage their employees to become involved in improving customer service by asking for suggestions and offering rewards for any suggestion approved and implemented.

Reward scheme – a system inside a company which rewards employees for good suggestions that help to improve sales or service

It is important to remember that improving customer service is the aim of all organisations, both in the private and in the public sector. In recent years, for example, the NHS and its services have come under close scrutiny and received criticism from both individuals and consumer watchdog organisations. Two of the major criticisms were the delays facing patients waiting to be seen in Accident & Emergency departments, and the poor facilities, resulting on occasion in patients being left on trolleys in corridors. Another area of dissatisfaction was waiting times for operations. It was apparent, from tables published as a result of analysis of facts, that some health authorities managed their budgets better than others and thus managed to provide a much better service. At present, targets have been set to bring the less efficient health authorities in line. When implemented, they should ensure that the standard of customer service in the NHS is greatly improved.

In customer service, as in other areas of business and private life, it is relatively easy to pinpoint shortcomings and to resolve to overcome them. It is much more difficult to implement the changes. It should also be remembered that the process of improving customer services is an ongoing one and therefore constant monitoring is necessary. If it is found that a particular technique does not bring the expected result, it often becomes necessary to revise and perhaps change the methods used.

CASE STUDY

Moments of truth – Yorkshire Electricity

Providing a good service involves meeting the expectations of your customers. This does not just involve the selling or supply process but includes every point of contact between an organisation and each and every customer. According to Jan Carlzon, Chief Executive of SAS Airlines in the 1980s:

Any time a customer comes into contact with any aspect of your operation he will make a judgement, positive or negative, on the quality of your organisation – these are the moments of truth.

Over recent years, many changes have taken place in traditional service organisations. There have been many reasons for theses changes. Some have been brought about by increasing customer choice, different consumption patterns, better lifestyles, increasing mobility, the process of privatisation and more competition. Where such changes have taken place, there has tended to be an accompanying influence on customer expectations. The net effect has been to create a far more knowledgeable and discriminating customer. However, as customers have become more sophisticated, they have also become more vocal. Customers are not willing to accept an inefficient service and, where competition is introduced, they always have the option to change their supplier.

After the 1988 Government White Paper recommended that the introduction of competition into the electricity industry would be in the best interests of customers, privatisation soon followed. In 1989, Yorkshire Electricity was one of 12 former Area Electricity Boards to become Regional Electricity Companies (RECs).

Customers can now choose their electricity supplier.

At the time of privatisation, OFFER (the Office of Electricity Regulation) was set up as an independent statutory body to regulate the electricity industry and to protect customers' interests by controlling prices and setting customer service standards.

Yorkshire Electricity's aim has been to provide electricity into the home, office or factory safely and at the right price, while providing a service which rates as one of the best when compared with other Regional Electricity Companies. Although it has been one of the top performing electricity companies, there has been growing concern that the results have been achieved without paying necessary attention to the customers of Yorkshire Electricity, the levels of service being provided and the overall level of customer satisfaction.

Although Yorkshire Electricity needs to continue to strive for further business efficiencies across all its activities, it also needs to ensure it retains existing customers and wins new ones in the new competitive market post 1998. According to the management gurus Drucker and Levitt, the purpose of every business is to create and keep a customer. **It also costs much more to attract a new customer than to keep an established one**. The key to success in this competitive marketplace will be for Yorkshire Electricity to differentiate from the competition with superior customer service and, at the same time, to provide a product at a reasonable price. To do this, Yorkshire Electricity has put in place its Customer Service Initiative.

It was recognised immediately that, for an organisation as large as Yorkshire Electricity to significantly improve customer service, the whole organisation would have to change and that this degree of change would only happen if the leaders of the organisation led the change and were seen to be supportive of it and the need for it. From the beginning, it was emphasised that this would not be a 'banner waving' exercise and that improving levels of customer service would also improve all aspects of Yorkshire Electricity's operations.

Yorkshire Electricity defines customer service as: *The product and service that Yorkshire Electricity provides at each point of contact with its customers and the standard to which these are delivered.*

Another reason for the Customer Service Initiative is that poor customer service is expensive. A recent exercise has shown that it costs Yorkshire Electricity at least £3 million a year to deal with unnecessary queries and complaints, compensation to customers for poor service and having to do jobs again.

Implementing the Customer Service Initiative involved careful preparation and planning through three distinct phases:

- **Phase One** – directors assessing current levels of service and deciding on objectives – how good the company wanted to be in delivering customer service
- **Phase Two** – developing the solutions through asking the customers what they want, measuring current standards and defining new standards

  This phase involved looking at the standards achieved by other electricity companies and related utility industries. As all 4000 staff at Yorkshire Electricity contribute in some way to customer service, they were all to be involved in the initiative. A survey of the views of all staff was undertaken, to collect their thoughts on customer service. As a result of this, six key success factors critical to achieving Yorkshire Electricity's mission were formulated:

  - Anticipating, listening and responding to our customers
  - Developing our people
  - Working together as a team
  - Providing inspirational leadership
  - Encouraging innovative ideas
  - Developing profitable businesses
- **Phase Three** – achieving the benefits

  Yorkshire Electricity then started looking at key areas that customers identified as needing improvement and set in motion plans for improvement. These so-called 'workstreams' included the development of customer skills training courses for over 300 managers and implementing more customer-focused business processes.

Implementation has a long time to run yet. It will bring together all the careful planning, research and development needed to deliver the improved levels of service. In the area of customer service, some improvements do not happen overnight and it may be some time before Yorkshire Electricity sees the results of some of the background work that has taken place.

Yorkshire Electricity's mission within five years is:

To provide the best levels of Customer Service against our competitors/comparators and so retain customer loyalty and win new business.

Source: Times 100

CASE STUDY

Linco Ltd

Linco Ltd is a medium-sized company, manufacturing and installing conservatories, situated in Buckinghamshire, and dealing mainly with customers in that county and West London. Linco Ltd was set up ten years ago by two brothers, Richard and Drew Wise.

Richard and Drew are well aware that, although conservatories are now popular as an addition to residential property, they are expensive and the market is somewhat limited. Furthermore, Linco Ltd is small compared to other, longer established and better known companies. They have resolved that, to succeed, they must ensure that their products are of the highest quality and that their customers receive the best service bar none. Their aims are shown in the company's mission statement:

> *Linco Ltd guarantees to provide all its customers with quality, reasonably priced products and a fast and reliable installation service. It is our aim to provide customer satisfaction at all times.*

Linco Ltd has been doing well and has increased its turnover steadily over the last ten years. The workforce has also grown steadily and now includes a marketing manager and several sales representatives. Richard and Drew have always selected all job applicants personally, and have insisted that each one must be told about the company's aims and objectives and the need to look after each and every customer. There has never been a formal training plan – the brothers did not think it necessary. All complaints were referred directly to one of the brothers who would deal with them as they arose.

Over the last year, Richard was becoming aware that the level of complaints had risen alarmingly. In the month of July, for example, almost half of the jobs in hand brought at least one complaint from the customer. He spoke about this to Drew and they tried to analyse what was going wrong. They found that as complaints made by telephone were taken by the receptionist on duty, some of them had not been properly logged and records were incomplete. Those that had been recorded, 44 in number, could be divided into the following categories:

- Twelve customers complained that the promised time for delivery and installation had been considerably exceeded.
- Seven stated that they had been given wrong information by the sales representative.
- Eleven said that the work carried out had been substandard, necessitating return visits by the installation crew.
- Five said that the finished conservatory differed in significant detail from the specifications agreed on.
- Two complained about the floors.
- Three stated that the workmen were slovenly and impolite.
- Four said that when they telephoned with a query while the work was being done, they were fobbed off by whoever answered the phone.

Eighteen of the complaining customers made it quite clear that they were not pleased with the service provided, and ten of those made a point of saying that they would never recommend Linco Ltd.

Richard and Drew were shaken by their findings.

'What's gone wrong?' said Drew. 'We are always so careful to explain to all the staff how important customers are. I was sure they all understood. After all, they all know our mission statement ...'

'Maybe the mission statement is not enough,' said Richard thoughtfully. 'Maybe we need a customer service policy. I've read somewhere that they are very helpful. And perhaps we should spend some money on training ...'

'What kind of training?' asked Drew. 'And what is a customer service policy?'

'I'm not sure myself,' answered Richard, 'so I think we must both find out as soon as possible and do something positive to improve our customer service before we lose all our customers!'

Activity

What could be done, and how?

Working with two friends, visit three organisations in your locality. (Perhaps you could start with your school or college, go on to a small shop or maybe a supermarket, and then a service business like a travel agent – the choice is up to you.)

- Make a list of facilities currently available to customers.
- If possible, spend some time observing customers.
- Discuss what you have found and what you have seen and draw up a list of possible improvements to existing services, and also any innovations that you think would be in the customers' interests. Explain how these could be implemented and make sure that your suggestions are practical and would not be too costly to introduce.

Revision Questions

1. What is a reward scheme? (1 mark)
2. Name four research methods that can help to evaluate existing customer services. (3 marks)
3. How can a company obtain feedback on its services? (2 marks)
4. What does a 'mystery shopper' do? (2 marks)
5. What is a mission statement, and what is its purpose? (3 marks)
6. Explain why all staff should receive customer care training. (3 marks)
7. With reference to the Yorkshire Electricity case study (page 146), explain how and why customers have changed. (5 marks)
8. Why does a small firm not need a complex communication system? (3 marks)
9. Why is it important that customers know a firm's customer service policy? (3 marks)
10. What are the advantages and disadvantages of customer questionnaires? (4 marks)

CHAPTER 5

Quality in Customer Service

KEY TERMS

Accessibility
Availability
Criteria
Customer retention
Value for money

In this chapter, you will learn about the need to assess the quality and effectiveness of customer service, and how organisations ensure that their service is meeting the needs of their customers. You will also examine how an organisation assesses performance against quality standards, and how necessary changes can be identified and implemented.

How can quality be assessed?

Criteria – principles or standards that a thing is judged by (singular – criterion)

To assess the quality of its customer service, an organisation must first identify the criteria against which such assessment can be made:

- Price/value for money
- Customer retention
- Consistency/accuracy
- Reliability
- Staffing levels/qualities
- Utilisation of experience
- Health and safety
- Cleanliness and hygiene
- Accessibility and availability
- Provision for individual/special needs.

Depending on the goods or services provided, different businesses might place these in a different order of priority.

Price and value for money

Value for money – worth what you are being asked to pay for it

This criterion is of paramount importance to all business organisations. While allowing for the necessary profit margin, prices must be reasonable. If prices are set too high, customers will look elsewhere. Competition is one of the great dangers to a business organisation, so most businesses regularly check the prices at which their main competitors sell their products, and often cut their own prices to attract customers.

One large supermarket chain has put notices in every store, informing customers that they check prices in other supermarkets every week and that they guarantee to provide a selection of goods more cheaply.

Once a **pricing policy** is set, it is relatively easy to adhere to it. Value for money is a more difficult concept. **Quality of the product** is of prime importance – a pair of shoes sold at a low price is not good value for money if the materials and workmanship are so poor that the shoes fall apart after a week. Value for money also includes such additions as pre-sales advice and after-sales service. (See the Marketing Unit). The easiest way to explain the concept of value for money is to say that the customer must be sure that the product he or she is buying is not only worth its price, but that it comes with reliable and efficient help and advice.

Customer retention

Customer retention – keeping regular customers who come back again and again

This **quality performance indicator** is regarded as one of the most vital. All businesses strive to ensure that their customers will come back again and again. We must remember, however, that this applies more to businesses whose customers have to buy their products regularly, or at least from time to time. One-off purchases, such as conservatories (see the Linco Ltd case study on page 148) are unlikely to be repeated.

Consistency and accuracy

To achieve customer satisfaction, a business must provide goods or services of a high standard at all times. This necessitates stringent quality control of manufactured goods and continual monitoring of services. Systems to ensure accuracy include procedures for dealing with enquiries and orders so that information given is always precise and accurate. All advertising and publicity must be based on fact, it must not promise anything that cannot be delivered. Failure to be consistent and accurate can lead to loss of customers.

Reliability

This quality is one that customers regard as of great importance. We all know how inconvenient, irritating and troublesome it is to find that the goods that were to be delivered by a certain date fail to arrive, and that there is little or no response to repeated telephone calls. A service engineer who does not come when arranged to repair your computer or washing machine does considerable damage to the image of his employer, and may contribute directly to your decision to switch to another company in the future.

Failure by front-of-house staff to pass on messages, and promises to deal with a problem that are not kept also create the image of an unreliable organisation which is not much concerned with providing a good service to its customers.

Another aspect of reliability has to do with the quality of goods. This must not change from batch to batch, and customers must be confident that what they buy is as described or seen.

Activity

Will they come back for more?

Which of the businesses listed below are likely to retain satisfied customers? Which cannot rely on customers returning time and again? Explain the reasons in each case.

- A corner shop
- A travel agent
- An estate agent
- A further education college
- A supermarket
- A window cleaner
- A double glazing firm
- An insurance broker
- A mobile telephone outlet
- A mortgage provider
- A newsagent
- A dentist
- An interior design company
- A hairdressing salon
- A roofing specialist

CASE STUDY

Problems at Fine Furniture Limited

Fine Furniture Limited, manufacturers of a wide range of good quality furniture, prides itself on excellent customer service. The company, which also has two retail outlets and a mail order department, has for many years successfully sold its products nationwide.

The directors of Fine Furniture know their market well. Their products are not cheap but very well made, and their customers know that the furniture will last. The customers range from the well-to-do, ordering one-off, specially designed pieces, to young couples who have saved enough to start buying quality goods. Recently, however, some goods have been returned, and several complaints about delivery, delays and lack of response to letters, faxes and telephone calls have greatly upset the management.

As a direct result of these events, Ivan Costello, the MD, decided to create a new post of Customer Services Manager. After a careful selection process, Miranda Ebro was offered the position.

Miranda was fully aware of the responsibilities of her new job. She decided to begin by holding meetings of employees concerned – those in the retail outlets, those in production and the front-line staff, whose job it was to deal with customer queries and complaints. Miranda was surprised to find that there were no set procedures for dealing with customer care, no established training for staff, and very little attention had been paid to feedback from both staff and customers.

She did find that, a few months previously, all customers on the company's database had been sent a questionnaire, asking their views and opinions about Fine Furniture's products and service, but the results – a whole pile of them – had not been processed.

Miranda decided that several urgent issues must be dealt with before an accurate assessment of customer care at Fine Furniture could be attempted and any improvements introduced.

Staffing levels/qualities

While there is a need to provide adequate training for all staff who deal with customers directly or indirectly, careful selection of employees comes before training, and the function of the selection procedure is to make sure, as far as is possible, that the right calibre of staff are employed.

However, even very good employees cannot provide high quality service if there are too few of them. It is not unknown for businesses to cut costs by reducing their staffing levels, resulting in inferior customer service. If, for example, a customer needing advice or assistance or wishing to place an order repeatedly tries to contact a telephone number and is always greeted by a recorded message, he or she might well decide to take their custom to another provider. Although, in many cases, employees are the greatest expense of a business, employing too few of them often proves to be a false economy.

Utilisation of experience

New businesses must establish the procedures and practices necessary to deliver quality customer service. These have to be checked and monitored carefully to establish if they are satisfactory. Once a business has been running for some time, it acquires experience on which it can draw to maintain and, whenever possible, improve its services.

Health and safety

Health and safety regulations for organisations are laid down by legislation, and there is no excuse for an organisation failing to provide an adequate level of facilities. Businesses whose customers visit their premises must ensure that those premises are safe and that the health of customers is not endangered. Such provisions range from a procedure set down to clean any spillages in a supermarket, to making sure that all fire exits are open and easily accessible.

Activity

The Customer Services Manager's role

- If you were in Miranda's position, what would you do, and why?
- How could new procedures help assess standards?
- What improvements might be necessary at Fine Furniture Ltd?

Cleanliness and hygiene

This follows on from health and safety requirements and includes maintaining necessary standards in the preparation of food and cleanliness in restaurants and other catering outlets, so that customers can have confidence in the products. Furthermore, facilities provided on the premises must also be of adequate standard. It would not be sufficient, for example, for a restaurant to impose stringent hygiene standards in the kitchen and to insist that the staff must be clean and tidily dressed, if the toilet facilities were not of comparable cleanliness.

Accessibility and availability

Availability – if something is available, you will find it – it will not have sold out or been withdrawn from sale.

If you ever watch TV programmes on consumer topics, you might have realised that, fairly often, customers complain that, having seen an advertisement or some publicity material, when they wish to purchase the product, they find it difficult to locate it. Sometimes, the product or service might have been withdrawn or replaced without this fact being communicated to customers. Sometimes the product might have sold out and the only option open to the customer is to wait. Both of these situations are unacceptable and business organisations must take steps to avoid them. When a product is unavailable, the customer will very likely look for it somewhere else.

Accessibility – if something is accessible, you will be able to find it easily.

Accessibility can be divided into two main areas.

- **Accessibility of communication**
  It is not in the organisation's interests if customers find it difficult, if not impossible, to contact the right person for information or advice. The manager who is 'at a meeting' every time a customer asks to speak to him or her, the unhelpful front-of-house member of staff, the forgotten messages – all of these are part of poor quality customer service.
- **Physical accessibility**
  This is also very important. Access for wheelchair users is now provided by many organisations, and additional facilities, such as special trolleys in supermarkets, wider parking spaces and toilets for the disabled are becoming more common. The layout of shops and stores should make it easy for shoppers to see and reach any goods they require.

Provision for individual/special needs

Apart from facilities for people with disabilities mentioned above, many organisations now provide chairs for the elderly shopper or perhaps one who is just very tired. The IKEA chain, among others, provides a playing area where mothers can leave their children while shopping. These areas are staffed by qualified attendants and precautions are taken to ensure the security and safety of the children.

> The HSBC bank provides leaflets about its services in Braille and also has a special facility for those with impaired hearing. Do you know of any other organisations that do this?

As you know, the needs of customers are constantly changing. In the case study about Yorkshire Electricity (page 146) you read about the way in which customers have changed in recent years. It is not enough for an organisation to know the criteria against which its level of customer care should be measured. It must carry out such assessment regularly and efficiently. In Chapter 4 we looked at the various ways in which customer feedback can help an organisation to find out how well it is doing and what else it could do.

Surveys of customers, staff, management and even non-users are a useful way of assessing levels of customer service, provided that they are well constructed, properly carried out and their findings are acted upon. The same applies to informal feedback from staff and customers, to staff and customer suggestions and to focus groups.

Organisations will achieve quality customer service if their procedures for dealing with customer issues are carefully structured and work efficiently. Such provisions must address matters such as communicating with the customer, responding quickly to enquiries, investigating any problems and complaints, and taking necessary action to resolve matters and to ensure that improvements are made as and when necessary.

It sometimes happens that the customer is unhappy because goods or services provided were not up to standard through no fault of the organisation. Delays might be the result of a supplier failing to deliver on time. Defective goods might be supplied by the manufacturer. If this occurs, the organisation must communicate directly with the supplier or manufacturer to try to ensure that the situation does not recur. Contacts with consumer associations can also be helpful as they can act in an advisory capacity.

Revision Questions

1. Explain what is meant by 'value for money'. (1 mark)
2. Why do companies need to retain customers? (2 marks)
3. How can a business provide for individual or special needs? Give three examples. (5 marks)
4. Why should organisations have set procedures for dealing with customer issues? (4 marks)
5. Why is experience useful when dealing with customers? (2 marks)
6. What is likely to happen if a business does not regularly assess its customer services? (2 marks)
7. List four ways in which the efficiency of customer services can be measured and assessed. (6 marks)
8. What is meant by 'providing for individual and special needs'? (4 marks)
9. Sometimes a business might not satisfy customers' needs through no fault of its own. Give two examples. (3 marks)
10. Why is assessment of performance not enough? What must be done as a result of such assessment? (4 marks)

UNIT 3

End of Unit Assignment

For this unit, you will need to study the customer services policies and practices of one organisation. The Assessment Evidence requires considerable detail on exactly how customer service works in the organisation, so it vital that you consider the following questions before you choose the organisation you are going to study:

1 Do you have really good access to the chosen organisation so that you can find out *all* of the details that you need to meet *every* part of the Assessment Evidence?

2 How easy will it be to obtain additional information if you find that you need more as you are writing up your investigation?

3 Is the organisation large enough to be practising all the parts of customer service that you have been asked to write about?

4 Does the organisation have a clearly stated customer service policy?

5 Does the organisation have a clear way of monitoring and improving its customer service provision?

When you know which organisation you will be studying, it is very important to explain clearly to your contact what information you will need.

You will be carrying out two major tasks:

1 An investigation into customer service practices in your chosen organisation

2 A report on how your chosen organisation could improve its customer service, which may be written, or presented orally or visually

The details that follow should help you to plan what you will need to research and write up – and present – your findings. They have been divided on the basis of the bullets points in the Assessment Evidence table of your unit (page 124 of the syllabus).

Task 1

For your introduction

- Provide a general introduction to customer service explaining how important it is to all businesses.
- Give a short outline on the organisation that you are studying, its main business, number of employees, location. etc.

For the body of your report

This list details what you must show and the grades.

- Identify the main customers of the organisation, including internal customers (**E1**).
- For each type of customer, outline their main needs (**E1**).
- Explain how the organisation uses its customer service to meet these needs (**E2**). Use real examples to back up the points you are making.
- Outline the customer service skills that staff use to meet the needs of customers (**E2**). Again, use real examples to show how these skills are used effectively.
- Describe the organisation's customer service policy and any objectives that it has in relation to customer service (**E2**). There may well be a published customer service document or manual.
- Explain why the customer service is effective in meeting the needs of customers, giving examples of good practice (**C2**).
- Check the main consumer protection legislation and codes of practice and explain how your organisation ensures that these requirements are met as part of its customer service policy (**E3**). This should be supported by examples of when the policy or practice meets the legal requirements and the codes of practice requirements.
- Produce an evaluation of the customer service in your organisation, highlighting the good and the bad points (**A1**).

- Ensure that your work shows that you have worked independently, both in the way that you have approached the assignment and in the way that you have extracted important facts and theories and have put them together to produce a quality piece of work (**C1**).

For your conclusion

- A summary that, again, emphasises the importance of customer service but, in this case, for the organisation itself rather than generally, together with comments on how well, or badly you felt the organisation has provided customer service (This will act as a good link into Task 2.)
- A full list of all sources of information that you have used, e.g., the contacts in the organisation, the customer service policy document, textbooks

Task 2

For your introduction

- Explain the importance of monitoring customer service provision in general.
- Outline the range of methods used for this, e.g., questionnaires, mystery shoppers, benchmarking, sales records.
- Explain how monitoring helps to improve customer service in the future and why it is so important to improve customer service in a competitive business environment.

For the body of your report

- Describe in detail what methods the organisation uses to monitor its customer service and explain how these techniques measure the level of customer service and help to identify any problems with it (**E4**).
- Consider carefully how useful each of these methods of monitoring are, and how useful they will be in identifying areas that need improvement (**C3/A1**).
- Having carefully examined the customer service provided by the organisation and the results of the monitoring processes, suggest improvements that could be made. Give examples of areas where improvements should be made (**A1**).
- Justify why these improvements need to be made. Explain how your study of the current level of customer service and the results of the monitoring processes have helped you to decide what needs to be improved and how it needs to be improved (**C4**).
- Ensure that the changes you are recommending are realistic and that they cover all the important areas where there are problems (**A4**).
- Explain how the changes that you are recommending will affect the way in which the organisation will have to operate in the future (**A4**).
- Ensure that your work shows that you have worked independently, both in the way that you have approached Task 2 and in the way that you have extracted important facts and theories and have put them together to produce a quality piece of work (**C1**).

For your conclusion

- A summary, which emphasises the importance of monitoring and improving on customer service, especially in your chosen organisation
- A full list of all sources of information that you have used, e.g., the contacts in the organisation, the monitoring feedback forms, textbooks, comments on the business from people outside the business (e.g., press reports)

UNIT 4

Information and Communication Technology

CHAPTER 1

What is ICT?

KEY TERMS

Accessibility	EFT	LAN	Receiver
Confidentiality	EFTPOS	Mail merge	Security
Cost	EPOS	Methods of communication	Sender
Durability	Feedback	Networks	Value for money
Ease of use	Fitness for purpose	Obsolescence	WAN
EDI	ICT	Quality	

In this chapter, you will learn what the term ICT means and how technology has become a vital part of the way in which businesses collect, store and communicate information.

This chapter looks at the process of communication and how technology is used to help this process. Examples of the range of information and communication technology available to businesses are considered, and the criteria on which good ICT should be measured are identified.

The meaning of ICT

ICT (Information and Communication Technology) has two distinct features: First, it refers to the many forms of technology which are used to collect, store, process, transmit or communicate information:

- The EPOS system, used by supermarkets, which collects data on sales and is used to help the stores decide what items are selling best, which customers buy what, when goods need to be re-ordered, etc.

EPOS – an **electronic point of sale** computer program which records information about goods as they are sold

- A **suppliers' database**, which stores information about the products that suppliers offer for sale – current prices, delivery times, credit facilities, etc.
- **Search engines** on the internet, which identify what people want to find out about and then select the most suitable matches from within vast databases
- **Automated railway timetables** which communicate the latest information to railway passengers waiting on station platforms

Second, ICT also refers to the many forms of technology that are used to aid communications systems:

- E-mail – modems – computers – the internet
- Telephones – fax – satellite – radio – television
- Tannoys – pagers – bleepers
- Networks – WAN – LAN – intranets – extranets – video conferencing
- E-commerce – telephone banking – media advertising

A **WAN (wide area network)** provides access to computer files and software outside of a single business.

A **LAN (local area network)** provide access to computer files and software within a business.

Most businesses use a wide range of ICT facilities and there are very few businesses in the UK that use no ICT facilities at all. The chapters that follow look at some specific examples of ICT as it is used by specific businesses, but most businesses tend to use ICT rather than manual systems for the same general reasons:

- Jobs such as recording and processing information can be carried out much faster.
- Calculations, checking data, re-ordering, etc. can be carried out more accurately.
- Using ICT allows businesses to communicate with many more customers.
- The cost of processing information and communicating is often much lower, e.g. an e-mail can be sent to a thousand customers at a fraction of the cost of sending it through the normal postal system.
- Many customers now have ICT and wish to use it to order goods, make payments, check accounts, etc., so ICT is necessary to meet customers' needs.
- ICT helps management to make the correct decisions more easily, based on a wide range of data, forecasts and statistical analysis.

Buying a camcorder at Dixons

In making one purchase at a store such as Dixons, a customer will find a wealth of ICT facilities being used.

- To check the store opening times, the telephone is used. If the store is closed an answer phone may provide recorded information.
- Details are also checked on the internet to see what special offers are available.
- When visiting the store, prices and availability of the selected camcorder are checked using the store's intranet and the stock database.
- The customer pays using a debit card which uses the EFTPOS system to transfer funds from the customer's account to Dixons's account.
- Details of the sale are recorded through EPOS so that the store can re-order if necessary.
- The automated till produces printed details of the purchase and a receipt for the customer's records.
- Details of the customer are taken and recorded on the customer database so that data on new products and offers can be sent out.

How ICT helps communication

The purpose of all communication is to pass information from a **sender** to a **receiver** (see Figure 4.1.1).

The methods of communication are very wide and include all forms of spoken, written, visual and electronic communication (see Table 4.1.1). The electronic methods of communication clearly use ICT but, in fact, all of the common methods of communication can now use ICT to enhance and improve them (see Table 4.1.2).

Technology has been improving the quality and efficiency of communication for hundreds of years. Recently, developments in technology have accelerated and many of the current changes were undreamt of even ten years ago. ICT now affects so many parts of

Figure 4.1.1 How communication works

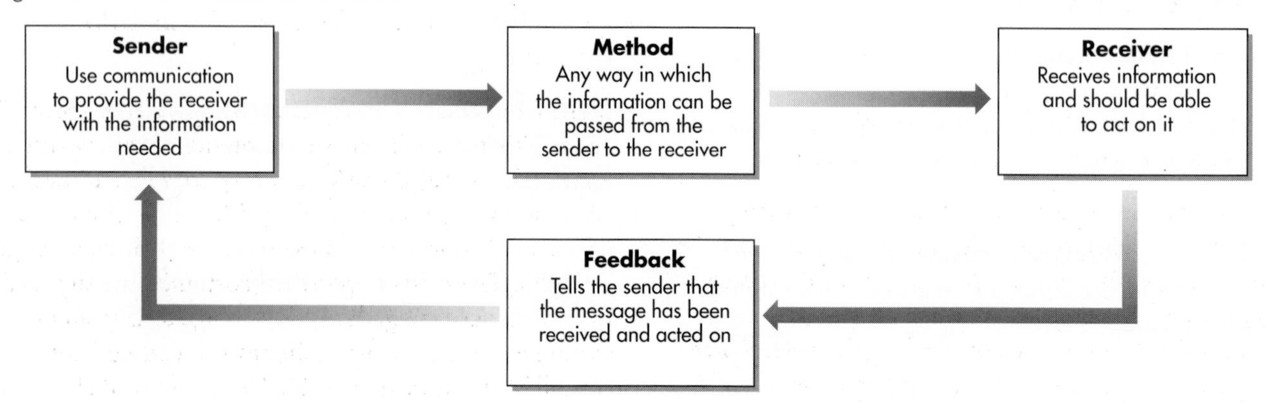

Table 4.1.1 Common examples of communication

Spoken	Written	Visual	Electronic
• Meetings • Speeches • Interviews • Talking to staff or customers	• Memos • Letters • Reports • Notices	• Sign language • Body language • Posters • Photographs	• EPOS • BACS • Surveillance cameras

Table 4.1.2 Using ICT to enhance and improve methods of communication

	Spoken
• Meetings • Speeches • Interviews • Talking to staff or customers	• Meetings can be conducted between people in different parts of the world using video conferencing. • A **public address** (PA) system can be used so that everyone can hear speeches. • Interviews can be conducted over the telephone. • Tannoys are used to talk to all staff at once in noisy factories, and PA systems are used to tell customers of current bargains in a supermarket.
	Written
• Memos • Letters • Reports • Notices	• Memos and letters are now frequently written using a word processor and sent by internal e-mail systems. • Reports and notices often include graphs, diagrams, photographs, etc., created in dedicated programs or scanned in and then combined with text.
	Visual
• Sign language • Body language • Posters • Photographs	• Optical sensors can now pick up body movements and computer software can interpret what they mean. • Posters have become animated with flashing lights, video clips, etc. • Photographs can now be taken with digital cameras, touched up and made to show what the businesses want to show.

our lives that it is impossible here to do more than scratch the surface of how it is used in business. Below are two examples that show why ICT has become so important to business and the function of communication: mail merge; and EPOS, EFT, EFTPOS and EDI. Many other examples are given in the chapters that follow.

Mail merge

Mail merge allows businesses to combine the functions of word processing with the use of a database.

When using mail merge a business may, for example, prepare a list of new products that customers might be interested in. This may be done using word processing facilities, adding graphics and scanning in pictures. Within the document, blank spaces will be left which identify, say, the name, address, and some other personal data about individual customers. What mail merge then allows the business to do is to personalise every letter that it will send out.

This is done by linking the 'blank' spaces in the document to specific fields in the database. When the mail merge is operated, letters will be created showing the individual name, address, etc., of each of the customers.

Many companies have very large customer files and mail merge allows these businesses to produce individualised letters, mail shots, e-mails, etc., very cheaply and easily. There is also a growing number of firms which buy lists of potential customers and use these for their mail merge activities. These lists of potential customers are supplied by other firms who gather a huge range of data about consumers, about incomes, interests, spending habits, etc. All of this is made possible by the use of ICT.

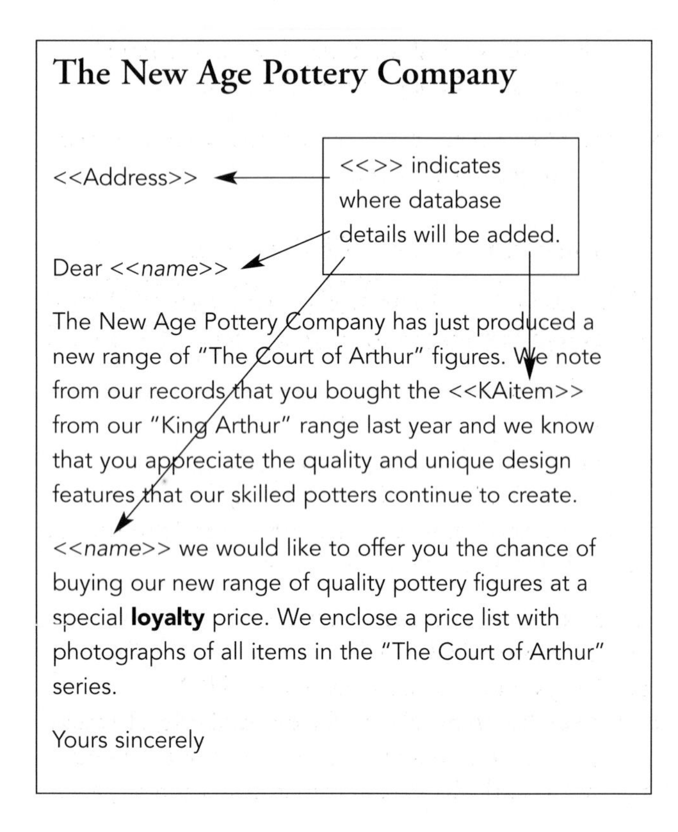

The New Age Pottery Company

<<Address>>

<< >> indicates where database details will be added.

Dear <<*name*>>

The New Age Pottery Company has just produced a new range of "The Court of Arthur" figures. We note from our records that you bought the <<KAitem>> from our "King Arthur" range last year and we know that you appreciate the quality and unique design features that our skilled potters continue to create.

<<*name*>> we would like to offer you the chance of buying our new range of quality pottery figures at a special **loyalty** price. We enclose a price list with photographs of all items in the "The Court of Arthur" series.

Yours sincerely

EPOS, EFT, EFTPOS and EDI

EPOS is the electronic technology used where products are being sold and paid for. Scanning bar codes is part of this technology, but it also includes scanning loyalty cards, scanning credit and debit cards and sending messages to a customer's bank so that the retail outlet is paid. Where payment is being made using this system, there will be **electronic funds transfer** (EFT), also known as **electronic funds transfer at the point of sale** (EFTPOS).

As the data is scanned into the system, it is processed and recorded. In many large stores, EPOS systems are now connected to centralised computers and to other software packages which will carry out a range of automated tasks. Where this data is being transferred from one system to another, it is undergoing Electronic Data Interchange (EDI).

EPOS systems will also help businesses by providing all of the following facilities:

- Creating bar code labels
- Scanning of bar codes
- Responding to keyboard instructions and pre-set keys for certain products
- Setting up prices, discounts, special offers, etc., that will register when the bar code is scanned
- Allowing payment by different methods, e.g. cash, cheque, credit and debit cards, and vouchers
- Converting prices between different currencies, e.g. pounds sterling and euros
- Creating a database on customers and what products they buy, when, how often, etc.
- Identifying individual customers and treating them differently
- Updating stock records and checking what stock is available

Figure 4.1.2 EPOS and EDI

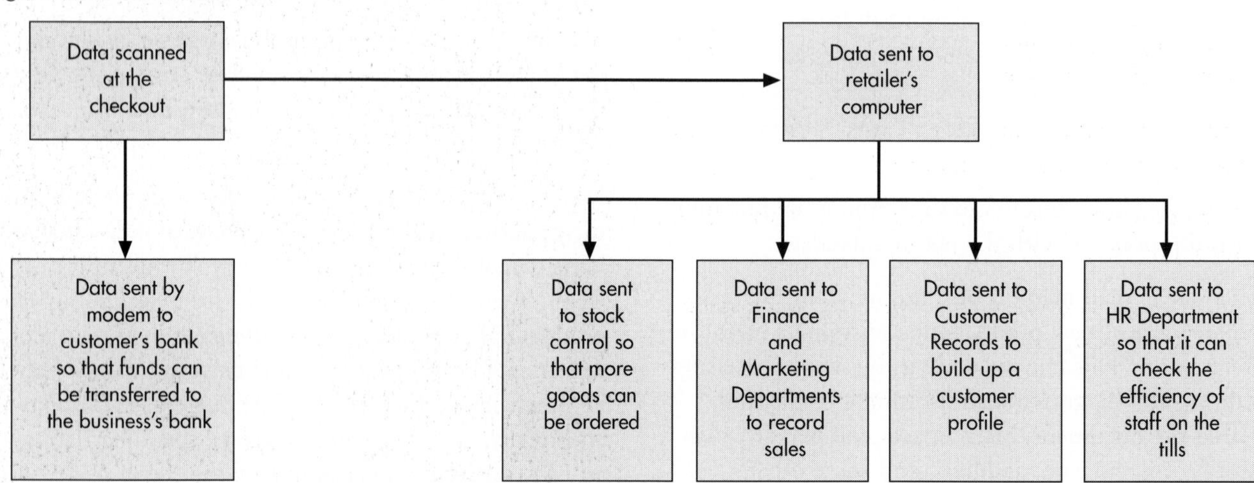

- Recording all details from each checkout, including who is operating it, what hours they work, how fast they work, and how much cash is taken

Using EPOS and EDI to manage stock and staff

When EPOS is used to manage stock, the checkout scanners are connected to a central computer. As the bar codes are scanned, data recording what has been sold is sent to the central computer. As deliveries of new stock are received, these are also scanned on the computer database. Staff in the office can then check all stock, order replacement stock, change the prices, etc.

Hand-held scanners can be used by staff in the store to check details about stock on shelves, e.g. what the price should be if the price tag label has come off, or if they want to check that stock is available in the storeroom.

The systems will allow all of the following stock control functions to take place:

- Checking and recording what stock has been sold
- Identifying what stock needs to be reordered
- Showing which products sell best
- Identifying which products are slow sellers and may need to be reduced in price or withdrawn from sale
- Printing out a list of stock that should be in the store so that it can be checked in the weekly or monthly stock-take
- Using hand-held scanners for the actual stock-take
- Using the data from customers' hand-held scanners to see how they move around the store and therefore where the best place is to put certain goods
- Preparing printed stock reports on what has sold, for how much, when, etc.

As well as controlling stock, the computer data can also be used to manage the checkout staff:

- Recording which member of staff is at which till and how long they have been working

  This can be used to calculate their pay and generate payslips, cheques, etc., automatically.

- Recording how fast staff scan products and take payment for goods

  If this time is too slow, it may lead to additional training, a cut in pay or even dismissal.

- Recording when tills are busiest and helping to plan when to put on extra staff

Electronic fund transfer (EFT) systems

EFT (electronic fund transfer) sends money electronically from one bank to another.

Part of the purpose of the EPOS system is to allow customers to pay for their purchases using credit or debit cards. This is done by connecting the scanning facilities at retail outlets, via a computer and modem, to the banking system (see Figure 4.1.4).

The connection is via the telephone system and is therefore electronic, hence its name: **electronic funds transfer system**. It is also known as EFTPOS (**electronic funds transfer at the point of sale**). Because it involves the business in sending details of payments to a bank and the bank confirming this, it is also part of EDI.

This system of electronic transfer of funds is not new. Automatic telling machines (ATMs or cash points) have allowed customers to access cash outside of banking hours for a long time. When the customer puts his/her card into the ATM, the account number and the bank sort code are scanned. The customer confirms it is

Figure 4.1.3 Printouts from EPOS allow management to make decisions on stock and staffing

Figure 4.1.4 Movement of data in an EPOS system

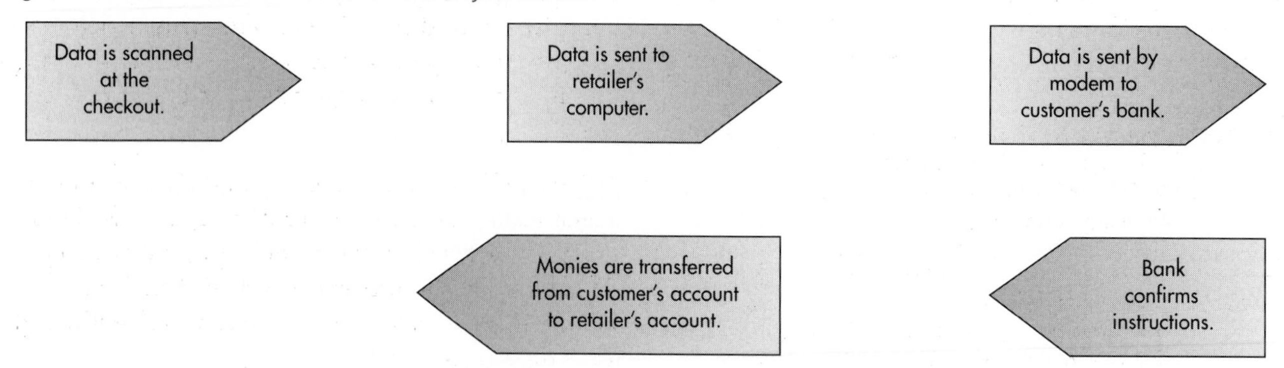

his/her card by keying in the correct personal identity number (PIN) and then selects withdrawal of cash, payment in, bank balance, etc. All of the data is checked electronically in the bank system and, if approved, the customer's requests will be met.

The EFT system in retail outlets is very similar. When the customer's credit or debit cards are scanned a message is sent to the bank to request payment. The customers confirm that the cards are theirs, and that they want to pay, by signing the printed payment slips.

With the huge growth in sales of products via the internet, EFT systems are now commonly used for this method of retailing as well. Customers can provide businesses with details of their credit or debit cards over the internet and businesses will use this information to request payment, using EFT systems, from the customers' banks. Because the internet lacks security, however, there is always a risk that dishonest people might obtain the credit card or debit card number and use it for their own purchases.

How to choose appropriate ICT facilities for a business

The benefits of good ICT facilities can be enormous but businesses must use the right criteria to judge these. Many smaller businesses have invested fairly heavily in ICT and they may have installed systems that are far too complex for their scale of business. These businesses are sometimes using less than 10 per cent of the features that the ICT facilities offer, especially where computers are involved.

Businesses need to consider all of the following criteria when they are deciding which ICT facilities to invest in.

Fitness for purpose

Will the ICT facility do the job that it is being bought for? Telephones may seem to be an obvious investment for a firm, but they will be of little use if their customers or suppliers have no telephones. Fixed telephone lines are of little use to a taxi firm trying to contact its drivers. If many people are going to be using the telephone at the same time, multiple connections will be needed.

Before a business invests in ICT it must:

- carefully assess the needs of the business
- draw up details of what it expects the ICT facility to do
- check with the ICT suppliers that these functions can be carried out by the ICT facility
- ensure that the new facility will be compatible with existing facilities
- think carefully about likely future needs and ensure that the new facility will either be able to deal with these as well, or that it can be easily upgraded.

Cost and value for money

Businesses need to make a careful judgement about cost. Clearly, the new facility must cost less than the benefit that it is going to provide, but getting the cost just right is difficult.

Cost is often related to quality and it may be worth paying a bit extra to ensure that the ICT facility will last and will do the job required. At the same time, many businesses seem to believe that, simply because it is ICT, high cost means good performance and will be worth it in the end. Frequently, these firms spend too

Table 4.1.3 Varying prices and facilities on some Compaq laser printers (Jan 2001)

Printer	Main features	RRP (£)
LN16	Mono Laser Printer, A4, 16 pages per minute, 600dpi, 12Mb, 2400 × 600dpi (software enhanced), PostScript level 2, PCL6, 500 sheet input, 250 sheet output	839
LN16N	Mono Laser Printer, A4, 16 pages per minute, 600dpi, 12Mb, 2400 × 600dpi (software enhanced), PostScript level 2, PCL6, Ethernet 10/100 Base-T and 10 Base 2, 500 sheet input, 250 sheet output	1126
LN32N	Mono Laser Printer, A3/A4, 32 pages per minute, 1200dpi, 32Mb, PostScript level 3, PCL5e, 30 pages per minute (duplex), printer management software, 10/100Base T and 10Base 2, 150 000 pages per month, 1050 sheet input, 500 sheet output	2304
LN40	Mono Laser Printer, A3+/A4, 40 pages per minute, 600dpi, 32Mb, PostScript level 2, PCL5e, 300 000 pages per month, 1500 sheet input, 500 sheet output	11 434

much and use only a proportion of what the facility can do. ICT facilities also tend to go out of date very rapidly and businesses need to include very rapid depreciation factors in their costing.

In looking for value for money, the business should be considering all of the following points:

- Cost
- How efficiently the job is done and the standard of work produced
- The speed at which the job is done
- The costs of training staff and the savings made by reducing the need for staff

Ease of use and accessibility

Many basic ICT products, such as telephones, fax machines, e-mails and EPOS scanners, are relatively easy to use. Staff training is therefore fairly quick and simple. Other ICT facilities, such as integrated accounting packages, programming EPOS systems and computer-aided design systems (CAD), are much more complex and require staff to be thoroughly trained and also to understand, to some extent, how the systems work.

Where staff do not have training in ICT, ease of use is a major factor. On the other hand, many ICT facilities can perform a wide range of additional and valuable functions. The business may decide that the best approach would be to buy a more complex facility and train the staff properly.

Businesses must also consider **accessibility** for their staff and for anyone else who needs to use the facilities. However, this must not compromise security and confidentiality (see page 166).

Access to computer files and software is now possible through networked systems. Internally these will be **LAN**s but access can also be created outside of individual businesses centres through **WAN**s. These allow all of the following situations.

- Retail staff accessing data to check prices, stock availability, etc.
- Memos, e-mails, etc., sent between staff

Figure 4.1.5 On-line help can make software easier to use

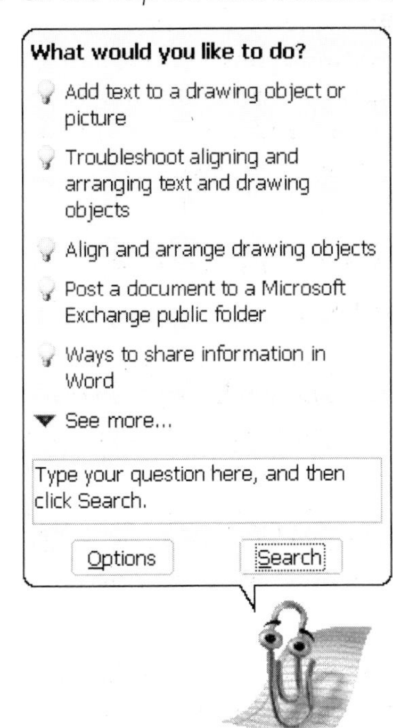

- Backing up data in various locations
- Multiple use of single facilities, e.g. many computers using a single printer
- Remote access, allowing staff to work from home
- Customers surfing the internet to check product details, the best buys, etc.
- Bank customers checking their accounts and making transactions on-line

Security and confidentiality

When customers and businesses use ICT facilities, they expect them to be secure and confidential. For businesses, these are major issues. Any facilities that involve the transfer of money must have safeguards to prevent unauthorised access, otherwise there is a danger that the transfers will be intercepted and funds stolen. Alternatively, thieves may be able to obtain card or bank details that will allow them to remove money from other people's accounts. Business information is extremely valuable and sales records, new designs, customer details, etc., also need to be protected. Where computer software is involved the business must also protect itself against viruses.

Firms also need to protect the confidentiality of their stakeholders and shareholders.

- Shareholders expect details of their holding to be kept secret, although the Companies Acts do insist that the names of shareholders with large percentages of holdings in PLCs are published.
- Suppliers expect that details such as price quotations, credit facilities, and transactions are treated confidentially.
- Customers expect their details to be kept confidential unless they give permission for the business to pass these details on.
- Employees expect personal details, such as their pay, number of days off work, addresses and bank account numbers, to be kept secure and confidential.
- The business expects that there will be restricted access within the firm to information such as accounts, details of taxation, etc.

Businesses will want to know that any ICT facility they are about to use meets their own, and their stakeholders', security and confidentiality needs.

Card fraudsters skim off £300m

Credit card fraud rose by more than 50 per cent in the past year to reach £300 million, with copied cards used to steal a third of the total, it was revealed yesterday.

Cloning or skimming of credit cards occurs when a card's magnetic strip is secretly copied by crooked staff in shops and restaurants.

Criminal gangs then transfer the copied strip to a counterfeit card which could turn up in the Far East or anywhere else in the world within a matter of hours.

Source: Metro 4th Jan 2001

Certain security and confidentially issues are covered by the legal requirements of using ICT facilities (see page 193).

Quality, durability and obsolescence

Quality measures how well the ICT facility meets what it is designed to do.

Durability measures how long the ICT facility will last and continue to function effectively.

Obsolescence measures when the ICT facility will no longer be useful and will need to be replaced.

Quality and durability are closely linked to fitness for purpose, ease of use and cost. An extra point that needs to be considered here is the environment in which the facility is going to be used, who will be using it and how it will be used. Scanners in a supermarket need to be robust because many different members of staff will use them and they will be used for much of the day. A mobile phone needs to be carried around and may be used in many different environments, e.g. on a building site where it is likely to be knocked, covered with dust, etc.

At the other end of the time-scale is the fact that most ICT products have a very limited lifespan before something better comes along and they become redundant. To buy the most appropriate product, businesses will need to balance these two factors.

CHAPTER 2

Basic ICT Packages

KEY TERMS

Automatic contents	Hardware	Teleconferencing
Automatic index	Input devices	Video conferencing
Central processing unit (CPU)	Output devices	Web connections
Database	Real time	Word processing
Formulae	Software	
Graphics	Spreadsheets	

In this chapter, you will learn what certain ICT packages can do and what software and hardware are required in order to run them effectively.

This chapter will look at examples of non-PC-based ICT packages, basic PC and computer hardware technology, the main software packages (word processing, databases, spreadsheets, graphics and presentations), and how businesses use these ICT facilities to improve the efficiency of their production.

What sort of ICT do businesses need?

If a business needs a mobile telephone it will, as a minimum, require the phone itself and the service provided by the telecommunication system. It does not have to buy any other **hardware** or **software** to use the phone. With many ICT packages, however, a range of different hardware and software facilities is required.

Hardware – pieces of ICT equipment such as the computer, VDU, printer, etc.

Software – the programs run on a computer

Most businesses which use conventional telephone services are likely to have all of the following:

- Telephone
- Land line connected to exchange
- Answering machine
- Facsimile machine (fax)
- Modem connection to computer
- **Database** of important telephone numbers
- Repair services if any of the equipment goes wrong

A **database** is a storage system used to keep information until it is needed.

All communication needs a sending device and a receiving device, and most modern communication methods also have a way of storing the information received. All of this requires hardware and software. Two examples are given below.

Computer hardware and software

Figure 4.2.1 shows typical hardware elements for a PC.

Input devices are used to put data into the computer. The data is then, stored, edited, combined and processed in the **central processing unit (CPU)**. When the data is needed from the computer it is accessed through the **output devices**.

Figure 4.2.1 Typical input and output devices for a computer

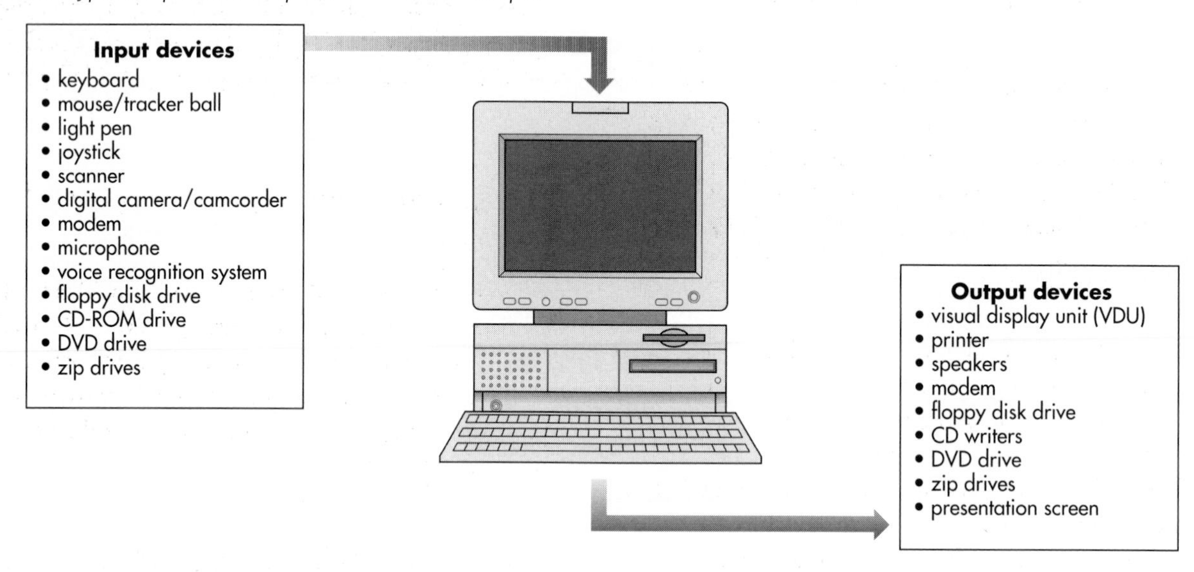

Most businesses require computers for multiple tasks: as data storage facilities, data processing facilities, communication channels between staff and between staff and customers, and presentational devices which produce high quality print outs, slides, reports, graphics, etc.

Computers process data and then present it in the form that is most useful to the business, but someone must tell the computer what to do – the **computer programmer**. This job requires considerable training and skill, and programming also takes a long time. It generally takes 1–2 years to develop a game like Final Fantasy IX, and involve a team of 10–20 programmers. Most businesses have no programming expertise, nor the time to create all the software needed. However, a wide range of relatively cheap programs is available, sufficient for most businesses.

Some software is specifically designed for one type of activity but can be used by most types of business: Sage, for example, to process a business's accounts. Other businesses need software to be created specifically, e.g. major insurance companies who all work slightly differently.

Increasingly, packages are designed to perform a wide range of important basic functions. Microsoft Word, for example, is primarily a word-processing package, but also offers a database facility, graphics, web tools and a programming language (Visual Basic).

Graphics are charts, artwork and non-written information produced by a computer program.

Figure 4.2.2 Toolbars in Microsoft Word

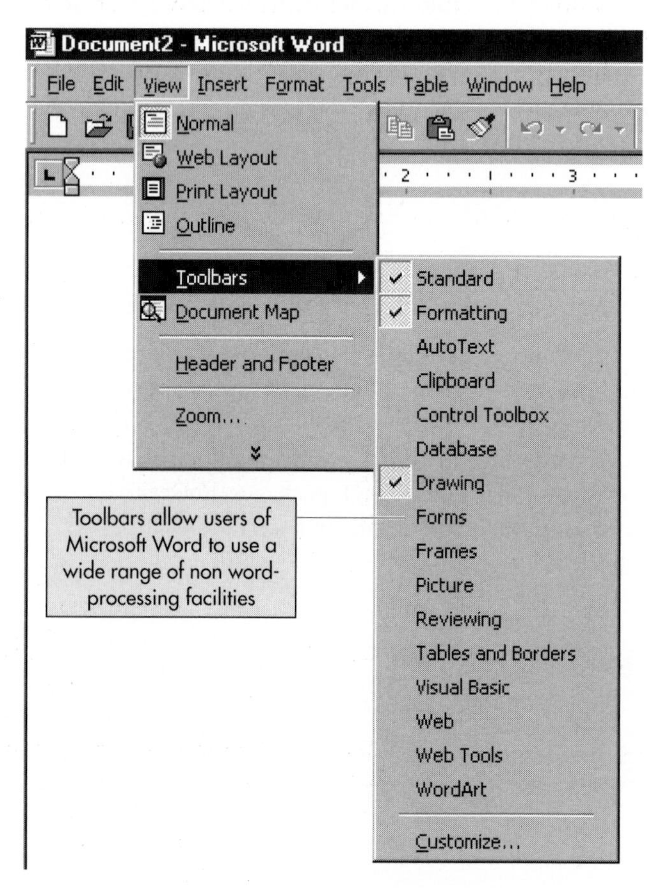

Teleconferencing (video conferencing)

Teleconferencing or **video conferencing** allows communication between different locations. This could be within a single building but it is really designed to allow people in different parts of the country, or even in different parts of the world, to talk to each other.

The way that **teleconferencing** works is for individuals, or groups, to sit in front of video cameras which record their conversation as though the various parties were actually sitting in one room having a discussion. The difference between this and multiple telephone links is that everything is being filmed and shown via a video link. This is why it is also referred to as **video conferencing**.

Teleconferencing allows people who cannot physically meet to discuss matters as though they were all in the same room. It does, however, require a combination of hardware items and supporting software (see Figure 4.2.3). Modern technology allows teleconferencing from individual PCs, with cameras mounted above them. When the computers are linked through cable or satellite, this is now just as fast as talking to each other in the same room (**real time**).

Real time – if a computer link is so fast that people using it think that it is happening with no time delay it is called real time.

The major software packages – word processing

A word-processing software package provides facilities for writing, typing and formatting text. Table 4.2.1 shows functions once carried out by three office staff. Today all of these functions are usually carried out by one member of staff using a computer and a word-processing facility.

Word processing provides all the functions that used to be carried out by a manual typewriter, and many of the functions that used to be carried out by the secretary using the typewriter.

Modern word-processing systems allow users to operate a huge range of facilities. Generally, however, even major companies, use only a relatively low percentage of what is available at any one time.

Figure 4.2.3 Basic hardware requirements for teleconferencing

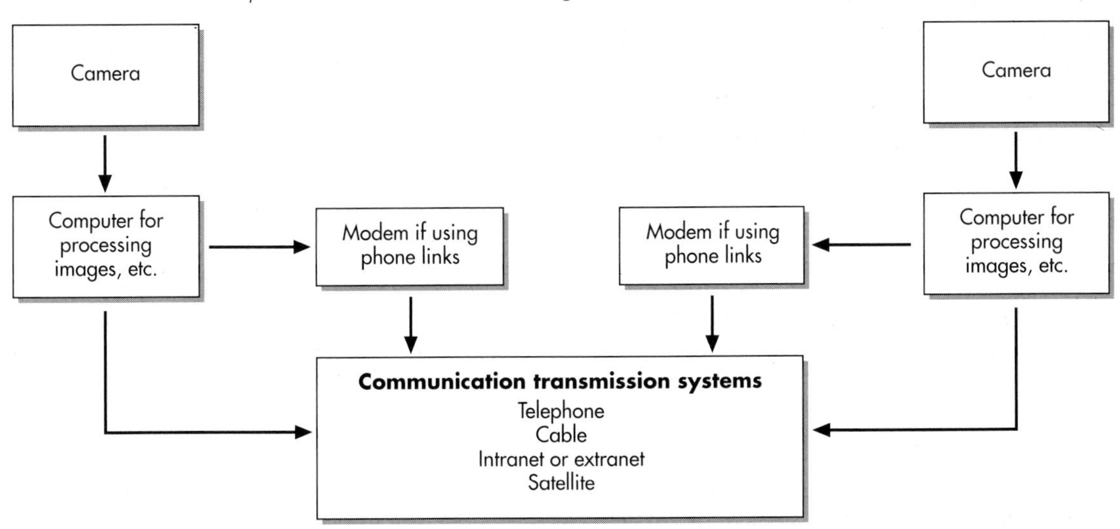

Table 4.2.1 Office functions now carried out by a computerised word-processing facility

Secretary
- Typing in the data, letters, reports, etc.
- Correcting any errors with white correction fluid, white ribbon, etc.
- Ensuring that everything is spelt correctly
- Setting the margins, working out spaces, etc.
- Checking that the correct grammar has been used

Filing clerk
- Storing copies of letters, reports, etc.
- Accessing files for checking, amendment, etc.
- Shredding old documents
- Duplicating documents using a photocopier
- Locking away documents for security

Mail office clerk
- Addressing envelopes
- Sending letters etc. to customers, suppliers, etc.
- Receiving mail and distributing it to the right people
- Recording details of all letters, etc. sent and received

Figure 4.2.4 Format menu in Microsoft Word

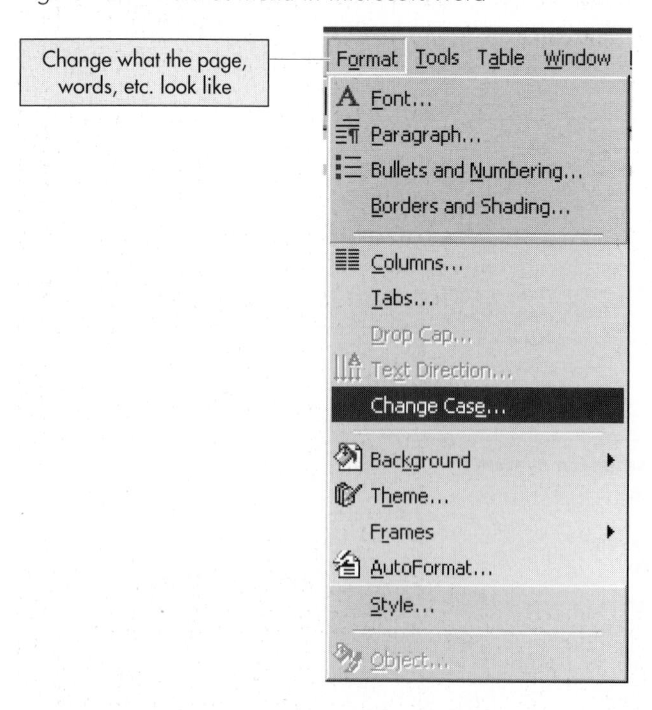

Microsoft Word is the most commonly used word-processing package throughout the world. Figures 4.2.4 and 4.2.5 show some of the facilities that are available. These are usually accessed by clicking on the 'drop down' menus (shown in Figure 4.2.4) or by using the 'tools' that are available. Figure 4.2.5 shows the buttons that will activate these tools. There are a great many of them and the best way to find out what each does is to click on them with the mouse to try them out.

Figure 4.2.5 Table menu in Microsoft Word

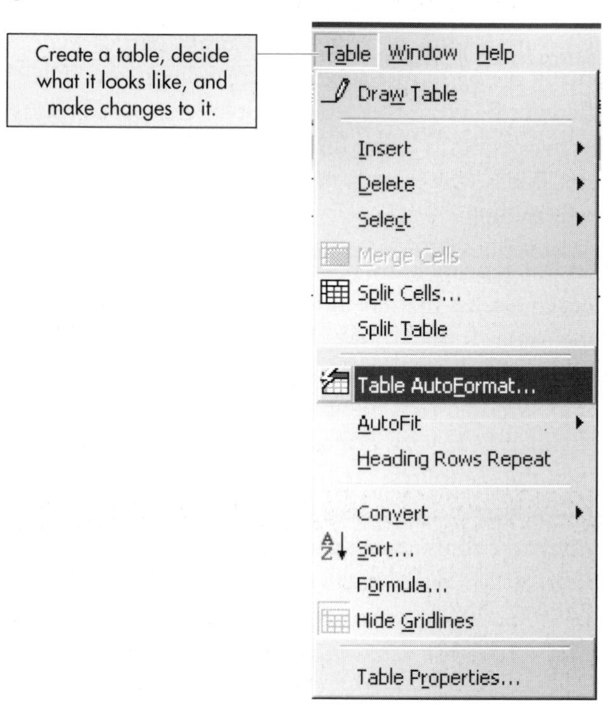

Common word-processing features

All modern word-processing packages allow the user to operate a keyboard and/or mouse to:

- input data
- change (edit) data
- merge, cut, paste and copy data
- save data – storing it in the computer on a hard drive or on a floppy disk, zip drive, etc.
- choose the way that the data will look
- check spelling and grammar.

Typical presentational features will include the following types of facilities.

Words can be made **bold**, put in *italics*, underlined, put as subscript or superscript and even given **shadow**. Word can be written in different sizes and in different styles called fonts.

Paragraphs, sentences or words can be:
Set on the left

or on the right

or placed in the centre

Other typical features include:

- justifying the text so that there is a straight margin on both the left and the right of the text
- spacing the lines to have single, double, or even greater spacing
- using bullet points, with dots (or other graphics) or numbers (as here!)
- indenting lines or sections
- giving text borders and shading around individual words, paragraphs and pages.

Specific word-processing features

Word-processing packages now have features that take them well beyond simply duplicating and improving on the functions shown in Table 4.2.1. Mail merge has already been discussed on page 161. Here are some more examples.

Generating a web-enabled document

On most modern word-processing packages it is possible to create web pages with all the features that you can find on a web site when you access the internet. Creating a web page can be done using the help feature provided by the software package. In Microsoft Word, this is called a 'wizard'. Alternatively, more adept users can create their own web pages using the word-processing facilities.

Web pages can be created from scratch by using the web page option when creating a new file. Figure 4.2.6 shows the web page options available. Using this facility, or saving a normal page as a web page, will convert the data into HTML, which is the format that can be read through the internet.

Figure 4.2.6 Web connections page from Microsoft Word

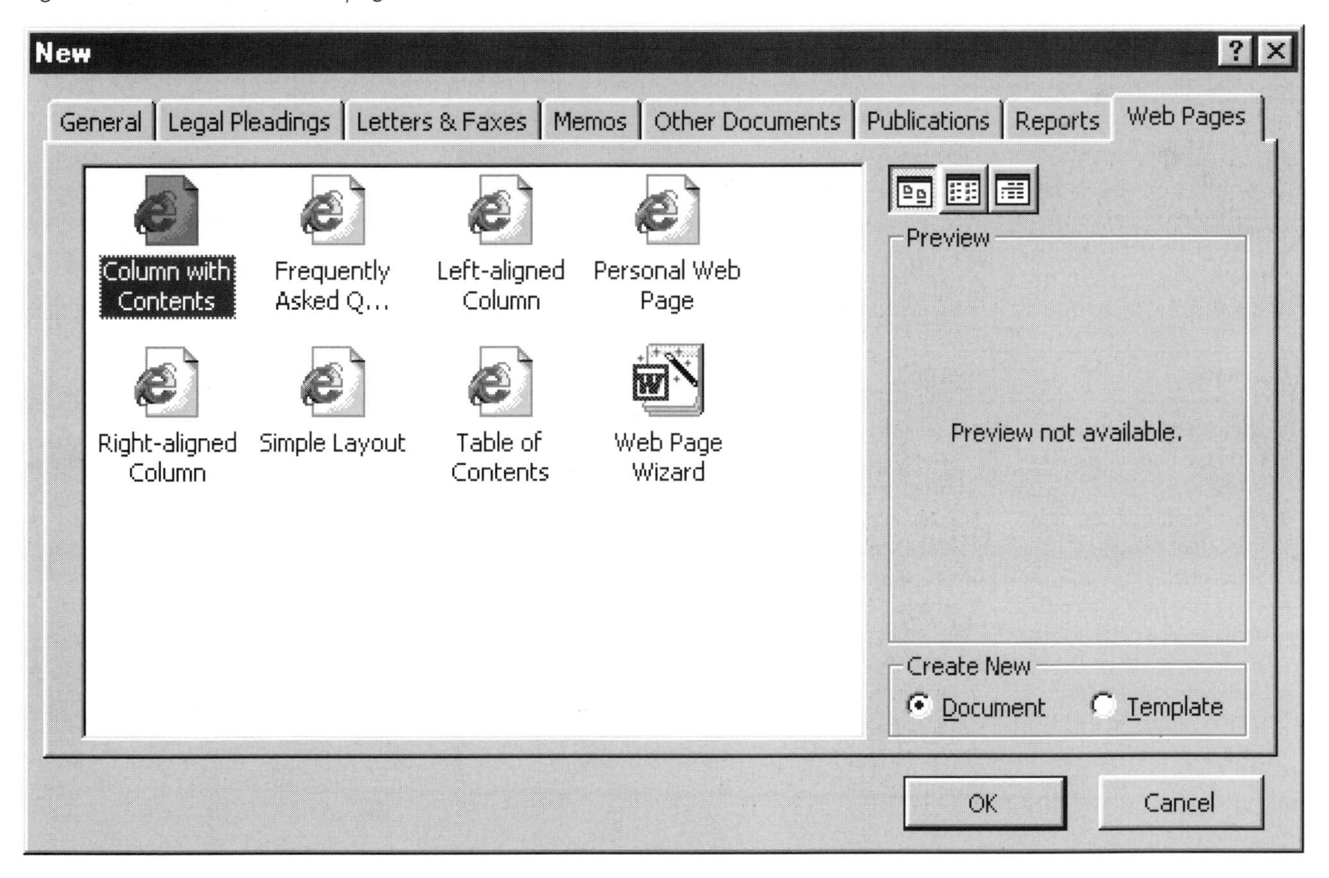

The following actions create a web page:

- Select drop down menu 'File'.
- Select option 'New'.
- Select card headed 'Web Pages'.
- Choose one of the options, e.g. 'Column with Contents'.
- Follow the instructions on the page and a web page will be created with links from one part of the page to another.

The links can also be set up to take the viewer to other pages and even other web sites.

Creating an automatic contents list and an automatic index

The contents section is usually placed at the beginning of a document and the index at the end. The **contents** will list all the major sections of the document. The **index** will list all the important words in the document. In both cases, it is important for the reader to know where in the document the sections or words can be found, so both contents and index have page numbers showing where the references are.

Because this is being done on a computer, it is possible to automate the process, save a great deal of time, and make it easier for the reader to use. Common features of what is provided are shown in Table 4.2.2.

Table 4.2.2 Features of automatic contents and index

Contents	Index
• Created automatically from the headings being used. • Most important and less important headings separated. • Page numbers created to show where each section starts. • An automatic link to take a reader to the section wanted.	• Created automatically by selecting the words that are wanted. • Selecting one word will identify every page on which that word occurs. • Allows subheadings in index. • Allows indexes to be written in a wide range of languages.

Creating a contents section in Microsoft Word

The easiest way of creating a list of contents in Microsoft Word is to use the headings provided. Each time a heading is written, the person typing in the text can decide what level of heading it should be. This can be done by highlighting the heading, and then selecting the drop down menu which contains the pre-set styles. (Figure 4.2.7) If you are not happy with the pre-set styles, these can be changed by using the drop down menu called '**Format**' and then selecting '**Style**'.

When all the headings have been chosen, the contents section can be placed at the beginning of the document, or anywhere else, using the following steps.

- Choose the place.
- Click on the '**Insert**' drop down menu.
- Choose 'Index and Tables'.
- Click on the folder entitled 'Table of Contents'.
- Make any changes needed to how the contents will look.
- Click on 'OK'.

The table of contents will then be displayed as you want it, with a list of page numbers. It will also have the added facility that if anyone reading the contents clicks on a contents heading, they will be taken immediately to that part of the document.

Figure 4.2.7 Style options in Microsoft Word

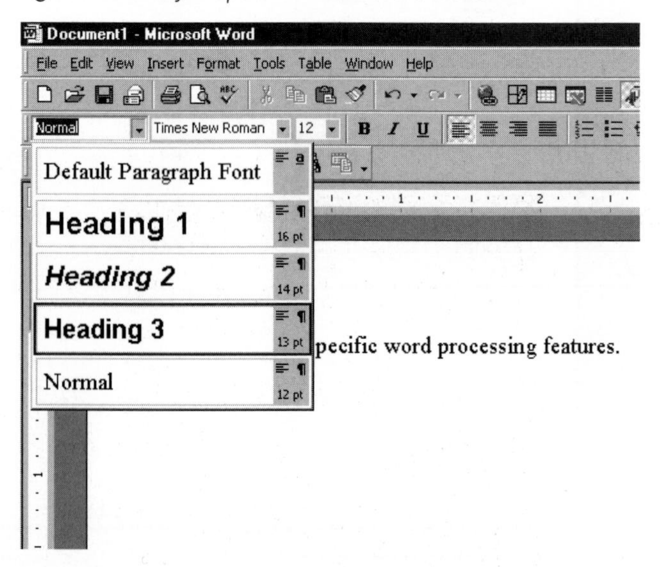

Creating an index in Microsoft Word

An index of all the important words can be built up by highlighting the word to be added and then carrying out the following steps.

- Click on the '**Insert**' drop down menu.
- Choose 'Index and Tables'.
- Click on the folder entitled 'Index'.
- Clicking on 'Mark Entry'.
- Decide if this a main entry or one that is to be listed as a sub entry under another main entry.
- Make any changes needed to how the index will look.
- Click on 'Mark All' and every page on which the item occurs will be recorded. It will also turn on the punctuation marker and if, say, the phrase 'fiscal policy' had been added, the indexed item will have {.XE 'index'.} after it.
- Close the index box.
- Press the punctuation display button to remove the punctuation marks.

This will add items to the index. To display the index (usually at the end of the document), some additional steps are needed.

- Make sure the punctuation display is off.
- Click on the '**Insert**' drop down menu.
- Choose 'Index and Tables'.
- Click on the folder entitled 'Index'.
- Click on 'OK'.

Figure 4.2.8 Creating an index in Microsoft Word

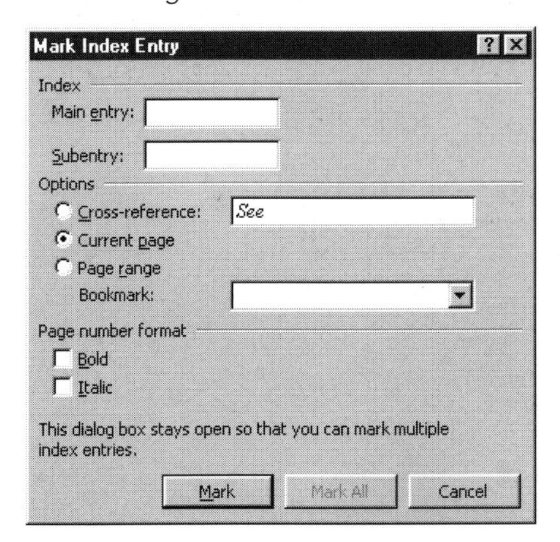

An index is expected in documents such as textbooks and major reports, but it is also a way of making your own assignments look more professional. It will, of course, require the addition of page numbers to your work. This can be done by clicking on the 'Insert' drop down menu, choosing the 'Page Numbers' option and then choosing where you would like the page numbers to be displayed. With Microsoft Word the numbers can be formatted to start at page 2, to appear in Roman numerals, etc.

The major software packages – spreadsheets

A **spreadsheet** is a display of numerical figures, such as a financial account.

A computer spreadsheet allows the user to employ all the following features that a manual spreadsheet would not have.

- Data in a spreadsheet can be edited, duplicated and saved without having to recreate the whole document.
- Cells may contain **formulae** to allow automatic calculations.
- Accounts can be set up so that the inputting of one set of data will automatically create other accounts.
- The figures can be used to create graphs, to improve the presentation of accounting data.

A **formula** (pl **formulae**) allows mathematical calculation to be worked out using a 'code'.

The spreadsheet package that will be considered below is Microsoft Excel.

Using formulae in Excel

The formulae in Excel allow mathematical calculations to be carried out automatically. You may add, subtract, divide, multiply, create percentages, work out standard deviations, etc. Table 4.2.3 shows a calculation for pricing individual items from boxes of items. The business wants a mark up of 20 per cent and, finally, needs to add on VAT of 17.5 per cent.

Table 4.2.4 shows the formulae used to calculate the cost/item + mark up and the final price with VAT. Formulae relate to cell references and use the data in that cell. With computerised spreadsheets, a formula can be copied to a range of cells with the relative cell references being used. Notice in the first part of the price column, the formula refers to D2, D3, D4, etc. Copying E2 to E3–5 creates these cell references automatically. However, the VAT cell reference must not change; it should always be B9. This is achieved by using an **absolute cell reference**, with a $ sign on either side of the letter for the cell reference, e.g. B.

If the VAT rate is changed, or the firm decides that it wants a mark up of 25 per cent, this can be done by changing only one cell and then all the other figures will be automatically recalculated.

Many financial decisions and monitoring processes are made from accounting data and it is very useful for the business to have spreadsheets that will automatically calculate the final accounts from basic original data:

- Trial Balances created automatically from books of original entry
- Trading and Profit and Loss Accounts and Balance Sheets created automatically from the Trial Balance
- Net Present Value calculations from the discount factors and the original purchase price of investment items

Table 4.2.3 Simple pricing routine in Excel

	A	B	C	D	E
1	**Item**	**Number/box**	**Cost/box**	**Cost/item + Mark up**	**Price with VAT**
2	Reams of paper	10	12.10	1.45	1.71
3	Biros	200	20.00	0.12	0.14
4	Pencil sharpeners	50	8.30	0.20	0.23
5	Pencil cases	40	26.00	0.78	0.92
6		**Percentage**			
7	Mark up	20			
8	VAT	17.5			

Table 4.2.4 Formulae for simple pricing routine

	A	B	C	D	E
1	**Item**	**Number/box**	**Cost/box**	**Cost/item + Mark up**	**Price with VAT**
2	Reams of paper	10	12.1	= (C2/B2)*(1+$B$8/100)	=D2*(1+$B$9/100)
3	Biros	200	20	=(C3/B3)*(1+$B$8/100)	=D3*(1+$B$9/100)
4	Pencil sharpeners	50	8.3	=(C4/B4)*(1+$B$8/100)	=D4*(1+$B$9/100)
5	Pencil cases	40	26	=(C5/B5)*(1+$B$8/100)	=D5*(1+$B$9/100)
6		**Percentage**			
7	Mark up	20			
8	VAT	17.5			

- Cumulative income figures from given interest rates
- List prices with discounts, VAT, mark ups
- Calculations of Income Tax, National Insurance Contributions, pensions and other deductions to be made from staff wages and salaries

Spreadsheets such as Excel also allow 'what-if?' statements which allow the user to program the spreadsheet to highlight potential problems. For example, it might indicate that if a supplier increased the price of raw materials above a certain figure this would significantly damage profits and a new supplier should be sought, e.g.

```
=IF(D2<1.5, "Buy", "Do not buy")
```

This is saying that if the cost + mark up of the reams of paper is less than £1.50 the business should buy the paper, but not if it is over £1.50. In Table 4.2.3, it is only £1.45 so a 'Buy' instruction could be displayed in, say, column F.

The major software packages – database

A database is a file of records which can be accessed to find specific details. In businesses, it is common for firms to keep computerised databases on customers, suppliers, staff and stocks.

Databases are made up of fields (columns), records (rows) and files (tables). **Fields** indicate the different types of data stored for each record. In Table 4.2.5, the fields are surname, initials, account number, etc. A **record** holds all the details for each field for one entry, e.g. for J Williams or for M Thompson. The **file** is all the records together.

The database package will allow a wide range of functions to be carried out on the data. Two important basic functions are **find**, or search for, data and **sort** data.

Figure 4.2.9 shows how a single record could be found by using one of the field details. Here King's record has been identified by the surname, but the account number could also have been used as each account should have a unique account number. This facility is obviously very useful when there is a very large number of records.

Searches or **queries** are more complex ways of finding records. Often two or more pieces of data are being looked for at the same time. For example, the business might want to know which customers who spend over £50/week use credit cards.

This command would identify all customers whose records showed weekly spends over £49 and who paid by credit card, and produce a list of these customers, showing details of the surname, initials and account number.

Table 4.2.5 Basic customer database

field name

Surname	Initials	Account No.	Weekly spend	Payment by
Williams	J	65876	54	Debit card
Hart	F	68845	212	Credit card
King	J	62534	71	Debit card
Thompson	M	64783	45	Debit card
Patel	A	64759	108	Debit card
Greenstone	N	62555	94	Credit card
Ingham	N	66897	38	Cash
Habid	I	64500	78	Cheque

one record

whole file = all records

one field

Figure 4.2.9 Finding one record by selecting a field detail

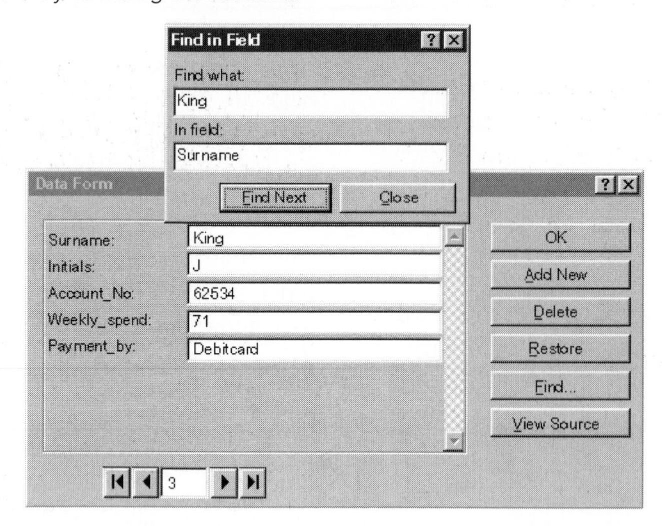

LIST Surname, Initials Account_No FOR
Weekly_spend>49. AND. Payment_by="Credit_card"

The **sort** facility allows records to be sorted by any field in the database. This can be done alphabetically for textual data, or numerically for numbers. For Table 4.2.5, the business might wish to know who spends most, so the data could be sorted with the highest weekly spenders shown first. For this table, sorting can be done simply by highlighting the column of the sort field and then clicking on the descending sort button. All the rows (records) will then be automatically reordered (as shown in Table 4.2.6) and Hart's record now appears first.

Figure 4.2.10 Sorting – ascending or descending

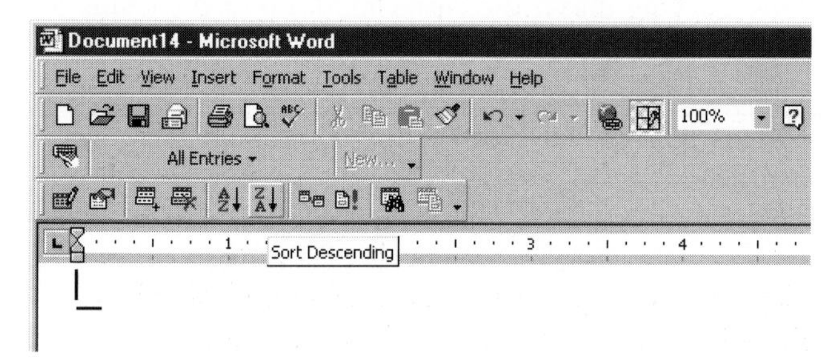

Most modern computerised databases are **relational**. This means the database comprises more than one table (file) and data within the tables are linked so that

Table 4.2.6 Basic customer database in order of Weekly_spend

Surname	Initials	Account No.	Weekly spend	Payment by
Hart	F	68845	212	Credit card
Patel	A	64759	108	Debit card
Greenstone	N	62555	94	Credit card
Habid	I	64500	78	Cheque
King	J	62534	71	Debit card
Williams	J	65876	54	Debit card
Thompson	M	64783	45	Debit card
Ingham	N	66897	38	Cash

reports and queries can relate to data from all relevant tables.

With compatible software packages, such as Microsoft, someone using a database in Word could also access data from files kept in Access or Excel, e.g. to find the price of a ream of paper (as on Table 4.2.3) using the Find option to access the data from the file in Excel as follows:

- Click on 'Insert Database' from the database toolbar.
- Click on the 'Get Data' button.
- Choose the data file from the listed files as you would when opening any file.
- Use query options to specify what data is wanted.

See Figure 4.2.11.

The major software packages – graphics

A graphic facility allows the user to create and edit diagrams, pictures, graphs, etc. Some packages are dedicated graphics package, such as CorelDraw and PaintShopPro. Others are part of another facility, e.g. Excel has a chart facility which creates graphs and diagrams from spreadsheet data. Microsoft Word and Excel both have a drawing toolbar that allows the user to create basic shapes. Microsoft Word also has a WordArt facility for creating special effects with words (see Figure 4.2.12).

Graphics are a valuable tool in communication. They often make the message easier to understand and they help to break up text and make it more interesting for the reader. Textbooks, reports, even letters and memos now often contain some form of graphic, e.g. a logo, or a map or a series of sales graphs.

Figure 4.2.12 Special effects using WordArt

Diagrams (such as Figure 4.2.13) may be relatively simple and constructed, using the basic drawing tool toolbar. This is relatively quick and easy to do and is fully compatible with the word-processing program.

Graphs and diagrams created in Excel can look more professional because the software program has been set up to produce good diagrams and charts from the numerical data. Figure 4.2.14 shows examples of the types of charts that can be created. All have been created from the same data.

The more professional graphics packages produce very high quality artwork, some of which can be created by relatively inexperienced users by following the help facilities. See Figure 4.2.15. Other effects require both a good knowledge of the graphics package and some artistic flair!

For some professions, the use of sophisticated graphics packages is vital, as the list below indicates.

Figure 4.2.11 Accessing data from Word

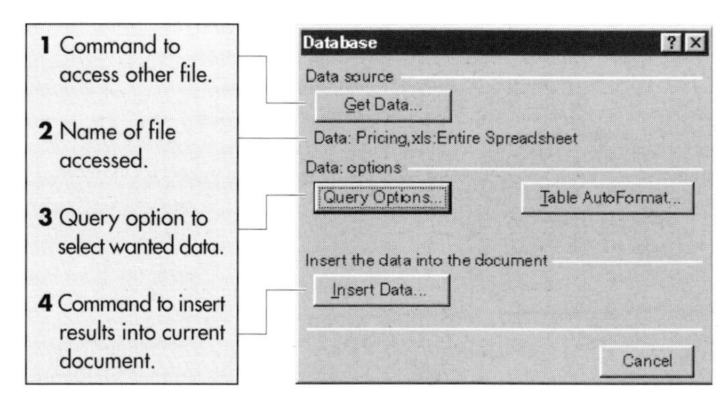

- Designers and architects produce very accurate drawings using **computer-aided design** (CAD) packages.
- Producers of titles for films and television use advanced graphics packages for the animation of text and graphics.
- Professional designers of web pages integrate text and graphics so that the web pages are both attractive and functional.
- Publishers of magazines, brochures and leaflets combine text and graphics so that their publications will stand out in a highly competitive market.

Figure 4.2.13 The effect of a tariff and a quota on imported products – an example of a simple line drawing

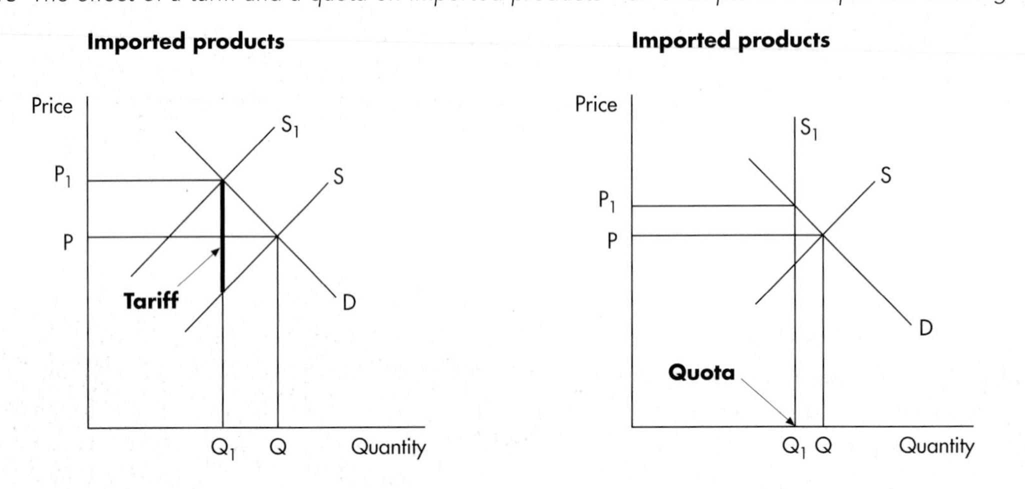

Figure 4.2.14 Examples of some graphical options available in Excel

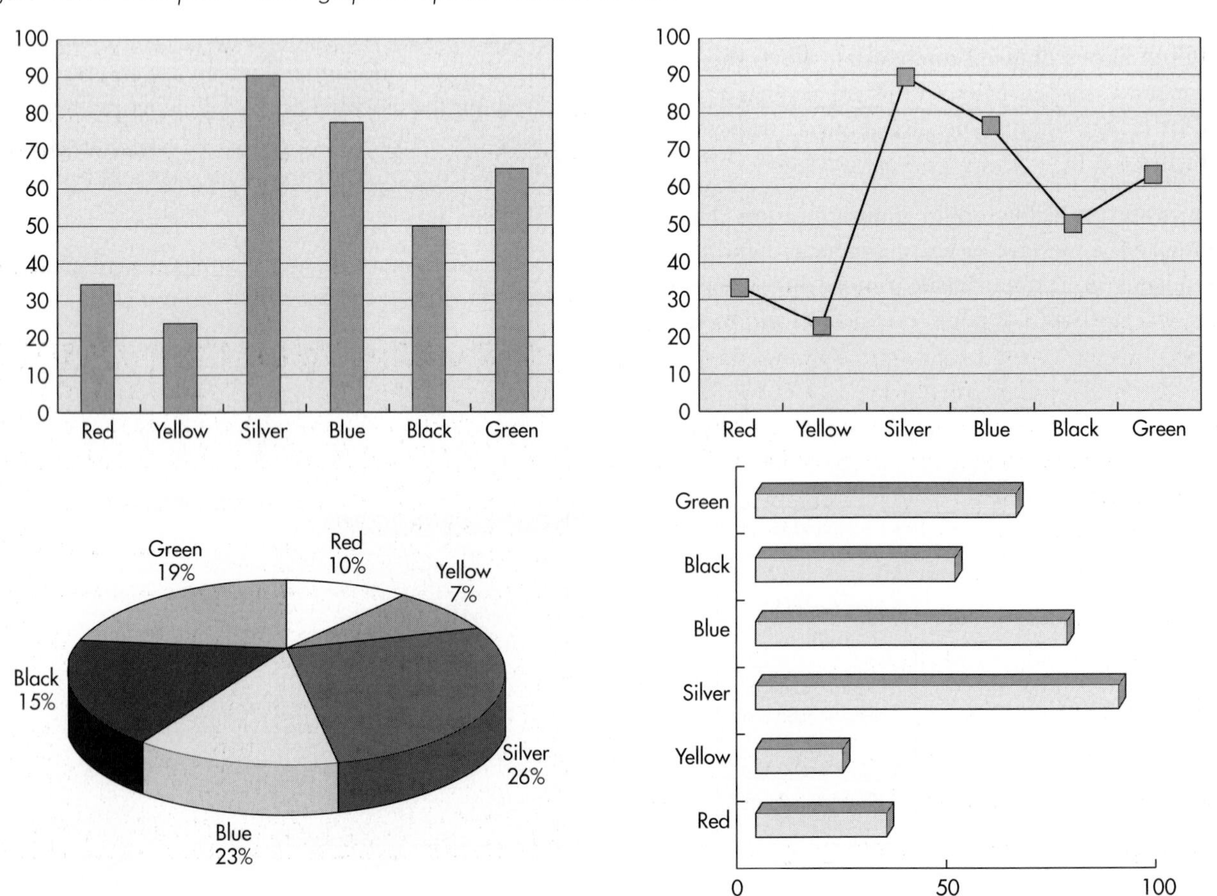

Figure 4.2.15 Graphic created using Bryce

Other common packages and facilities

The uses and developments of ICT are growing at a phenomenal rate. Below is just a brief mention of some of them.

Scheduling

Many general packages offer the possibility of drawing up a schedule of planned activities and informing other members of staff of timings of meeting, trips, important events, etc. This is called **scheduling**. For this to be effective, the computers need to be on the appropriate network so that the schedule can be posted and all staff who need access to it will either be informed or can check the schedule for themselves. In Microsoft Word, this facility can be used by:

- clicking on the drop down menu 'Tools'
- selecting the 'Online Collaboration' option
- selecting 'Schedule Meeting'
- filling in the 'My Information' section
- saving in a file to which all relevant staff have access.

The message can be sent or read through e-mail and Microsoft Outlook. Outlook provides the connection with the other users if e-mail is to be used, and the connections will have to be set up in Outlook first. (See Figure 4.2.16.) Where internal LAN systems are being

Figure 4.2.16 NetMeeting screen from Microsoft Outlook Express

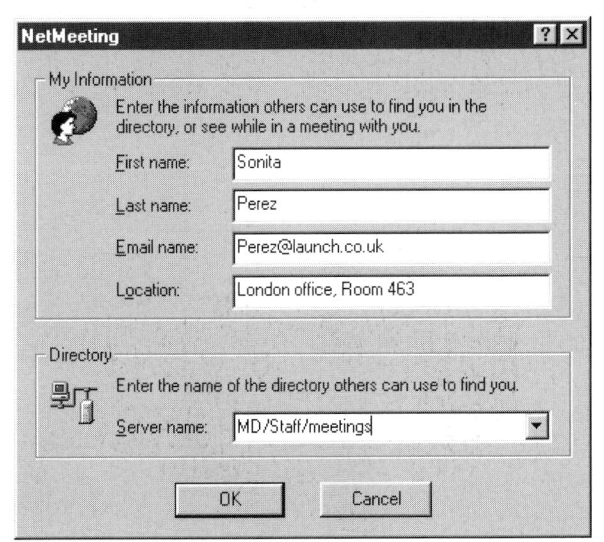

used, **bulletin boards** and e-mail delivery systems can be set up so that all staff receive details.

Many schedules are planned well ahead and have to fit in with other staff commitments. To ensure that these do not conflict and lead to double bookings, missed meetings and considerable anger and frustration, meetings and other activities are frequently noted on a centrally available calendar. This ensures that staff cannot book themselves into two events at the same time, but it also allows managers, their assistants or any administrative staff to check if everyone who needs to be present at a meeting can actually attend. This facility is known as **calendaring.**

Presentation slides

In the past, presentations from management to staff, or from businesses to customers, used to rely upon on pre-printed materials, OHPs and flip charts, etc. Today, many businesses use computer-generated slides to enhance their presentations.

The slides are created individually and then linked together so that they can be presented one after the other at the click of a button. This technique is used by television weather forecasters.

Packages such as PowerPoint allow users to create slides using simple text and graphics editing. Users can also import graphics, pictures, etc., from other packages and support the slides with basic animation and sounds.

E-mail

E-mail (electronic mail) provides an electronic version of a paper-based mail system. It can carry out all the functions of ordinary mail but combines this with the many advantages of a computerised system:

- It is very much faster.
- It can send multiple messages all at the same time.
- It allows the receiver to copy, edit, download, reply, etc., all on the computer.
- It is cheaper because all the data is sent electronically.
- Files can be attached and downloaded by the recipient.
- Senders can be informed automatically if the message has not been received.
- It is usually combined with an address book to allow the user to compose, address and send messages easily.

To send e-mails, the business will need a modem and internet connection. Only very large firms have their own internet service facility, so most businesses will also need to subscribe to an **internet service provider** (ISP) who will also provide a facility to store messages before they are passed on, and a connection to the internet itself and the world wide web.

Figure 4.2.17 Emailing using Outlook Express

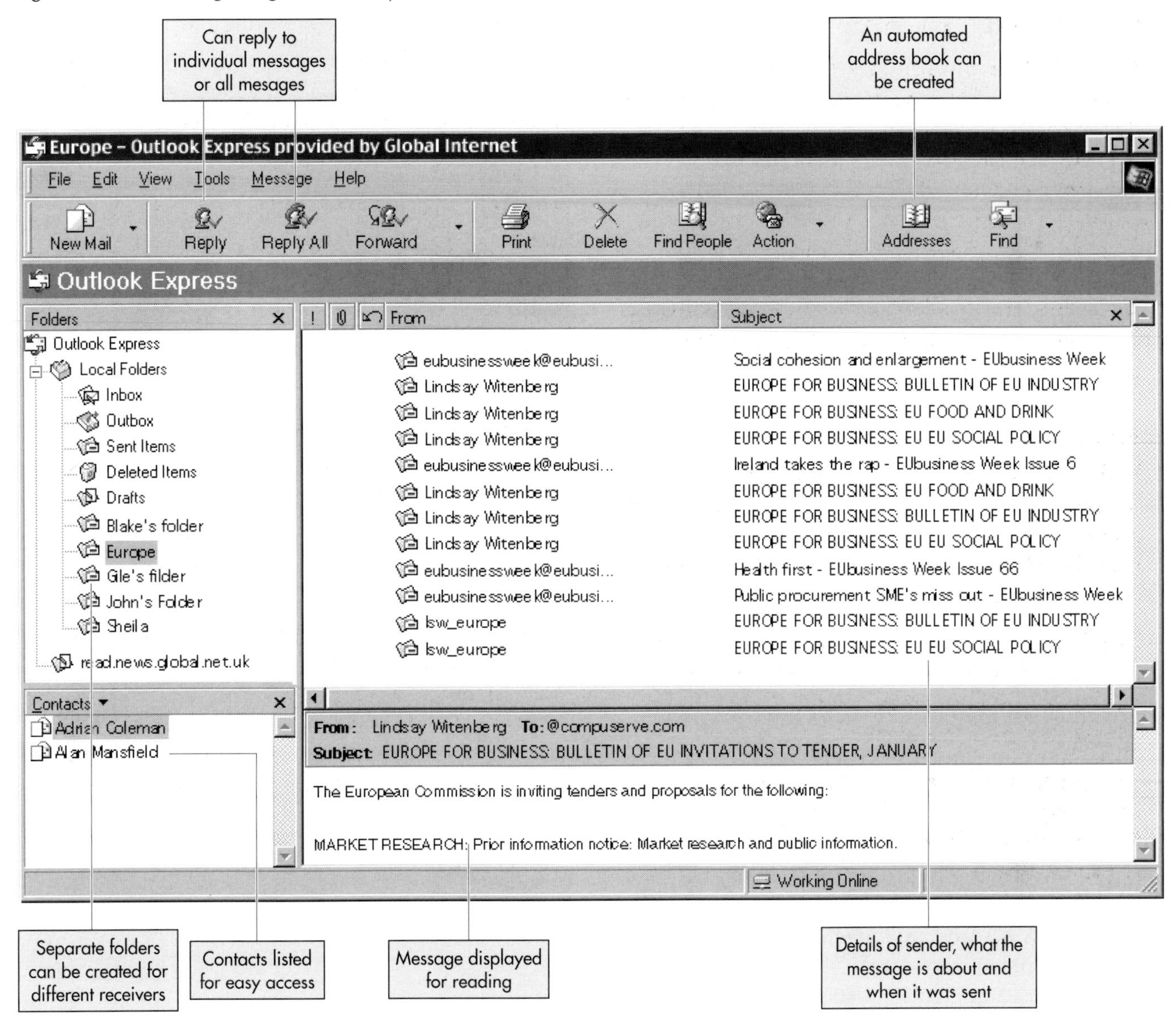

CHAPTER 3

The Internet

KEY TERMS:

Bookmarking
Data Protection Act
E-commerce
E-mail
E-mail file attachments
Internet service provider (ISP)
Legal and security aspects
Modem
Search engines
Web browsers
Web pages
Web sites
World wide web (www)

In this chapter, you will learn about the internet and some of the major business uses of it. You will also be given basic guidance on how to access the internet and use it effectively.

This chapter will look at the meaning of the internet, the meaning and use of the world wide web, the use of e-mails and the importance of e-commerce.

What is the internet?

The internet is a communication network that connects computers and users across the world. The computers are connected by phone lines, cables, satellite links, radio waves, etc. Before users can connect to the internet they usually need a **modem** and an **internet service provider** (ISP).

The internet allows users to carry out various activities, many of which involve businesses, but a growing number of users access the internet purely for social communication:

- The world wide web (www)
- **E-mails**
- Chat-lines
- Newsgroups
- **E-commerce.**

A **modem** converts the information that is stored on a computer into an electronic signal that can be transmitted to another modem. The second modem converts the information back into its original format so that the receiver's computer understands it.

An **internet service provider (ISP)** provides the connections which allow people to communicate through the internet.

E-mail (electronic mail) allows written messages to be sent via the internet.

E-commerce allows people to buy and sell products via the internet.

This chapter looks at the parts of the internet that are most important to business: the world wide web, e-mails and e-commerce.

Figure 4.3.1 How users connect to the internet and to other users

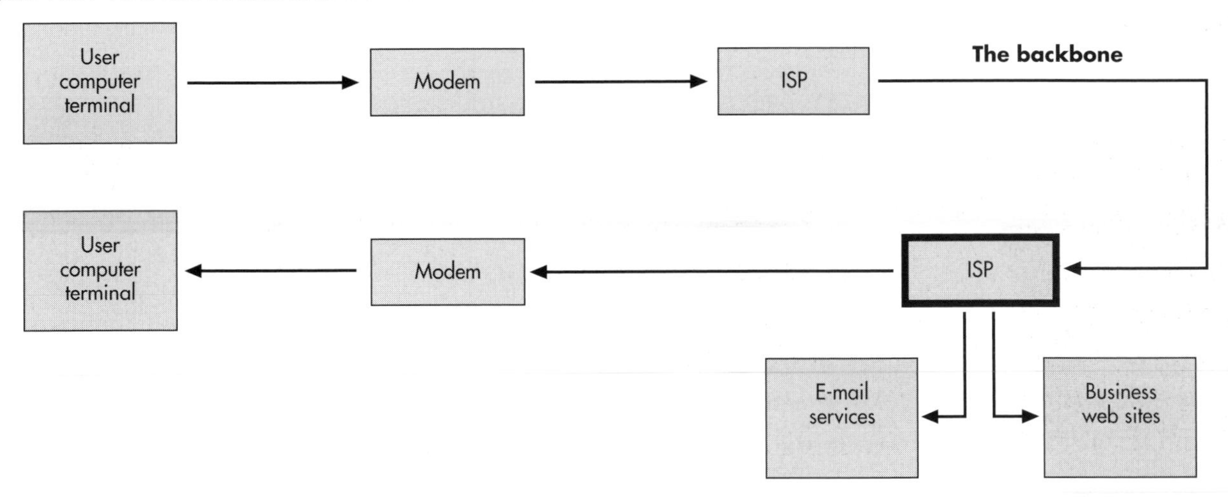

Internet Service Providers (ISP)

The internet is rapidly becoming the major form of business and personal communication between individuals, firms and organisations, especially where people are in different locations. For many businesses and individuals the two most important factors are:

- that the communication is **fast**
- that it is available **24 hours a day**.

For individual users, and most businesses, the cost of keeping communication links open 24 hours a day is usually too expensive. For high-speed transmission, communications need to be open all the time and they also need expensive connections to ensure that the messages are passed on as fast as possible.

The major links, which carry messages across countries and across the world (called **backbone network services**), transmit data at 9.6 billion bits per second. For many messages, that is essentially instantaneous. In a world where 'time is money', businesses need to be linked to this backbone via connections that operate almost as fast. Individually, they cannot afford to do this unless they are very large businesses, but ISPs provide the links for them.

ISPs specialise in providing users with a 24-hour connection to the internet and advanced technological connection, such as fibre optic cables, satellite or an ISDN (integrated services digital network) lines, which mean that message are transmitted very rapidly. Because these ISPs also provide connections for households, many of the providers are very well known, such as AOL (America On Line), Global Internet, and Compuserve. Connections are now also offered through large companies such as BT, Dixons and Tesco.

The world wide web (www)

The **world wide web** is only one part of the internet but it is the part that is growing fastest and the one that most people think about when the term 'internet' is used. The world wide web is like a giant spider's web of interconnected pages of data which users can access through their internet connections.

The **world wide web** is a huge network of data which can be accessed through the internet.

Web pages contain data in the form of pictures, text, sound and even video. They also frequently contain links to other pages and other **web sites** – internet addresses where web pages will be found.

To access the world wide web, the user needs these facilities:

- A computer
- A **web browser** software package
- A modem
- Connection to the internet (see Figure 4.3.1)

Figure 4.3.2 A web page for Longman, written in HTML

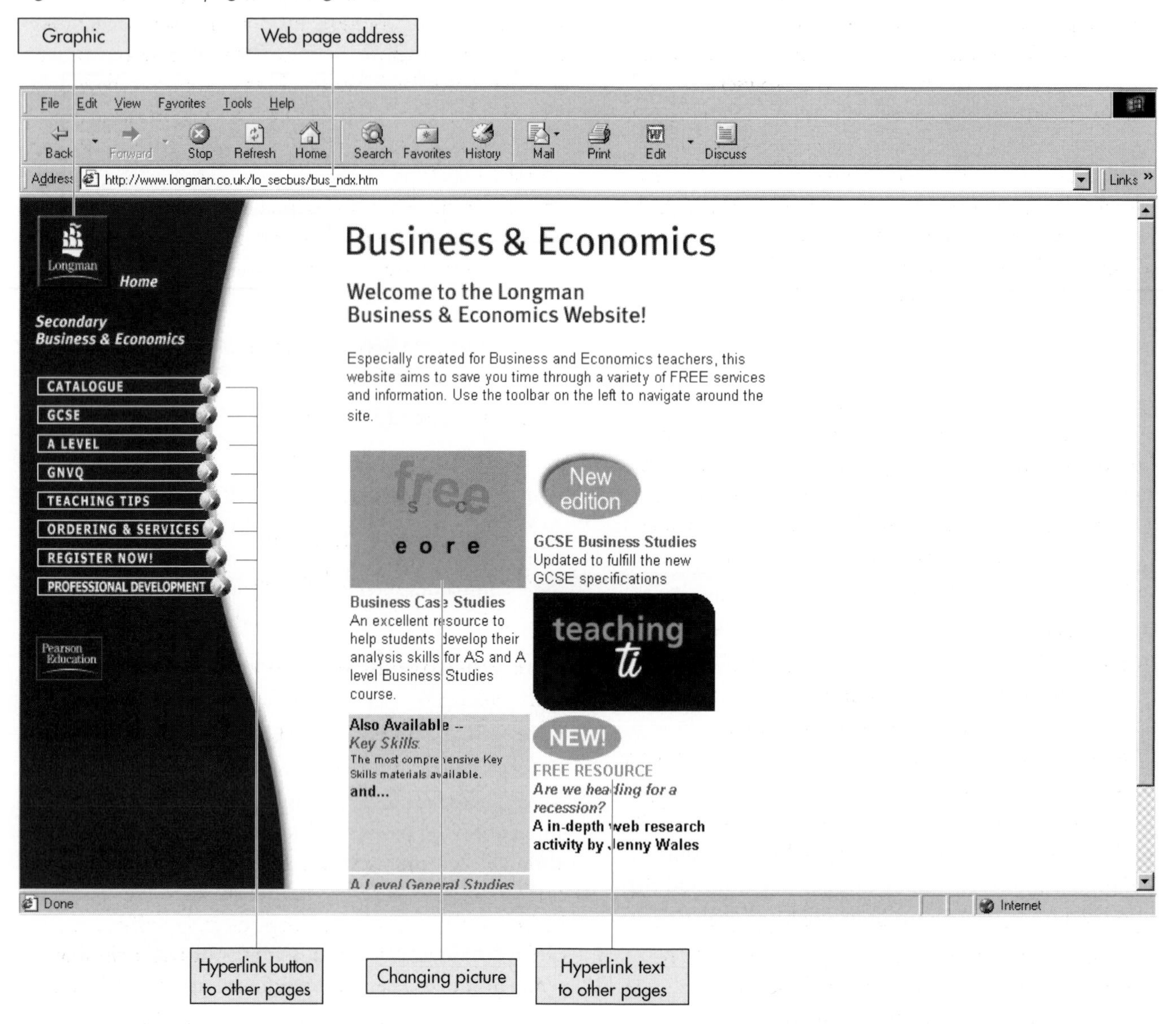

- Possibly a **search engine**
- A web host server
- Web pages and links (hyperlinks)

A **web browser** is a tool or package which allows users of the internet to connect to a website.

A **search engine** is a tool which helps users of the internet to find websites.

Web browsers

A web browser is a software package that allows users to connect to a web site through the internet and then receives the web pages and displays them on the user's computer. Today, it is possible to connect to the web from many different packages, such as word-processing packages, through the browser to the web pages you want. The most commonly used browsers are Internet Explorer and Netscape.

Web page data is written in a language called hypertext markup language (HTML) and the browser will read this language and display the data in a form that the user understands, as shown in Figure 4.3.3. The coding used in HTML tells the browser whether the data is text, graphics, video, etc., and also how and where to display the data on the user's computer. Some data on web pages cannot be accessed by the browsers and will require additional software applications before the data can be viewed. A very common example of this is 'PDF' files which need the Adobe Acrobat Reader before they can be viewed. This reader is available free through the internet, but it only allows the user to view the file, not to edit it. The full, purchase, version of Adobe Acrobat can be used to create and edit PDF files.

Search engines

Finding and connecting to the web page that you want is rather like finding someone's address or telephone number and then contacting them and receiving a reply. In the case of web pages, however, there are millions of addresses and hundreds of millions of pages which can be downloaded and viewed. Finding the right address can therefore be difficult.

For addresses known to the user, all the user has to do to contact the site is to connect to the ISP and type in the web site address. Each site has a name (its **domain name**) and an address (known as a **web uniform resource locator** (URL)). Typical web site addresses are www.hm-treasury.gov.uk and www.dixons.co.uk, which will bring up the web sites as in Figure 4.3.3. Having contacted the web site, downloading the web page is very simple.

For people who do not know the address of the web site, especially when searching for new material, indexes of specialist topics and more general indexes are available at **http://ukdirectory.com** and **http://www.yahoo.co.uk.** These include millions of items but the user needs a way of searching: a search engine.

Search engines – sometimes referred to as 'search tools', 'web crawlers' or 'spiders' – have stores of the millions of web sites, all classified in terms of the main topics that they deal with. Anyone wanting to find a particular topic or site will type in key words and the search engine will then search through its database, find relevant sites and display a list of them. Figure 4.3.4 shows the first result of a search for holiday homes in France. The search via Alta Vista found 30 web pages which specifically used the phrase 'holiday homes in France'.

None of the major search engines charge either individuals or businesses for using their search facilities, but it clearly costs them a great deal of time and money to create their databases and keep them up to date. Their money is made by selling advertising space on their web sites which will be seen by everyone who logs on for a search. As million of users log on, selling advertising space is very profitable. This has also encouraged many new providers of search engines to join the more traditional providers. The following firms are providers of on-line search facilities:

- Alta Vista at **www.altavista.com/** or **www.uk.altavista.com/**
- Lycos at **www.lycos.co.uk/**
- Excite at **www.excite.com/**
- Yahoo at **uk.yahoo.com/**
- Google at **www.google.com/**
- Ask Jeeves at **www.ask.co.uk/**
- WebCrawler at **www.webcrawler.com/**

When searching for specific data it is vital that the right questions are asked. If only one word is being used then this can be typed into the search box, e.g.

bized

This will create a search for all references in the search engine's database for all sites that use this term including the Biz/ed home page itself. Good search engines prioritise the most important sites, including home pages. Where more than one word is used, e.g.

population figures for the EU

most search engines will look for all of the main words separately. References will come up for 'population', 'figures' and 'EU'. If the whole phrase is put in inverted commas then the search engine should try to match the whole phrase.

Conjunctions OR, AND and NOT can be used to refine searches, limiting what the search engine looks for. On Alta Vista typing in different words results in the following number of pages being located for UK GDP data.

Figure 4.3.3 Sample web pages accessed by typing in the web address

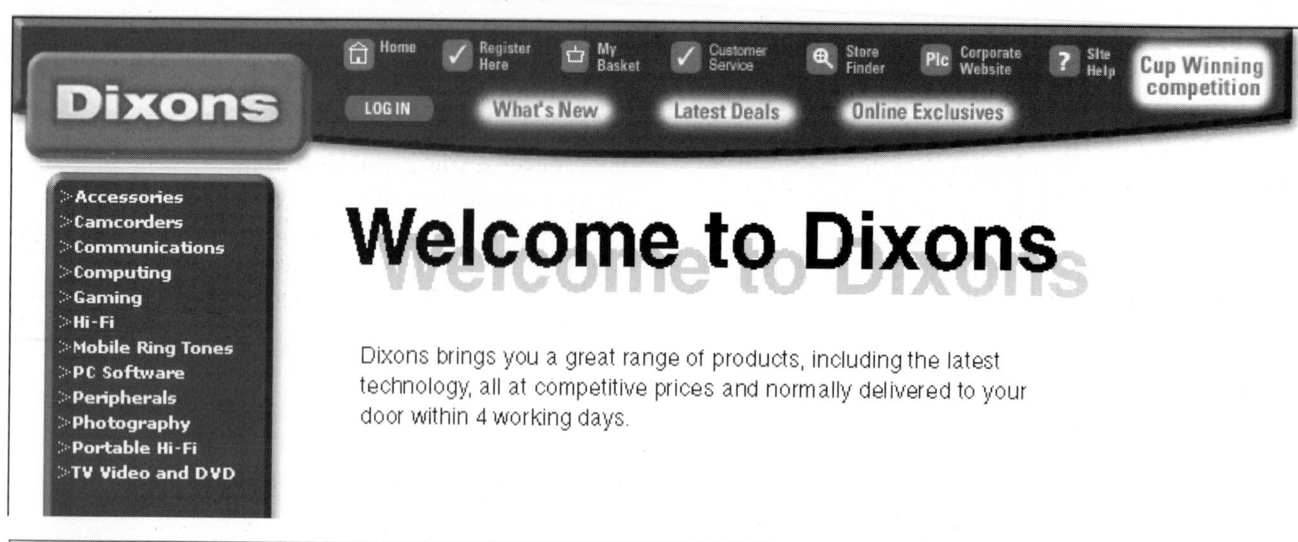

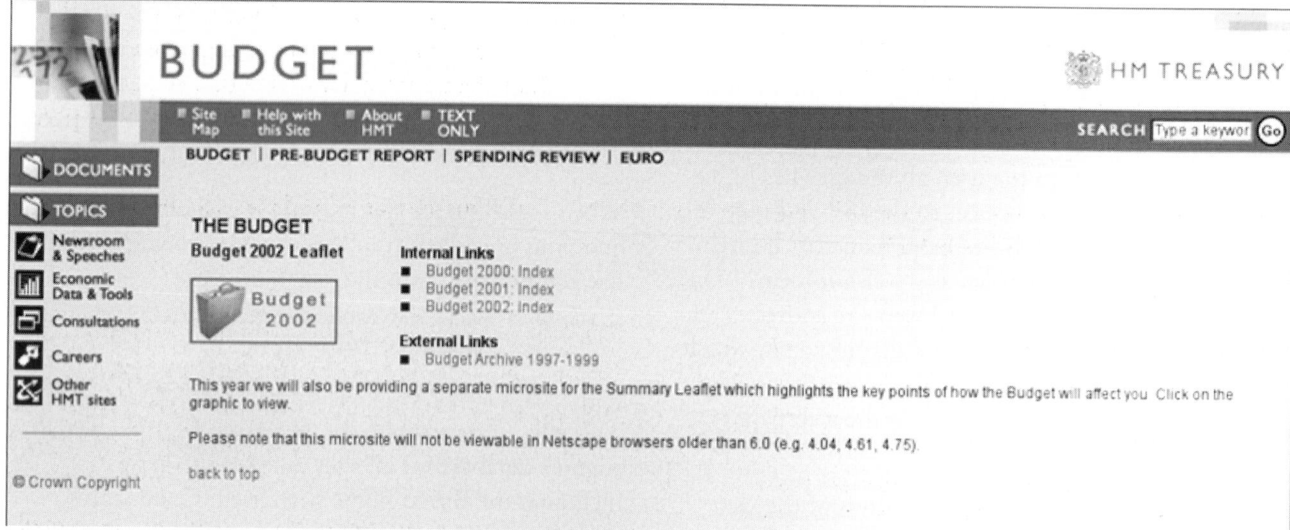

Figure 4.3.4 Using the Alta Vista search engine

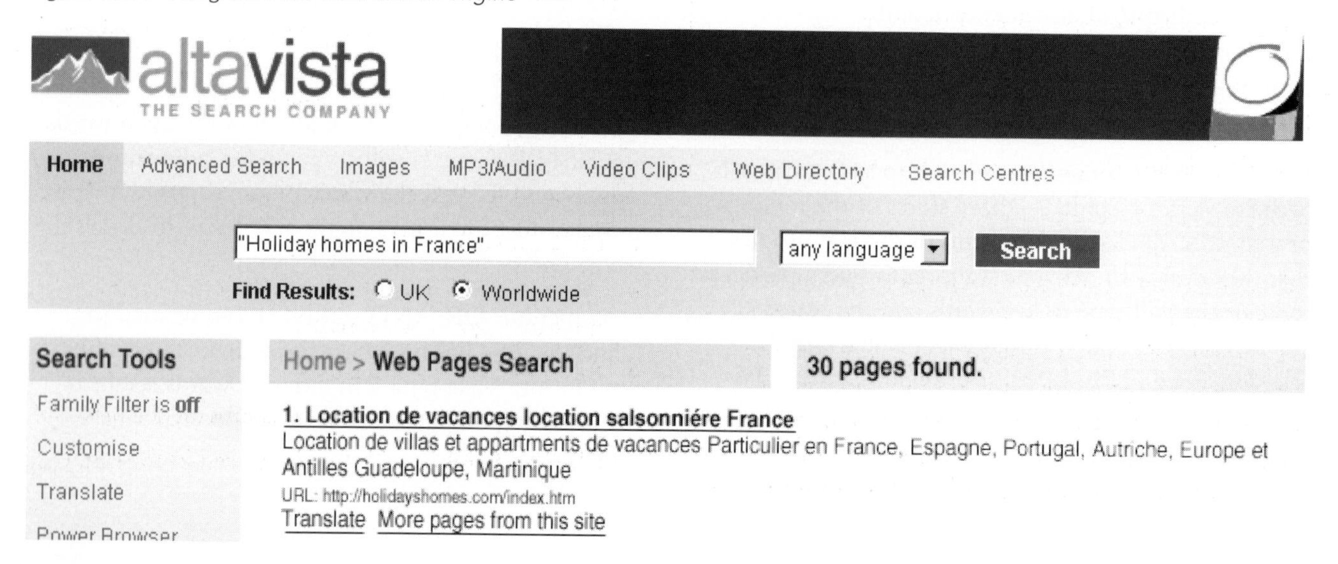

GDP	locates 295309 pages
GDP AND UK	locates 36963 pages
GDP in the UK	locates 99 pages
'GDP in the UK' AND figures	locates 36 pages

Even then, these may not be the best pages and better data would be found by going to the Biz/ed site, the ONS site or even the Eurstat site.

Bookmarking/favourites

Bookmarking – placing addresses that are used often in a file for easy access

Searching the web can be a very time-consuming process and when you have found a really useful site you do not want to waste time searching for it again the next time you need it. You could simply note the address. Alternatively, you can use the computer software to **bookmark** it for you.

Using 'favourites' in Internet Explorer.

To add a web page:

- Access the web page.
- Click on the **favourites** drop down menu.
- Click on **add to favourites**.
- Choose the folder where the details are to be stored, or create a new folder.
- Save the address with a suitable file name.

To connect to the web site from favourites:

- Click on the **favourites** drop down menu.
- Go to folder, subdirectory, where address is stored.
- Click on the file (web page) that is to be loaded.

When web sites are bookmarked, their addresses are placed in a file, i.e. your own directory system. To access the site another time, you need not go through the search process again, you just go to the bookmarked files, select the address that you want and load it. Figure 4.3.5 shows some bookmarked files for Internet Explorer. (Note that the US spelling is favorites.)

Web addresses can also be placed within data, such as a word-processed text. In many packages, such as Microsoft Word, this is done automatically as the address is keyed in. For example, keying www.altavista.com/. the characters will turn blue and be underlined www.altavista.com/.

To download the page, however, the computer must be connected to the internet.

By clicking on this underlined text the software will immediately try to connect to the Altavista web site.

E-mail

Electronic mail (e-mail) is like the normal postal service except that messages are sent between computer terminals. Messages can be sent internally around the same business or they can be sent externally all over the world. Like the postal system, each user requires a unique e-mail address. This uses the @ symbol as part of the address:

joesomeone@globalnet.co.uk

The user's name, which can be anything the user chooses.

The host name where the e-mail account holder has an internet account.

To send an e-mail, the user needs to load up the e-mail software and write the message to be sent. E-mail software packages have features that allow the user to open and save files, edit, copy, format, check spelling, etc. The main features are for creating message (see Figure 4.3.6), sending and receiving messages and searching for messages.

To create new messages (Figure 4.3.7):

- Click on **New Mail**.
- Fill in the addresses of the people to whom the message is going to be sent.
- Write the e-mail message.
- Attach any files that are to be sent with the message.
- Click on **Send** (it will then be placed in the outbox).

Figure 4.3.5 Favourites directory in Internet Explorer

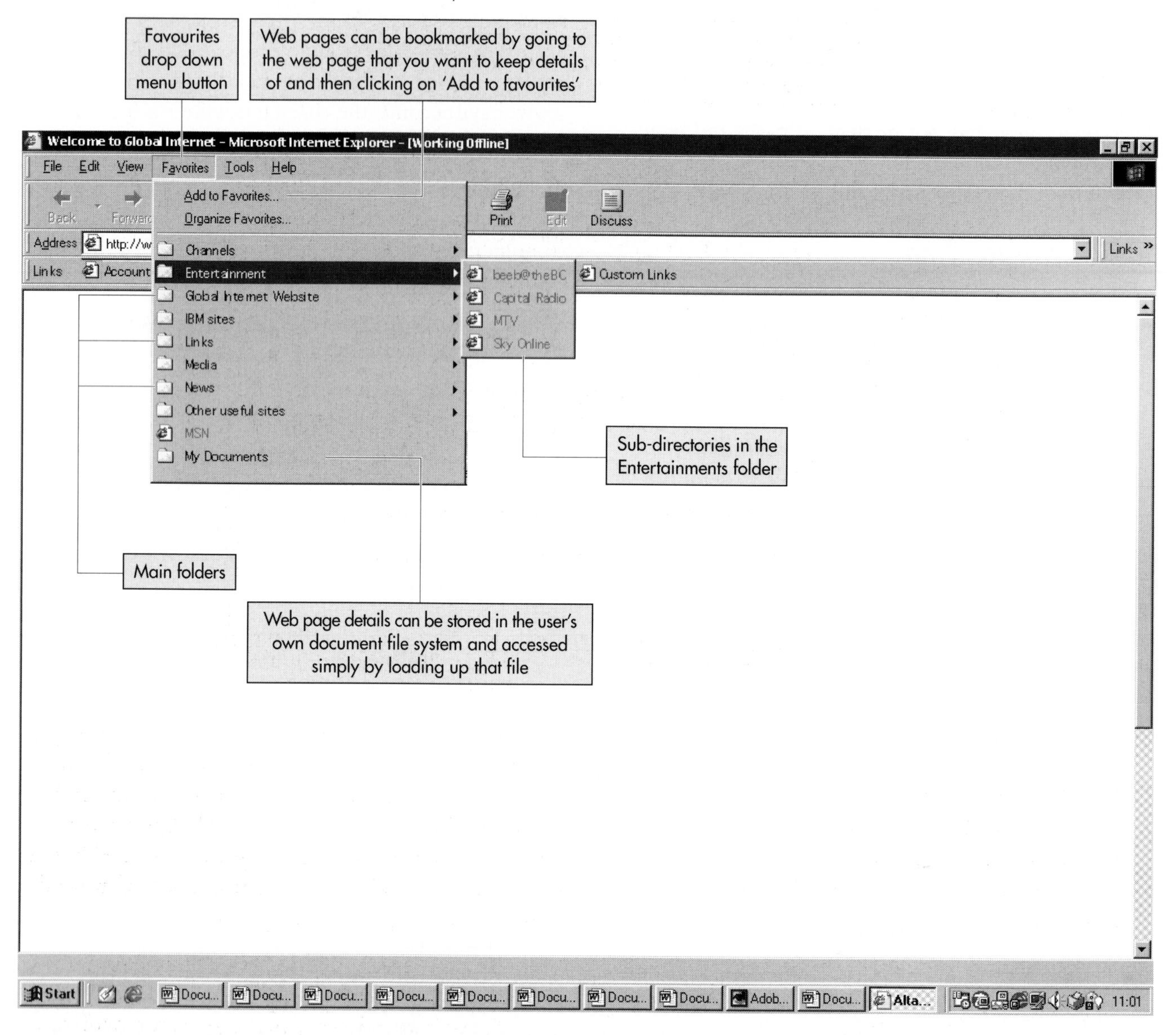

Figure 4.3.6 Some main facilities of Outlook Express

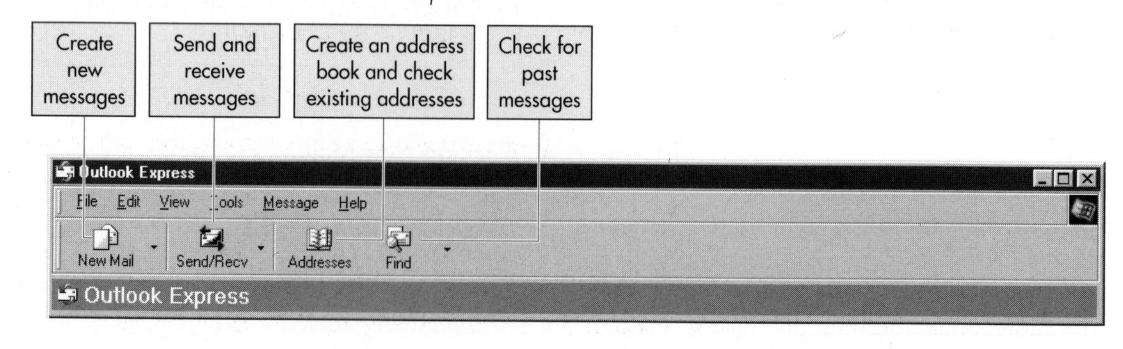

Figure 4.3.7 Creating a message in Outlook Express

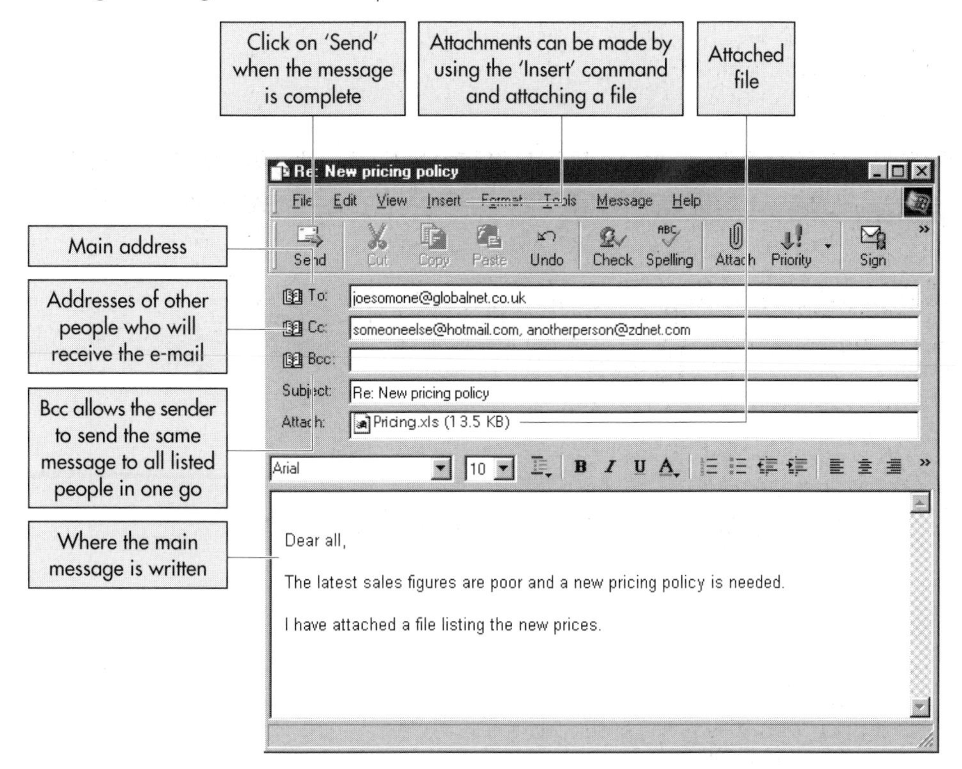

To send and receive e-mails:

- Connect to the internet.
- Click on **Send/Recv**. This will send all messages waiting in the outbox and receive all messages and place them in the folders to which they are addressed.

To set up or find or edit addresses:

- Click on **Addresses**.
- Use the buttons and drop down menus to create new addresses, edit old ones, find contacts, print addresses, etc. (Figure 4.3.8).

To search for past messages (Figure 4.3.9):

- Click on **Find**.
- Enter details of the message that is being looked for.
- Click on **Find Now**.

The address book can also be set up to allow contacts to be shared by different users. This also means that when messages are received they will automatically be sent to all users connected to the shared area. This is very useful for sending and receiving general messages.

Finding past messages can be done in a variety of ways. If you know who the message was to or from, this can be typed in. If you know any word that was written in the main subject line, this can be used. Alternatively, typing in any main word or phrase that was used in the message itself will pick out all messages with that word or phrase in it, e.g. 'EU social policy'.

The search can be made very specific by typing in a combination of details such as who it was from, a word from the subject section and a phrase from the message section. It can be refined further by limited the dates between which it was received and whether or not it had an attachment or was flagged.

Advantages of using e-mail

The use of e-mail by both individuals and businesses is now commonplace. In businesses, it has almost totally replaced the fax machine and, to some extent, it has also replaced the old postal and telephone services for many messages. The reason way it has become so popular is because it has many advantages:

- It is very fast, operating at the speed of the telephone, cable or satellite link.

Figure 4.3.8 The address book facility in Outlook Express

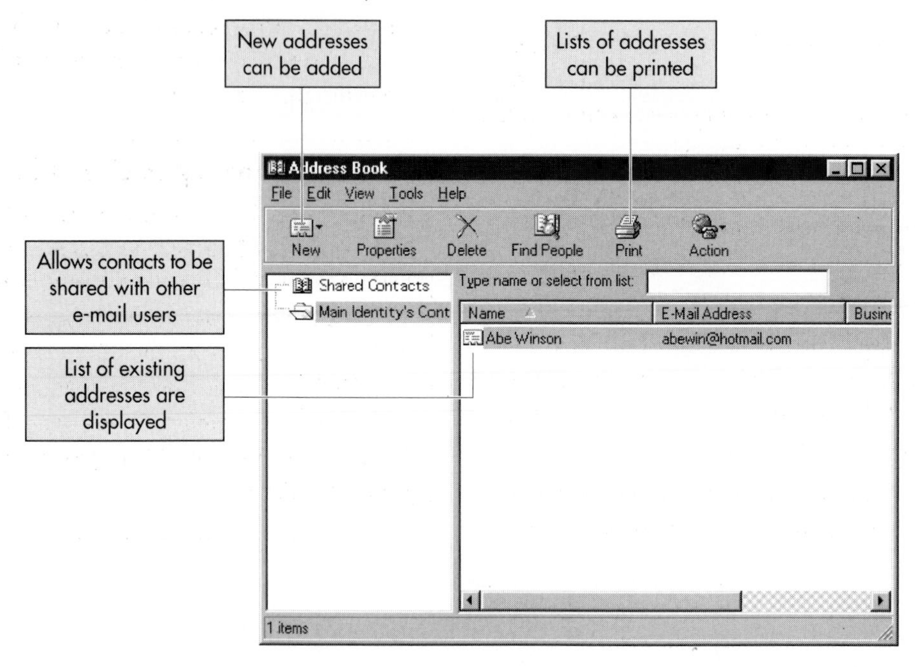

Figure 4.3.9 Finding past messages in Outlook Express

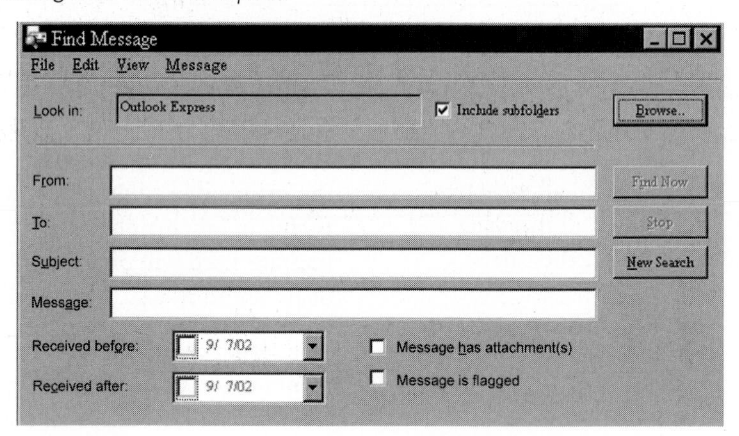

- The way that e-mail messages are written tends to be much less formal than traditional business letters and this allows them to be written and sent more quickly.
- It can carry huge amounts of data, especially with attachments, and this makes it cheap to use.
- Messages are stored in the ISP's mailbox waiting for the receiver to log on.
- Messages can be sent to tens, hundreds, even millions of people all at the same time.
- Because messages are received into the computer they can immediately be read, editing, saved, printed out, etc.

Disadvantages of using email

- The receiver may not read the message immediately, whereas when communication is by telephone the sender knows whether the message has been received and may expect an immediate reply.
- Often, junkmail is sent through e-mail and it can be time-consuming sorting out what is important. It is possible to set up the e-mail so that it will only accept messages from known sources.
- Sometimes message come with viruses attached. These are usually only annoying, but sometimes they can destroy vital data on the computer, and, in the worst cases, make the computer unusable.
- Messages can be intercepted and read by people who should not have access to personal or sensitive data.

It is possible to set up password systems and to use encrypted messages that can only be read by those with the key to turn the encryption back into meaningful language.

Viruses still coming thick and fast

Two key dates for the launch, or spread, of new viruses have been April Fools Day and any Friday the 13th. The Melissa virus arrived at the end of March 1999 via the e-mail and, if opened by users, had the ability to destroy the user's hard drive. The I Love You virus of May 2000 shut down computers across the world and caused over £6 million pounds worth of damage. The Anna Kournikova virus of February 2001 was potentially just as damaging.

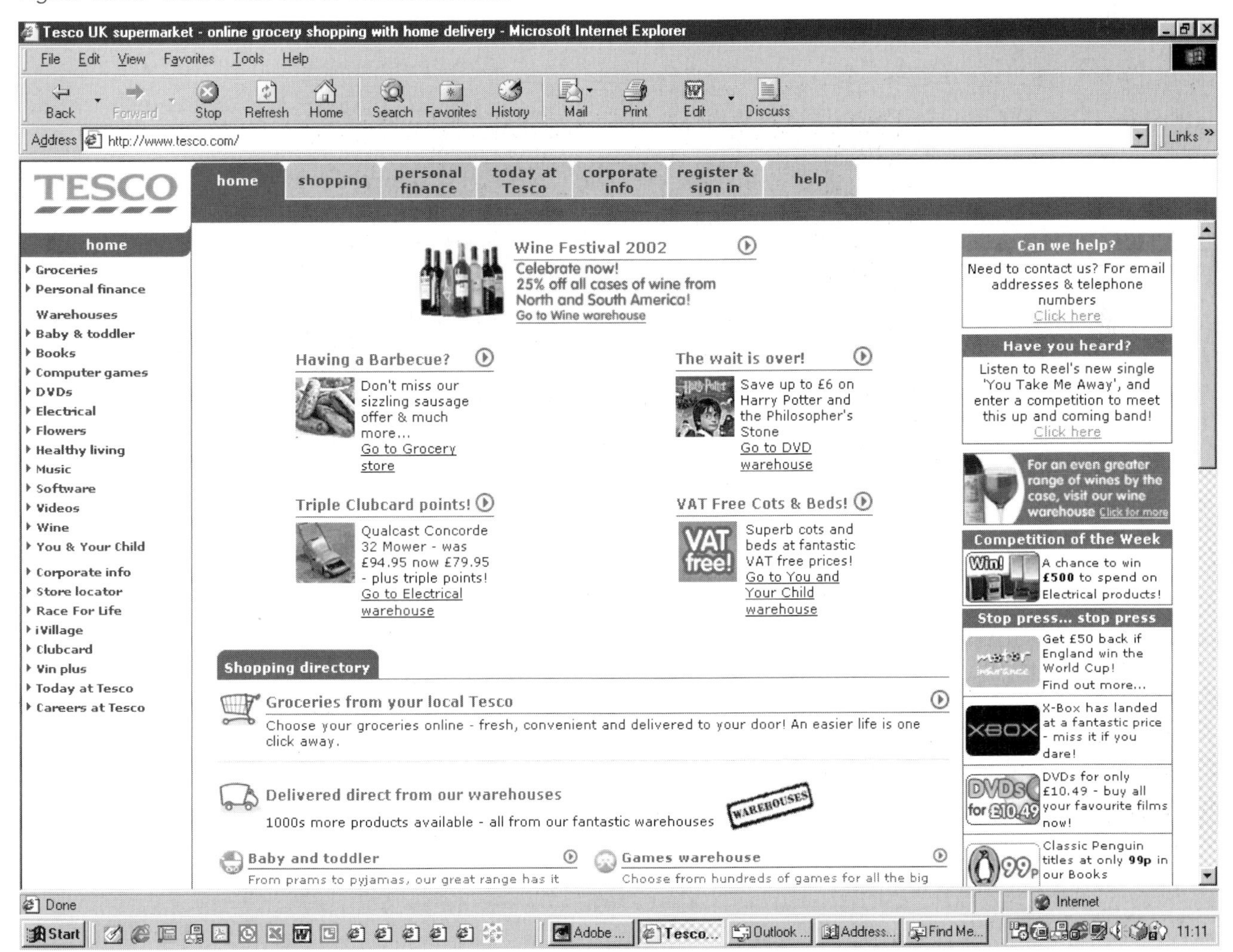

Figure 4.3.10 Tesco's web site at www.tesco.co.uk

E-commerce

Many web sites provide details of how huge the term e-commerce has now become, e.g. check out: **www.wilsonweb.com/**

E-commerce (or electronic commerce) has a variety of meanings, which is often the case when a new and popular term first appears and is then used by different interest groups. We consider the term e-commerce only as it relates to trading on the internet:

- Advertising to customers using web pages
- Sending e-mail shots to new or existing customers, offering them goods or services
- Selling goods and services on-line
- Accepting payments on-line
- Carrying out market research on-line
- Providing customers with support and information for products already bought
- Using the internet to confirm details with other firms, as travel agents do, when selling goods or services to customers

For small companies, there are great benefits in using the internet for contacting customers and selling products. The cost of creating web pages and establishing a presence on the internet is relatively low. It also has the benefits that premises, advertising and vast stocks are not required. Businesses can respond to customer inquiries as they come in and provide products on demand.

The rapid growth of internet companies scared the major companies and they responded by setting up e-commerce facilities of their own. Most major businesses in the world now have internet sites and many of them offer their customers the option of buying products on-line

The advantages of e-commerce for businesses

- The internet and the world wide web are international and connect businesses to literally millions of potential customers.
- The cost of creating and maintaining web pages is relatively low.
- Many customers, especially in businesses such as banking, now expect internet services. This provides an audience for selling additional products.
- Businesses can operate solely on the internet and this means that they do not need expensive offices or shops. Instead of premises all around the country, or the world, they can operate from a single location and that location can be anywhere they please.
- Companies with popular web sites which are visited by large numbers of users can sell advertising space to other businesses.
- The internet is available 24 hours a day and this allows customers to buy when they want.

The barriers to e-commerce

Although the advantages of e-commerce are potentially very great there are also major barriers.

- The use of the internet requires some technical knowledge:

  How to set up web pages

  How to protect customers who are paying by credit or debit card

  What laws and regulations govern trade on the internet
- Because there are millions and millions of web pages and addresses, it can be difficult, initially, to make customers aware that your business exists.
- Where customers are not asked to pay in advance, especially if they are in different countries, it may be very difficult to obtain payment if they simply do not pay. On the other hand, the customers may refuse to buy from the business if it insists on being paid in advance.
- Many potential customers do not trust the internet because they are worried that details about their credit or debit cards might be intercepted by criminals and used to withdraw funds from their accounts illegally.
- Businesses can be affected by viruses, technical failures, etc., and if the internet is the only way in which they trade, this can stop all sales completely until the problem is resolved.
- Where businesses are successful on the internet, it is very easy for other firms to copy what they do and compete their advantage away.

Help available to businesses developing e-commerce

For businesses that are uncertain about how the internet operates and how to set up e-commerce facilities, there is a vast amount of support available. Many businesses now offer other businesses the expertise required to set up e-commerce facilities. Advice and services are available through books, on-line support centres, specialist businesses and government support agencies:

- Businesses which will design, create and service every aspect of e-commerce for the business
- Advice on how to create web pages (including the required programming) that will be attractive to customers and effective in providing persuasive information
- Advice on how to set up a payments system for the internet and how to protect customers from hackers intercepting personal and financial data
- Full details of the legal requirements and controls related to trading on the internet

> **UK online for business** provides advice for small and medium-sized businesses, including general advice on e-commerce and details of important changes that are occuring in the regulations.
>
> UK Online for Business can be found at **www.ukonlineforbusiness.gov.uk/**

Major legal issues of using the internet

The internet is considered by many as the last totally free system of communication in the world where there are few or no rules and regulations governing what can and cannot be transmitted. For some businesses and users, this is almost true. Many of the laws that protect customers and individuals inside countries cannot be used to protect people from what is being done in other countries. For businesses within the UK, selling to the UK, many of the general laws of commerce apply equally to using the internet:

- The Trade Descriptions Act 1968
- The Sale of Goods Act 1979
- The Sale and Supply of Goods Act 1994

There are also laws that relate more specifically to the use of computers and the internet:

- The Copyright, Designs and Patents Act 1988
- The Computer Misuse Act 1990
- The Data Protection Act 1998

The Copyright, Designs and Patents Act 1988

This Act extends the rights already given to authors, designers, inventors, etc., in the non-computer world, to people who create computer programs. Generally, computer software is not sold to the user but is sold under licence so that the user can use the software as agreed in the contract. This act makes it illegal to:

- copy software, unless permitted in the contract
- use a program code without authorisation (although this is often difficult to prove because the basic numbers cannot be copyrighted)
- copy designs, e.g. for web pages, without the author's agreement.

The penalties for breaking this law can be severe, with an unlimited fine and up to two years in prison.

The Computer Misuse Act 1990

Computers and the internet have opened up a vast world of communication that should be of benefit to individuals and to businesses. Unfortunately, there are people who abuse these systems, either for commercial gain or for personal satisfaction. Their actions can seriously damage the benefits that individuals and businesses should be gaining from this new computer technology. The Computer Misuse Act 1990 was passed to protect computer users from these people.

Under the Act people cannot:

- hack into programs that they are not authorised to access
- alter any data held in a computer system without authorisation
- modify any computer material unless authorised to do so
- use a computer at work for personal use, unless authorised
- copy computer programs without authorisation

- prevent or hinder access to any program or data held in a computer.

Essentially, this Act makes the unauthorised misuse of computer software or hardware illegal. This includes hacking into machines, changing files or deleting files, introducing a virus into a systems, altering the setup of a system, etc. Different offences carry different penalties but, for certain actions, such as introducing a virus or modifying systems files, there is an unlimited fine and a possible prison sentence of five years.

The Data Protection Act (DPA) 1998

This replaced the Data Protection Act of 1984 and was required because the development of the internet had been so rapid and introduced new problems. The new Act covers both the holding of data and the processing of data. It is based on certain principles which must be followed by businesses:

- Personal data must be obtained and processed fairly. This may require the person's permission or be vital data such as that held by the Inland Revenue for tax purposes. Some personal data, such as political opinions, religious beliefs and membership of a trade union, can only be processed if explicit consent is given.

Processing data refers to the collection, amending, deleting, re-arranging of, or extracting from, any data held.

- Personal data must only be obtained for specified and lawful purposes and further processed for that legal purpose. Data cannot be disclosed to unauthorised people.
- The personal data collected should be no more that is needed for the registered legal purpose. Any unnecessary data must not be held or processed.
- Personal data must be accurate and it must be kept up to date if this is important.
- Personal data must not be kept for longer than is necessary.
- The rights of the person whose personal data is being held or processed – the data subject – must be upheld. This includes the right of that person to see any personal data held about them. There are exemptions to this (see below).

A **data subject** is anyone about whom personal data is held or processed.

- The holder of the data must make certain that no unauthorised or unlawful processing of the personal data takes place. This includes preventing access and preventing accidental loss or damage of personal data.
- Personal data must not be transferred to any country or territory outside of the European Economic Area unless that country or territory can ensure similar data protection.

For many business purposes, such as keeping data from loyalty cards or the results of questionnaires, this Act is very important. The data controller will be responsible for ensuring that the Act is followed.

A **data controller** is anyone who has control of the data and who decides its purpose and how it will be processed.

Certain types of data and uses are already classified, but where personal data is being held or processed for other, new, uses, the data controller must notify the Data Protection Commissioner who will decide if this use is allowed.

Breaking any part of the Act can lead to an unlimited fine.

Some personal data that is held and processed is *not* subject to the Act. This includes data held within a family. The rights of the individual to see personal data is also restricted in certain cases, e.g. if the data is being used:

- to prevent or detect crime
- to collect taxes
- in some medical reports
- personal references for jobs.

UNIT 4

End of Unit Assignment

For this unit, you will need to produce evidence of your practical ICT skills and two reports. For each part, you will need to consider how it relates effectively to specific business situations. This assignment, as a whole, is testing how well you understand and can use ICT **in a business context**.

There are four main tasks that you will need to complete:

1 Produce computer printouts showing your skills at word processing, spreadsheets and databases.

2 Produce computer printouts showing that you can effective use the internet, e-mailing, scheduling/calendaring and presentational graphics.

3 Produce a report on how a medium-sized business uses e-commerce and is affected by the law and by the IT decisions of the business itself.

4 Produce a report on recent developments in the use of IT.

For Tasks 1 and 2, you can use IT materials that have produced for other units, such as Finance or Business Planning. They must, however, meet the full IT requirements of this unit and that may mean that you will have to make some changes to what you have produced for the other units

Task 1

This task tests your skills in the use of the three main office software packages: word processing, spreadsheets and database. You must show that you can use all of these packages effectively and you must demonstrate this by showing that you can use them in specific business situations or to solve specific business problems.

To show that you can do this, you will need to choose appropriate situations or problems and then show how you can use the facilities of the IT packages to deal with them. For example, if a business needs to record and compare its profit and loss account from one year to the next, and present the results in an effective graphical way, you should choose a software package such as Excel, which can be set up to work out the profits and calculate the percentage changes and, finally, display them as charts. With each situation, you will need to apply some **general points**:

- Decide what skills you are trying to demonstrate.
- Decide on a suitable business situation or problem, and write about this in detail.
- Use your skills in IT to deal with the situation or problem effectively.
- Explain how you have dealt with the situation or problem, and why this was the best way to do this. This should include screen dumps (print screen) annotated to show what you did.
- Explain how the business will benefit from what you have done.

The grade that you will achieve for this part of your work will depend on these factors:

- How well you have used the software package
- How many different features you have included
- How well you have met the needs of the business
- The accuracy of your work

Spreadsheet work should include the production of at least three monthly or weekly financial reports, with a summary report combining or comparing this data and forecasts for the future using appropriate formulae. All elements in the 'What you need to learn selection' should be included.

Database work should include a relational database and this should be used to produce a report that has extracted data from at least three related tables. You need to show your ability to create the databases themselves and to use sorts and searches to include data in a report.

Word processing work should use a variety of presentational skills including the use of headings and sub-headings using the 'style' option.

Task 2

This task expects you to show effective use in each of these topics:

- Internet browsing
- E-mailing
- Scheduling or calendaring
- Using presentational graphic as in a PowerPoint slide show.

Each of these skills will need to be demonstrated in a suitable business situation, for example, showing your ability to browse the web by checking competitor prices and products for a named business, and compiling a short report for the benefit of the marketing department.

For each of the elements named below, you should also carry out the **general points** listed for Task 1.

Internet browsing work should show that you can locate specific data rapidly and extract the parts that you need, and that you can bookmark important sites. You also need to show that you can carry out simple and more advanced searches using standard search engines (e.g. Google).

E-mail work should show your competence in using e-mail facilities to send and receive messages. This should include proof of your ability to use file attachment facilities and to open attached files when they are sent to you. You should also show that you can create and use the address book facility effectively.

Scheduling or calendaring work should show that you can use one of these software facilities to carry out these procedures:

1. Book an appointment for yourself.
2. Book an appointment to which you invite other network users.
3. Access the schedules of other users so as to check their availability for an appointment, a meeting, etc.
4. Monitor replies from people you have invited to attend appointments, a meeting, etc.
5. Book an appointment or meeting that is to be repeated on a regular basis.

Presentational graphics work should show that you can create an appropriate IT presentation and then set up an effective way of presenting it. The slide show should have at least twelve slides and use at least six autolayouts (one offered by the software package itself). The presentation should also show that you can effectively use combinations of text, graphics and sound within the slide show to support your own spoken presentation. High grade presentations would include special effects and a well thought out order.

Task 3

IT is not simply a tool designed to make the work of businesses easier; it is a very powerful tool. For that reason, it needs to be controlled. Task 3 requires you to look at the controls that are placed on IT by the government (through laws), and by the business itself (through corporate policy and objectives).

For this part of your assignment, you must study one particular business with these characteristics:

- It must be a **medium-sized business** (i.e., a business with 50–250 employees or an annual turnover of £1.4 million to £5.75 million per year).
- It must **operate on one site.**
- It must be **involved in e-commerce.**

The **legal aspects** will require you to show that you know the basic legal constraints that are placed on businesses using IT. For an 'E' grade, this is likely to be fairly *descriptive* and will include the main requirements of the Data Protection Act (both versions), copyright law, Codes of Practice for e-mail usage and EU directives, such as that relating to working with VDUs. All of these aspects need to be applied to a particular situation, one that a business is likely to find itself in, e.g., a decision to sell its products through the internet or a decision to advertise using web pages. This part of the unit expects you to show that you understand the growing importance of e-commerce.

For a 'C' grade, you will need to provide some *explanations* of how these laws restrict the ways in which businesses operate but, at the same time, protect businesses. As with all parts of this task, the explanations must relate to a specific business situation.

For an 'A' grade, you must consider the positive and negative effects that the law has on the business and how that is likely to affect the business's current and future use of IT. For example, how much information should a business keep on its customers? Should it, can it, offer these details to other business? How would its customers react if they knew this was happening?

The **corporate aspect** expects you to have researched and understood the ways in which your chosen business has decided to set its IT objectives for the business and what standards, policies and procedures have been set up for controlling the use of IT within the business. To meet the Assessment Evidence Criteria, you will need to consider factors such as these:

- The confidentiality of customer, employee and business data and how the business prevents unauthorised access
- How software and hardware should be used correctly to protect it against damage, loss, viruses, etc.
- What training should be given to staff using IT

Business will decide to use IT for different purposes. You should examine at least one major system that the business is using and write a report with these details:

- What it is used for
- How it helps to improve the efficiency of the business
- What special hardware and software requirements it creates

Five examples of systems are given in the unit content, business/management information systems, business decision-making systems, financial management systems, financial modelling and forecasting, and planning/production/scheduling systems.

Task 4

This part of the assignment requires that you look at a range of IT developments and how they are affecting business, and to produce a report on this. You could consider any new major developments, but one of them should be the growing importance of e-commerce. The depth and detail of your study and report will dictate the grade you will be able to gain for this part.

For an 'E' grade

- Some recent key developments
- Some potential uses of these developments
- Descriptive details of current and future uses of e-commerce

For a 'C' grade

- Most recent key developments
- Many potential uses of these developments including e-commerce
- All uses shown in a particular business situation

For an 'A' grade

- An evaluation of how important recent IT developments have been for specific business situations
- An outline of what future changes are likely to occur soon
- An evaluation of the potential benefits of e-commerce for business

UNIT 5

Motivating and Developing People

CHAPTER 1

Motivation in Management

KEY TERMS

Disincentive	Incentive	Manager
Hierarchy	Job enrichment	Motivation
Hygiene factor	Management	Motivator

In this chapter, you will learn about motivation, its history and its importance for individuals and organisations. You will also learn about motivation theories and about incentives that can be used in the workplace.

What is motivation?

Motivation – an attitude defined by goal-directed behaviour

> Motivation takes place when people expect that a course of action is likely to lead to the attainment of a goal and a valued reward.

Source: M. Armstrong: *Personnel Management Practice*

All organisations have aims and objectives. In the case of business organisations, the main objective is to produce and sell their goods and services at a profit. However, there are other objectives. Businesses fulfil the needs and wants of people, have legal obligations and affect or contribute to the environment in which they operate.

To be successful, organisations must be efficiently and effectively managed. The unit *Business at Work* introduced different ways of managing, depending on an organisation's size, line of business, and the people who run it.

Management – the professional administration of organisations

Manager – a person controlling or administering an organisation or part of an organisation

Even the best of managers, however, will not succeed if the workers, for whatever reason, are unable or unwilling to work. All management theories have tried to establish how managers can best motivate their labour force, but the views as what makes the best motivators have differed widely.

Motivator – a factor which motivates

Before the Industrial Revolution of the eighteenth and nineteenth centuries and the emergence of the factory system, the agricultural society had little need to think about management. There were very few places and situations where groups of people had to work together and therefore had to be managed. When the new order was established, however, the factory owners became concerned with the problem of how to make their workers more productive. This led to a number of people – management experts – carrying out extensive research to try to find out what made workers work harder. Of the resulting theories, not one can be said to be 100 per cent correct, but most have contributed significantly to our knowledge of what makes people at work 'tick', and have helped to shape today's attitudes and motivation practice at work.

In the early twentieth century, it was believed that the only 'valued reward' which motivated workers was money. Today, we know that although money is of very great importance, it is by no means the only motivating factor.

We now look at the most important contributors to the theory of management, and how their work has changed the ways organisations are managed today.

F. W. Taylor and scientific management

F. W. Taylor, an American, published his book, *The Principles of Scientific Management*, in 1911. The beginning of the twentieth century was a time of rapid industrial growth in the USA, but the administration of work was haphazard and, in most factories, was left to the foremen or even to the workers themselves. Taylor saw that this was an unsatisfactory situation, with managers not aware of what was going on in the workplace and workers often doing as little as possible.

Taylor believed strongly that people are only motivated by money. He set out to lay down principles which, if followed, would enable workers to earn more and therefore encourage them to work harder.

Taylor also believed that workers should receive 'a fair day's pay for a fair day's work', and that this could be achieved in a 'scientific' way. He advised that managers should observe workers at work, eliminate any unnecessary activity, and then select the quickest way to carry out a particular task in the shortest possible time. Once the sequence had been decided, the workers then had to carry out their tasks – usually very simple ones on an assembly line. The managers' job was to supervise the workers closely at all times.

Taylor's approach can be summed up by saying that, in his view, workers were there to work, and managers to manage. He saw no connection between the attitudes and aspirations of the two groups. Although his principles were adopted by many organisations at the time (and perhaps are still followed in some organisations today), many weaknesses of his 'scientific' methods became apparent.

Taylor regarded people more as machines than as human beings, and totally disregarded their individual needs. He seemed unaware of the fact that people are not all the same. He believed that breaking each job into small components and making each worker carry out only one simple repetitive task would solve all problems, both for the managers and for the workers themselves. Little training would be needed as the tasks were simple and easy, and constant repetition would make the workers more and more efficient and productive. The more they produced, the more they would earn, and this would motivate them to even greater efforts.

In spite of its shortcomings, Taylor's 'scientific' principles were the first serious attempt to try to explain how management at work could be improved and how people could be motivated. Some businesses which tried to introduce his methods found that they resulted in workers' unrest, rising absenteeism and a high labour turnover. Other firms were more successful, but very gradually people began to realise that money was not the only motivator for workers, whatever their position.

Elton Mayo and the Human Relations School

Another American, Elton Mayo, working during the 1920s and 1930s, carried out a study of workers at the Hawthorne Plant of the Chicago-based Western Electric Company. This study, now known as the Hawthorne Experiment, took five years to complete. During that time, frequent changes were made to the workers' conditions at work. Heating and lighting levels, rest periods and other factors were altered from time to time. The effect of each change on the workers' output was carefully measured. The results were unexpected. Productivity rose each time a change was made, even if that change was not particularly beneficial to the workers.

Elton Mayo concluded that the changes themselves were not very important. The rise in productivity following a change was due to the change in the workers' perception of the relationship between themselves and the management. Each change meant communication with management, making the workers feel noticed and therefore more valued by the company. They began to think that the managers were interested in them as individuals, and also as a special group, and this made each team strive to perform better.

Mayo's experiment is the cornerstone of what became known as the **Human Relations School of Management**, and he was the first to realise that people respond to factors other than financial rewards.

Although the results of the Hawthorne experiment were a valuable step forward in the study of motivation, Mayo's conclusions were far from perfect.

The main criticism of his theory is that it is biased towards management. Mayo said that managers could manipulate workers to make them work harder. He also assumed that all individuals, workers and managers alike, want the same things. Another of his assumptions was that all workers would welcome frequent communication with their superiors whereas, in reality, those low down in the workplace hierarchy might not want it at all.

Hierarchy – a system in which grades of status or authority are ranked one above the other in a pyramid shape

Elton Mayo's importance lies in his recognition that there are human needs other than money. It was not until some years after the end of the Second World War that the first attempt was made to list, explain and classify such needs.

Abraham Maslow

In 1954 Maslow published his theory, which he called the *hierarchy of needs*. He divided human needs into separate categories and tried to explain how these are related to each other.

Maslow's theory is usually shown as a pyramid (Figure 5.1.1).

Maslow believed that the physiological needs of human beings are so basic that they are common to all. Safety needs apply to most of us, and freedom from physical or other harm is of great importance. Job security is one of the safety needs, and since we need a job to satisfy our physiological needs, we need job security as well. At the next level in his hierarchy, he placed the need to work with supportive colleagues and a sense of being part of a group. This is important to the majority of individuals, but not to all. Recognition of effort and praise were placed even higher, while at the top level in his hierarchy we find the need to realise one's full potential. A minority of workers feels this need, although most of us could attain it.

In Maslow's opinion, the achievement of the various levels of needs must be progressive. Until one level is

Figure 5.1.1 Maslow's hierarchy of needs

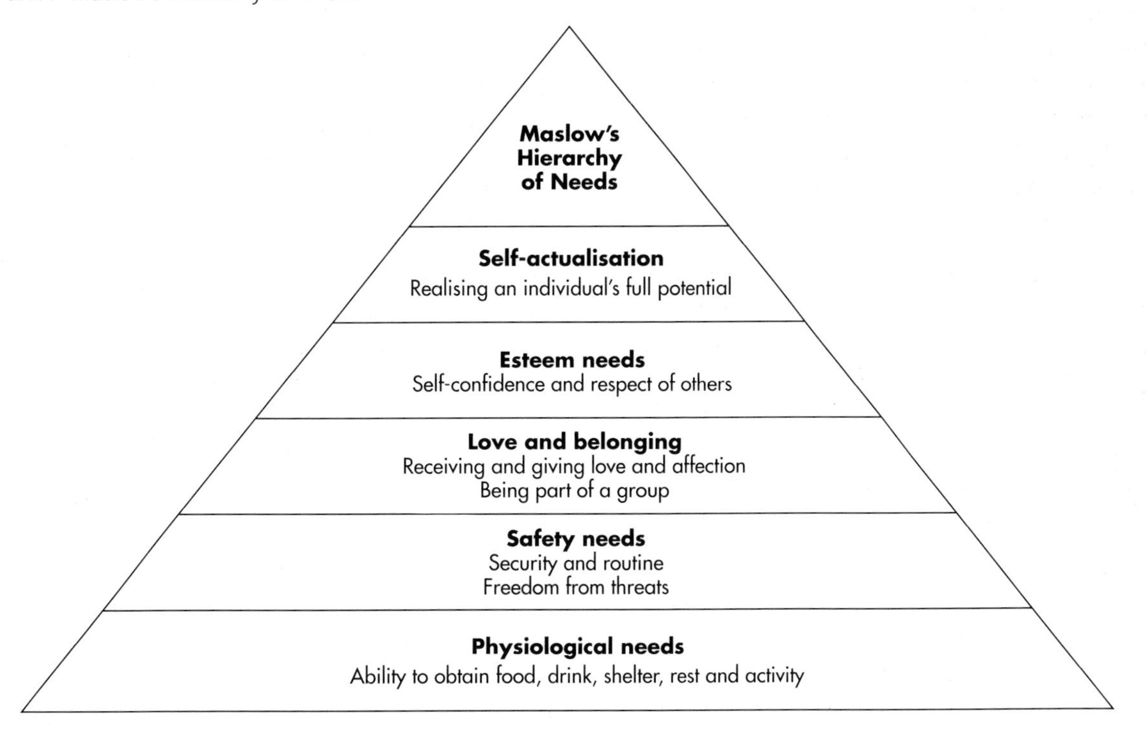

satisfied, workers will not strive towards the next. When they have achieved one level, it becomes of less importance and they become interested in the next.

Maslow's theory gained great popularity but, like others, it has some weaknesses. His categories are far too rigid – some of the levels only apply to some individuals, while the same rewards might be appropriate for more than one level. One such reward is money which is needed for such essentials as food and drink at the lowest level, but which is also valued by people at higher levels, sometimes as a symbol of status or personal worth.

Douglas McGregor and his Theory X and Theory Y

In *The Human Side of Enterprise*, published in 1960, McGregor attempted to show how the hierarchy of needs could be used in business. By then, the idea that people are only motivated by money had come to be seen as too simplistic and wholly inaccurate. McGregor set out to explain the reasons why people work and summarised two diametrically opposite attitudes, calling them Theory X and Theory Y.

McGregor's Theory X is similar to Taylor's theory of scientific management. It assumes that people are motivated solely by money and that they must be coerced to work. Forcing people to work can only be achieved by threats of punishment. Threats only work if they can be carried out. Today, such methods are not only considered to be wrong and counter-productive – they would also be illegal.

Table 5.1.1 Theory X and Theory Y

Theory X	**Theory Y**
Workers are lazy and dislike work.	Workers can enjoy work.
Workers are motivated by money.	Workers have many different needs which motivate them.
Workers are selfish and lack ambition.	If motivated, workers can organise themselves and take responsibility.
Workers need to be controlled and directed.	Management should create a situation in which workers can show creativity and use their job knowledge.

Theory Y goes to the other extreme of the motivation spectrum. It assumes that individuals are not inherently lazy, lacking in ambition and without interest in their jobs, nor motivated by monetary gain alone. According to Theory Y, most people respond to higher motivators, are committed to their jobs, like responsibility and want more out of their jobs than the wage packet. In other words, Theory Y has much in common with the higher levels of Maslow's hierarchy.

Herzberg and the Two-factor Theory

Herzberg's Two-factor Theory, published in 1966, was based on research into motivation at work. Herzberg wanted to find out what gave people most satisfaction at work, and also what made them most dissatisfied. He asked a group of professional people to provide him with their views. The result was his theory, in which he identified two categories of factors that affect motivation at work:

- **Motivators** give **job satisfaction**. Rewarding workers for a job well done raises their self-esteem and is likely to make them work harder. This does not always happen, however, because other factors often affect productivity.
- **Hygiene factors** cause **dissatisfaction**. They include poor facilities, cramped conditions, lack of comfort, etc. While improvements, will remove the cause of the dissatisfaction, hygiene factors themselves do not actively motivate people.

We can see that Herzberg's motivators are similar to the higher levels of Maslow's hierarchy of needs. One of the criticisms of Herzberg's theory was that his research had dealt only with professionals who were more likely to be motivated by praise, recognition and power.

Herzberg and his ideas introduced the concept of **job enrichment**.

Job enrichment – a process in which jobs are redesigned to allow workers to become more involved in the production process
Giving individuals more responsibility and recognition makes them more motivated and therefore more productive.

Activity

Why do we work?

This activity should be carried out in pairs. Working with a friend will enable you to talk to more people, so that the results of your mini-survey will be based on a larger number of responses.

Each of you should ask at least ten people these ten questions:

1. What is the main reason why you work?
2. Do you like working on your own or with other people?
3. Does your job give you satisfaction?
4. If you had the opportunity for further training, would you take it?
5. Do you hope for promotion? (Give reasons for your answers.)
6. If your boss offered you the choice between a salary increase or a more responsible position, which would you choose, and why?
7. Do you think a manager should praise a worker for a job well done?
8. Does your manager keep you informed about what is going on in your place of work?
9. If you could change anything about your job, what would it be and why?
10. On a scale of 1 to 10, how do you rate your job? Please explain your answer. (10 would be your perfect job!)

Now analyse the answers and write a short report on your findings.

Critics of the Two-factor Theory said that hygiene factors, although important, only remove workers' dissatisfaction once – when they are first improved. For example, if the quality of food served in the works canteen is poor, workers will complain about it and demand an improvement. A new, better selection of meals and snacks will, at first, make the workers happy but, after a time, they will take this for granted and might soon become dissatisfied again.

Job enrichment schemes, which have been tried by a number of organisations, are costly to introduce and it takes a long time for results to come through. Many businesses simply cannot afford to invest in such projects.

Other theorists

David McClelland said that people had three basic needs:

- Need for achievement
- Need for affiliation
- Need for power

He was interested in how to motivate people in managerial positions, and he concluded that organisations should recognise the differences between individuals and use them accordingly. Those who are motivated by the need for achievement like to take responsibility, are not afraid of taking risks, can be very successful, but do not work very well in teams. The need for affiliation is found in individuals who are often very successful, but like working with others. Power seekers are often regarded as those who want to control others. This is a negative view as those who seek power are often very skilled at influencing and leading people.

All of the above motivation theories tried to find a blueprint that would enable management to motivate workers to work as hard and as efficiently as possible. **Vroom** and **Lawler**, and also **Porter**, pointed out that the assumption made by Maslow, McGregor and Herzberg, among others – that people would always try to satisfy their needs by meeting certain goals – are unrealistic. Each individual has different needs, and these often change over time due to changing circumstances. Also, people will only try to achieve goals if they think that there is a good chance of success. Finally, the reward for achieving a particular goal might have different values for different people.

While it is true that motivation at work is of paramount importance, there is no one theory that an organisation can put into practice and be sure that it will work. There are merits in each theory, even in F. W. Taylor's belief that the best and only motivator is money. In some business organisations, because of their management style and the type of work involved, hard cash might well be the answer. Any organisation must be flexible when trying to motivate people, and must try to understand the views of its workers before deciding how to motivate them.

Incentives

Incentive – a motive for action, a reward that can be gained for performing a task well

All people are different so they do not all respond to the same motivators. A business organisation can offer a number of incentives to its employees:

- **Financial incentives**
  Pay rises, productivity bonuses, profit-sharing schemes in which workers benefit if the business performs well in a given period are all powerful incentives, welcomed by workers throughout an organisation. A wage increase for an individual who is young, inexperienced or simply in a low-paid job can make a great difference to his or her standard of living. For those in higher, better-paid positions, the need for more money may not be so crucial, but everyone likes to be paid more; a financial reward is seen as recognition of status and achievement.
- **Promotion**
  The chance to climb the promotional ladder is important to those individuals who are ambitious and look forward to gaining higher status and responsibility within the organisation. Conversely, a 'dead-end job' – one where chances of promotion do not exist – often demotivates people.
- **Career prospects and development**
  Ambitious individuals often look further than straight promotion. They hope that their present job will lead to a full and rewarding career. This might mean a change of direction and the possibility of switching from one department or section to another.
- **Training**
  The importance of training is well recognised. Training schemes for employees, on or off the job, are welcomed by many.
- **Autonomy**
  This is an incentive for those who are confident enough to want to be able to work without too much supervision, and to make their own decisions.
- **Responsibility**
  Not everyone wants responsibility but it is a strong incentive for those individuals who are ambitious, self-confident and eager for promotion.
- **Praise**
  Some critics say that praise for a job well done should be unnecessary in the workplace, as the worker is paid to do the job and the payment should be reward enough. Human nature being what it is, however, most people like their efforts to be noticed, and recognition and praise are generally good incentives. There are many ways of praising someone – from a few words from the individual's manager to a mention in the company's newsletter or in a memo to senior management.
- **Shared ownership**
  Many businesses now offer their workers shares in the company, sometimes given free or at a preferential price. The idea behind shared ownership

CASE STUDY

A Reunion

Asha, Charlotte and Kurt first met at the age of 11, when they arrived at high school. After their GCSEs, they all went on to study business at college. At the end of their course, which all three successfully completed, Kurt found a job as a management trainee at a large manufacturing company in the neighbouring town; Asha, who had always been interested in advertising, joined a small but growing advertising company in their home town; and Charlotte became a receptionist at a five star hotel.

The three friends kept in touch but had not met for some time. Last month Kurt telephoned the other two and told them that he was coming home for a few days. 'It's not really a holiday,' he said. 'They're sending me on a training course which happens to be here, so I thought we might all meet up and have a meal or something.'

The next weekend, they all met at their favourite pizza restaurant. After some catching up on personal news gossip, conversation turned to their respective jobs.

'You're doing well, Kurt,' said Asha, 'being sent on a course so soon. What's it like, working for that huge company?'

'Actually, it's great,' said Kurt. 'True, it's a big place, but it's very well organised. My line manager is always there if I need help, and we have regular meetings to discuss progress. We are often told what's going on, what the company is producing and so on.'

'I suppose you're not earning much, though,' said Asha.

'No, the money is low – after all, I'm only a trainee, but when I finish the training I'll receive a hefty pay rise. Anyway, money is not the most important thing! I like the way I'm treated, and the prospects of promotion are good if you show that you can work hard and produce results. In a couple of years' time I hope to have a job with much more responsibility. But that's enough about me. What is your job like, Asha?'

'Not as good as yours,' Asha replied. 'When I started, I thought it would be a great opportunity for me to learn all about advertising and perhaps to do some work independently. It's a small place and I was sure that it would not be too impersonal. I was wrong. Rowena Smart, the MD, isn't at all interested in what her employees want. Each person has to do exactly what she tells them and, as the most junior there, I'm just given the boring jobs like filing and answering the phone. My supervisor, Gary, can't even see her when he needs advice, so he is quite frustrated, particularly when he is blamed if things go wrong. I've tried asking about more training and whether there is any chance of having more responsibility, but it was useless. Rowena just told me that she pays me well – which is true – so I should be happy. I don't know what to do.'

Charlotte, who had been very quiet, chimed in. 'Count yourself lucky, Asha,' she said. 'At least you are paid well. At the hotel, the wages are really low and the hours are long and hard. The manager is not interested in us at all, and the only perk is the uniform. There is no question of training, and it's a real dead-end job . . .'

'But Charlotte,' said Asha, 'you had no interest in a career. You wanted to work in the hotel because you thought it would be glamorous!'

'Well, I was wrong,' snapped Charlotte. 'I hate the hotel, I hate the job, and I can see no way out.'

'Of course, there is a way out,' said Kurt. 'If you want a job with prospects, look for one, but this time think carefully about what you want. What are your priorities? Do you want an interesting job? More responsibility? Better money? Are you willing to work harder?'

'It's easy for you to talk,' grumbled Charlotte. 'You're lucky, your job sounds ideal.'

'Yes, it is,' said Kurt. 'But I know that to succeed I must work hard and I'm willing to do that.'

'Listening to you two,' said Asha, 'has made up my mind. I'm going to look for a job that will offer me more than just high wages. I want a career and, like you, Kurt, I'm willing to take a job that will eventually give me job satisfaction and the chance to show what I can really do.'

'Good for you, Asha,' said Kurt. 'What about you, Charlotte? Will you be looking for another job too?'

But Charlotte was not sure that she wanted to try.

is that a worker holding shares in the employer's company will feel that he or she is more than just an employee. If the company does well, he or she will receive some financial benefit. This will make the new shareholders, however minor, more interested in the affairs of the company and more willing to make a greater effort to be productive.

- **Fringe benefits**
  These can be very useful to workers. Although when times are hard many organisations cut back on fringe benefits, many consider them to be valuable incentives. Fringe benefits include subsidised meals in the works canteen, company cars (with or without a petrol allowance), private health insurance, membership of the company's sports clubs, and so on. Marks & Spencer, for instance, provides workers with a free medical and chiropodist service, and bank employees can obtain mortgages at preferential rates.

Disincentives

While incentives motivate people, disincentives have the opposite effect. One of the greatest disincentives is the threat of redundancies or fear of closure. Unfriendly or unhelpful treatment by managers can also demotivate workers.

Managers and motivation

All the motivation theories concentrate on the needs of the individual and how satisfying those needs will ensure that he or she will respond by working harder and being more productive, all for the benefit of the employer. There are many incentives that management in the workplace can offer, and managers should be aware of the need to motivate – and most of them are.

However, this does not mean that managers should respond solely to what the individuals in their team need. The responsibility of the managers is to the organisation, and their most difficult task is to reconcile the objectives of the business with the needs of their workers. This conflict often causes problems and difficulties.

Aims and objectives of the organisation

If the objective of an organisation at a particular time is to increase production as quickly as possible, this might make it difficult, if not impossible, for the manager to allow workers time off for training and career development activities. Pressure of work can also prevent the manager from spending time with the workers, or communicating with them as often as might be desirable. Some businesses, particularly those in manufacturing industries, might find that the only incentives that managers can offer workers are financial ones – this can demotivate workers who are looking for other, higher rewards.

Conflicts of interest

However much a manager may want to enable workers to satisfy their needs, a conflict of interests might arise and make this impossible to achieve. If a flu epidemic lays low several key members of a team at a time when a deadline is approaching, the manager will have no choice but to tell another member, who is due to attend a course or participate in a conference, that he or she must cancel those arrangements and come in to work instead. This could be either a minor and temporary inconvenience to the individual, or a major disappointment.

Dealing with conflicts

Communication is the key to successful management of a conflict situation. If the manager takes the time and trouble to explain the situation to the employee, there is a much greater chance that the situation will be amicably resolved. A curt order or instruction is much more likely to result in upsetting, and possibly demotivating, the worker.

Designing organisational objectives

These should take into account people's individual needs. Different organisations have different objectives. These depend on their products, their customer base and their overall aims. The objectives can change as time passes and circumstances alter. When designing objectives, managers should consider the individuals in the organisation and make sure that each is entrusted with the task or tasks that best fit with her or his individual needs. This can be difficult if objectives have to be redesigned and tasks are allocated to workers whose needs are in conflict with those objectives.

Revision Questions

1. Explain what is meant by motivation at work. (1 mark)
2. What was the main conclusion about motivation drawn by F. W. Taylor? (2 marks)
3. What were the results of the Hawthorne experiment? (3 marks)
4. What were the criticisms of Mayo's theory? (2 marks)
5. McGregor's Theories X and Y are both too extreme. Do you agree? Give reasons for your answer. (6 marks)
6. According to Maslow, what is self-actualisation? (2 marks)
7. What are 'hygiene factors', and how important are they? (2 marks)
8. Name three incentives that can be used to motivate people at work. (3 marks)
9. What are disincentives? Give two examples. (3 marks)
10. No motivation theory is 100 per cent correct. Why? (5 marks)
11. Which theory is most likely to apply to the majority of workers? Give reasons. (4 marks)
12. Which incentives do you personally consider most important? Why? (5 marks)

CHAPTER 2

Groups at Work

KEY TERMS

- Formal group
- Group
- Group conflict
- Group dynamics
- Group norms
- Informal group
- Long-term groups
- Quality circle
- Short-term groups
- Social groups
- Team
- Team roles

In this chapter, you will learn about groups of people working together. You will learn about different types of groups and how they can be of benefit to the individual and to the organisation as a whole. You will also learn about teams, their characteristics and membership, and how teams differ from groups.

A **group** is 'a collection of two or more people who:

(1) interact with each other;

(2) perceive themselves to share some common interests or goals;

(3) come together or are brought together to accomplish some work activity'.

Source: Feldman and Arnold, 1983

How people work together

Chapter 1 of this unit looked at individuals at the workplace, and why it is important for an organisation to motivate them. However, in most organisations, you will find people working together to achieve a common goal.

Groups bring many advantages to an organisation, but it is important for managers to recognise that group members often have needs that are different from the needs of individuals. A group that fails to work well together, for one reason or another, can seriously impair the performance of the organisation.

Formal groups

Formal groups are established for a particular purpose. The structure and membership of a formal group depend on the nature of the task involved and on the way in which the organisation is managed. Each group member is chosen for his or her skills and experience, and there is a clearly defined leader.

Communication between members of a formal group is essential for its success.

One example of a formal group is a department of a large company. The Marketing Department, for instance, has the Departmental Manager as the leader of all the other department members. The task of the department is to carry out all marketing functions necessary for the organisation as a whole. Since these functions are diverse and require different areas and levels of expertise, people with a variety of skills are needed. The group will, therefore, include market research specialists, advertising staff, public relations people, etc. Only by working together can the Marketing Department achieve its objectives.

Informal groups

As the name implies, these groups are not set up by management, but consist of people within the organisation who, for one reason or another, have some need to come together. According to Lita de Alberdi (*People, Psychology and Business*), people usually join an informal group to fulfil a special need:

- **To accomplish goals**
  People working in different parts of an organisation might find that, by helping each other, they can achieve their goals more easily. Having a personal assistant to the manager as a friend can give one staff member an advantage over others – for instance, the PA is able to pass on informant information before it becomes public knowledge. The advantage of this relationship to the PA might be simply the friendship of a senior employee who will spend time relating office news and gossip.
- **To advance their careers**
  Information and help received from people in other parts of the organisation can result in tasks being completed earlier and better than expected, thus earning the worker a reputation for efficiency.
- **To enhance their reputation**
  Being a member of a group seen as high flyers can earn a worker the reputation of being ambitious and career-minded.

Informal groups can sometimes be detrimental to the organisation. This was demonstrated by the Hawthorne Experiment (page 202). Workers taking part in the study showed clearly that they could regulate their own activity and output themselves, without considering the wishes of management.

Short-term and long-term groups

Often groups are set up to carry out a task that has a specific deadline. Such groups exist only until the project is completed. The length of time involved can vary.

- **Marketing a new product**
  When a company wishes to launch a new product, a group of members of the Marketing Department might be assigned to work together to ensure that all that is necessary to sell the product is done. The group will work together solely on the new product and will disperse as soon as this task is finished.
- **One-off objectives**
  An inter-departmental group may be set up to organise and carry out all the steps that are necessary for the organisation to reach a one-off goal, such as membership of the Investor in People scheme.

Social groups

These are groups that exist for purposes seemingly unconnected with the organisation. People tend to form relationships with colleagues that extend to shared coffee breaks, and sometimes to activities outside working hours. These groups might have a beneficial effect by making members of feeling secure and valued by others.

Quality circles

Quality circles are small groups of workers in related work. They meet informally to discuss progress and suggest ways of improving methods and performance. Membership of quality circles is voluntary; so, by definition, all members participate because they wish to.

Group dynamics

Group dynamics – the way that people in a group behave, and the changes that belonging to a group brings to their behaviour

Being in a group can make an individual work harder than when he or she is alone. The opposite, however, can also be true. The presence of others may be a distraction, leading to worse performance, or an individual might think that other members should do more.

Group dynamics refers to the interaction between group member and the resulting outcomes. This interaction depends on several factors. Personal traits and differences affect the way in which group members work together. The leader of the group often exerts great influence on the cohesion, or otherwise, of the group.

Group norms

These are unwritten and unspoken rules about acceptable behaviour within the group. They vary from group to group but, for a group to work well together, all members must conform to the norms.

Group norms can include levels of co-operation with management, standards of timekeeping and even standards of dress. Acceptable levels of performance are also often a norm of a group. If the majority of the group are well motivated and work hard, this will also be expected of any new member. On the other hand, a new, hard-working member might find that he or she is

CASE STUDY

Friends or foes?

Taiko Asekura was very excited when she was offered a job in the Accounts Department of Teeny Treats plc, a manufacturer of baby foods and drinks. Taiko has studied accounts at college and is working towards her professional qualifications. After leaving college, Taiko worked for a while for a small business where she was in sole charge of day-to-day book-keeping and general administrative duties. She very much wanted a job that would be the stepping stone to a career in accountancy. She was also fed up with working on her own and was looking forward to joining the staff of the Accounts Department.

On the first day at work, Gareth Black, the Departmental Manager, introduced Taiko to the rest of the members of the department. He then went into his office and shut the door, leaving Donna Paige, the Senior Accountant, to show Taiko the ropes. Donna was very pleasant and explained things to Taiko, but she made it quite plain that the junior accounts clerks were supposed to carry out their assigned work and not bother her or Gareth.

'But,' said Taiko hesitantly, 'what if I need some help or advice?'

'Oh, you can always ask Miriam, one of the other clerks, or Jeremy. They have been here long enough and know exactly what to do.'

The first time that Taiko had to ask for help, she approached Miriam. Miriam seemed very pleasant and told Taiko all she needed to know. On the second occasion, Miriam was out of the office, so Taiko asked Jeremy. He looked at her coldly and said, 'I don't know why you're asking me. You didn't bother to talk to me when Miriam was around.'

'Oh, it wasn't like that,' said Taiko. 'It was just that she was here and I had to ask somebody . . .'

'It's no good making excuses,' snarled Jeremy. 'Miriam always thinks that she is more important than the other clerks, and now you have made her even more sure of herself!'

Taiko tried to say something, but Jeremy walked away.

When Miriam came back to the office. Taiko went to her with her question. To her astonishment, Miriam refused to talk to her.

'I've just met Jenny in the canteen,' she said, 'and she told me that as soon as my back was turned, you went crawling to that Jeremy . . .'

Taiko tried to explain, but Miriam would not listen.

Taiko was most upset. She had thought that working in a large department would mean making friends and helping each other but things did not seem to be like that at all.

At the first meeting of the department, Taiko discovered that things were, in fact, much worse. Jeremy would not sit next to Miriam, and he and his friend Adam made snide remarks about her throughout the meeting. Miriam sat with Lucy and Terry. When asked about the progress of a job that all five of them were working on, Miriam complained that Jeremy was slacking and made it impossible for her to complete her part of the task. This infuriated Jeremy who refused to say anything and sat glaring at everybody.

To Taiko's surprise, Gareth seemed unconcerned about the situation, although the atmosphere at the meeting was thoroughly unpleasant. He spoke mostly to Donna, and then gave the rest some further instructions. He made no attempt to discuss any problems and, after closing the meeting, disappeared again into his room.

Taiko tried to talk to some of the others but no one seemed interested in anything except getting through the day and going home.

After two weeks, Taiko decided she had made a great mistake in taking the job at Teeny Treats.

breaking the performance level norm. This might well make him or her unpopular with the rest of the group.

If there is a good relationship between management and workers, however, group norms will encourage good performance.

Group effectiveness

In the 1950s and 1960s, **Rensis Likert** was involved in applying human relations theory to the theory of management, and was the first to develop a theory of the 'group pattern of organisation'.

Like Elton Mayo, Likert believed that small groups at work formed the best organisational structure, exerting positive influence and achieving goals. He believed that there are overlapping groups in an organisation which, together, link the activities of the whole and help to achieve co-ordination.

Likert's conditions for group effectiveness are extensive and, in real life, it would be difficult to achieve such a perfect set of working characteristics in any group, large or small. Trust and loyalty to each other, to the leader and to the organisation are of undisputable importance if a group is to work well together, but these conditions are frequently difficult to achieve. In a group situation, individual personalities are often at loggerheads, and managers find it difficult to gain the total trust of the workers.

In addition, when a number of people are working together, there is ample room for personal antipathies to emerge, and for misunderstandings, incidental or otherwise, to disrupt co-operation.

Likert's view of group effectiveness

The properties and performance of the ideal, highly effective group are as follows:

1 The members are skilled in the various leadership and membership roles required for effective interaction.

2 The group has been in existence sufficiently long to have developed well-established, relaxed working relationships.

3 The members of the group are loyal to it and to its leader.

4 The members and leaders have a high degree of confidence and trust in each other.

5 The values and goals of the group are an expression of the values and goals of its members.

6 The members of the group are highly motivated to abide by the major values and achieve the important goals of the group.

7 All the interaction, problem solving and decision making activities of the group take place in a supportive atmosphere.

8 Insofar as group members perform linking functions with other groups, their goals and values are in mutual harmony.

Source: R. Likert, *New Patterns of Management*, 1961

Group decision making

'Many heads are better than one'.

There are distinct advantages of groups making decisions in a workplace.

- Members of groups have a variety of skills and expertise. This means that group decisions can be taken after all members have had a chance to contribute, and the outcome is likely to be a sound one.
- It is more likely that possible errors and mistakes will be spotted before any decision is made.
- Good decisions require all aspects of the task or project to be examined and considered in detail. This is more likely to happen during group discussions.

Group decisions carry some disadvantages as well.

- They take time. When a decision has to be reached quickly, the time needed for discussions and airing of views of group members can be against the organisation's interests.
- Even within a group, one individual with special knowledge and experience may be in a better position to make a particular decision.
- Individuals within the group may have different personalities and points of view, making it difficult for the group to act as one when making decisions. This can lead to inefficiency.

- Groups are sometimes prepared to take riskier decisions than individuals would, as the responsibility and criticism for a wrong decisions does not rest on one individual.

Group conflict

Likert's conditions of group effectiveness, while sound, are often not achieved in real life. Groups do not always share exactly the same goals and values with other groups, or wholly share those of management. Individual needs and aspirations also block the way of smooth operation of groups.

Conflict within a group is the inevitable result when individuals with different skills, experience, personality traits and attitudes are put together and expected 'to get on with it'. Group conflict can take different forms. Sometimes two members find it difficult to rub along, and their mutual antipathy may divide the whole group into opposing factions. Group members may express their dissatisfaction with others by refusing to co-operate, at the same time implying that they could help the group to achieve its goals but, instead, refuse to disclose how this could be done, and causing public disagreements, criticising others, avoiding discussion of any controversial issues and so on.

Group conflict can have very negative results. It can

- make the group lose sight of its objectives and focus instead on the problems of working together
- make people refuse to discuss the immediate problem by adopting defensive tactics
- reduce co-operation between members
- lead to a fall in productivity
- in extreme cases, cause the group to fall apart.

Group conflict, however, is not always destructive. It can have positive effects for the group as a whole. In 1981, **Hunt** listed the beneficial effects of conflict within a group:

- A difference of views or opinions may bring about new solutions to a problem.
- Conflict can define the balance of relationships in the group.
- It can force group members to listen to individual points of view which might be worth considering.
- It can bring personal animosities into the open and allow them to be dealt with.

It is the role of the group leader to resolve any difficulties within a group. We shall look at how managers can try to achieve this later in this unit.

Teams

The terms 'group' and 'team' are often thought to be interchangeable. However, in 1988, **Honey** suggested that they are quite different, and then **Katzenbach and Smith** provided another definition of a team in 1993.

> A group is a collection of individual people who come together to serve some purpose .... A team is a small group of people (6 to 8 people is a typical size) who co-operate together in such a way that they accomplish more than the sum total of the individuals.
>
> *Source*: Honey, 1988.

> A team is a small number of people with complementary skills who are committed to a common purpose, performance goals and approach for which they hold themselves mutually accountable.
>
> *Source*: Katzenbach and Smith, 1993.

Teams are composed of people who are different, while members of a group are often similar in some way. Teams are often essential for the carrying out of difficult, complex and non-routine tasks. Thus it would follow that teams are more important to organisations than groups but, in practice, the difference between them is often ignored and leaders of groups frequently refer to the group as 'the team'.

Within a team, there is a clear pattern of different roles, each of which is important for the efficient functioning of the team.

Meredith Belbin, a British psychologist, identified eight distinct roles found in teams. Seven of these, said Belbin, are needed for a team to function efficiently. Belbin, basing his conclusions on extensive observations of management teams at work, concluded that the roles emerge naturally in any team, although the 'chairperson' and the 'shaper' are both leadership roles and only one of them is needed.

Team Roles

1 **The chairperson or co-ordinator**
The chairperson is good at organising people and using them productively. He/she commands respect but may often come across as unfeeling and impersonal.

2 **The shaper**
The shaper likes to influence group decisions and to introduce ideas, and is not afraid of criticism or unpopularity. The shaper has drive and self-confidence, but could be intolerant towards others.

3 **The contacts person**
Bringing new ideas, developments and people from the outside, this person likes fresh ideas and is the first to see possibilities, but is sometimes over-enthusiastic, or fails to follow up on own ideas.

4 **The ideas person**
The innovator – independent, intelligent and imaginative – often brings new solutions to old problems but is sometimes impractical and unable to communicate well with others.

5 **The critic**
This careful, sometimes slow, analyser and evaluator of other people's ideas, while very useful to the team – as he or she makes sure that decisions are not taken until all the facts have been considered – is not usually very creative.

6 **The implementer**
The practical team member who can be relied on to carry out plans and achieve objectives, the implementer tends to be inflexible and to resist new ideas.

7 **The team builder**
Best at working with people, and supportive to the ideas of others, the team builder can, however, be indecisive and lack toughness.

8 **The inspector**
With a fine eye for detail and acting as the conscience of the team, the inspector checks for any errors that might have been made, and thus protects the reputation of the team, but is often impatient and intolerant.

Based on *Team Building* (1985) by Meredith Belbin

Although his findings are of interest, and his roles are recognised by those with experience of working in teams, not every team will automatically produce all the roles outlined. Belbin said that if one or more of the seven roles is missing, the team's efficiency is impaired.

Innovations at Whipp & Bourne Ltd

Whipp & Bourne of Rochdale manufacture heavy electrical switchgear for customers worldwide. A new initiative at Whipp & Bourne is the **Team Enterprise** approach.

> Implementation is now focused on a Team Enterprise approach – authority is delegated to production teams. Team Leaders facilitate training of their team members and are responsible for liaising with the leaders of other teams. The teams manage quality and production levels and bring in specialist help from support functions within the Company to help resolve production problems.

Source: Times 100

The importance of teams

Teams are the basic units of performance in most organisations. The experience, skills and knowledge of all the team members come together in teamwork, making a team effort more productive than individual efforts would be.

Teams are particularly valuable in situations that demand a high degree of knowledge and expertise.

A well-knit team is also capable of adjusting to the internal and external changes that inevitably occur, while team meetings provide a forum for an exchange of ideas, mutual support and decision making.

To be fully effective, a team must have the right structure and leadership, and be fully committed to the task in hand. It is not easy to ensure that this always happens, and there are also some reservations about decisions made by teams. Quite often, whatever the theorists say, team decisions, while not worse, are not better than those made by individuals.

It is important to remember that, however cohesive a team is, its members are individuals with different attitudes and needs, and a team leader should not lose sight of the differences between them.

Revision Questions

1. What is a formal group? Give two examples. (2 marks)
2. Why do people join informal groups at work? (2 marks)
3. What are quality circles and what is their purpose? (2 marks)
4. Explain how group norms come into being, and what is likely to happen if a group member does not conform to the norm. (5 marks)
5. Give a definition of group dynamics. (3 marks)
6. Explain how group conflict can have positive effects. (4 marks)
7. How does a team differ from a group? (3 marks)
8. Why did Belbin believe that the roles of the 'chairman' and the 'shaper' in a team are mutually exclusive? (4 marks)
9. What are the advantages to an individual of working in a team? (3 marks)
10. What are the advantages of teams to the organisation? (3 marks)

CHAPTER 3

Functions and Styles of Management

KEY TERMS

Autocratic style	Laissez-faire style	Management functions
Contingency model	Leadership styles	Organisational culture
Democratic style	Management by objectives (MBO)	Systems theory

In this chapter, you will learn about different functions that managers must carry out, about different leadership styles that are used in organisations, and factors that affect the choice of a leadership style. You will also learn about skills that managers should possess.

Management functions

The first two chapters of this unit have established that, to be efficient, people must be motivated, and that leaders are needed to direct, control, encourage and motivate workers.

The unit *Business at Work* showed that there are different management structures.

- The tall management structure has more levels of management than the flat one.
- Centralised structures need different methods from those required by decentralised organisations.
- Strict hierarchical structures tend to be managed 'from the top down'.
- Matrix structures introduce a much more liberal approach to management.
- Whichever model is adopted, managers are necessary for the success of the organisation.

P. F. Drucker was, for many years, a business adviser to several US companies. Although, if asked about the purpose of business, many would probably reply that it was making a profit, Drucker took a much wider view. According to him, the purpose of a business is *not* just to make a profit.

Its purpose must lie outside the business itself. In fact, it must lie in society, since business enterprise is an organ of society. There is only one valid definition of business purpose: *to create a customer* . . . Customers are the foundation of a business and keep it in existence. They alone give employment. To supply the wants and needs of a customer, society entrusts wealth-producing resources to the business enterprise.

Source: P. F. Drucker, *Management*

Organisations must create and keep customers, and must also be aware of the social environment in which they operate. This is not to say that profit is not important – without profit a business will inevitably fail – but that businesses should realise how they must go about creating, maintaining and increasing their customer base.

Much has been written by management experts about the functions of management.

Henri Fayol, the French theorist, listed the following functions in the early part of the twentieth century: planning, organising, commanding, co-ordinating and controlling.

Planning

Planning is vital and is one of the major tasks of managers. Objectives must be set, and then plans made how to achieve them. There are several types of planning:

- **Strategic planning** is the overall plan prepared by top management, and includes long-term aims. It tryies to answer the question: 'Where are we going?'

- **Policy planning** is deciding on the best ways to achieve the organisation's strategic aims. It answers the question: 'How are we going to get there?'
- Lower down the line, plans must be made about programmes and procedures in different parts of the organisation, which, together, will enable the strategic objectives to be met.

Many people believe that planning is something that only the most senior managers have to do. Nothing can be further from the truth. All managers have to plan, but the scope and extent of their plans vary.

- A first-line manager might only have to plan the duty rosters of his or her workers.
- A departmental head will produce plans that will ensure that the department participates fully in the strategy of the whole company.
- The Board of Directors will try to anticipate the future, by deciding on a well-thought-out strategic mission.

Organising

Managers have to set tasks for their workers and make sure that these are carried out efficiently. This means that jobs in the various department of sections have to be organised. This, in turn, leads to **delegating** some of the tasks to others and giving them the responsibility for the work.

One project often involves many tasks, all of which must be done well and completed on time. It is the responsibility of the manager to allocate the jobs, and to make sure that the work is carried out, deadlines met and customers satisfied.

Commanding

Fayol recognised that managers must have the authority to give instructions to their subordinates, and that it is the managers' responsibility to see that the instructions have been carried out.

Co-ordinating

Activities of the individuals and groups within the organisations must be brought together. Sometimes, an individual or a group might have a different goal to that of the company. Managers must ensure that all concerned have a common approach; otherwise, the company's aims will not be achieved.

Controlling

By controlling, Fayol meant the need for managers to monitor and measure the performance of individuals and groups, and to correct any actions that fall short of the expected standard.

There are several other management functions: motivating, problem solving, information handling, training and mentoring, and providing feedback.

Motivation

This function is the topic of Chapter 1 of this unit.

Problem solving

Problems, big and small, occur at all levels in all organisations. Some can be solved easily and quickly. Others need consultation and discussion with others. Solving problems is an inherent part of a manager's responsibility.

Information handling

A modern business organisation, whatever its products, generates and receives a large amount of information. This includes instructions, personal data and communications with customers, suppliers and workers. Managers must be able to deal with and use all information efficiently, and to pass on to their subordinates the information that they need to perform their jobs efficiently.

Training and mentoring

This managerial function has a two-fold purpose. It is beneficial to the individual to receive training and any additional help that his or her manager may provide. It is also beneficial to the organisation if its workers are fully supported and are given the opportunity to improve their performance through training. This function is closely related to the wider function of motivation.

Providing feedback

Managers do not operate in a vacuum. A manager should provide his or her own managers with feedback on the state of affairs in his or her own area of activity, and should also ensure that workers receive feedback on their efforts, achievements, ideas and suggestions.

Activity

What do they actually do?

Working in a group, organise a meeting with one of your school or college managers. (They probably would not much like to have a dozen or more individuals coming separately to ask the same questions!)

Ask the manager to focus on these four functions of his or her job.

1 Planning

2 Motivating people

3 Organising

4 Controlling

Ask the manager to tell you briefly which function he or she:

- spends most time on
- finds most difficult (and why)
- finds the most rewarding (and why)
- considers the most important to the smooth running of the school/college.

Write a short evaluation of your manager's answers.

Skills of managers

It is dangerous to assume that an individual without any managerial experience will make a good manager just because he or she is a very efficient worker. To be effective, managers should have certain skills:

- **Good interpersonal skills**
  A manager should be able to deal with different individuals in a variety of situations, without becoming angry, impatient or losing interest.
- **The ability to organise**
  As this is one of the most important management functions, a manager who cannot organise is not going to be successful.
- **A good communicator**
  This includes verbal, non-verbal and written communication skills.
- **Having a good knowledge and understanding** of the organisation, its products, aims and objectives.

Theories of management

Several important management theories were discussed in Chapter 1 of this unit. All the theorists were concerned with the ways in which that managers should manage the individuals in their charge. Their conclusions were different, but all had a great influence on management today.

Other contributors in the field of management theory are covered below.

Peter F. Drucker

Peter Drucker was born in Austria and emigrated to the US where, for 30 years, he was a leading management expert and business adviser. Drucker argued that management involves four skills, which can be learned, and does not rely on experience or ability alone:

- Planning and setting objectives
- Organising – which involves the ability to analyse, describe and authorise

- Motivating and communicating
- Measuring

Drucker introduced the concept of **management by objectives** which is still used by some organisations today.

Management by objectives – a system of management in which every individual should be given objectives or targets to reach

These targets should be reviewed regularly after assessment of the worker's performance.

Fred Fiedler and the Contingency Model

Fred Fiedler was a psychologist who concerned himself with the problem of the best management style. He came to the conclusion that different situations demanded different solutions, and called his proposals **the Contingency Model**. Fiedler believed that there is no one 'best' method of management. He advised that different situations demanded different managers, and that managers should be matched to the situation.

Von Bertalanffy and the Systems Theory

Von Bertalanffy was a German biologist who, in 1968, published his general systems theory. His work was concerned with systems that 'cover a broad spectrum of our physical, biological and social world'.

Von Bertalaffy defined a system as 'an organised, unitary whole composed of two or more interdependent parts', which can, and do, function well together. His ideas were taken up by management theorists who identified systems within organisations and concluded that every system is composed of subsystems of a lower order, and that each system is also a part of a superior system. Thus, a department of an organisation is a system, with its sections or teams as subsystems, and the whole organisation as the suprasystem.

Styles of leadership

All managers are leaders, but there are several distinct styles of leadership: autocratic, democratic, laissez-faire:

Autocratic style

The manager sets objectives and allocates tasks and then expects subordinates to do what they are instructed to do. This style does not allow workers to participate in decision making, and can lead to worker dissatisfaction and unrest. This, in turn, can reduce productivity because of low motivation, even though an autocratic manager supervises his workers closely. Today, the autocratic style is out of favour and few managers would like to admit their preference for tight control of workers. In practice, quite a few managers would probably rather like to be able to manage autocratically. Some situations demand an autocratic approach. The armed forces and the police are good examples of organisations where decisions must be made quickly, often without any consultation, and orders carried out without question. Another example of a situation in which an autocratic style would be appropriate is of an organisation in difficulties which, in the view of management, can only be resolved if workers follow instructions and carry out their allotted tasks without discussion.

Democratic style

A democratic style of leadership includes workers in decision making. The leader consults the workers before the decision is made, and their views influence the final decision. This style of leadership makes the workers feel that they are valued members of the organisation, and leads to greater motivation and therefore to greater productivity.

Since communication is a vital part of this style, managers must have excellent communication skills, be prepared to explain what is required to workers, and he willing to listen to their views and ideas. One disadvantage of this leadership style is the time taken to reach decisions.

A variant of the democratic style is the **persuasive** style of leadership. Here the decisions are made by the manager, but the workers are told why such decisions were necessary and persuaded that they were beneficial, not only to the organisation but to them as well.

Laissez-faire style

The laissez-faire style of leadership allows the workers a lot of freedom and gives them few directions. While this results in a stress-free atmosphere, many workers

CASE STUDY

Enthusiasm is not enough

Charlotte Jones is a bright, enthusiastic 22-year-old. She has a business qualification and has now been working for Tall Orders plc, a company manufacturing and selling clothing for very tall men and women, for over two years. Charlotte is ambitious and has worked very hard to achieve good results. She was delighted when the post of manager of the mail order section became vacant, and decided to apply.

At her interview, Charlotte impressed the panel with her enthusiasm and ideas. Her immediate boss, Perry Stretton, asked her how she would go about managing a group of ten workers, all engaged in different jobs, and suggested that she might benefit from some management training. Charlotte took it in her stride. 'I read all about management theories on my course,' she replied. 'I know exactly what a manager should do.'

Perry still had some doubts about Charlotte's suitability for the job, but the other panel members did not agree with him and Charlotte was offered the position.

That evening, Charlotte telephoned her father to tell him the good news. Mr Jones congratulated her warmly and asked how she was going to go about managing so many people.

'No problem, Dad,' said Charlotte. 'It's going to be easy.'

During her first week as manager, Charlotte was surprised at the amount of information that arrived daily on her desk. She found it difficult to cope with all the problems that had to be dealt with on a daily basis, and most of her paperwork was left unfinished at the end of the day.

Several of the workers asked for help in getting a large mail order out on time, but Charlotte told them to do the best they could. She also found the regular weekly meetings of the departmental managers irksome. She had so much to do! She resented having to spend several hours every week discussing future developments and plans when she needed to be in her office, dealing with more pressing matters.

When Charlotte missed two meetings, the Departmental Manager called her in and told her in no uncertain terms that attendance at the meetings was compulsory.

'These meetings make it possible for us to agree our plans for the future, provide an opportunity to compare notes, and discuss ways and means of improving things in the department,' he said.

'But I have no time for planning,' wailed Charlotte. 'I'm too busy trying to deal with routine matters. I was hoping to reorganise some of the ways in which things are done in the section, but the staff don't want to co-operate with me! As for monitoring their work, I haven't even started!'

Charlotte was very upset and called her father again. He was sympathetic but seemed to think that the difficulties she was in were largely of her own making. 'It's your own fault, Charlotte,' he said. 'Being a manager is not as simple as you thought. You haven't bothered to find out exactly what would be required of you, haven't tried to learn anything about planning, organising or dealing with people. No wonder you are having problems.'

'Is there anything I can do now?' Charlotte asked tearfully.

become demotivated because they feel that management is not interested in them as individuals. Productivity tends to decrease as a result.

Today, most people believe that the democratic style of leadership is the one most likely to motivate workers and achieve best results for the organisation. It is also in line with present-day legislation which lays down the rules for ensuring workers' rights in the workplace. As mentioned above, there are situations where the democratic style is not the right one.

Supportive and **collaborative** styles place great emphasis on the need for managers to create an atmosphere in which workers are given support whenever needed and, in the latter case, are actively encouraged to work together with management to achieve common objectives. These two styles are related to **democratic** leadership.

Reasons why managers adopt a certain leadership style

Different styles of leadership are often adopted by an organisation because of a particular need within the organisation.

- The **culture** of the organisation
- The **type of workers**
  For example, the more skilled and mature the workforce, the better it will respond to democratic leadership.
- The **work itself**
  As we have seen, when quick decisions are imperative, and the success of a project depends on the work being done quickly, even those managers who intrinsically tend to the democratic style may adopt the autocratic style.
- The **personality** of the manager
  All managers are not the same, and some will automatically tend to adopt the democratic style, while others are happier leading their group democratically.
- **Size of groups**
  For practical reasons, very large groups are difficult to manage democratically.

Other factors also affect the choice of a leadership style. An internal or external change in circumstances may cause a company to change its leadership style to fit in with the requirements of the new situation. Finally, in many organisation a mixture of two, or even three leadership styles may sometimes be used.

Organisational culture – all the beliefs and values of a business, including expected ways of behaviour and acceptable attitudes

Revision Questions

1. What, according to Drucker, is the main purpose of a business? (2 marks)
2. Name three management functions. (2 marks)
3. Why should a manager have good communication skills? (2 marks)
4. Explain, briefly, the theory of MBO. (4 marks)
5. What were the main points of the contingency model? (3 marks)
6. What is meant by 'strategic planning'? (3 marks)
7. Why do managers need to be good organisers? (4 marks)
8. What are the benefits of training to the organisation? (2 marks)
9. What is 'organisational culture'? (2 marks)
10. What are the main features of democratic leadership? (4 marks)
11. Explain the usefulness of the autocratic style in some situations. (4 marks)
12. With reference to the 'Enthusiasm' case study on page 221, explain why Charlotte was failing as a manager. (10 marks)

CHAPTER 4

Communication in the Workplace

KEY TERMS

Barriers to communication	Grapevine	Means of communication
Communication	Horizontal	Two way
Formal	Informal	Vertical

In this chapter, you will learn about communication in the workplace and about its importance. You will also learn about the ways in which communication can be achieved.

What is communication?

Communication is vital to the success of all organisations. Good communication systems are a powerful tool of management. We have already seen that it is impossible to motivate people without communicating with them, and that good communication skills are a prerequisite of good managers. Communication is the link between people at all organisational levels, which enables the whole organisation to function smoothly. When F. W. Taylor was formulating his principles of 'scientific management', the only communication regarded as necessary between workers and management was the issuing of orders and instructions. We have come a long way since then.

Communication is the sending and receiving of information.

In a business organisation, communication takes place all day, every day, but to be effective it must not only be sent and received, but must reach the right recipient and be understood.

Communication as a two-way process

In all organisations, managers communicate with their subordinates, and workers communicate with their bosses. While some communication needs no response or feedback – e.g. information from management about a routine matter – most businesses now recognise the need for two-way communication. This enables recipient of a message to respond to it, and allows the sender to find out its effect on the recipient.

Two-way communication should also encourage the lower levels of an organisation to make their views and comments known to their superiors. The democratic style of leadership actively encourages, and relies on, regular communication throughout the company.

The need for communication systems

A small organisation has no communication problem. The owner of a newsagent's shop, employing two assistants and three or four paper boys and girls, does not need to set up elaborate communication system. Any information that he or she must give the employees can be done face to face. They, in turn, can speak directly to the owner about anything that concerns them.

The situation in a large company is different. Not only are there hundreds or even thousands of people who all need to communicate with others, but the structure of the business means that there are many departments and sections, all needing information, help with problem solving, praise, instruction and reassurance. In many cases, different parts of the organisation are located in different buildings, maybe in different towns or even in different countries. Without proper systems, communication would fail.

Communication originating with management

There are two ways in which management may choose to communicate with workers:

- On a '**need to know**' basis
  This assumes that workers, whatever their position, should be told only what is absolutely necessary for them to know in order to perform their work efficiently. Autocratic leaders are likely to follow this method.
- **Inviting response**
  Democratic managements aim to encourage workers to comment on information received, offer suggestions and even influence decisions.

Management needs to communicate with workers on a variety of topics, vertically and horizontally.

Vertical communication travels from one level to another in an organisation.

- Senior management must inform workers about company policy and, more and more frequently nowadays, about the organisation's strategic plans and objectives. This can be done by top managers informing middle managers who, in turn, pass the information on to their subordinates. Another way is for all workers to be informed directly, in meetings, or through memos or newsletters.
- Middle managers must communicate with their workers about all aspects of work to be done. Again, this can be achieved in different ways.
- Lower down the line, supervisors or foremen communicate with their operatives about day-to-day requirements or problems.

In organisations with a flat management structure, there may be fewer levels of communication, but the content of the communications remains much the same.

Horizontal communication takes place between people on the *same* level of the organisation. Messages sent from one department to another are an example of horizontal communication.

As you can see, the channels of communication can be different. Both horizontal and vertical communication can be formal or informal.

Means of communication

Not so many years ago, communication in the workplace was limited to face-to-face meetings, telephone conversations, memos and letters. New technology has brought us faxes, and e-mails, giving a much greater choice of means of communication. None of these methods, however, will guarantee efficient receiving and sending of information if the organisation fails to set up efficient systems.

Oral communication

There are many opportunities for oral communication in the workplace. They include meetings, one-to-one interviews and discussions during performance reviews. Oral communication has a number of advantages. It is direct, there is no delay in waiting for a reply, and it is less impersonal than any other medium. However, there is often no permanent record of what had been said.

Many managers operate an 'open door policy' to encourage workers to speak to them directly.

Communication can take place not only between managers and workers, but also between workers and their representatives, such as union officials, and between the representatives and management.

Written communication

Written communication can take many forms:

- Memos
- Letters
- Reports
- Newsletters
- Financial statements
- Facsimilies
- E-mail
- Notice boards
- Posters
- Forms

CASE STUDY

COMMUNICATIONS – THE KEY TO SUCCESS!

FKI Group of Companies

Organisations communicate with their workforce:

- To help employees to understand fully what they are required to do
- To provide feedback on how well they are meeting that requirement
- To give them an opportunity to share ideas on how products and services can be improved
- To let them know how well the company is doing and about its plans for future development.

FKI is a multinational company engaged mainly in engineering. It has member companies in the UK, the USA and Europe. FKI member companies have customers throughout the world and have earned an international reputation as leaders in their field. Building and maintaining a reputation such as this is gained by dedication to quality and technical excellence – a clear priority when meeting customer needs.

This means that the companies must stay ahead of competitors in aspects of quality and innovation. But it is the people within these companies who are vital to its success in rapidly changing markets. Employees at all levels need to cope with a rate of change unlike anything they have known before – a pace of change which will go on increasing.

Meeting the challenge of change has meant that restructuring within parts of the group has been necessary in recent years. This has caused uncertainty and anxiety among some employees .... Managers throughout FKI companies acknowledge that success comes through people at all levels working as a team ... working together to solve problems. **If they are to do this, they need to communicate properly**. This means **TALKING**!

Talking

Communication needs to flow in all directions in a successful organisation. The board needs to devolve their objectives through management to all employees but needs to be able to receive ideas and input from all corners of the business. Here are some ways this is done at FKI:

Annual reports

Each employee receives an annual statement from the Managing Director of his or her company, which summarises successes or problems in the previous year. It provides an outline of changes planned for the year ahead and how these fit into the company strategy for the medium and long tem. It also summarises the financial progress of the company.

Team briefings

Messages about new developments and changes in production methods or the solutions to problems can be rapidly cascaded by team briefings. The Board agrees key messages, these are communicated face to face with managers, managers pass these on in face-to-face meetings with supervisors and they, in turn, pass on the messages through similar meetings with production teams.

Notice boards

An old and far from 'high tech' medium, but, if used properly, posters and notice boards can provide accurate and speedy information on production achievements, safety records and quality performance. This can help to correct some of the misinformed and exaggerated stories that will flourish on the unofficial 'grapevine' in every workplace. Saturation poster campaigns can be used to support drives on particular issues such as quality or safety.

Some examples of communication used successfully in FKI Engineering Companies:

- **Whipp & Bourne Ltd, Rochdale**
  An **active communications** policy has been adopted by the Board. Directors use **half-yearly meetings** to keep employees informed of long-term strategies, future developments for the company, how it will get there and what role the employees will play. The meetings also provide an opportunity for questions to be asked of directors.
  Weekly meetings of directors and middle managers enable messages to be cascaded quickly through the company. Middle managers, in turn, pass the information obtained to supervisors and work teams, varying in size from 6 to 30 people.
- **Bristol Babcock, Kidderminster**
  Directors address all the workforce together at a **quarterly meeting.** The meeting provides an explanation of business plans, forecasts, progress and problems. Questions and suggestions are encouraged.
- **Laurence Scott & Electromotors, Norwich, Bedford and Worcester**
  The Management Team puts a heavy emphasis on **top-down communications** to keep workers informed about what is happening in the company.
  Senior managers attend regular **monthly meetings** with directors and then cascade information given throughout their own departments. Whatever methods of communication are used, formal or informal, written or spoken, they should contribute to keeping employees continually informed on the key questions:

  What do I need to do?

  Where does my work come from and go to?

  Why is my job important?

  Who is my line manager?

  What are my work targets?

  What changes are being made and why?

  How can I help improve what is done?

There is a role in the workplace for every method of communication, but any successful communication strategy cannot omit face-to-face communication and the spoken word. Messages are much more readily absorbed when received this way.

Source: Times 100

Formal and informal communication

Communication can be formal or informal.

- **Formal communication** takes the form of meetings, notices, letters, etc.
- **Informal communication**, often called the **grapevine**, exists in all workplaces. Workers meet, chat and exchange information.

The grapevine often has a negative effect, so that information becomes distorted as it is passed around, much as in a game of Chinese Whispers. This can lead to anxiety and unrest unless managers clarify the situation.

Conversely, the grapevine can be useful to management as it can bring information about competitors or alert managers to potential problems.

IT and communication

IT has revolutionised the ways in which we can communicate. The sending of messages and storing and retrieving of information no longer rely on the traditional methods.

- Telephone messages can be recorded on answerphone machines if somebody is out of the office and unable to take the call. For example, someone in London who needs to communicate with someone in New York or Tokyo, can call and leave a message even though nobody is there to receive it, due to the time difference.
- Individual managers can use mobile phones to check on their mail, or to find out what has been going on even when they are out of the office.
- Faxes and electronic mail provide quick and accurate methods of transmitting messages in written form.

- Videos are another form of sending and receiving information and are useful in many situations. For example, a travel agency will use videos to acquaint its employees with new holiday locations. This is much more effective than sending written descriptions illustrated with photographs.
- Videoconferencing gives individuals in different locations the opportunity for discussion and an exchange of ideas exactly as if they were all sitting together in one boardroom.

Matching the medium for the message

Not all communication media are suitable for all purposes. Confidential data must be sent securely to ensure that it is not received by the wrong people. If speed is of the essence, e-mail or oral communication is best. However, oral communication should not be used if it is necessary to keep a record of it. Cost is also a factor in choosing how to communicate. Videos and films are expensive and, in many instances, other media must be chosen.

It is important to remember that **external communication** must also be efficient. Companies must communicate with their suppliers, customers and clients, as well as with outside agencies such as financial institutions, the Inland Revenue and the local authority. Care should be taken that the right medium is chosen for this type of communication.

Barriers to effective communication

Communication is effective if:

- the sender makes the message clear
- the recipient understands the message
- the correct medium is used.

Here are some barriers to effective communication:

- **Unclear messages sent**
  Telling a worker that a job must be finished soon when the exact deadline is in two days' time, will probably result in a delay.
- **Use of jargon**
  Many technical terms, known as jargon, make sense to those engaged in production but not necessarily to those whose job it is to advertise the products. Use of jargon should be avoided unless it is certain that the recipients understand it.
- **Wrong choice of medium**
  Telling one individual to pass an important message to his or her workmates orally is not an efficient way of ensuring that the correct message is received and understood.
- **Style used**
  This must be suitable for the recipient. When informing shopfloor workers of the firm's strategic plans, simple and clear language must be used and it should not be assumed that everybody understands the finer points of management planning.
- All communication should be **clear, concise and to the point**
  Too much information in a memo or fax may lead to the recipients failing to understand the main purpose of the message.
- **Personal prejudices**
  One person's view of another may prevent him or her from responding correctly to a message received.

Care should also be taken that all messages are conveyed to the right people; otherwise the results can be embarrassing.

CASE STUDY

You should have known!

Patrick works in the Marketing Department of Fine Houses Estate Agency. It is his first job after leaving college and Patrick is determined to make a success of it. To prove to his manager, Erwin, that he is dedicated to his job, Patrick makes sure that he is always the first to arrive, does not clock watch at the end of the day, and carries out Erwin's instructions to the letter.

Last week, Patrick was delighted when Erwin, who had to go out to show a property to a client, asked him to 'look after things' during his absence. (On previous occasions, Erwin had requested other members of staff to cover for him.)

There were several calls for Erwin. Patrick wrote down all the details, and assured the callers that Erwin would be in touch shortly. Two prospective clients came in and Patrick gave them the information they required. Patrick began to feel rather pleased with himself.

A bit later, the firm's accountant rang, asking for Erwin. On being told that Erwin was out of the office, he said that he had still not received Erwin's expenses claim. Patrick promised to pass the message on but, just as he put the phone down, he was handed a fax. The sender was requesting immediate response to his earlier fax. He wanted to know the details of a deal that Erwin was about to complete. Patrick rummaged on Erwin's desk and found the relevant paperwork. He then faxed the information to the caller. He was a little surprised that the address was that of another estate agency, but thought no more of it.

When Erwin returned some time later, Patrick proudly told him all that he had managed to achieve on his own. Erwin was quite impressed until Patrick mentioned the fax. He went red in the face and seemed about to choke. 'What on earth made you give that man the information?' he shouted. 'Don't you know he is a competitor? Anyway, such information is always confidential. Why didn't you ask somebody what to do? You should have known better!'

Patrick was most upset, and felt that he had been unfairly treated.

Activity

Too Little or Too Much?

Ask two people who have a job to tell you:

- how they communicate with their line managers
- how their line managers communicate with them
- how often they have meetings with their colleagues at work
- if, and how, they are informed about what goes on in their workplace
- what methods of communication are used at their place of work
- if they feel that they receive too little, enough or too much information
- how communications at their place of work could be improved.

Write a short summary of the information you have gathered.

Revision Questions

1. What is communication? (1 mark)
2. Why is communication important to a business? (2 marks)
3. Explain the difference between vertical and horizontal communication. (5 marks)
4. Why should communication be two way? (4 marks)
5. Why are regular meetings important? (2 marks)
6. Give two examples of oral communication. (2 marks)
7. How has IT changed business communication? (6 marks)
8. What are barriers to communication? (1 mark)
9. Name two barriers to communications, and explain how they can be avoided. (5 marks)
10. Why are formal communication channels needed in large organisations? (4 marks)
11. What is a 'grapevine' and how does it operate? (3 marks)
12. What are likely to be the results of a breakdown of communication in the workplace? (4 marks)

CHAPTER 5

The HR Department and its Work

KEY TERMS

Career development	Human resource management	Off-the-job training
Critical incident analysis	Human resources (HR)	On-the-job training
Disciplinary procedure	Induction	Performance appraisal
Equal opportunities policy	Job description	Person specification
Fault analysis	Manpower planning	Recruitment
Grievance procedure	Needs assessment	Selection

In this chapter, you will learn about the work of the Human Resources (HR) Department and its responsibilities, including selection, recruitment, assessing the needs of the individual and providing training.

What are human resources?

Human resources – all the employees of an organisation, from managers to production workers and from office staff to cleaners

The growth of the HR Department was the direct result of organisations gradually coming to understand the value and the needs of workers. All the main management theorists, from Taylor, Maslow and Herzberg onwards, were concerned with the needs of individuals and groups in the workplace. Labour is now generally accepted to be a factor of production like no other and, to succeed in their quest for higher levels of production, organisations must select the most suitable workers and look after them well.

Today, most middle-sized and large companies have HR Departments, and HR managers are usually members of the senior management team. However, there are still some widely held misconceptions about the role and functions of HRM.

Human resource management (HRM) – an organisational function concerned with all aspects of people's lives at work

The HR department does not work in a vacuum. It must work closely with top management and other departments and its work must reflect the needs of the organisation. Strategic and operational plans and the implementation of the policies of the organisation shape the way in which the HR function will be carried out.

The main functions of the HR department are manpower planning and HR planning.

For a firm to be efficient and effective, it has to employ the right number of employees with the requisite job knowledge and expertise: **manpower planning.** It involves knowing the current employment needs, forecasting future needs, both short- and long-term, and analysing the availability of workers.

Short-term manpower planning deals with such tasks as filling existing vacancies. Long-term planning is concerned with forecasting, and making provision for the future needs of the business. Forecasting is based on the company's long-term plans and on any data available, including past figures, work study and research into external factors that might affect both the need for workers and the supply of workers available.

HR planning is concerned with ways in which the organisation can improve working relationships, respond to workers' needs and provide them with training opportunities. This part of the planning process includes plans to change and improve the **organisational culture** of the business and to introduce changes in the way in which employees are supported and trained.

HR and manpower planning is not a static activity. Changing circumstances often dictate a change in planning. These circumstances may be internal, like the need for retraining workers so that they can cope with modern methods of production, or having to reduce staff levels because of a recession.

Predicting future events is never easy and, however carefully plans about manpower resources are made, there is no guarantee that the results will be correct.

Recruitment and selection

This is a crucial function of the HR department and is carried out in conjunction with other departments. If the Marketing Department needs to expand, and must recruit two additional workers, the Marketing Manager will give all the details of his or her requirements to the HR people so that they can set up the recruitment process. Throughout the process, HR must work closely with the department on whose behalf they are recruiting.

The objective of the recruitment process is to select and appoint the best candidate for the job. Appointing the wrong person can be detrimental and costly to the organisation, so the process must be very carefully carried out. It is important that HR know exactly what kind of person is needed. The process will proceed through several stages:

- Gathering and analysing information about the job
- Job description
- Person specification

Gathering and analysing information about the job is done through the **task analysis, activity analysis** and **skills analysis** of the job in question.

Task analysis is a study of those tasks that the appointee will have to carry out in the job.

Activity analysis studies all the activities involved in the tasks.

A manual job might include activities, which do not seem to be directly involved with the job itself; e.g. a storekeeper might have to be computer literate to be able to input and retrieve information.

Skills analysis involves identifying skills necessary for the job.

Skills can be manual, technical or even interpersonal skills if the person will be required to work with others.

A job description includes information about the contents of the job, tasks to be performed and responsibilities to be taken on, as well as information about working conditions.

A person specification summarises the qualities required in an applicant for a particular job, e.g. the ability to work on one's own initiative, have some previous knowledge of a particular area of work, or a proven ability to work as an effective team member.

Person specification: Supermarket Cashier

The successful candidate will:

1 Have at least GCSE Grade 2 in Maths

2 Have some experience in the retail food trade

3 Show ability to work under pressure

4 Be meticulous in his/her approach to the job

5 Be willing to learn new skills

6 Enjoy working with people

7 Have a friendly and positive outlook

8 Be committed to the company's Equal Opportunities Policy

9 Be flexible – the hours of work are sometimes unsocial, and Sunday working is required

Activity

Find three job advertisements in your local paper, and compare them. Then answer the following questions.

1 Do they all contain the same information? (If not, summarise the differences.)

2 Is any mention made of the kind of person the employers are seeking? If so, what are the required personal characteristics?

3 What instructions are given about applying for each job?

4 Which advertisement is the best, in your opinion, and why?

Recruitment methods

Recruitment can be **internal** or **external**.

- Internal recruitment occurs when people who are already working in the organisation are appointed to a new job.
- External recruitment is used to acquire new employees from outside.

To recruit from outside, the vacancy must be advertised. The advertisement must be carefully worded and all the relevant information included. Depending on the job, it is possible to advertise in Employment Centres, in the local and national press and in trade and professional journals, as well as on local radio and, *very occasionally*, on television. The cost of advertising plays an important part in which advertising method is chosen.

If **application forms** are used, these must be designed and agreed across the organisation.

All applications must be carefully scrutinised, and a **short list** of those to be called for interview must be decided together with the head of the relevant department.

Interviews vary from job to job and from organisation to organisation. It is the responsibility of HR to organise the interviews, inform all concerned and provide interviewers with relevant information.

After the interview, the successful candidate/s must be given information regarding contracts, start dates, etc. Debriefing or feedback is often offered to those who were unsuccessful.

Induction and Training

Induction programmes are organised for new employees with the aim of introducing them to the organisation and making them feel that they belong. During induction, new appointees meet members of the management team and other personnel, have a tour of the premises and are given additional information. They are told about employee benefits and services, if any, disciplinary and grievance procedures and safety rules and regulations. Good induction programmes have the merit of cutting down the number of new workers who might leave very soon after starting a job. Induction also can start the process of integrating the new workers into the company and giving them a sense of security.

Training is one of the major tasks of the HR department and is an ongoing process. Training is necessary for the individual if he or she is to be able to learn new tasks and to progress. It is also advantageous for the organisation. Planning training is a complex job that must understand and reconcile the needs of the worker and of management.

Training must be planned in line with the needs of the organisation. For example, when office technology was introduced some years ago, HR departments had to plan and deliver training in the use of personal computers to all secretarial and administrative staff. To be able to plan training, HR personnel must know the policies of the organisation and the needs of the individual workers.

HR managers work closely with top management to assess the needs of the firm, and with departmental managers who have their own requirements as far as training is concerned. In many cases, however, the full programme of training that HR managers might consider necessary, after careful analysis of the firm's current and projected needs, cannot be delivered due to budget restrictions, and choices have to be made as to what training should take priority.

Assessing individual needs

To provide training that will benefit both the individual and the organisation, individual needs must be assessed. There are various ways of achieving this:

- **Observation** by line managers
- **Skills audit** – finding out, through questionnaires and interviews, the skills that individual workers have, and establishing what additional skills they need to acquire
- **Self-observation** i.e. finding out from the individuals themselves what training they consider necessary and why
- **Performance appraisals and reviews**
  Unfortunately, individuals at work often see appraisals as being a forum for criticism by their managers. If properly structured and carried out, performance reviews allow the worker and the reviewer to have a frank and constructive exchange of views. The performance review should include an assessment, by both parties, of any training and development needs of the worker, and the results of performance reviews should form the basis of training plans.

Organising training

Once the needs of the worker have been assessed, decisions can be made on the type of training most suitable fort him or her. The training must then be agreed with the worker's manager, and organised by the HR department.

There are many types of training; some are more difficult than others.

On-the-job training is carried out at work. The person being trained by another worker might have to spend time observing the activities of that colleague. Another way of training on the job involves a manager or another experienced worker instructing a new worker in the use of equipment or tools. This might arise, for example, when an assistant at a delicatessen counter must learn to operate a bacon slicer safely and efficiently. Sometimes, a new worker is paired with another, move experienced one who acts as a 'mentor' and is on hand to provide help and advice.

Job rotation, used for training managerial recruits in some large organisations, involves the person spending some time in each department. At the end of the rotation, the individual will have acquired a range of knowledge and skills.

Apprenticeships have declined in line with the decline in manufacturing industries. The apprentice trainees were given a thorough training in their particular craft or trade over a period of time, and were then taken on by the firm at the end of the apprenticeship.

Off-the-job training means sending employees on courses. The courses may be short (a day or two) or long (six months or more). Off-the-job training can be provided on the employer's premises. Special courses may be organised as and when the need arises. The Finance Department might ask for a course on the use of the latest computerised accounts packages, for example, or managers might be asked to attend an assertiveness course or a course on interpersonal skills.

Many companies send their employees to schools or colleges offering vocational courses such as GNVQs. Many courses are available in many areas of training, so the choice is there. While such courses do not have to be organised by the employer, the HR Department is responsible for liaising with the employees' managers, arranging course places and monitoring those attending.

Evaluation of training

It is vital that the results of all training programmes are evaluated, to establish their worth to the organisation and the individual, and to find out if the costs involved have been justified by the results.

Career Development

Any training that successfully increases an individual's skills and knowledge is a step in his or her personal development. Career development goes further, by offering the person the opportunity to work towards higher goals. Not everyone sees his or her job as a stepping-stone to a career, but those who do should receive support and help from the organisation. Trainee managers, for instance, are often given the opportunity to learn about the work of all departments before they decide on their preferred career route.

Tools used to review and assess performance at work

Faults analysis

If many faults occur during the performance of a task, they should be identified, and individuals should then be told how to recognise the faults, what causes them and how they can be avoided.

Critical incident technique

This is a way of obtaining information about effective or less effective behaviour related to an actual incident. Workers are asked to provide information about the incidents and when they occurred. Analysis of the data makes it possible to list the competences required to eliminate or at least reduce such incidents.

Such techniques are useful in enabling individuals to become more effective in their jobs.

Statutory Requirements

Another responsibility of HR management is to ensure that the organisation understands and implements legal requirements with regard to equal opportunities at work. Most organisations now have an equal opportunities policy which is communicated to all workers, but such policies are not enough. All aspects of equal opportunities must be constantly monitored and reviewed to ensure that no one in the organisation is discriminated against on the grounds of race, religion, disability or gender.

Reviews

The activities of the HR Department are many and far reaching and include in their scope the interests of individuals, groups, departments and the organisation as a whole. This necessitates reviews, one of which, the **performance appraisal review**, has already been mentioned.

Other reviews include **departmental reviews**, at which the efficiency and performance of the department is assessed and the results analysed, with a view to introducing any necessary improvements.

Reviews of performance are valuable at all levels of the organisation and are often requested by managers and senior managers.

Disciplinary and Grievance Procedures

However well an organisation looks after its employees, problems do sometimes arise. Much of the work of the HR Department is aimed at satisfying the needs of individuals, and a sound selection process, good induction and training opportunities are instrumental in making employees feel that the organisation cares about them.

Sometimes, however, an individual does not fit in with the organisational culture, or simply refuses to obey the rules. The trouble might be confined to the job in hand or might escalate into fully fledged conflict with colleagues and/or managers. In the first instance, it is the individual's line manager who has the job of trying to find a solution to the problem. In this, help and advice can be given by the HR personnel.

If matters are not resolved, it might prove necessary for a disciplinary procedure to be taken by the line manager. If so, the HR Department can assist and advise on the correct procedures to ensure that the procedure is carried out fairly.

The other side of the coin is a grievance procedure taken by an employee against a member of management. Again, if the matter cannot be resolved informally, the HR Department has a role to play, not only as adviser, but also often in negotiations with the trade union of which the employee is a member.

The functions of the HR Department described in this chapter show clearly the scope of its activities in selecting, recruiting, training and developing individuals, and also in looking after their interests by providing fair and unbiased support in any difficulty or dispute. The HR Department acts as a link between senior management and other departments on one hand, and individuals on the other, and, as such, has a unique position in the business organisation.

CASE STUDY

An unfair advantage

Juanita joined the administrative team at Foster & Co. Ltd straight out of college. Foster & Co. is a large firm which manufactures and sells plastic novelties. Juanita was quite happy in her new job for some months. Then her friend in the office, Lynn, told her that the office manager, Paulette Rigson, had suggested that she should join an NVQ in Business scheme.

'It's brilliant,' said Lynn. 'I can do some of the things needed at work, then I'll have time to learn new skills, and then I'll get a good qualification. Couldn't be easier!'

'That's lovely,' said Juanita, but she was far from pleased. She could not understand why she had not been offered the same opportunity. She did not want to ask her manager directly, but made an appointment to see one of the HR managers.

She then met Laura in the HR suite and told her about her disappointment.

'I couldn't believe what Lynn told me,' she said. 'It's so unfair! We both work in the same office, our jobs are the same, why can't I do the NVQ?'

Laura looked very surprised. 'I don't know what Lynn told you exactly,' she answered, 'but your situation is very different. You already have a business qualification, and there are other reasons as well, which I can't discuss with you. Believe me, Juanita, you are doing well, and we are all aware of this fact. Remember your performance review. What did we decide about further training?'

Juanita felt rather foolish. 'We agreed that I didn't need further training at the moment, but that if I worked hard it might be possible to transfer me to a management training scheme,' she said.

'Exactly,' said Laura.

Juanita fled.

Revision Questions

1. What is 'manpower planning'? (1 mark)
2. How can developing the skills of individuals be beneficial not only to them but to the organisation? (5 marks)
3. List and describe the stages of a selection and recruitment procedure. (5 marks)
4. How does a job description differ from a person specification? (3 marks)
5. What is the purpose of an induction programme? (2 marks)
6. What is off-the-job training? Give two examples. (3 marks)
7. Explain the purpose of critical incident analysis. (3 marks)
8. The HR Department is said to be a link between management, workers and all other departments. Explain. (5 marks)
9. What is an equal opportunities policy, and why is it important? (4 marks)
10. How does a grievance policy work? (2 marks)
11. How can an individual's needs be assessed? (5 marks)
12. What is the purpose of performance reviews, and how can they benefit the individual? (5 marks)

UNIT 5

End of Unit Assignment

CASE STUDY

Real Leather Co. Ltd

Real Leather Co. is located on the outskirts of London, not far from Heathrow Airport. It manufactures good quality leather travel goods, as well as handbags, purses, wallets and credit card holders. In the last few years, the company had suffered some setbacks. In addition to competing with other manufacturers in the same line of business, it also lost customers who switched to cheaper artificial leather goods. During that time, the MD, Noel Norris, the son of the firm's founder, reluctantly decided to change the style of leadership in the Production Department. He was sure that the only way for Real Leather Co. to survive was to introduce a new, dynamic manager who would cut costs and improve productivity without consultation with the workforce.

The new Production Manager, Vassilis Yannis, proved efficient although unpopular. The workers, warned of possible redundancies or even closure, complained among themselves, but eventually settled down. Productivity increased, and this, together with an improvement in the economic climate, allowed the company not just to survive, but also to increase its profits.

Two hundred and sixty people are employed in the Production Department at Real Leather. They are divided into teams of eight, each with a supervisor who acts as team leader. The rates of pay are good, and a productivity bonus is paid once a year, in December.

The company has an equal opportunities policy, which is made known to every worker. There is also a grievance procedure, and the workers are given details of this, as well as of the firm's disciplinary procedure, during their induction programme. The induction is organised by the HR Department under the leadership of Nancy Meadows.

Real Leather provides its workers with a subsidised canteen and free tea and coffee during their morning and afternoon breaks.

There is a contributory pension scheme for all workers, into which the company pays a sizeable amount. On reaching retirement, workers receive a lump sum and a pension. The amounts depend on length of service and final salary. Shopfloor workers are paid weekly, but the supervisors and all managers are on monthly salaries. Overtime is regularly worked during busy periods, but is entirely voluntary.

All workers have annual performance appraisals, during which their individual targets and achievements are discussed. In recent years, there has been little training in the company, as Vassilis considered it of low priority.

All departmental managers meet regularly, to ensure that policies, plans and their implementation are agreed and carried out. However, the old practice of all line managers, including the supervisors, meeting on a weekly basis with their workers to hand down information and listen to suggestions, has been abandoned. In the last few months, this has led to some dissatisfaction among the workers.

Questions

1 We are told that Vassilis Yannis proved to be efficient but unpopular. Explain why Noel Norris felt he had to appoint Vassilis when the company was in difficulties. Why would a more democratic style of leadership not have been the best choice at the time? (5 marks)

2 Why are the workers at Real Leather divided into teams? How can the way in which the supervisors manage their teams be improved? (5 marks)

3 In addition to discussing performance and setting targets, performance appraisals should also identify training needs. Explain how the failure of the company to provide training can be detrimental to the firm and demotivating for the individual workers. (8 marks)

4 Real Leather has a tall structure. Explain what that means, and why it is important that communication within the structure should be two way. (3 marks)

5 There appears to be a breakdown in communications at Real Leather. Identify where the problem occurs and suggest how it could be resolved. (5 marks)

6 With reference to Maslow's hierarchy of needs, explain which levels of needs are provided for at Real Leather. (6 marks)

7 The company provides its workers with some of Herzberg's Hygiene Factors. Identify these, and explain why, although important, they are not likely to act as motivators. Which motivating factors seem to be lacking at Real Leather? (10 marks)

8 A new supervisor has asked her line manager for guidance on how to conduct appraisals. She is under the impression that the only correct method is for the line manager to ask questions and the appraisee to answer them. Write a memo to the supervisor, explaining in detail the procedure of performance appraisal. (10 marks)

9 Whenever possible, promotion is internal in the company. A vacancy has arisen for a management trainee in the Production Department. The person appointed will initially be working for the Production Manager. Here are some details of the job:

- Hours: Monday–Friday, 8.30 a.m.–5.30 p.m.
- Holidays: 3 weeks per annum
- Responsibilities: day to day as assigned by the manager
- Qualifications: Vocational A Level Business or equivalent
- Opportunities for further training
- Rate of pay: £10,000 p.a.
- Productivity bonus : 1/10 of annual salary
- Must be enthusiastic, willing to learn and like dealing with people
- Clean driving licence an advantage
- Conditions: modern office, working in a small, dedicated team
- Previous work experience in a busy office would be an advantage.

The above information can be used to create a job description and a person specification. Which pieces of information should be used in the person specification?

The HR Manager needs a job description that can be used to advertise the position. Write the job description. (12 marks)

10 Why are the workers in the Production Department dissatisfied? Suggest what could be done to improve their morale. (6 marks)

11 Noel Norris has spoken to Vassilis and suggested that he should try to be less autocratic in his dealings with the workers. Vassilis replied that he could not agree to a laissez-faire style of management. What would be the dangers of laissez-faire in the company? Is it the only choice available to management? (7 marks)

12 At present, all workers in the Production Department are full time. It has been suggested that some of them might welcome the opportunity to work part time. Some of the senior managers, however, are of the opinion that part-time workers are not motivated, and they oppose the proposal. Explain why part-time working might be beneficial both for the workers and to the management. (5 marks)

13 At the last meeting of departmental managers, the Head of HR said that unless a planned and structured programme of training for staff at all levels is introduced soon, Real Leather is going to find itself lagging behind its competitors. What did Nancy Meadows mean?
(5 marks)

14 Noel Norris has suggested to the senior management team that quality circles should be introduced in the production department. Some managers consider such an innovation to be a waste of time and oppose this idea. Write some notes, explaining:
a) what quality circles are and how they work
b) how they could be of benefit to everyone.
(6 marks)

15 Vassilis has upset Noel by saying that all workers are basically lazy and need nothing more in addition to wages. He seems to believe in McGregor's Theory X. How does Theory X differ from Theory Y, and which, in your opinion, is more likely to motivate the workers in the Production Department?
(6 marks)

16 Because of inadequate communication, speculation and rumour are rife at Real Leather. Some supervisors are concerned that the grapevine is active and often used to pass on inaccurate information. While this may well be detrimental, name two ways in which the grapevine can be useful to management. (3 marks)

17 Noel Norris would like to introduce a job enrichment scheme at Real Leather. Explain how this can be done, and what the disadvantages might be. (3 marks)

18 According to Meredith Belbin, in every team there are usually several different team roles. Noel Norris has read Belbin's theory and has said that, in the senior management team, Nancy Meadows is a *team builder* while Vassilis Yannis is an *implementer*. Explain what Noel means. (4 marks)

UNIT 6

UK Business and the EU

CHAPTER 1

The Development of the EU

KEY TERMS

Common Market
Community law
Customs Union
Enlargement
EU citizenship
European Economic Area (EEA)
European Economic Community (EEC)
European Union (EU)
Inter-governmental conferences (IGCs)
Single currency
Subsidiarity
The Amsterdam Treaty
The Commission
The Council of Ministers
The EU Structural Funds
The European Court of Justice
The European Parliament
The four freedoms
The Single European Act
The Treaty of Rome
The Treaty on European Union (Maastricht)

In this chapter, you will learn how and why the EU developed in the way that it has and how the existence of the EU as a unique market place affects UK businesses.

This chapter will look at why and how the EU developed; the major Acts and Treaties that have bought the EU into existence; the main institutions of the EU; and what changes are likely to take place in the future.

Figure 6.1.1 The Member States of the EU (2001)

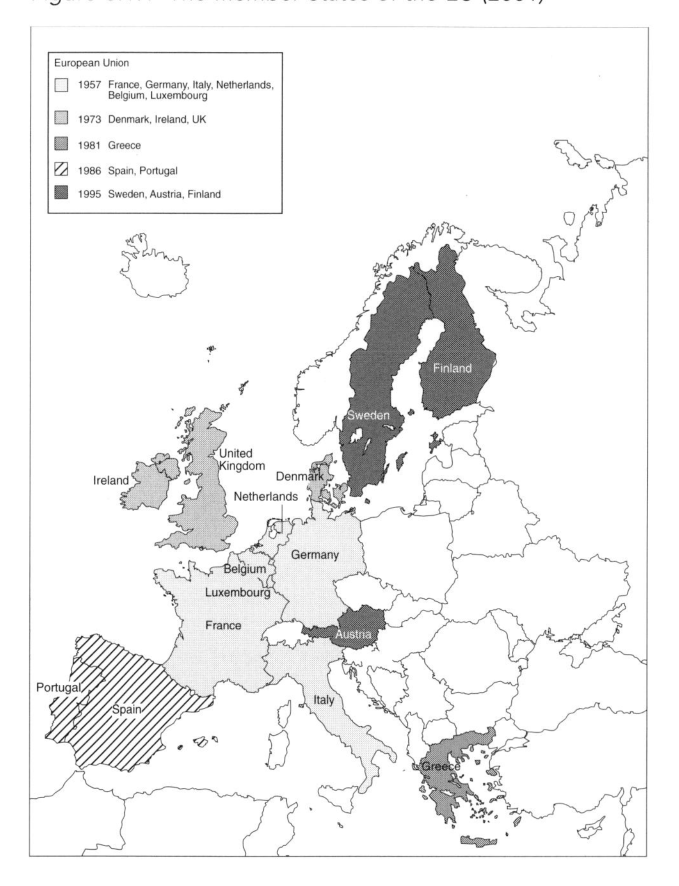

Why and how the EU developed

The desire to create closer integration among European nations arose as a direct result of the devastation of two world wars centred in Europe. The leaders of these nations decided that uniting Europe through economic and political ties was the surest way of preventing such devastation from ever happening again.

> If Europe is to be saved from infinite misery, and indeed from final doom, there must be an act of faith in the European family. To recreate the European family and provide it with a structure under which it can dwell in peace, safety and freedom, we must build a kind of United States of Europe.
>
> **Winston Churchill, 1946**

What is now called the **European Union (EU)** was set up by the **Treaty of Rome** in 1957. The member states have confirmed their commitment to their common objectives by agreeing to changes that will affect all of the EU countries. These changes have been created through new laws and regulations that apply to all the member states.

The **EU** is a formal organisation of European member countries which have common economic, social and political objectives.

The term **EU** is comparatively new and has been used only since the Treaty on European Union (Maastricht) in 1992. Before that the Union was called by various names: the **EEC (European Economic Community)**; the **Common Market** and the **European Community**.

The number of member countries has also changed over the years, growing from six major members in 1957 to 15 major members in 1995. This expansion is shown in Figure 6.1.2.

Although the name has been changed, the basic objectives of the EU have remained the same as when it was first established in 1957:

- The creation of a customs union with free trade between member states
- The creation of a common market for factors of production
- The ultimate integration of the separate national economies into a single European economy
- Significant integration of the member states toward political union

The first definite step on the economic front was in 1945, when Belgium, the Netherlands and Luxembourg established a single **customs union**, generally known as 'Benelux'. This union was designed to reduce trade barriers such as import tariffs and quotas among the three countries and thereby encourage trade.

Customs union – a group of member countries which have no internal barriers, such as tariffs, between themselves and have common external barriers to non-member countries

When the EEC was created in 1957, it established a customs union for all EEC member states, and every new member state has had to agree to remove all tariff and quota barriers between it and the rest of the Community. The long-term objective, however, has always been to create a real **common market**.

Common market – a group of member countries where all internal barriers to trade have been removed and a common set of regulations control trade including the currency, movement of goods and people and levels of taxation

Figure 6.1.3 shows the difference between free trade area, a customs union and a common market.

In 2001, the EU was still some way from achieving this objective, but it had removed many of the barriers, as the examples below demonstrate. It is now possible, in theory, for EU citizens:

- to work in any EU country if they wish
- to have their professional qualifications recognised in all EU countries
- to invest in firms in any EU country
- to sell their products in any EU country on the same basis as national firms sell their products
- to buy goods and services for their own use from any EU country and only pay the taxes charged by that country
- to live in and own property in any EU country
- to be paid and buy products with a currency, the euro, which has the same value in 12 of the member states.

Figure 6.1.2 The history of the EU

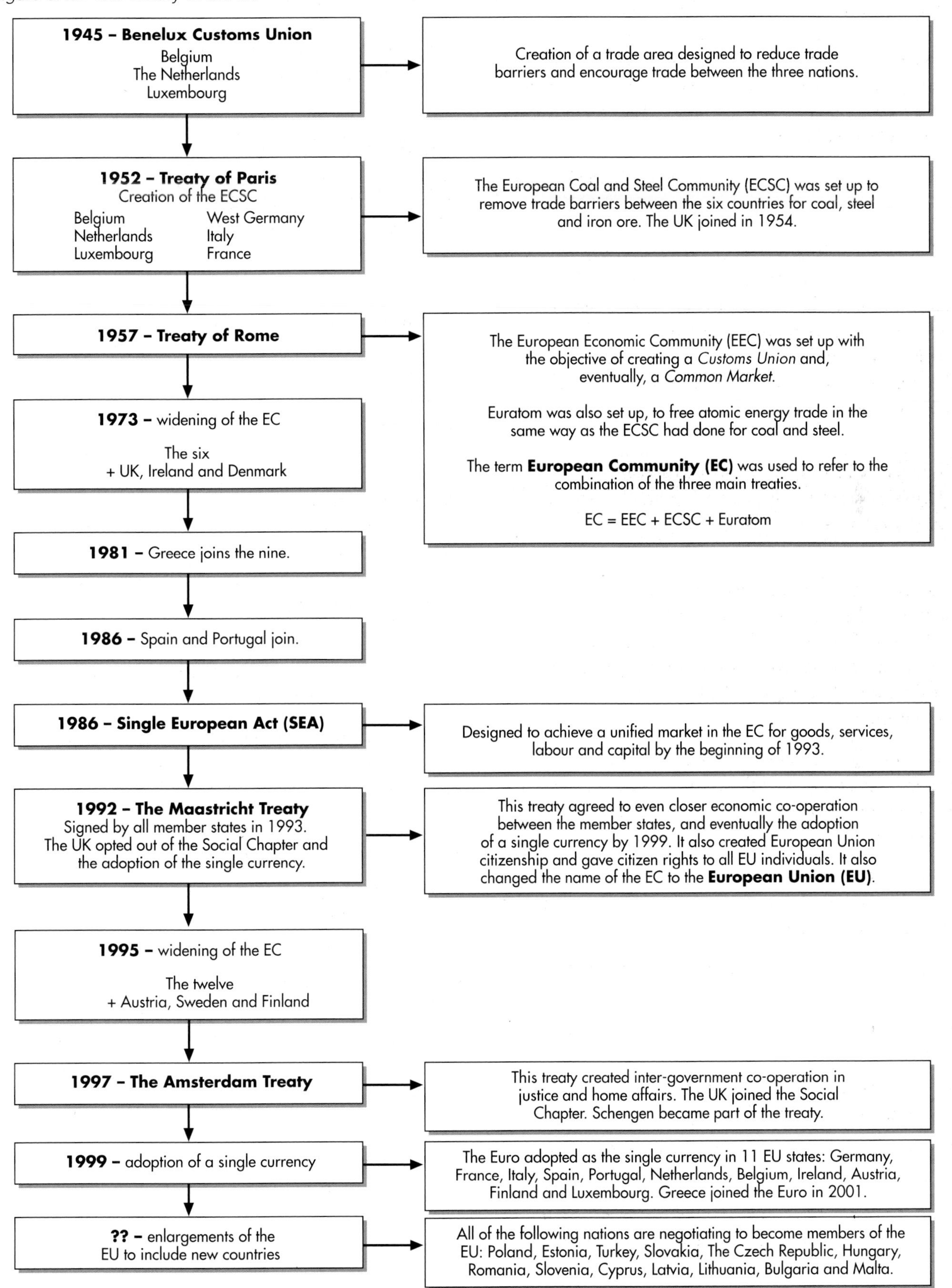

Figure 6.1.3 The difference between a Free Trade Area, a Customs Union and a common market

For the EU to achieve full **common market** status, all the countries would need to treat their citizens and businesses in the same way. All EU citizens and EU businesses would have the same opportunities, rights and responsibilities. That would require common taxes and social benefits, common education and training facilities, common working conditions and a common form of money across the whole of the EU. So far, the EU has only moved part of the way towards a full common market.

The EU has moved toward its final objectives through three major agreements. Details of these are given below, as well as the latest major agreements taken at Amsterdam and Nice.

The Treaty of Rome 1957

The **Treaty of Rome** created the basic objectives and philosophy of the EU – the belief that nations working together for a common end could achieve more than the same nations working separately and for their own ends.

The Treaty gives:

- the Community the right to make laws, which apply to all member nations
- the individual the right to take any other individual, business or government to court if they break Community law.

The Treaty of Rome established the EEC with the following specific objectives:

- To remove all tariffs and quotas on trade between member nations
- To create common external tariffs on agreed imports into any part of the Union
- To remove all barriers to the movement of people, services and capital between member nations
- To create a common policy for agriculture and transport
- To monitor and control competition to make it fairer
- To create a European Social Fund to improve employment opportunities and raise workers' standards of living
- To create a European Investment Bank to support new developments in the Union

The Single European Act 1986

The **Single European Act 1986** built on the Treaty of Rome and accelerated the move toward a completely free area of trade where the EU could act as a single market place with no artificial barriers to trade.

This treaty established the following rights and benefits:

- The right to free movement of goods and services so that EU citizens can buy goods and services from any part of the EU and pay only the local rates of tax
- The right of EU citizens to work in any part of the EU with the same rights, protection and duties as nationals

- Increased consumer protection
- Improved health and safety controls in the workplace
- The right for any EU citizen to set up a business in any EU country
- The movement towards European standards for products in terms of quality, labelling, safety, etc.
- Allowing businesses from other EU countries to compete for government contracts (public procurement)
- Closer levels of VAT and excise duties (e.g. on alcohol, tobacco and petrol) across the EU

All of these objectives have now been met except the objective of unifying the taxes on goods and services. The effect of the Single European Act has been to encourage EU countries to trade even more with each other rather than with non-EU countries. UK trade with the EU has risen from 16 per cent to 58 per cent in the latter half of the twentieth century. Our major trading partners in the EU are shown in Figure 6.1.4.

The Treaty on European Union 1992 (Maastricht)

The **Treaty on European Union 1992 (Maastricht)** created the concept of Union citizenship.

Thanks to the Maastricht Treaty, we are all now not only UK citizens, but also EU citizens with clear rights in the EU. These were the main objectives of the Maastricht Treaty:

- To create Union citizenship and the rights that go with this

The rights of EU citizens

- The **right to free movement** throughout the EU
- The **right to reside** in any EU country that they want to live in
- The **right to work** in any EU country where they want to work
- The **right to vote and stand as a candidate** in municipal and EU elections in any EU country

- To give the Union additional powers in terms of transport, communications, education and vocational training, consumer protection and health
- To move towards and establish a **single currency** for the EU (see page 261)

Single currency – one currency used by different member states (in the EU, this is the euro)

- To develop a common foreign and defence policy
- To establish closer co-operation on legal matters, immigration policy and police forces
- To adopt the conditions laid down in the **social chapter** to protect workers (see page 267)

The UK opted out of both the agreement to move towards a single currency by 1999 and the adoption of the social charter.

The Treaty also established the 'three pillars' (see Figure 6.1.5) on which the whole of the European Union is now based.

Figure 6.1.4 UK's major trading partners in the EU (1999)

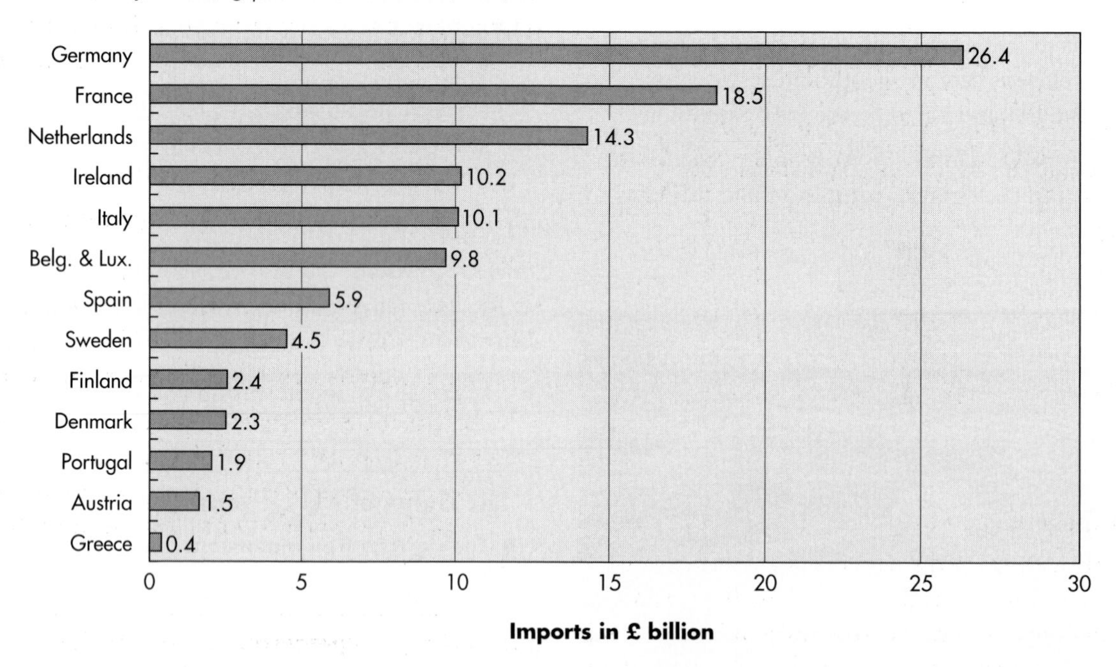

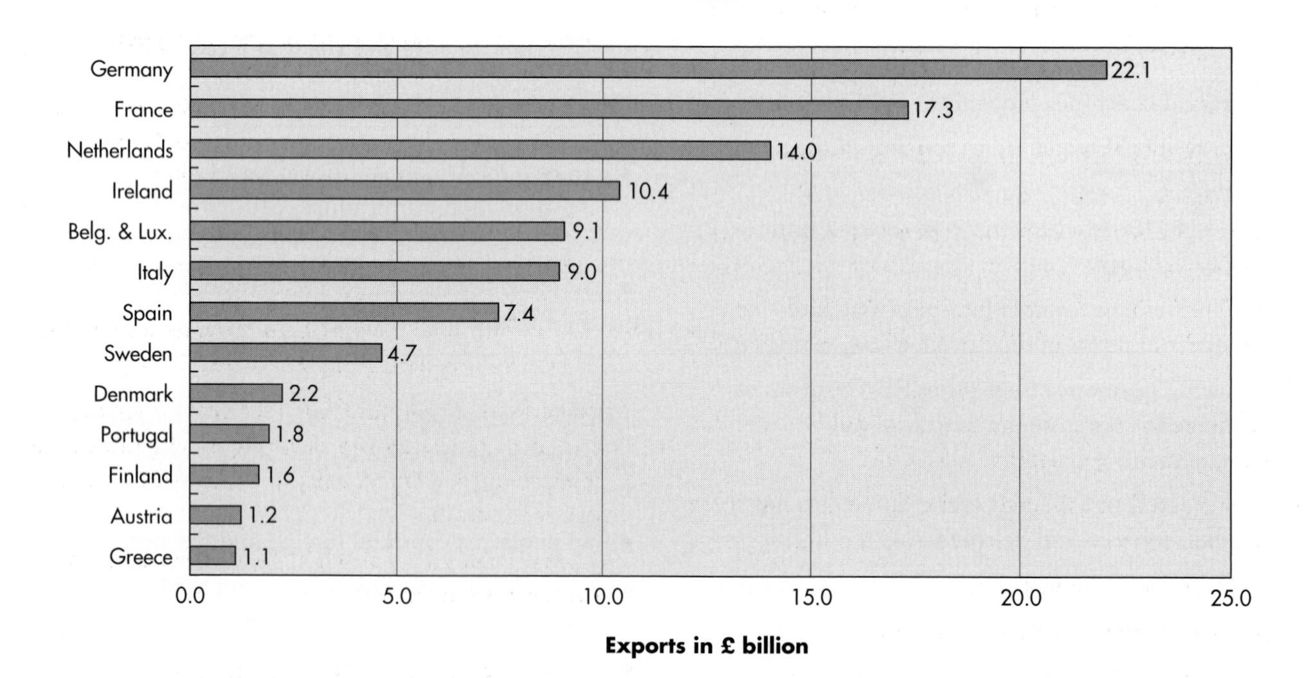

Figure 6.1.5 The three pillars of the EU

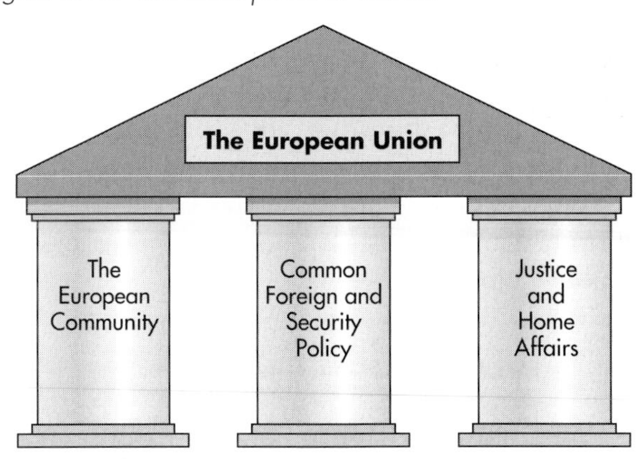

The European Community

The first pillar confirmed that the main agreements on which the EU is based are economic. The **European Community** incorporates the three economic agreements of the European Coal and Steel Community (1951), the European Economic Community (1957) and the European Atomic Energy Community (1957). The European Economic Community was extended to include economic and monetary union (EMU).

The Common Foreign and Security Policy

The second pillar finally accepted that the EU needs to be more than just an economic agreement if it is to last and achieve the dream of political stability that its founders envisaged. At Maastricht the member states agreed to work towards **Common Foreign and Security Policies** which:

- safeguarded common values and interests of member states and the independence of the EU
- strengthened the security of the EU and the member states
- helped to preserve world peace
- promoted international co-operation
- promoted and preserved democracy, ensuring fundamental human rights and freedoms.

Co-operation in the fields of justice and home affairs

The third pillar recognised that a stable and secure society is based on certain controls and safeguards that affect **justice and home affairs.** The member states agreed to work out common policies and co-operation on immigration, various criminal activities, such as drug dealing and fraud, and closer co-operation between the police forces of each country.

The Amsterdam Treaty 1997

In this treaty, the following major agreements were made:

- To create inter-governmental co-operation in justice and home affairs and create conditions to combat crime and create better links between police forces
- To create the **Schengen Agreement** as part of the treaty, and hence part of EU law. Special consideration was given to the UK, Ireland and Denmark who still do not follow the full Schengen agreement

> ***The Schengen Agreement***, set up in 1990, gives citizens the right to move freely between the states which have signed the agreement.
>
> Citizens from Schengen countries display a green sticker on their vehicle windows and can then drive across borders with no checks at all. Frontier controls at ports and airports have also been removed. Norway and Iceland, both non-EU nations, are part of Schengen.

- For the UK to adopt the **Social Chapter** and end its opt-out of that part of the Maastricht Treaty
- To establish a charter of human rights outlawing discrimination based on race, origin, religion, sexual orientation, age or disability, parts of which came into force in 2000

The Amsterdam Treaty also laid down clear rules on **subsidiarity** (see page 248)

The Nice Summit – December 2000

The Nice Summit prepared the way for the enlargement of the EU and was a major step in allowing additional countries to join the EU. Here are just two of the agreements made:

Subsidiarity – the principle that 'decisions should be made at the lowest possible level and that it is for each member state to decide how its powers should be exercised domestically'. This should mean that the Community will only be creating laws and regulations that could not be decided on at national level because they affect other nations. The new rule provides that:

- Community action is only justified when its objective is achievable by the Community but cannot be achieved by the separate member states alone
- Community action should be as simple as possible, leaving the individual member states to implement the details so that the laws and procedures are appropriate for their own requirements
- Community action should be justified with facts and figures wherever possible
- the Commission must consult widely before proposing new legislation and should assess the likely impact of the legislation; this must be done to ensure that as the objectives of legislation are met, no unnecessary burdens are placed on member states and the principle of subsidiarity is followed.

- A change in the voting power of the existing member states gave the larger countries more voting power in matters that are decided by a qualified majority vote. These are matters that are not considered to be vital for each individual country.
- The number of areas of policy in which qualified majority voting will be accepted, rather than unanimous voting, was extended. This was not extended to setting taxes, mainly because the UK objected.

New laws and regulations

New laws and regulations are being added to Community law all the time. Much of this comes from the Commission as it implements the agreements of the major treaties. There are also periodic meetings of all the member states, called **Inter-governmental Conferences (IGCs)** (see page 250), which decide on other major changes. These sometimes lead to new treaties and new rules.

The major institutions of the EU

The laws and regulations of the EU have come about through various different procedures. Some have been agreed through major treaties, some have been passed as a result of regular IGCs, others have come from the four major institutions of the EU: the Commission, the Council of Ministers, the European Parliament and the European Court of Justice.

The Council of Ministers

The Council of Ministers is the institution which decides on all major laws and policy changes and represents the individual nation's interests.

The Council of Ministers is made up of ministers from each member state. Which government minister attends the meeting will depend on what is being discussed. If, for example, the discussion relates to monetary union or overall budgets, the finance minister will probably attend.

The Council of Ministers decides on all major matters. Most proposals have to be agreed unanimously before they can be passed, but decisions of less importance can be passed by majority vote, and sometimes by a qualified majority vote (one that is weighted in terms of the size of the member countries).

The leaders of the member states and the President of the Commission also meet twice each year at a summit called the **European Council**, as well as at the IGCs. Each country takes the presidency of the Council of Ministers in rotation for six-month periods and often uses this period to push forward their own interpretation of how the EU should be developing.

Order of the Presidency of the EU

	First half-year	Second half-year
1998	UK	Austria
1999	Germany	Finland
2000	Portugal	France
2001	Sweden	Belgium
2002	Spain	Denmark
2003	Greece	

The Commission

The Commission is the institution which represents the interests of the EU as a whole and is responsible for ensuring that EU laws and policies are carried out.

The Commission is responsible for implementing the decisions of the Council and Parliament. It is mainly responsible for **proposing or starting new legislation and measures**. All major proposals are finally decided on by the Council before they can become law. There are, however, many minor areas of legislation over which the Commission has direct control. The major treaties often merely outline what changes need to be made and the Commission is then given responsibility for ensuring that the objectives of the treaties are brought into effect.

The European Parliament

The European Parliament consists of 626 members (MEPs) directly elected by the people in each member state. The number of seats that each nation has reflects, generally, the size of the population. Germany has 99, the UK 87 and Luxembourg just 6.

Unlike the UK House of Commons, the **European Parliament** has very little power to create new laws.

The **European Parliament** is responsible for discussing and making recommendations, but it cannot actually pass laws nor change them unless the Council of Ministers agrees.

Following the Maastricht Treaty, the European Parliament now has the following main roles:

- Parliament has the right to veto certain proposals if no agreement can be reached by the Council of Ministers (**Codecision Procedure**).
- Parliament is consulted twice on legislation and can propose amendments (**Co-operation Procedure**).
- Parliament simply gives its opinion on proposed legislation (**Consultation Procedure**).
- MEPs can ask the Commission and the Council questions about legislation matters and these organisations must reply. This helps to make the Commission and the Council more accountable.
- Parliament can request that the Commission introduces certain new legislation.
- Parliament has to approve the overall budget of the EU and can change how the money is spent (except for the agricultural budget).

The Court of Justice of the European Community

The **European Court of Justice** is the supreme court of justice for cases that involve Community law.

The Court is made up of 15 judges, one from each member state, and three to five judges will sit to decide on each case. The Court of Justice rules on all major disputes. It is now supported by a **Court of First Instance** which hears less important cases.

European Court overturns decision by the Commission

The Commission had imposed a fine on the German Drugs company Bayer because it had restricted supplies to its Spanish and French wholesalers. The wholesalers had been selling the drugs on into the UK where prices were up to 40 per cent higher. This had meant that Bayer's sales direct to the UK were being undercut by their own products coming from Spain and France.

The Commission felt that, in a free market, restricting sales in this way was anti-competitive and created an unnecessarily high price in the UK market. A spokeswoman for the Commission said that consumers should have the chance to benefit from lower prices in the EU.

The European Court of First Instance dismissed the case, not because it approved of the clear anti-competitive situation, but because it was not clear that Bayer had a specific agreement with the wholesalers in the first place.

Oct 2000

Part of the role of the Court of Justice is to rule on details of Community law where there is some uncertainty. Once the ruling has been passed, the new interpretation will become part of Community law and all EU countries, businesses and individuals will be bound by it.

Community Law

The general rule accepted by all member states is that if Community law and national law conflict, Community law will have priority and must be obeyed. It is, therefore, very important to know how Community law is created. Figure 6.1.6 shows the main sources of Community law.

Community law is law created by the EU and has to be obeyed by all EU member states and their citizens.

Inter-governmental Conferences (IGCs)

Changes to the treaties cannot be made by any of the institutions of the Community. The member states must meet to decide on such changes.

Inter-Governmental Conferences (IGCs) are periodic meetings between senior representatives of all EU member states called to discuss and decide on major changes to the EU.

The latest ICG started in February 2000 and closed in December 2000. Representatives from the member states were considering these topics:

- How enlargement of the EU (see page 253) can be made to work
- How the number of votes that each member state has should be changed so that the new member states, which generally have small populations, will not upset the voting power that the major nations already have
- A change in the number of commissioners so that a workable group will be created; major nations have two commissioners each and this may be reduced to one each
- An increase in the areas where majority voting, rather than a unanimous vote, will be used.

Figure 6.1.6 Main sources of community law

Sources of Community law

Community law is created in four ways:

1. When the member nations create new laws by **signing major treaties** and **conventions**, e.g. The European Convention for the Protection of Human Rights (1950), The Treaty of Rome (1957), The Single European Act (1986), The Treaty on European Union (Maastricht), 1992.
2. Through **regulations** passed by the Council of Ministers and/or *the Commission. These* regulations automatically become Community law and all member nations must obey them, e.g. regulations that give powers to the Commission to control and prevent mergers of large firms (1992).
3. Through **directives** issued by the Council of Ministers or the Commission. These directives are binding on member states, but the exact details are left up to the governments of each country, who make them into national laws, e.g. the European Directive on Product Liability has been made part of UK law in our Consumer Protection Act 1987.
4. Through **decisions** issued by the Council of Ministers or the Commission. These decisions are made about specific matters and relate to specific people, companies, etc. They are binding on those people.

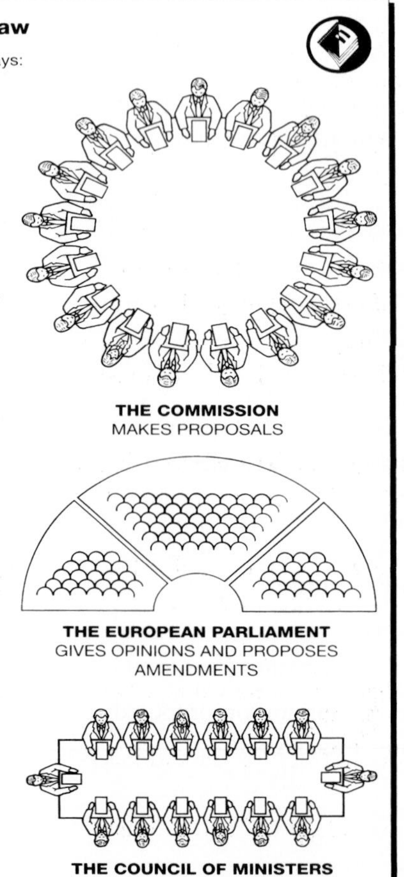

Source: DTI The Single Market – 'Brussels can you hear me?'. Crown Copyright

Other major institutions in the EU

The institutions mentioned above are the most important in the EU, but there are many others that have been set up to deal with particular aspects of the EU. Details of some of these are given below.

The EU Structural Funds

The **EU structural funds** support areas within the EU that have social or economic problems.

One of the objectives of EU policy is to support areas that have particular social and economic problems. This is mainly done through the four **structural funds** outlined below. To raise the money required to pay for this support, the EU uses three sources of revenue:

- A percentage of each member country's VAT is paid to the Community.
- A percentage of each member country's Gross National Product is paid to the Community.
- Tariffs are placed on the import of non-EU goods into the EU.

The funds that are raised from these sources of revenue are used to support specific objectives of the Community. The objectives of the structural funds are set for a number of years. In the period 2000–06, it is estimated that the funds will spend the equivalent of £161 billion.

The objectives for the 2000–06 period had not been finally agreed at the time of writing this book but the main changes have been hinted at. The objectives will resemble those of the 1995–99 period and will most likely be as follows.

1 To provide support to regions of the EU which have a per capita GDP of below 75 per cent of the EU average
In the UK, these regions are Northern Ireland, the Highlands and Islands of Scotland and Merseyside.

2 To help to redevelop regions or areas which have high unemployment levels due to industrial decline, with funding for industrial, rural, urban and fishing areas
In the UK, these areas are likely to include South Wales, North East England, West Cumbria, Furness, Greater Manchester, Lancashire, Cheshire and Plymouth.

3 To provide training and assistance to help the long-term unemployed, the young, the socially excluded and people affected by changes in industrial and productive systems
These measures will apply anywhere in the UK other than those covered by the first two objectives.

These three objectives will be met out of the four fund areas outlined below. Each fund can be used to support any of the three objectives.

The European Regional Development Fund (ERDF) provides funds to help to reduce unemployment and create and maintain jobs. Assistance is given to fund infrastructure projects, such as transport links, but also to help businesses to set up and expand in areas of high unemployment. Funds are also available for education and training schemes for local businesses, research and development and investment into environmental projects.

Examples of aid provided by the ERDF and the ESF:

- Improvements to the Greater Manchester motorway network
- Improved insulation in houses in Glasgow to conserve energy
- The provision of computer access for small and medium-sized businesses at North Lincolnshire College so that they could test product designs on computers which, individually, they could not afford
- The provision of training courses in Ballymena for the unemployed to ensure that they can achieve appropriate NVQs at levels 1 to 4 and are then qualified for work

The European Social Fund (ESF) was set up in 1960. If provides funds for vocational training, retraining and job-creation schemes. It helps the long-term unemployed, young job-seekers and people excluded from the labour market. It helps to promote equal opportunities and provides funds for equipping workers with new skills as industrial processes change.

The ESF will provide funds directly for training and re-training schemes, but it will also supply funds indirectly through improving teacher training or supporting changes to the curriculum. Funds are also available for improving the quality of research, science and technology services and providing a skilled workforce to deal with these new technologies.

Details about the ESF can be obtained from the Department of Employment EU Branch, European Social Fund Unit, Level 1, Grays Inn Road, London WC1X 8HL. www.esfnews.org.uk.

The European Agricultural Guidance and Guarantee Fund (EAGGF) provides funds for the EU's **Common Agricultural Policy (CAP)**. Through this, it aims to support agriculture and work towards changes that will make it more efficient. One branch provides funds to help to keep agricultural prices stable and, through this, to stabilise farm incomes. The other section provides support to help to modernise farming.

This support combines to help farmers in poor farming areas, such as the Welsh Hills. It is also used to encourage new young farmers, the creation of producer organisations which will market their own farm produce and investment in the tourist sector, heritage and village protection.

The main benefits have been produced through providing farmers with a minimum guaranteed price for certain products such as grain, milk, wine and beef. This has led to massive overproduction which has made large farms very wealthy but has done little for the small, low-production farms. As a result of growing 'mountains' and 'lakes' of surplus products which cost a great deal to store and frequently have to be sold off at a loss to governments, the CAP is now being radically changed. This is also changing the role of the EAGGF.

Six new policy objectives have been created for the CAP for the twenty-first century:

- To improve the Union's competitiveness through lower prices
- To guarantee the safety and quality of food to consumers
- To ensure stable incomes and a fair standard of living for the agricultural community
- To make production methods environmentally friendly and respect animal welfare
- To integrate environmental goals into its instruments
- To seek to create alternative income and employment opportunities for farmers and their families

Source: European Commission

The Financial Instrument for Fisheries Guidance (FIFG) was set up in 1994, and carries out a similar role for the fishing industry as the EAGGF does for agriculture. It regulates the amount of fishing that can be carried out so as to preserve stocks for the future. It also provides funds to develop fish farming, develop port facilities, promote fish products, and help people who earn their living from fishing to move into other forms of employment as the industry declines.

PESCA operated between 1994 and 1999 to help the fishing industry to restructure as fish stocks declined and market conditions changed. Measures provided by the fund included aid to find and develop new markets and to find alternative ways for fishing communities to earn income, e.g. through the development of tourism.

EU environment policies

Articles 2, 3(k) and 130r of the Treaty of Rome established a clear aim in the Community to work towards better protection of the environment in the EU:

- To protect and improve the quality of the environment
- To protect the health of the population
- To ensure the careful and rational use of natural resources
- To promote levels of environmental control at an international level so that vulnerable regions will be better protected from inter-country pollution

Many parts of the work of the structural funds listed above have an environmental element within them. The CAP, for example, tries to reduce the use of unnecessary fertilisers and pesticides and thereby protect rivers, etc. from pollution. In the 1990s, there were some very specific EU initiatives some designed to protect the environment:

- The introduction of a common environment tax on energy and CO_2 emissions
  This was not actually passed but many individual countries have introduced their own taxes. In the UK, we have increased taxes on hydrocarbons well above the rate of inflation.
- The **Altener programme**, designed to encourage the use of alternative, and renewable energy sources
- The **SAVE programme**, designed to encourage methods of saving energy, both in the home and in businesses
- The banning of **CFC production** by mid-1995, as a measure to protect the ozone layer
- The provision of funds for projects that help to improve the environment
  The funds are distributed through the **LIFE Financial Instrument for the Environment**, set up in 1992.
- Loans from the **European Investment Bank** for the creation of waste disposal plants and sewage treatment plants

Businesses are affected either directly or indirectly by all of the initiatives introduced by the EU. Grants to help fishing communities to build up tourism or craft industries will directly affect the fishing industry, but they also indirectly affect businesses that provide the new tourist area with postcards or the new craft industry with its clay, paint, wicker, etc. Look back over all of these ways that the EU affects the Community and its member states and think how these measures will affect individual industries.

Enlargement of the EU

Enlargement – is the term used when refering to more countries joining the EU.

The EU has already expanded from six nations to 15, and 12 other nations are moving steadily towards joining. This does not include the members of the **European Economic Area (EEA)** who already enjoy many of the benefits of being in the full EU (Figure 6.1.7).

The **EEA** is an area of free trade that exists between the EU and the EFTA countries.

The European Economic Area (EEA) came into existence on January 1994. It linked the members of the EU with those of the seven members of the other main economic area in Europe, the **European Free Trade Association (EFTA)**. Since then three EFTA countries have joined the EU and two EFTA countries, Switzerland and Liechtenstein, decided not to join the EEA. The EEA is therefore currently an agreement between the 15 members of the EU and Norway and Iceland.

The EEA extends the four basic freedoms of the European Community to all EEA countries so that Norway and Iceland now have no trading barriers with the EU and also have free movement of goods, services, capital and workers. Norway and Iceland also have to meet the agreements of the EU safety standards on products.

Thirteen countries have applied to join the EU as full members, most of them from Central and Eastern Europe (Figure 6.1.8) Some of them, particularly Turkey, have been waiting a long time to be accepted.

Some benefits of enlargement

- A larger market for member states, particularly for the new members
- Greater choice of products and increased competition
- A further increase of the importance of the EU in world affairs
- Greater political stability in Europe as a whole, which should help to ensure democracy and make conflict less likely
- Support for the economies of these new members, which will also help to improve standards of living and ensure better environmental standards across Europe
- Agreed actions on justice and home affairs, which should help to reduce cross-border crime, including drug smuggling
- A better understanding between the peoples of Europe

Figure 6.1.7 Enlargement of the EU

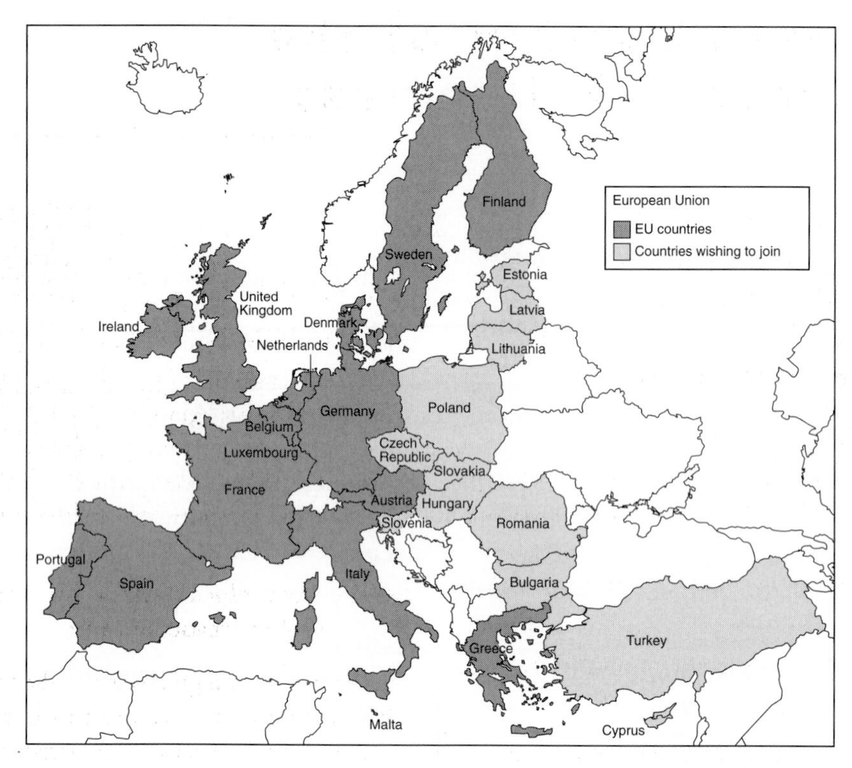

Figure 6.1.8 Countries waiting to join the EU

Date of first application	
1987	Turkey
1990	Cyprus
	Poland
1994	Hungary
	Slovak Republic
1995	Bulgaria
	Estonia
	Latvia
	Lithuania
	Romania
1996	Czech Republic
	Slovenia

Enlarging the EU is an historic opportunity, both for the EU and its new members. It will fulfil the challenge set a decade ago when the Iron Curtain was brought down and create a prosperous and peaceful Europe.

Robin Cook (Foreign Secretary) Nov. 1997

Some drawbacks to enlargement

- Many of the new members would be relatively poor and require considerable financial support. A high proportion of the budget available for the European Structural Funds might have to go to these new countries.
- Costs of production in these new countries are likely to be below those in the existing EU countries and this may well lead to production moving to these new countries. That would cause unemployment to rise in places like the UK.
- Enlargement will change the voting procedures in the Community and this may either make it harder to reach agreements or lead to agreements that some countries do not want.

CHAPTER 2

How Membership of the EU affects UK Business

KEY TERMS

Comparative advantage
Competition policy
Economic and Monetary Union (EMU)
Economies of scale
Free market
Import tariff
Import quota
Single currency
The Social Chapter

In this chapter, you will learn how membership of the EU affects UK businesses, both positively and negatively:

- The size of the EU in comparison with other major trading blocks and the UK
- The pattern of UK trade with the EU and other countries
- The benefits of membership and the drawbacks, including the theories behind free trade, Economic and Monetary Union (EMU), legislation which affects working conditions, and competition policy.

The importance of the EU

The economic importance of the EU can be judged in a variety of ways. The most common measure, however, is **gross domestic product (GDP)**. GDP records the total amount of goods and services produced in a country in a set period of time, usually one year. GDP is a particularly useful measure because it shows:

- how much is produced in each country, and can therefore provide the inhabitants with information about their standard of living
- how much income people are receiving and therefore how large the potential market is for domestic producers and importers
- how powerful a country is in terms of being able to control international trade.

Countries with high levels of GDP and large markets have the power to dictate terms to their trading partners, offer incentives to attract foreign investment, gain economies of scale and lower production costs, and invest in research and development to find the high selling products of the future. On their own, the EU nations have found this difficult but, working together, pooling resources and sharing their markets, they have been able to build a union that now has considerable economic strength.

Since the Second World War, the USA, Germany and Japan have dominated world production and trade. Individually, these countries have outstripped the rest of the world in terms of economic growth, income, wealth, investment, technological innovation and a host of other indicators that economists put forward as important measures of economic success. In the four years from 1994 to 1999, the fortunes of Japan and Germany have suffered compared to the USA, but their GDPs still remain relatively high. Figure 6.2.1 shows the relative strength of the different nations in terms of GDP. The national GDP figures have been converted into pounds sterling to make comparison easier.

Individually, the EU countries' production is far below that of the USA. Even Germany's GDP for 1999 was only 21 per cent of the USA's GDP. When combined together, however, the output of the EU places it right back among the world leaders.

Figure 6.2.1 GDP for the USA, Japan and EU countries, 1999 (£ billion and PPP)

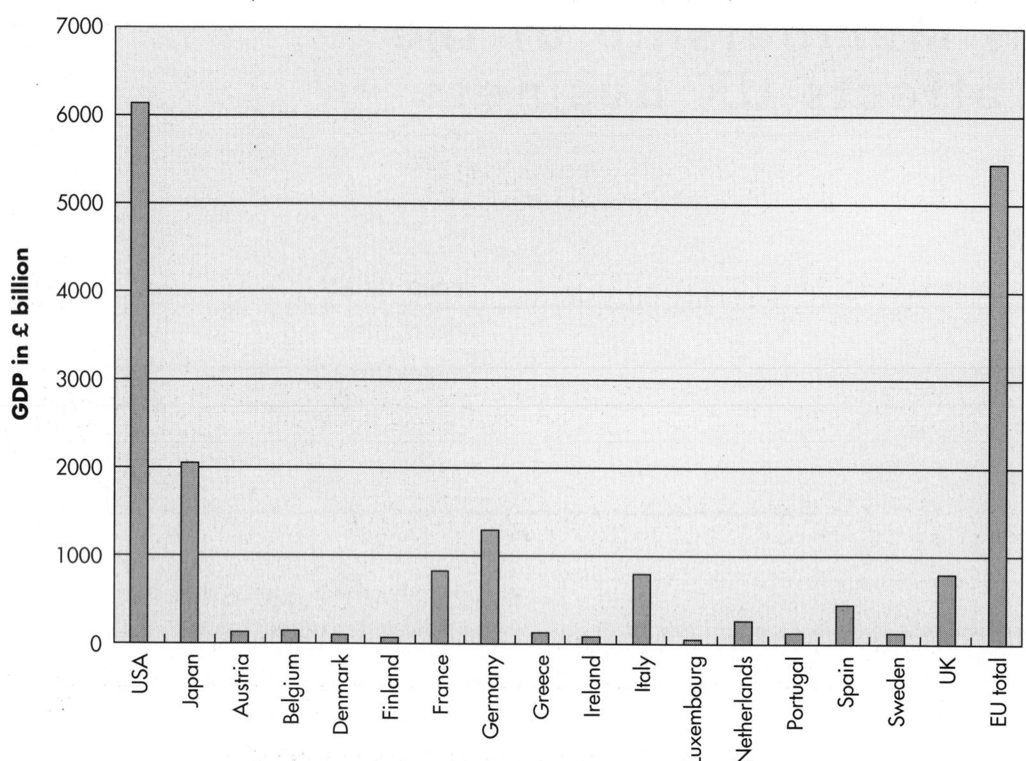

Source: Adapted from *Main Economic Indicators* (OECD).

When individual types of production are taken, the EU often leads the world. The EU has the world's largest production of wine (over 60 per cent), olive oil (over 75 per cent) and cars (over 30 per cent). Figure 6.2.2 shows that the EU also holds its own against the USA in many of the major areas of manufacturing.

The importance of the EU for the UK

Figure 6.2.3 shows the growing importance of the EU countries as trading partners for the UK. The graph shows how our percentage of trade in exports and imports with the other 14 countries of the EU has risen since 1962. The UK actually joined the EU in 1973 but it had already built up close trade links by 1962. After 1973, the UK also benefited from the removal of tariffs and quotas between itself and the other EU countries. By 1999, all of the benefits of free trade listed on pages 257 to 261 applied and this has made trade with other EU countries more attractive for many UK businesses.

The pattern of UK trade with the EU and the rest of the world is shown for 1999 in Table 6.2.1. The trade of goods with the EU is a very much higher percentage than the trade of services. This is because it is much easier to transport goods to the EU than to other parts of the world, whereas services, such as finance, insurance, shipping services and travel services, can be sold to all parts of the world with little additional cost.

The EU is also important because of its size. Figure 6.2.1 showed the relative size of each country's GDP and the EU total. For businesses, the size of the population is also important because these people are the potential market and also provide the workforce. Figure 6.2.4 shows how the size of the EU's population has grown as each set of countries has joined. The diagram shows the population for the EU in terms of the size of each country's population in 1999.

The EU now has a considerably larger population than the USA (273 mil.). It does not, however, yet match the size of the new trading area of the **North American Free Trade Association (NAFTA)**. NAFTA (401 mil.) is made up of the USA, Canada and Mexico, and was set up in 1994 specifically because the USA was worried about the growing importance of the EU. If enlargement of the EU (see page 253) takes place, the total population of the EU will be greater than NAFTA. Turkey, alone, has 66 million people.

Figure 6.2.2 Manufacturing industries where the EU outperforms the USA

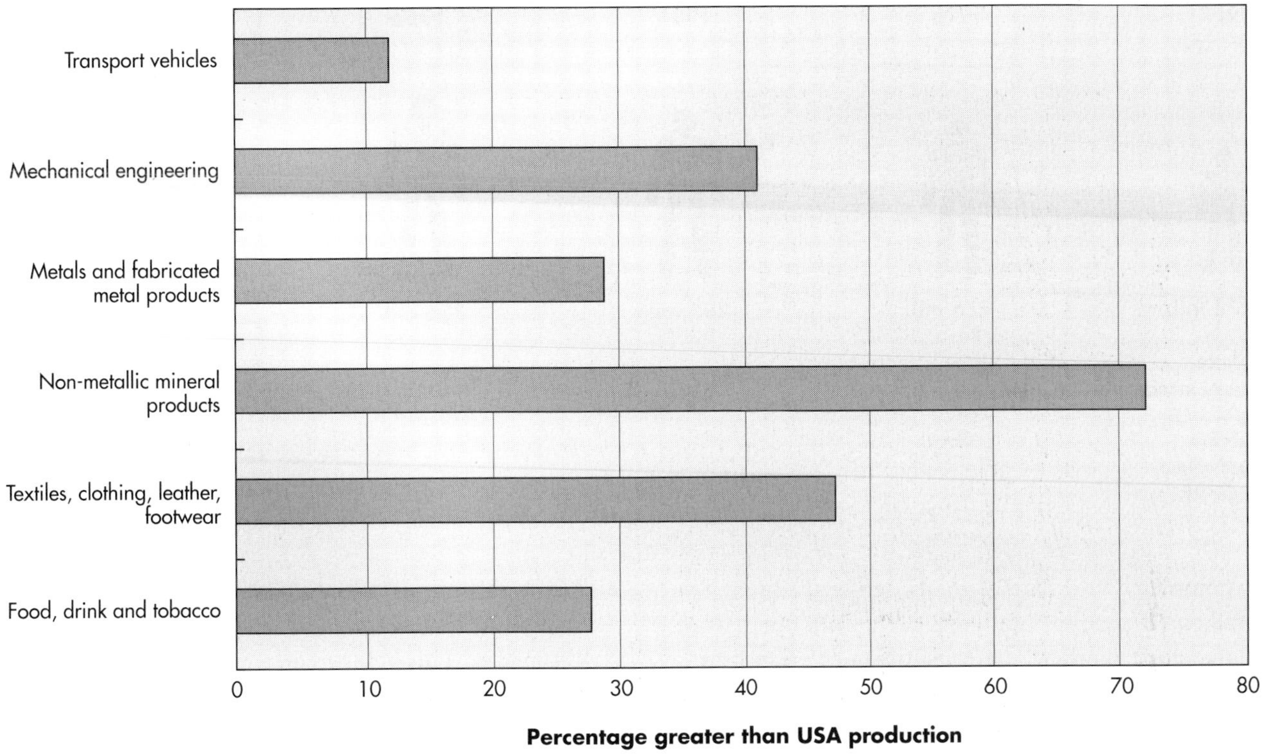

Transport vehicles
Mechanical engineering
Metals and fabricated metal products
Non-metallic mineral products
Textiles, clothing, leather, footwear
Food, drink and tobacco
0
10
20
30
40
50
60
70
80
Percentage greater than USA production

The importance of the EU to UK businesses is also shown by the changes that UK businesses must make to sell their products in the EU and how they must react to EU businesses selling their products in the UK. Details of these are given in Chapter 3.

Figure 6.2.3 UK exports and imports with the 14 EU member states, 1962, 1973 and 1999

Exports
Imports
Percentage of total UK trade
70
60
50
40
30
20
10
0
1962
1973
1999

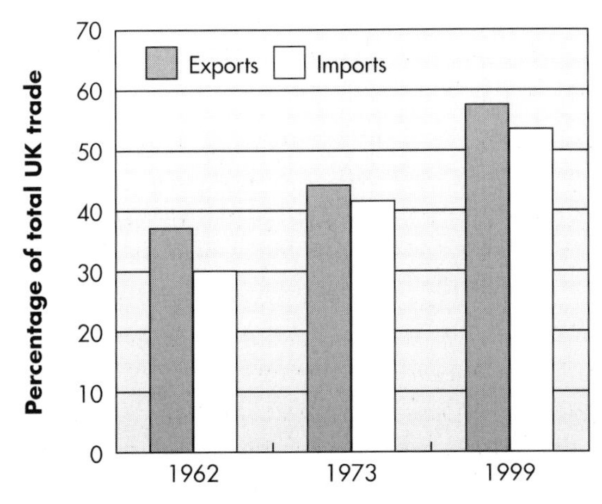

The benefits of a free market

Free market – a market in which there are no artificial barriers to trade

Table 6.2.1 Percentage of UK trade with EU and non-EU sectors (1999)

	Goods		Services	
Sector	Exports	Imports	Exports	Imports
EU	55.6	54.0	33.5	33.0
Other Western Europe	4.7	5.4	11.9	13.0
North America	15.2	15.1	25.4	36.3
Other OECD countries	5.4	8.2	5.3	4.9
OPEC countries	4.6	1.9	9.1	3.9
Rest of world	12.2	15.4	14.7	8.9

Notes: 80–90 per cent of the figures for North America is for the USA. Other OECD countries include Japan. The OPEC countries are the Oil Producing and Exporting Countries.

Figure 6.2.4 The expanding population of the EU from 1957 to 1995

1957	1973	1981	1986	1995
208 mil.	**276 mil.**	**287 mil.**	**336 mil.**	**375 mil.**
France West Germany Italy Belgium Netherlands Luxembourg	*plus* UK Ireland Denmark	*plus* Greece	*plus* Spain Portugal	*plus* Sweden Finland Austria East Germany (1990)

In a completely free market goods, services, labour, capital and businesses can move freely from one part of the market to another. There are, of course, transport costs but there are no artificial barriers to trade, such as import taxes, quotas, special regulations on how goods are packed or advertised, etc. If the EU was a completely free market, UK producers could make their products in the UK, or any other EU country, and sell them anywhere in the EU with no additional costs other than transport.

The EU is not yet a free market but it has moved a very long way towards becoming one. All of the following changes have been put into place at different times since the Treaty of Rome in 1957:

- All import taxes and quotas have been removed for trade between member countries.
- Uniform standards have been agreed to ensure that goods are safe and of an acceptable quality.
- The documents that were needed for transporting goods have been reduced to a minimum.
- Twelve of the EU countries have a single currency (the euro) so prices can be easily compared.
- Businesses and workers can move to any EU country that they wish to (with some limitations). This has made production and labour markets much more competitive.
- Businesses can now bid for government contracts in any EU country, in the past, government contracts generally went to the country's own businesses.
- Many rules about how businesses are run and how they must treat their workers apply to all EU businesses. This helps to create 'a level playing field'.

Creating a completely free market where there are no artificial barriers to trade has benefits and drawback for businesses and individuals (Table 6.2.2).

A completely free market can also be justified in economic terms.

Removal of tariffs and quotas

> An **import tariff** is a tax placed on an imported product that has to be paid by the importer.

Tariffs and quotas act as barriers to international trade and make it more difficult for the importers to compete with home-produced products. The tariff is like any other tax. It increases the costs for the importer and this causes the supply to decrease, S to S_1 (see Figure 6.2.5). This causes the price to rise, P to P_1, and therefore customers buy less of the product, Q to Q_1. When tariffs are removed, the prices will fall back to P and more goods will now be imported. This is good for the businesses selling the imports but it does increase competition for the home producers of similar products.

> An **import quota** is a physical limit placed on the amount of a product that can be imported into a country.

Table 6.2.2 Benefits and drawbacks of a free market

Benefits	**Drawbacks**
• Businesses can compete on an equal footing.	• Individual businesses will now face more competition.
• Efficient businesses will do well in competitive markets.	• Smaller firms may be forced out of business because of larger competitors.
• Competition should make prices lower for customers. • Customers have a wider choice of products.	• The best firms may get rid of their competitors and then form monopolies. They can then increase prices, reduce choice, etc.
• Workers can take jobs in whichever country they want.	• Workers from other countries can come in and compete for jobs in the home country.
• Goods can be transported with no restrictions.	• It is easier to smuggle illegal goods such as drugs.

In Figure 6.2.5, the import quota is Q_1. Because less is allowed into the country, the price is bid up to P_1. Removing the quota would again cause prices to fall, back to P, and more imports to be sold, back to Q.

Comparative advantage

The theory of comparative advantage explains why trade takes place even when one country is better at producing products than another country. For this to work, there must be completely free trade between the countries. Table 6.2.3 shows how comparative advantage works and how both countries will benefit from trade.

> **Comparative advantage** shows that one country can produce products relatively more cheaply than another country. The cost of production is measured in terms of what other products would have to given up in order to produce it.

If we assume that Germany can produce cars and wine more efficiently than the UK, the amount of production that each country can produce with the same input of labour, raw materials, land, etc., might be as shown in Table 6.2.3.

It would appear that Germany would gain no benefit from trading with the UK because it is better at producing both products. Germany has the **absolute advantage** in producing both products.

Comparative advantage considers which country gives up least to produce each of the products. If Germany wanted to produce 200 more cars, it would have to give up producing 300 units of wine, or, for each 1 car that

Figure 6.2.5 The effect of a tariff and a quota on imported products

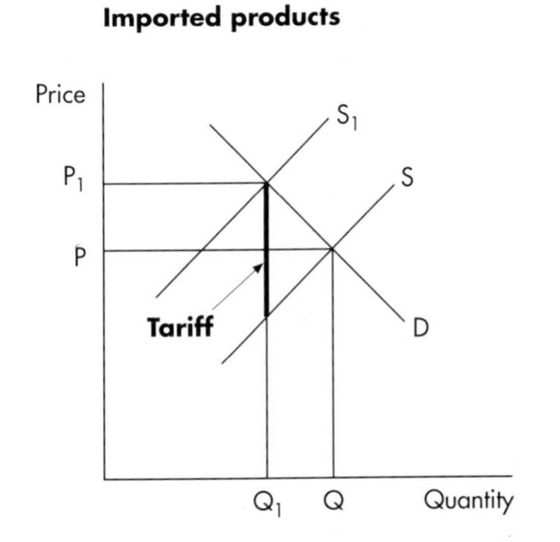

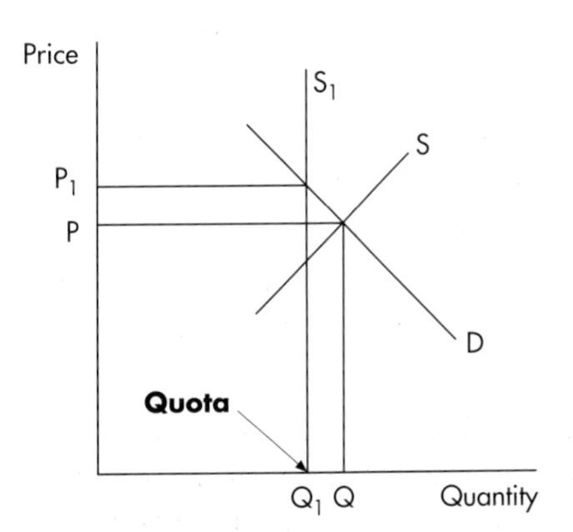

Table 6.2.3 Germany with an absolute advantage for both products

	Cars	Wine
Germany	200	300
UK	100	100
Total production	300	400

would be 1.5 units of wine. The UK, on the other hand, can produce 1 extra car by giving up only 1 unit of wine. In terms of what has to be given up, the UK is more efficient than Germany in the production of cars, i.e. it has the **comparative advantage** in the production of cars.

This also means that Germany has the comparative advantage in the production of wine. To produce 1 unit of wine Germany must give up producing 2/3 of a unit of cars, but the UK would have to give up producing 1 unit of cars.

If the UK stopped producing wine altogether, it could produce 200 more units of cars. If Germany gave up producing 80 units of cars, it could produce another 120 units of wine. Table 6.2.4 shows that if this was to happen total production for the two countries would rise.

In total, car production and wine production have each increased by 20 units. However, the UK now has no wine and Germany may have fewer cars than it needs, but this will be sorted out by importing and exporting. We can sell cars to the Germans and buy wine from them and we will all be better off. For this to work, however, there must be no significant costs of importing and exporting and definitely no tariffs or other major barriers.

Economies of scale

Before the UK joined the EU in 1973, we had only one market in which there were no significant barriers to trade. That was the UK. In 1973, we had a population of about 55 million people. That was the immediate market for UK businesses. Now we have a potential market of 375 million people. This allows businesses to benefit from economies of scale.

Economies of scale mean that as the output of a business grows the cost/unit of producing products falls.

Table 6.2.4 Germany with an absolute advantage for both products

	Cars	Wine
Germany	120	420
UK	200	–
Total production	320	420

If UK producers are selling into a market of 375 million people, instead of into a market of 55 million people, their costs/unit will, in most cases, be lower. There are many reasons for this, but the easiest reason to grasp is the spreading of fixed costs.

If a business has to pay rent and rates of £50 000 on its factory, it will have to pay this irrespective of how much the factory is actually producing. As the output from the factory increases, the cost of the rent and the rates will be spread across more and more goods and the cost per unit will fall. This is shown in Table 6.2.5.

As the number of units produced increases, the cost/unit can very rapidly decrease. This helps the business to keep its prices low and gain more customers, or to keep its prices the same and make more profit per unit.

Some economies of scale – **internal economies of scale** – occur because the individual businesses now have a large output:

- Fixed costs are being spread.
- Large firms can borrow money more easily and at a lower rate of interest than small firms.
- Large firms can afford to employ specialists who produce more output and reduce costs.
- Large firms benefit from lower costs from their suppliers. Discounts are usually given for bulk buying.
- Transport costs can fall if full lorry loads of products are being delivered rather than partly full lorry loads.

Table 6.2.5 Economies of scale gained by spreading fixed costs

Number of units produced	Cost of the rent and rates/unit
10 000	£5.00
20 000	£2.50
50 000	£1.00
100 000	£0.50
500 000	£0.10

- When one market is performing poorly, other markets may be expanding, so the risk is spread more.
- Production can be divided and specialist labour used to produce each part. This **division of labour** increases the output per person and reduces costs per unit.
- When marketing occurs some of it will promote the whole firm, as with McDonald's where a single television advertisement will promote every branch in the television reception area.

Other economies – **external economies of scale** – occur because there is now a larger market and more businesses in the market:

- The labour force will now have developed specialist skills that will be useful to the individual firm, e.g. there will be more sales personnel who can speak European languages.
- Specialist firms will have been set up which can help businesses, sometimes called **ancillary firms**. There will, for example, be specialist exporters, agents and distributors who know each EU market very well and can help UK firms to sell into the EU.
- Specialist publications are set up which help businesses to find markets or find out what is going on in markets. The internet now also provides a wealth of specialist information as with **www.europe-for-business.co.uk**.

Economic and Monetary Union (EMU) and the single currency (euro)

The **Economic and Monetary Union (EMU)** is an objective in that the EU should operate as a single integrated market place with one economic and monetary system.

The movement towards EMU

The EEC was set up with the express intention of forming an economic area in which, eventually, there would be a common market. From the start, it was given the nickname of the 'Common Market'. As was explained on page 242, for a common market to exist, there must be full integration of all the economic controls. For this to happen, there must be:

- no barriers to trade
- free movement of goods, services, labour and capital
- a uniform tax structure
- a single currency.

The EU has moved towards all of these objectives and has achieved some of them. As yet, however, there has been little progress on establishing a uniform tax structure. National taxes are different, but people are not expected to pay any additional taxes if they take products out of the country. As the alcohol taxes in France are well below those in the UK, many people go to France to buy their beer, wines and spirits and do not have to pay any additional tax when they bring them home.

The development of a single market for goods, services and factors of production (i.e. labour, capital and enterprise) has been covered in Chapter 1, pages 241 to 254. Here we will look briefly at the development towards a single currency for the EU.

A **European Monetary System (EMS)** is where the EU currencies are all linked together. Today, that has occurred with the creation of a **single European currency** (the euro). The basic objective of tying European currencies together stems from the Werner Report in 1970, which proposed full monetary union for the European Community as early as 1980. It has taken another 20 years to create a single currency in the EU and that only applies to 12 of the 15 EU countries.

In 1999, 11 countries joined the single currency. Greece wanted to join but failed to meet all of the required criteria; it was allowed to join in 2000; see Figure 6.2.6.

Figure 6.2.6

Euro Countries 1999		
Germany	France	Ireland
Italy	Spain	Austria
Portugal	Netherlands	Finland
Belgium	Luxembourg	
Greece joined in 2000		
Non-Euro Countries 2001		
UK	Denmark	Sweden

Countries, including the UK, and businesses have been able to trade in **euros** since 1999, but there were no actual notes or coins until 2002; see Figure 6.2.7. The national currencies were then phased out so that now euros have become the national currency of all 12 member countries.

The benefits and drawbacks of a single currency

Changing money from one currency to another is not only time-consuming and inconvenient but it is also expensive because the bank or *bureau de change* will charge for doing this. The cost of changing pounds into other currencies makes it more expensive to buy a foreign product than to buy a UK product.

Having a single currency offers many benefits:

- **No transaction costs**
  There would be no cost for changing one currency into another.

Figure 6.2.7 Progress towards a single currency

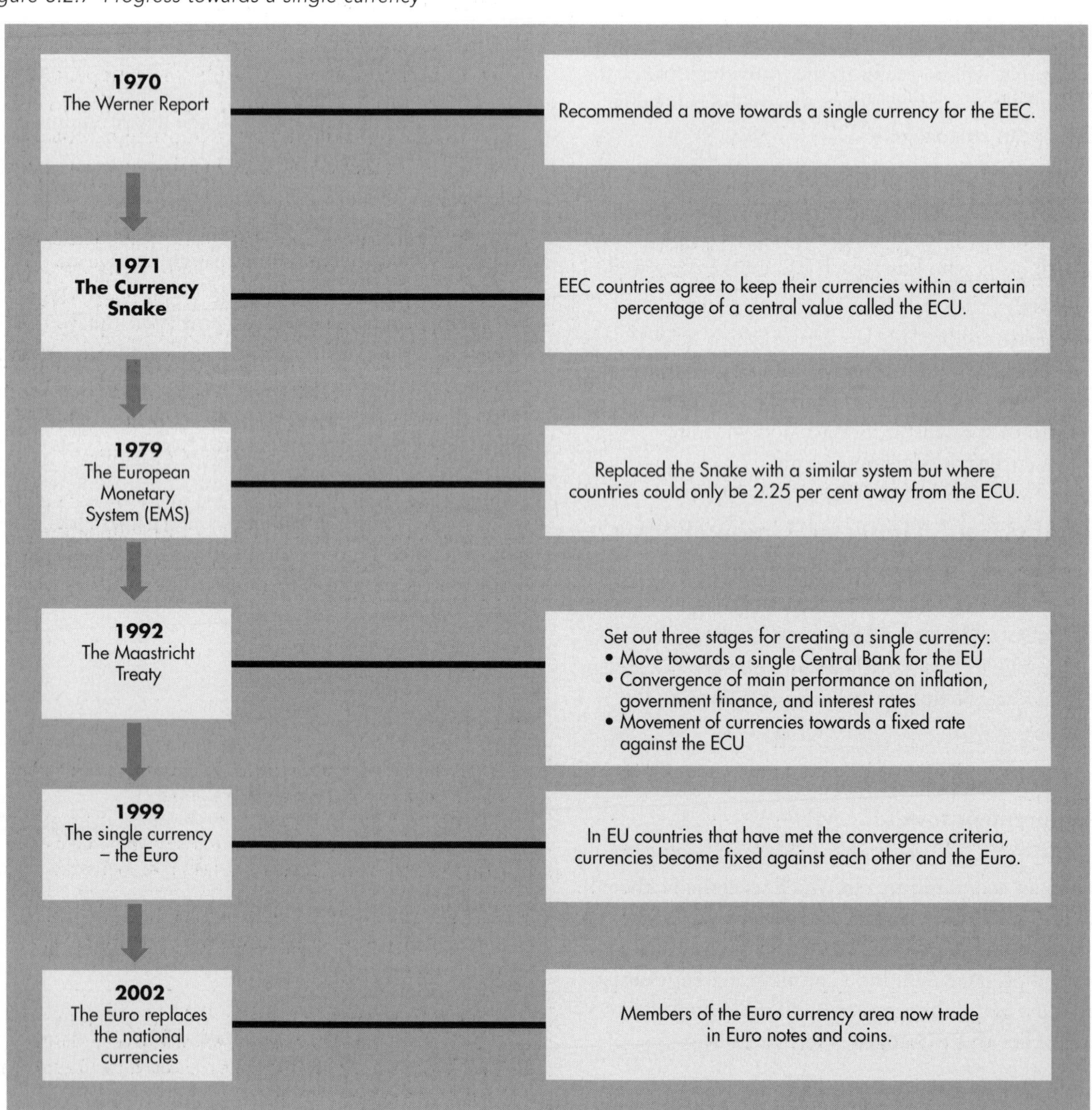

The cost of exchanging currencies

When changing money from one currency to another people, and businesses, will be faced with two exchange rates: the **buy rate** is the rate at which the bank will buy currency from the customer; the **sell rate** is the rate the bank will charge the customer when providing currency. The buy rate is always below the sell rate, e.g. on 17 Dec 2000, a typical high street bank had these rates for exchange against the French Franc:

Sell: £1.00 = 10.46F **Buy:** 11.31F = £1.00

A tourist, changing £1000 into francs and then straight back into pounds, would have received only £924.85 pounds in return.

At the sell rate: £1000 = 10 460F

At the buy rate: 10 460F = only £924.85

In addition to making money on the buy and sell difference, the banks also charge a commission on changing money, usually between 1 per cent and 2 per cent; as well as losing £75.15, this tourist would have been charged between £19.25 and £38.50 in commission.

- **Easy to compare prices**
  All prices would be in the same currency so it would be very easy to compare prices.
- **Incomes worth the same**
  For example, a worker earning a monthly income would now be paid, say, €1800 but could spend it in any EU country with the euro without having to pay any transaction costs.
- **Centralised monetary policy**
  The single currency cannot work if individual countries have the ability to control their own money supplies and interest rates. A necessary part of a single currency is to give up national control of monetary policy and allow this to be controlled by a **European Central Bank**. Monetary policy for individual countries will be impossible. Until we join the Euro, UK monetary policy will still be run through the Bank of England.
- **Interest rates will be the same**
  Interest rates will be dictated by the European Central Bank and will be the same for all euro countries. This will increase competition between banks and other lenders, and probably bring interest rates down.
- **Stability in payments for importers and exporters**
  Before the single currency, an importer or exporter might make a contract to buy or sell goods with a price set in one of the currencies. Then, if the currency changed, the price would also change. This made it very difficult to plan costings for the future. A single currency will remove this problem for importers and exports within the euro area.

The countries that have adopted the euro will gain all of these benefits. For UK businesses, there will be both benefits and drawbacks of having a euro area but not being part of it (Table 6.2.6).

Table 6.2.6 Benefits and drawbacks of the Euro zone for UK businesses

Benefits	Drawbacks
• Pricing, from 2002, will be in one currency for 12 EU countries.	• UK businesses will still be faced with transaction costs that will make their products less competitive.
• If the pound is weak, UK businesses will be able to sell more exports.	• If the pound is strong, UK prices will be higher for Euro countries and UK businesses will sell fewer exports.
• The UK will be able to control its own monetary policy and fix interest rates at a level that can be of benefit to UK businesses.	• The Euro zone will be stronger than the UK acting on its own and may have better control over monetary policy than the UK has.
• UK businesses can trade in euros if they wish and will therefore appear the same as any other Euro country.	• UK businesses selling in the UK will still be selling in pounds so tourists, for example, will still have to change their Euros into pounds and the extra cost may discourage them from coming to the UK.

> **Brussels threatens fine over plan for takeover**
>
> The European Commission has warned Hutchinson Atlantic, a subsidiary of Hong Kong's Hutchinson Whampoa, that it could be fined for trying to take over a Rotterdam container company without the Commission's approval.
>
> *Source: Financial Times*, 27 October 2000

There is no doubt that the creation of the euro zone will have a very great impact on UK businesses, whether they like it or not. Nearly all of the large businesses in the UK have already taken note of the changes and prepared themselves for the impact. Many small and medium sized businesses (SMEs), on the other hand, have not. A survey conducted in April 2000 showed a worrying level of ignorance and lack of planning by the SMEs; see Figure 6.2.8.

Figure 6.2.8 SMEs' opinions about how important the Euro zone is to them

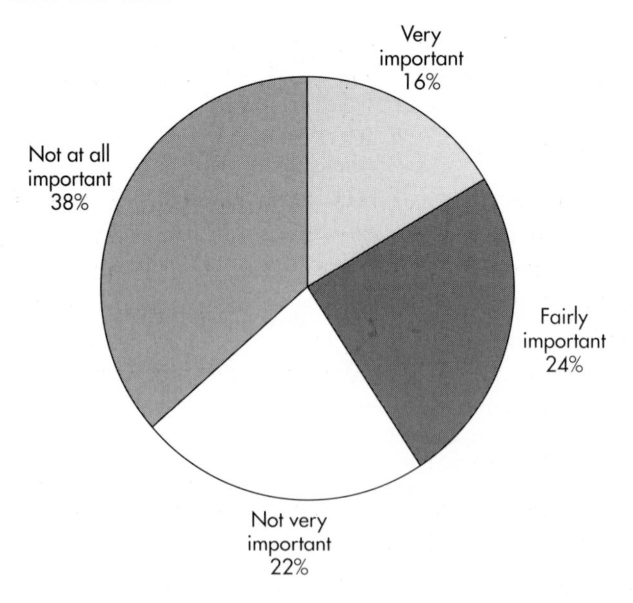

The results of the survey were, unfortunately, little more encouraging when only those SMEs that already have EU connections were asked about euros; see Figure 6.2.9.

Competition policy

One of the major reasons for the original creation of the EU was the belief that greater competition would be good for the Union, that it would increase production, keep prices down and encourage innovation and enterprise. To achieve greater competition, quotas and tariffs were removed, free movement of goods, services, labour and capital was allowed, and now there is a single currency in 12 countries. Unfortunately, when firms compete, they tend to drive other firms out of business and move towards becoming monopolies. To prevent this happening and to ensure that competition continues to take place, the EU has had to create controls that prevent actions that stop competition.

> The **Competition Policy** has been created by the EU and national governments to encourage greater competition between businesses in the EU.

The objectives of Competition Policy were set out in

Figure 6.2.9 Percentage of SMEs, with EU connections, which had already made specific preparations for the euro zone in April 2000

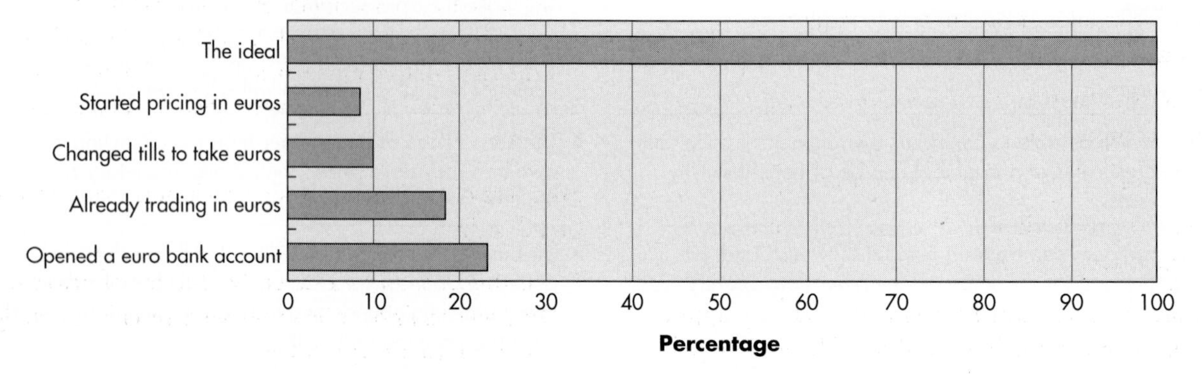

the Treaty of Rome in 1957 which prohibited agreements between firms that:

> ... may affect trade between Member States and which have as their object or effect the prevention, restriction or distortion of competition within the common market ...

The controls that have been set up are in addition to those which the UK itself operates. The Commission is responsible for ensuring that EU competition rules are followed. It has wide powers of investigation, can insist on inspecting a business's premises and seeing relevant documents, and may start an investigation for any of these reasons:

- If it feels that this is justified
- If there has been a complaint from a member state, business, or individual
- If the firms involved inform it of, say, a merger or takeover – the firms will do this to ensure that their agreement will not break EU competition rules
- If state aid is being given by a member state to one of its businesses – the government will inform the Commission to ensure that the state aid is permitted under EU competition rules

Businesses or countries that are found to be in breach of competition policy will be made to stop their anti-competitive actions and may also be fined. Decisions may be challenged in the Court of First Instance and the European Court of Justice.

Actions that are, and are not, anti-competitive

Actions that are against EU competition policy include agreement between firms:

- To fix prices
- To set restrictive conditions of sale
- To restrict sales of products in certain areas or to certain customers
- To control markets through dividing them up to limit competition
- To boycott certain suppliers or customers
- To limit production or deliveries so as to limit competition.

There are, however, some agreements that may appear to be anti-competitive but are allowed because it is felt that, overall, they help to increase competition. These include agreements:

- To improve production or distribution of goods
- To share new technologies
- To carry out joint research and development
- To run franchises.

Investigation into Time Warner/EMI merger

On 14 June 2000, the European Commission announced that it had decided to open a full investigation into the proposed merger between Time Warner Inc. and EMI Group plc. It was recognised that the merger would limit the market for recorded music (and digital delivery of music via the internet) to an oligopoly of four firms: Time Warner/EMI, Universal Music Group, Bertelsmann Music Group and Sony Music. These firms would control about 80 per cent of the market in the European Economic Area. Time Warner/EMI would also become by far the largest of these four firms and this could lead to unacceptable dominance of the market.

Planned **mergers** are also considered as anti-competitive if this is likely to give unacceptable monopoly power to the new, larger firm. When the Commission investigates mergers, it takes into account how dominant the new firm is likely to be in the market. The Commission considers a great many mergers each year, but very few are prevented, mainly because the businesses involved already know what will, and will not, be permitted.

Business that are already large are also covered by competition policy if they **abuse their dominant position** in the market. The Treaty of Rome states that:

> any abuse ... of a dominant position within the common market or in a substantial part of it shall be prohibited as incompatible with the common market in so far as it may affect trade between the Member States

Examples of businesses abusing their dominant position would include:

- treating customers differently in terms of prices or trading condition when they were receiving exactly the same goods or service

Glaxo Wellcome's double price not allowed

The European Commission has insisted that Glaxo Wellcome end its practice of charging Spanish wholesalers different prices for pharmaceutical products they intend to sell in Spain and those they intend to re-export. Glaxo Wellcome had been doing this to prevent the wholesalers from selling to the UK market at prices that were lower than the company was selling at itself. This should mean lower prices for the UK market.

Spanish tax credits are anti-competitive

On 31 October 2000, the Commission decided that Spanish tax credits allowed for foreign investments were anti-competitive and broke the rules on state aid for the EU steel sector. The credits allowed Spanish firms investing in other EU countries to pay less tax and therefore gain an unfair competitive edge.
The French government provides temporary tax-free provisions for setting up branches abroad and this will now also be investigated.

- refusing to sell to certain customers.

Where **state aid** is given to businesses, governments must ensure that this aid does not:

> ... distort or threaten to distort competition by favouring certain undertakings or the production of certain goods ...

However, state aid is permitted in certain circumstances:

- There has been damage caused by natural disasters or exceptional occurrences.
- The aid is granted to individuals and is not designed to support specific products.
- The aid is provided to businesses in designated 'assisted areas'.
- The aid is for cultural or heritage conservation.
- The aid is to support small and medium-sized businesses.
- The aid is for research and development, environmental protection or employment and training.

Details and a wide range of data on EU competition policy can be found through European Community publications and at:

- http://europa.eu.int/comm/competition/index_en.html
- http://europa.eu.int/pol//comp/index_en.html

Also businesses are now allowed to compete for contracts to run what used to be state-owned industries, such as telecommunications in countries other than their own. They may also compete to provide national governments with goods and services through what are called 'public procurement contracts'.

Legislation on working conditions

The EU has affected working conditions in many ways:

- The right to work in any EU country
- Free trade which has made wages more competitive
- A single currency in 12 member states
- The rights given to EU citizens under the various treaties

Figure 6.2.10 The stages of opening up national telecommunications to international competition

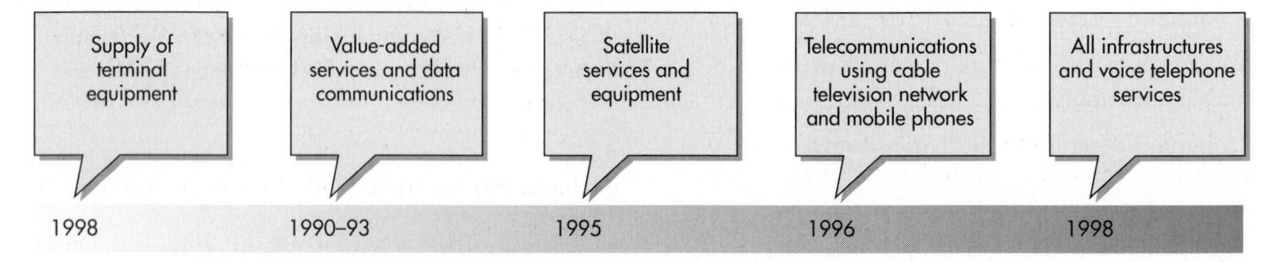

- The protection and aid provided through the structural fund

This section concentrates on other important effects that EU legislation has had on working conditions.

The Social Chapter

In May 1989, the European Commission approved the **Community Charter of Fundamental Social Rights of Workers**. This was initially known as the Social Charter but as it then became one of the chapters in the Maastricht Treaty it is now referred to as the **Social Chapter**.

The **Social Chapter** – originally **The Social Charter** – is part of the Maastricht Treaty which ensures basic rights for workers and for some people in society, e.g. the elderly.

These were the main points of the Chapter:

- The right to work in the EU country of one's choice
- The right to a fair wage
  This has lead to the introduction of a minimum wage.
- The right to continuing improvements in living and working conditions
- The right to adequate social protection, generally through social security benefits
- The right to belong to a professional organisation or a trade union, and the right to be represented in collective bargaining
- The right to receive vocational training throughout one's working life
- A guarantee that men and women will be treated equally in the workplace
- A guarantee that workers will be consulted, provided with relevant information and be allowed to participate in decisions of firms, where appropriate
- The right to satisfactory health protection and safe working conditions
- A guarantee to protect children and adolescents, to include a minimum working age of 15 years, fair pay, and reasonable hours
- A guarantee of a minimum decent standard of living for the elderly
- A guarantee to bring about changes that will make it easier for disabled people to become part of the workforce

The UK did not initially adopt this charter but, as we already had most of these rights in place, that made little difference. The Chapter was finally adopted in 1997, followed shortly by the introduction of the minimum wage in 1999.

Despite objections by the UK Government, it has now been forced to introduce the Working Time Directive. This limits the maximum number of hours an employee can be made to work to 48 hours per week,

Again, in March 2000, the UK Government delayed the implementation of new laws to protect workers. In this case, it tried to delay implementing equal rights for part-time workers. This would give them the same kinds of protection as full-time workers already receive. As before the government will, eventually, be forced to pass these laws.

Equal opportunities

For men and women

Article 119 of the Treaty of Rome (1957) stated that:

> Each member state shall ... ensure and ... maintain the application of the principle that **men and women** should receive **equal pay for equal work**.

Since the 1957 Act, there have been many changes and directives designed to remove the substantial inequalities that existed between men and women. These have included measures to ensure that women and men are treated equally in these ways:

- **Equal pay for equal work**, including equal pay for equal value
- **Equal access to employment**
  In the past, women were not allowed to be on the

floor of the Stock Exchange, which barred them from becoming stock market traders. This is now illegal.

- **Similar working conditions**
  All facilities that are provided for one sex, e.g. toilets, time off work to look after children, pensions rights, must be provided at an equivalent level for the other sex.
- **Time off from work** for the birth of a child
  This may need to be given primarily to the woman, who must be guaranteed the right to return to work, but fathers must also be allowed parental leave.
- **Vocational training**
  Men and women doing the same job have the right to receive the same training and educational opportunities.

The principle of equal pay for equal work extends to job that have **different titles**, such as an air hostess and a cabin steward. If they carry out the same job they are entitled to the same rates of pay. They must, however, work for the same business and have the same qualification.

Work of **equal value** means that even if the jobs are different, but are equally demanding, men and women should receive the same rate of pay. Again the employees must work for the same business and have similar qualifications.

- **Promotion**
  Employees should be promoted solely on the basis of factors such as their performance, seniority, skills and qualifications.
- **Social security**
  Generally men and women doing the same type of work must receive the same social security provision for sickness, invalidity, pensions, industrial accidents, and unemployment. These provisions do vary from country to country and in some cases men and women can be treated differently as in the case of the retirement age for men and women. In the UK men officially retire at 65, but women can retire at 60 or up to 65.

For all employees

Equal opportunities have tended to concentrate on establishing equal rights for men and women. Unfortunately, there are many other forms of discrimination. The EU has recognised this and has set up provisions to try to ensure that all forms of unfair discrimination are covered.

The Treaty on European Union (Maastricht) gave the EU the power to take appropriate action to combat discrimination. The possible grounds of intervention are discrimination based on sex, race or ethnic origin, religion, belief, disability, age or sexual orientation.

Equal opportunities in the EU now cover all of these situations:

- Men and women being treated differently
- Workers being discriminated against on the basis of gender, race, religion, colour, ethnic origin, religious beliefs or age
- Employees working full-time or part-time
- Payments into pension funds and other social security protection schemes being safeguarded as workers move from one country to another

Legislation on consumer rights

The UK has a strong set of consumer rights, as have most of the other EU countries. What Community law has done is to confirm most of this, ensure that it is uniform across all of the member states and, in some places, increase the rights.

Five basic rights now apply and must be met by all producers and retailers selling goods in the EU:

- **Protection of consumers' health and safety**
  No product that is likely to endanger a consumer's health or safety can be sold in the EU. The regulations set specific standards of quality and safety codes, e.g. uniform colours for all electric wiring.
- **Protection of consumers' interest**
  Businesses must consider the consumers' interests when they produce and sell products and should not use unfair methods of selling products. This

would include using misleading advertising or pricing.

- **Consumers' rights to information and education**
  Consumers have a right to be fully informed about details of the products that they are buying, e.g. details on prices, ingredients, how to use products efficiently and safely.
- **The right to redress**
  If consumers are treated unfairly, the products are not up to standard, the products cause injury, etc., consumers have a right to have something done to compensate them. This may range from having the product replaced to taking the business to court. Member states must ensure that procedures are in place to help consumers and that gaining redress does not cost too much.
- **The right to representation and participation in major decisions**
  Consumers must be represented at all levels of local, national and EU legislation on all topics that are likely to affect them.

> David Byrne, the European Commissioner for Health and Consumer Protection, has praised the work of EU scientists on BSE testing. He confirmed that the introduction of more advanced tests will help to ensure that the real picture of how widespread BSE is in EU herds is known. In the long run that will allow additional protective measures to be introduced for the benefit of the consumer.
>
> Dec. 2000

CHAPTER 3

Differences in the EU

KEY TERMS

Activity rates	Culture	Language
Agents	Customs	Logistics
Common market	Distributors	Product, price, place and promotion
Competitiveness	EU markets	Religion
Consumer spending	Exports	The family
Country profiles	Imports	Trade with the EU

Nearly every business in the UK is affected by our membership of the EU and by the increased level of trade that this has created. Some businesses have decided to expand their sales and sell to one or more EU countries. Other businesses have decided not to take up the challenge of selling to EU countries but they are still affected because EU businesses are selling in the UK.

This chapter will look at:

- how UK businesses are affected by trade with the EU
- how UK businesses choose which EU countries they will trade with
- what changes they need to make to their products
- the differences between EU countries.

EU business in the UK

Figure 6.2.3 (page 257) shows that not only do nearly 60 per cent of our exports go to the EU but 54 per cent of our imports come from the EU. In total, we import over £110 billion of goods and services from the EU and all of these are entering the UK market to compete with UK goods and services. Figure 6.1.4 (on page 246) shows where those imports come from.

Germany is the UK's largest EU trading partner but it is easy to find examples of products from all of EU countries on sale in the UK and competing with our own home produced products (Table 6.3.1).

With many imports, producers in the EU are able to produce the products more cheaply than we can in the UK. There are various reason for this:

- Lower labour costs (Figures 6.3.1 and 6.3.2)
- More efficient production, allowing foreign factories to produce more output per worker
- Better climate, which increases yields for vegetables, fruit, grain, etc., and also makes holidays abroad more attractive
- Lower taxes

UK shoppers also want to buy EU imports simply because they come from other countries. Most people in the UK have been to an EU country in the last ten years. They have experienced different lifestyles, different foods and specialist products. These people now expect to find similar products at home. Most major supermarkets now stock globe artichokes, tuna fish, Parma ham, sundried tomatoes, rye bread, Danish beers and Belgian chocolates.

UK businesses are forced to compete with a growing number and variety of imports. They need to react to ensure that they will survive and continue to make acceptable profits. All of the following actions will help them to do this:

Table 6.3.1 Typical products from other EU countries

Country	**Import**
Germany	Cars, beer, sausages, insurance, iron and steel
France	Wine, clothes, fruit and vegetables, machinery
Netherlands	Flowers and bulbs, natural gas, plastics, poultry
Ireland	Dairy products, beef, beer, chemicals, tourism
Italy	Olive oil, wine, footwear, textiles, tobacco
Belgium	Chocolates, beer, tractors, vehicle parts
Luxembourg	Glass, chemicals, rubber products
Spain	Wine, cars, fruit and vegetables, tourism
Sweden	Cars, machinery, matches, paper products
Finland	Timber products, mobile phones, textiles, ships
Denmark	Bacon, pork, fish, dairy products, machinery
Portugal	Wine, paper, cork, leather, clothes, footwear
Austria	Machinery, electronic equipment, paper products
Greece	Olive oil, citrus fruits, footwear, tourism

- Carrying out detailed market research on the new businesses, checking their products, where their products will be sold, what price they will set, the type of advertising they will use, etc.
- Modifying their own prices, promotion and, if necessary, the products themselves, and where and how they will be sold
  Good defensive action will make it hard for new businesses to enter the UK market.
- Reviewing the production process to see if costs can be cut anywhere, but not if this will reduce the quality of the product
- Going on the offensive and making efforts to start selling products into the EU

Declining competitiveness

As the pound has risen in value against the euro, UK industry has become less and less competitive. The cost of production in most EU countries is now below that of the UK.

This has made it more and more difficult for UK businesses to compete against EU firms. This is partly because businesses find it difficult to compete in EU countries because their labour costs are often well below ours, but also because firms producing and selling in the UK now find that cheaper imports are invading what used to be secure markets.

Understandably, UK manufacturers are concerned and

Where does our fresh fruit come from in October?

By October, the UK fruit-growing season is essentially over. Some UK fruits, such as apples, can be stored for a short time and are still available in shops, but most of our fruit is imported and much of it comes from the EU.

Table 6.3.2 EU countries that are still able to produce fruits in October, and are the main exporters to the UK

Fruit	UK	France	Italy	Spain	Greece	Portugal	Belgium	Netherlands
Apples	✓	✓	✓					
Avocados				✓				
Grapes		✓	✓	✓	✓	✓		
Kiwifruit			✓					
Melons			✓	✓				
Nectarines		✓		✓				
Pears			✓	✓			✓	✓
Plums		✓	✓					
Strawberries							✓	

Figure 6.3.1 EU countries with lower labour costs (%) than the UK for unskilled manual workers in industry (Year 2000)

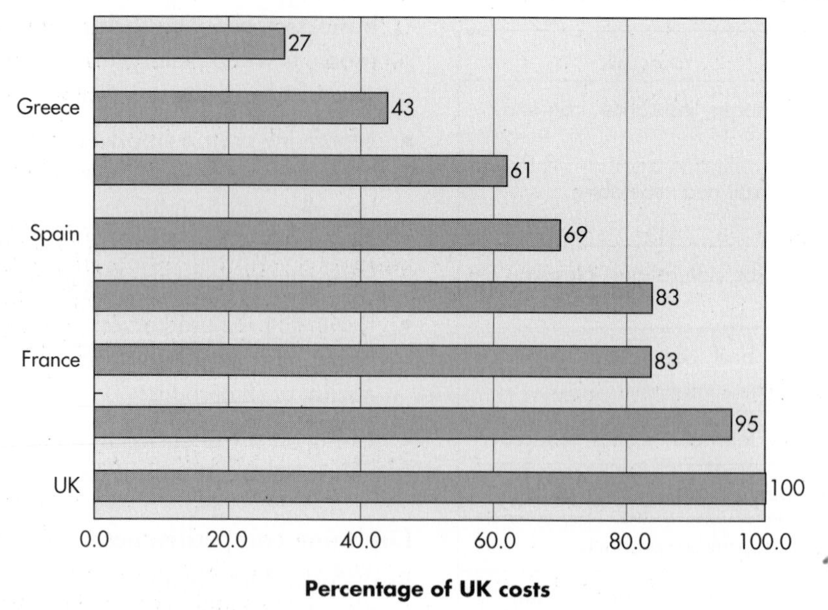

Source: Adapted from *Main Economic Indicators* © (OECD), 1999.

Figure 6.3.2 EU countries with a lower labour costs (%) than the UK for skilled workers in manufacturing industries (Year 2000)

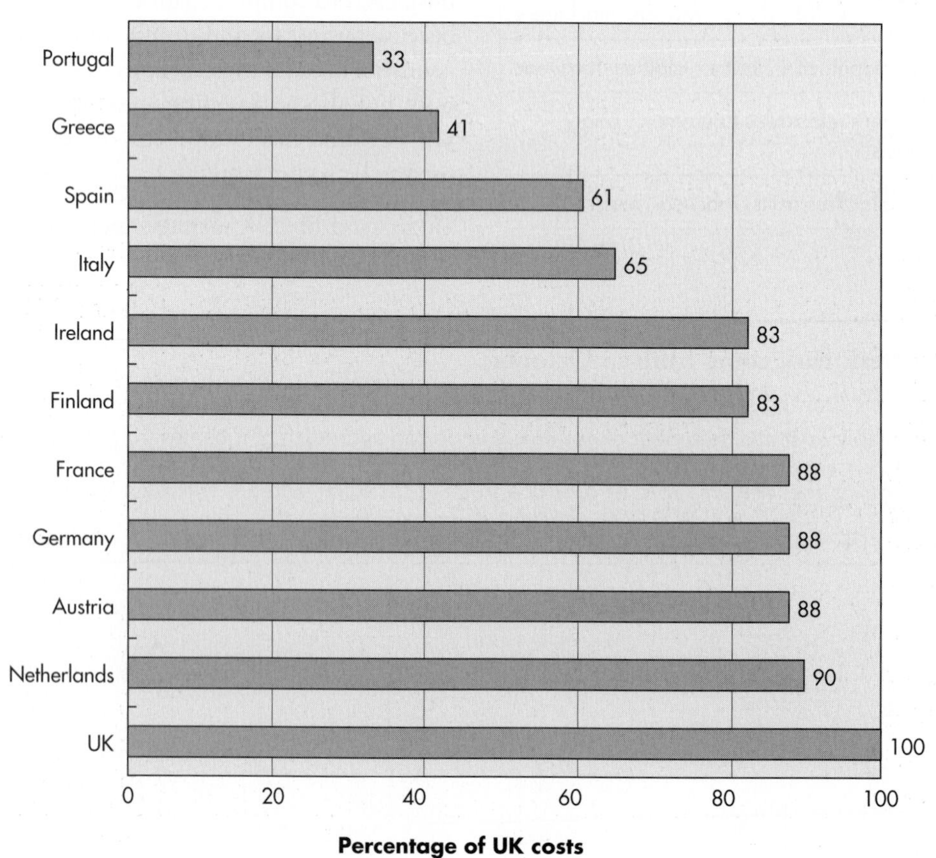

are asking the UK Government for answers. The very high value of the pound is not simply reflecting the success of UK business, it also reflects the fact that UK interest rates are higher than those in Euroland. This has created an artificially high value for the pound and UK businesses are suffering. Many UK business would like the Bank of England to lower interest rates, allow the value of the pound to fall and, through this, create a more level playing field. The cost of production would then compare much more favourably with most EU countries.

UK business expanding into the EU

One of the major arguments put forward by the Conservative Government under Prime Minister Edward Heath for joining the EEC in the early 1970s was that it would increase the potential market for UK businesses from 55 million (the UK domestic market) to 270 million (the total EEC market in 1973). Details of how the size of the EU market has continued to increase are shown on Figure 6.2.4 (page 258).

In the twenty-first century, the EU has become a trading area where UK firms can buy and sell products almost as though the EU was, in fact, a single market place. Many UK firms now see their market as European rather than just in the UK. Figure 6.3.3 shows where the UK sold products in the EU in 1998 and how important each EU country was for total UK business.

Selling into any foreign country requires firms to alter their products or marketing in some way. There are also **logistics** problems, such as how to transport goods, how long delivery will take, etc. Below we consider some of the important factors that a business planning to sell, or increase sales, in the EU will have to consider.

Logistics refers to the movement of goods or people from one place to another and includes transport, storage, delivery schedules, transport documents, etc.

Which countries to sell to

EU countries are not all the same. Some of the major differences are detailed on pages 279–85. It is therefore important that UK businesses which wish to start selling abroad should choose their markets carefully. It may be felt that the most important factor is how much money each country has to spend. Details of the GDP for each country were given in Figure 6.2.1. There are, however, many other factors that could, and should, be considered:

- The **total GDP** of the countries
- The **GPD/head** of each country
  This shows how much income each individual, on average, has to spend.

Figure 6.3.3 Export of goods and services from the UK to EU countries by destination, 1998 (£ billion)

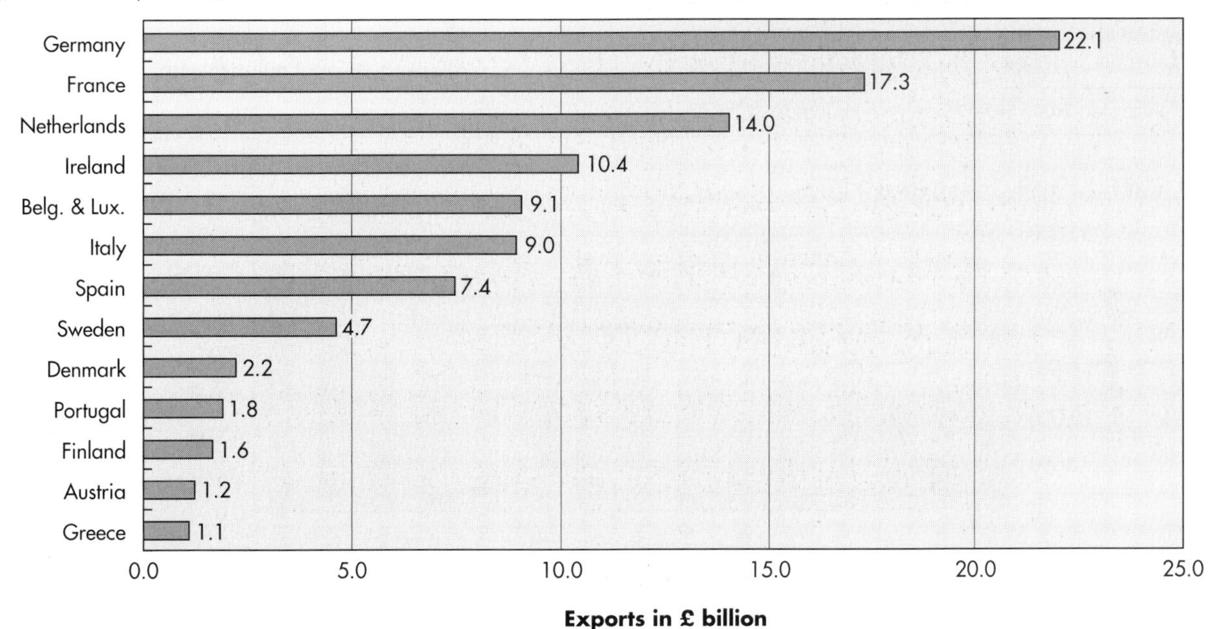

- The **total number of people** in the country
  This gives some guidance as to the size of the potential market.
- The **density of the population**
  This indicates how easy it will be to get the products to the potential customers within the country.
- The **age structure** of the country
  This will be important if the business's products are aimed at particular age groups.
- The **language**
  Advertising, packaging, instructions, etc. will all need to be translated.
- **How far the markets are from the UK**
  This will affect transport costs and how quickly goods can be taken to the customers.

Table 6.3.3 shows the total GDP, the GPD/head, the total population, the population density and the official languages of EU countries. Figure 6.3.4 charts the total GDP and GDP/head for EU countries in 1999.

The characteristics that a business should take into account will depend on what type of product it is selling. If a business is selling luxury items, it will be more important to target countries with high income than with high populations or high GDP. Figure 6.3.4 makes the point very clearly. Luxembourg has the lowest total GDP but the highest GDP/head. There are, however, only 426 000 people in Luxembourg. Germany, with the highest population and highest total GPD, actually has more people with high incomes than Luxembourg. As a niche market Luxembourg may be very attractive, but for a mass market, even of luxury

Table 6.3.3 Some major characteristics of EU countries (1999)

Country	GDP (£ billion)	GDP/head (£)	Population (millions)	Population density (km²)	Official languages
Austria	133	16 459	8.1	96	German
Belgium	167	16 348	10.2	335	Dutch/French/German
Denmark	93	17 389	5.3	123	Danish/German
Finland	78	15 121	5.2	15	Finnish/Swedish
France	887	14 625	59.1	108	French
Germany	1292	15 743	82.1	230	German
Greece	104	9 864	10.5	80	Greek
Ireland	62	16 569	3.7	53	Irish/English
Italy	849	14 726	57.1	190	Italian
Luxembourg	12	26 787	0.4	164	Letzeburgesch/French/German
Netherlands	265	16 758	15.7	385	Dutch
Portugal	109	10 864	10.0	108	Portuguese
Spain	475	12 043	39.4	78	Spanish
Sweden	135	15 254	8.9	20	Swedish
UK	880	14 791	59.2	242	English/Welsh

Source: Adapted from *Main Economic Indicators* (OECD)

Figure 6.3.4 Total GDP and GDP/head for EU countries (1999)

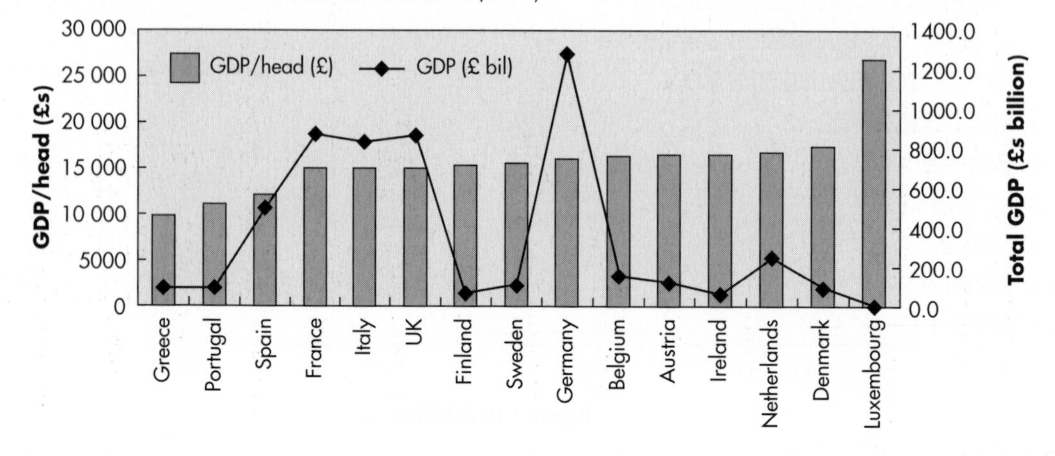

products, Germany would be much better. Businesses need to make sure that they are in possession of the correct data.

If a business wanted to concentrate on selling to one language group across the EU they would probably choose German, English or French. These are the languages that are most widely spoken in the EU (Figure 6.3.5).

It must, however, be remembered that customers will expect certain details, such as ingredients, sell-by dates and instructions to be in their national language. On that basis, German is the most attractive language as it is the main official language of Germany and Austria, with a total combined population of over 90 million people.

Figure 6.3.5 Total number of people able to speak German, French or English in the EU (2000)

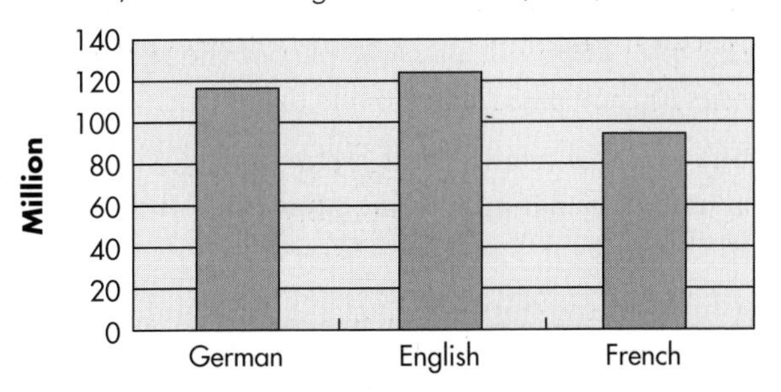

> **Luxembourg**
>
> Luxembourg, the wealthiest of the three (Benelux) markets with the highest GNP per capita in the world, is often overlooked by exporters, according to Sarah Martin, Export Promoter for IT and Telecoms in Western Europe. She comments: 'Insurance services are high on its list of imports from Britain, together with luxury goods and high quality clothing.'
>
> *Source: Overseas Trade*, October 2000

Consumer spending

If businesses are to sell successfully into EU countries they need to have a good understanding of what their customers want. If they are selling to consumers they need to know what consumers in each of the EU countries typically buy. Choosing a country without carefully checking what customers spend their incomes on could mean that loss-making markets might be chosen instead of profitable markets.

Figure 6.3.6 shows which countries have the highest and lowest percentages of consumer income being spent on major types of product. For food producers Greece

Figure 6.3.6 Extremes of consumer spending in the EU

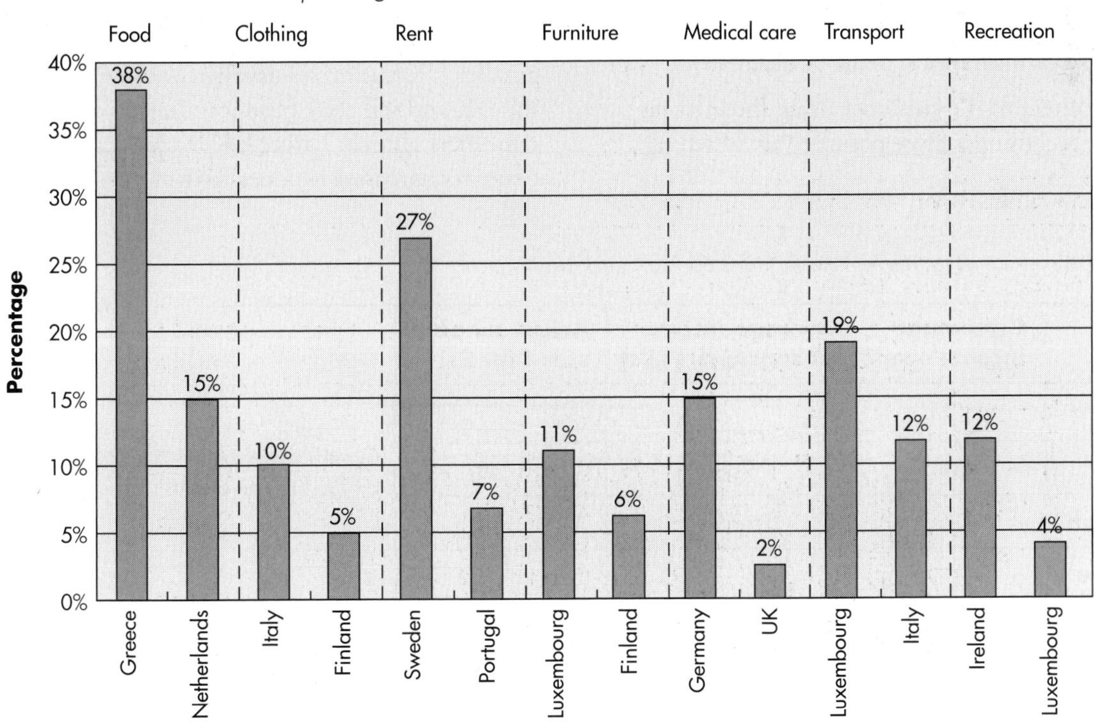

Source: Adapted from EUROSTAT

would appear to be the obvious country to target, but it must be remembered that Greek citizens have a much lower income than Dutch citizens. UK businesses need to take this into account.

The basic data suggests that Greeks spend 2.5 times as much on food as the Dutch. Table 6.3.4 shows the real difference in terms of the actual amount of expenditure (given here in pounds). Some figures, calculated in terms of how much is actually spent (in pounds), can make the gap wider, as with consumer expenditure on furniture. Luxembourg seems to spend 1.8 times as much as Finland, but the corrections on Table 6.3.4 show that it is actually 3.2 times greater.

Full details of countries' spending patterns can be found in individual national statistics or from general sources such as EUROSTAT.

How the goods will be sold

Businesses planning to sell into the EU also have to consider how the products will be sold. They may be produced in the UK and exported, or produced in the EU country itself.

Producing in the UK and selling abroad

- Selling direct to the customers by visiting them This is very difficult and time-consuming for consumer products but is quite common practice when selling products such as machinery, computer networks or insurance systems to businesses.
- Selling direct to the customer using the internet This is becoming a more popular way of selling abroad.
- Using **agents** who act on behalf of the business to find places or customers where the products can be sold abroad
- Using **distributors** who will buy the goods from the business and then find their own customers to take the goods

Advantages of this approach:

- Expansion may be easier as it is essentially home based and does not initially need new factories, etc.
- Less expense is involved if the attempt to break into EU markets is unsuccessful.
- Agents and distributors often deal with more than one country and arrange sales of products in many countries fairly quickly.

There are also disadvantages:

- Distributors do not work for the firm and can be unreliable. They will also take part of the potential profits as they pass the products on.
- Many national retailers still prefer to deal with firms that are either national or are producing in their own countries.
- For firms in the north of England, Scotland or Wales, transport costs can be very high.

Setting up production in the EU country and selling the products direct to the customers

Smaller UK businesses usually continue to produce in the UK and sell their products directly or indirectly to customers abroad. Larger UK businesses often set up branches abroad. This does have certain advantages:

Table 6.3.4 Correcting figures for expenditure on food and furniture

	Percentage income spent	Average income of consumers (£s)	Actual amount spent (in £s)	
Food				
Greece	38	9864	3748	Greeks spend only 1.5 times as much in £s on food as the Dutch.
Netherlands	15	16 758	2514	
Furniture				
Luxembourg	11	26 787	2947	People in Luxembourg spend 3.2 times as much in £s on furniture as the Finns.
Finland	6	15 121	907	

French businesses move to the UK

While some UK businesses are keen to set up in France, a growing number of French businesses see the UK as an attractive country in which to base their businesses. The UK is seen as a country with a lenient tax regime and a business-friendly environment. French businesses complain that French taxes on business, and the cost of the social security provision that they have to pay, are just too high.

In France, social security charges are 48 per cent of the employee's gross salary, compared to 21 per cent in the UK. France's tax on business profits for most small to medium-sized firms is 36.6 per cent, whereas in the UK it is only 20 per cent.

Olivier Cadic moved his business from Paris to the UK in 1996 and now employs 15 people producing printed circuit boards in Ashford, Kent. He was so incensed at the punitive tax regime in France that he set up a website to tell the French Government, and anyone else who wishes to access the site, just how foolish the French tax structure is.

Cadic's website can be found at **www.francelibre.org**

- Lower transport costs
- Producing in the actual market so that it is easier to carry out market research, advertising, selling, etc.
- Closer relations with customers, which makes it easier for the business to respond to their needs
- The ability to monitor closely what competitors are doing and to react to any aggressive changes
- Usually employing nationals who are likely to have a better understanding of the market
- Labour costs may be cheaper, especially in countries such as Greece and Portugal

Setting up the business abroad can also have disadvantages:

- Labour costs in some EU countries, such as France and Belgium, are higher than in the UK.
- Taxes on profits are higher in many EU countries than in the UK.

Many businesses print details or instructions in a number of languages so that the product may be sold more easily in many countries.

CONSUMIR PREFERENTEMENTE ANTES DEL: VEASE TAPA.

A CONSOMMER DE PREFERENCE AVANT LA FIN: VOIR LE COUVERCLE.

BEST BEFORE: SEE LID

MINDESTENS BIS ENDE: SIEHE DECKEL.

- It may be possible to gain better economies of scale by producing all of the products in one place instead of in different centres in different countries.
- There may be language barriers with staff which will make production more difficult.
- Working conditions, laws, rules and regulations are different and this means that businesses may find it much more difficult to run their businesses efficiently without making mistakes about taxes, pensions, social security, hours of work, etc.

Changes that need to be made to production and marketing for selling abroad

When businesses sell products abroad, either from the UK or by setting up production units in a foreign country, it is likely that changes will need to be made to the products and the way that they are marketed. Some of these changes are obvious, but others are not and need to be thought about carefully before the business decides to expand its sales into foreign markets:

- **Language**
  What parts of the product packaging, instructions, advertising, etc. will need to be printed in another language? When this is being done, should the business plan ahead and add other languages at the same time?
- **The product**
  Will the product need to be changed to meet the needs of the different market conditions? For example, cars sold in most EU countries (not Ireland) will need to have left-hand steering; garden

Figure 6.3.7 New businesses in France (1999) by key sector

In 1999, in France, 268,919 new businesses were set up. About 75 per cent of them were sole traders with no employees, but 6760 were businesses with more than five employees. Some of these businesses were British.

The main areas of production are shown here and should give UK producers some idea of which areas are expanding in France and where there are competitive markets.

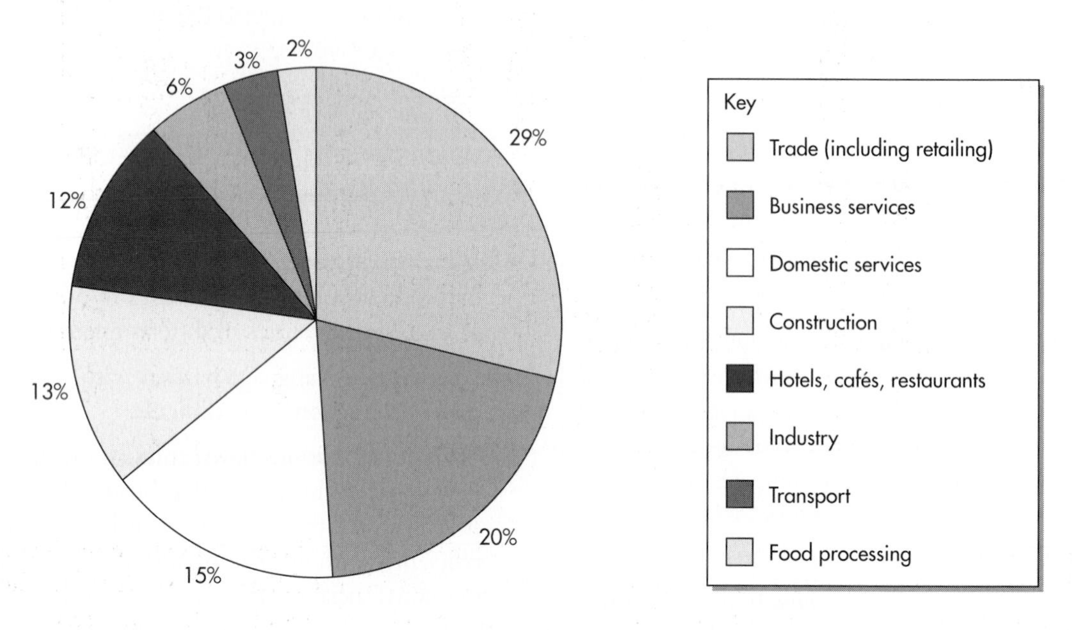

Full details of how to set up businesses in France can be found at **http://www.apce.com/**

gnomes sold in Sweden or Finland will have to withstand much colder winters; beef sold in some EU countries (November 2000 – France) must be sold off the bone.

- **Advertising**
  Many advertisements that might be allowed in the UK would be banned in other EU countries. In Italy, where religion is still very important to most Italians, any advertisement that made fun of Christianity would be banned.
- **Pricing**
  When UK firms sell their products in other EU countries, they usually charge slightly different prices in different countries. This reflects important factors which change from country to country:
  - The level of sales tax that the country insists is put onto the product
    This will include VAT, but also specific taxes on alcohol, tobacco, etc.
  - The GDP/head that different EU countries have (see Table 6.3.3)
    It may, for example, be necessary to have lower prices in Greece, Portugal and Spain than in Luxembourg, the Netherlands and Ireland.
  - The level of competition in each country
    Where UK products are unique there will be no competition and the UK business can charge what it likes. Where similar products already exist the UK business will need to set it prices at the same level, or even use penetration pricing.
- **Transport costs**
  When UK businesses producing goods in the UK are selling those goods to EU countries, there is immediately an added cost for transport. This will affect prices and profits, and may influence where the business wishes to sell (Figure 6.3.8). These businesses also need to consider what method of transport they will use. Will it be road, rail, air or water?

Figure 6.3.8 Distance by road from London to other EU capital cities (miles)

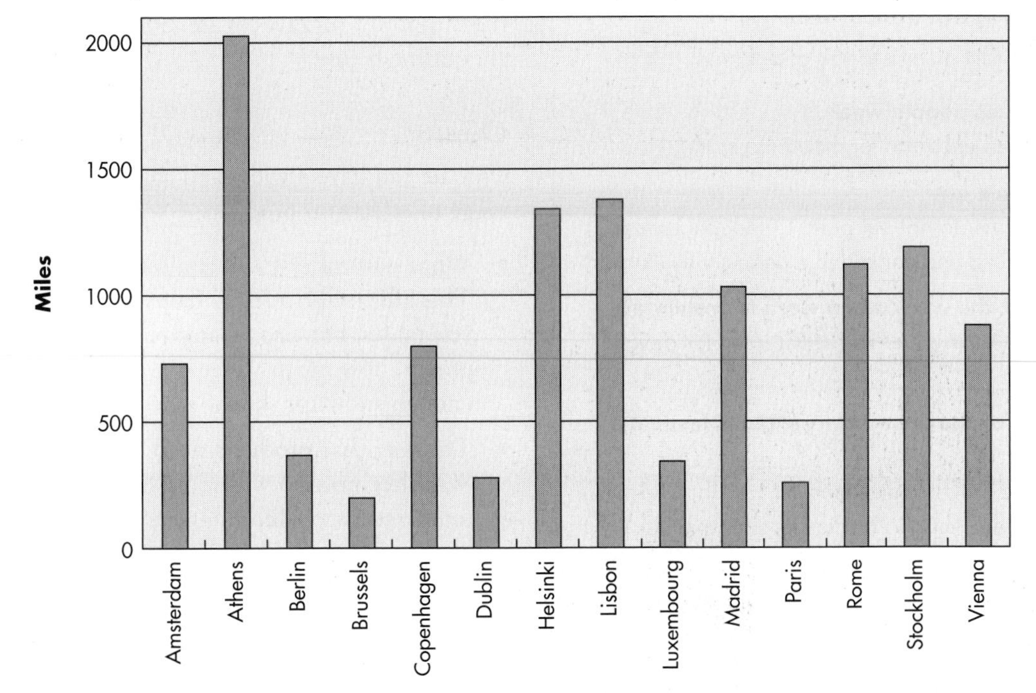

- **Different cultures**
  In the UK we do not tend to bargain with people selling goods, except occasionally with double-glazing salesmen and at car-boot sales. In other EU countries, bargaining is more common. In Portugal, Spain and Greece, street markets are still a common way of selling products, and bargaining about prices, quantities and quality is normal practice.

Differences and similarities in the EU

Many of the changes that have taken place in the EU in the last 40 years have tended to make markets, businesses and workers more similar. Some laws apply to all EU countries. Consumer protection and workers' rights are very similar. Some products are sold across the EU with almost no change to the product, e.g. the Big Mac, bottles of Champagne and Tippex. Many businesses are now so well established in the EU that they need to make little or no change when they sell into different markets.

There are, however, very important differences between the EU countries and most businesses need to consider these differences before they can successfully sell their products in other countries. We have considered some of them above, e.g. language, incomes, the level of competition and different laws and taxes. There are also more fundamental differences which reflect the different **customs** and **cultures** of the EU countries.

Customs are ways of behaving that have become so well accepted in a society that people in that society are expected to behave in that way all of the time.

Culture reflects the intellectual side of society and shows how tastes, manners, behaviour, etc. have developed.

The closure of shops and businesses on a Sunday developed out of the Christian religious culture of 'a day of rest' which should be dedicated to giving thanks to God. Over many centuries this has become a custom, generally backed by law, which forbids certain businesses to operate on Sundays. In the UK, where religion is no longer as dominant a part of our lives as it used to be, Sunday trading is now allowed. There is, however, legal protection for any employee who does not want to work on Sundays, and this was specifically included in legislation to protect people who still feel that Sunday is a special religious day.

How does religion affect business?

Religion can affect many aspects of business:

- **What clothes people wear**
  Black clothes are worn for mourning in Italy.
- **What people eat**
  Strict Muslims do not eat pork. Orthodox Jews only eat food killed and cooked in a certain way (kosher).
- **The day of the week when work is prohibited**
  Sunday for devout Christians; Saturday for devout Jews.
- **The times of the year when religious festivals take place**
  Christians expect to have time off work at Christmas and nearly all shops to be closed on Christmas Day.
- **What motives business have**
  Many businesses with religious connections operate on a not-for-profit motive.

In other EU countries, Sunday trading is still banned for many businesses. These tend to be countries where a strong religious (usually Catholic) faith still exists, e.g. Italy, Spain and Greece. Even in these countries, however, trade is breaking down the barriers, and in all countries tourist businesses, such as cafés, restaurants, bars, and hotels, will be open seven days a week.

When businesses sell abroad they need to know what the important differences are. Some of these differences are outline below.

Climate

Climate can have a wide, and sometimes unforeseen, range of effects on products:

- **What natural raw materials are available**
  This affects agricultural crops such as fruit and vegetables, but also what type of timber can be grown, how much water is available, whether there is enough snow for skiing, etc.
- **The way that products need to be made**
  Will they need to withstand extremes of temperature, or differing levels of humidity?
- **What products will be demanded**
  In hot countries, more drinks, air conditioning, skin protection, etc. will be needed. In cold countries, more warm clothes, double or treble glazing, higher carbohydrate meals, etc. will be needed.
- **How people live**
  In northern Europe people tend to work throughout the day with a short lunch break and then a fairly early supper. In the Mediterranean area, where the days are long, a two or three-hour-lunch break is taken and people work into the evening, eating late.

Figure 6.3.9 shows the extremes of normal daily temperatures in Helsinki and Athens. Normal daily

Figure 6.3.9 Range of daily temperatures in Helsinki and Athens (°F)

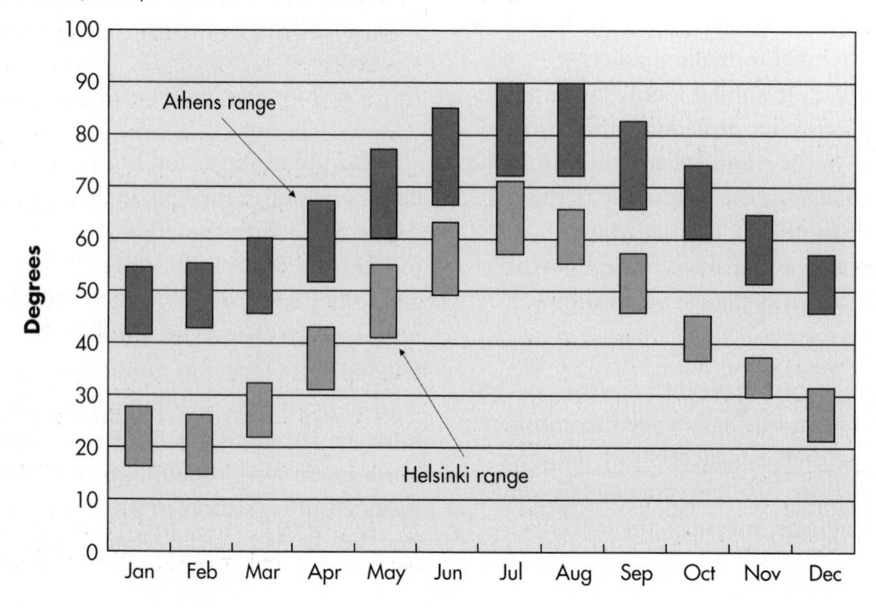

Figure 6.3.10 Average monthly rainfall (inches) for Nice and Madrid

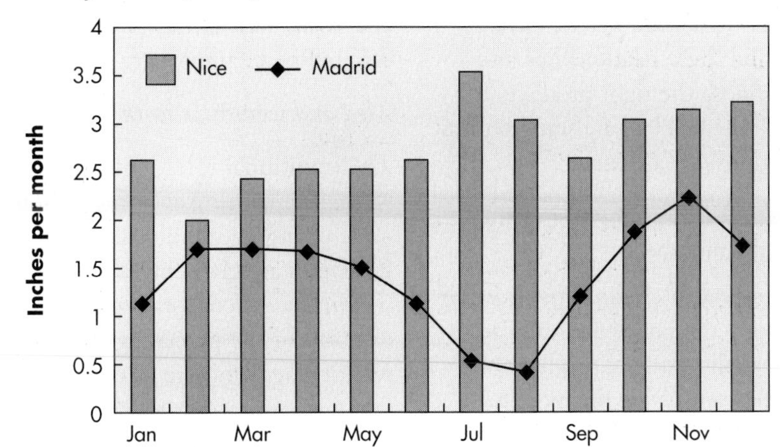

Figure 6.3.11 Average daily hours of sunshine for Gibraltar and Glasgow

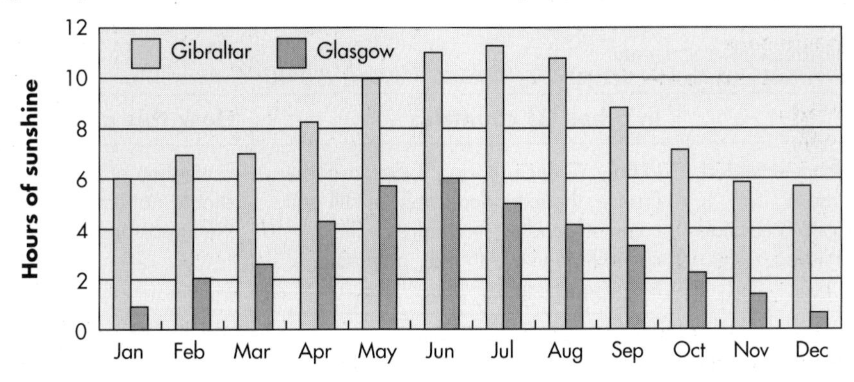

temperature in Athens ranges from 42°F to 90°F across the year. At no point is it below freezing point of 32°F. In Helsinki, the range is from 15°F to 71°F, with four months of the year where temperatures do not rise above freezing point.

Figures 6.3.10 and 6.3.11 show similar extremes for rainfall between Nice and Madrid and for daily sunshine between Gibraltar and Glasgow.

National customs and culture

Customs and cultures are very important parts of national identities. They affect how people live and behave, what they find acceptable and unacceptable, what foods they eat, what they wear, their social ties, how they look at the family, what conditions they expect at work and how they treat customers. Below are just a few examples of how customs and culture in the UK differ from, or are similar to, other EU countries and how that affects products and labour markets.

The family

The Family in Greece

The family is at the heart of Greek society in both the town and the country. Sons and daughters live with their parents until they are married, and married couples will often live with the family for a year or two after the marriage. In some regions, it is expected that the couple will live with the wife's parents and the husband will move to his wife's village. This practice is also found in cities.

Often each generation carries on the family business and the primary purpose of marriage is still to have children and carry on family traditions.

Details of business in Greece can be found at:
www.internationalist.com/business/Greece.php

The family remains an important feature of our lives, even if we have left home. The relationships between partners, brothers, sisters, mothers, fathers, grandparents, aunts, uncles, etc. are some of the strongest we have. Businesses need to understand these relationships and use them to help them to choose the right products to sell and the right way to sell them. Here are some typical examples of how these relationships are used:

- Selling insurance, understandably, emphasises the need to provide for family members.
- Toy producers have to appeal to children by showing how exciting and necessary the goods are but also to the parents (who will actually buy the products) by emphasising quality, safety and value for money.
- Food products frequently show positive family situations, as with OXO, and suggest that the food products will help to cement family relationships.

UK businesses selling into the EU will need to appreciate that other EU countries view the family differently. Examples are given in Table 6.3.5.

Men and women at work

The traditional roles – of men as the breadwinners and women remaining at home as housewives and mothers – are changing rapidly across the whole of the EU. Examples are given in Table 6.3.6. There are, however, still major differences between EU countries, especially in terms of the percentage of men and women of working age who are in the labour force (Figure 6.3.12).

In Scandinavian countries, the percentages of men and women in the workforce are very similar and all three countries offer a high level of support to mothers to

Table 6.3.5 How EU countries view the family

In the UK	In other EU countries	How this affects markets
We have moved away from extended families where three or more generations live together, to a nuclear family of parents and children.	In Italy, Greece, Portugal, Spain and France, the extended family is still quite common, and often children will continue to live with their parents after they are married.	Promotion of products to these EU families should not emphasise independence, but the importance of family.
The gender role of housewife at home and husband at work is breaking down because both partners work. UK couples now often shop together.	In Italy, Greece and Portugal, the woman is in charge of the home and makes the decisions about what food, cutlery, crockery, etc. will be bought.	Sellers of food products, cutlery, and crockery must target the woman, not the man. Prices need to be set so that they are acceptable on a limited household budget.

Table 6.3.6 The roles of men and women

In the UK	In other EU countries	How this affects markets
Men and women both work, with some women taking out time to raise a family. Women now tend to follow specific careers and expect to progress within those careers.	In Italy, Greece, Spain, Ireland, Belgium and Luxembourg, far fewer women are working.	Women who work and earn their own incomes are much more independent shoppers. Where there are high activity rates, products can be targeted specifically at the women. Where there are low activity rates for women, the men may need to be persuaded to buy the products.
A very high proportion of working women work only part time.	In Italy, Greece, Spain, Finland and Portugal, a very high proportion of working women work full time.	Working full time provides higher levels of income and more spending power for the individuals.
24.9 per cent of the UK workforce is part time.	In Greece, Spain, Italy, Luxembourg, Portugal and Finland less than 12 per cent of the population work part time. In the Netherlands 38.8 per cent of the workforce work part time.	The hours that people work will affect their incomes, when they can shop, the amount of leisure time that they have, and their lifestyles. All of this will affect businesses trying to sell their products.

Figure 6.3.12 Activity rates for men and women in EU countries (1998)

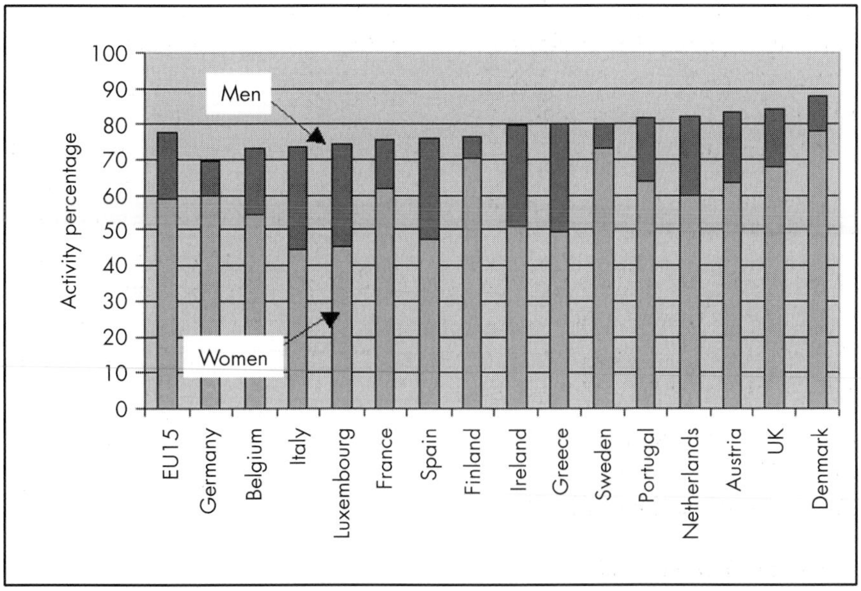

Source: Adapted from *Employment in Europe* 1999, European Commission

help them back into the workforce. In the Catholic countries of Italy, Spain and Ireland, and in Greece, where the Greek Orthodox Church is still very important, the tradition of women in the home remains very strong.

Figure 6.3.13 shows the percentage of men and women working part time. In all EU countries, a higher percentage of women work part time than men. This is because many retailing jobs are part time and retailing jobs are often done by women. Part-time work fits in

Figure 6.3.13 Proportion of the workforce working part time, men and women (1998)

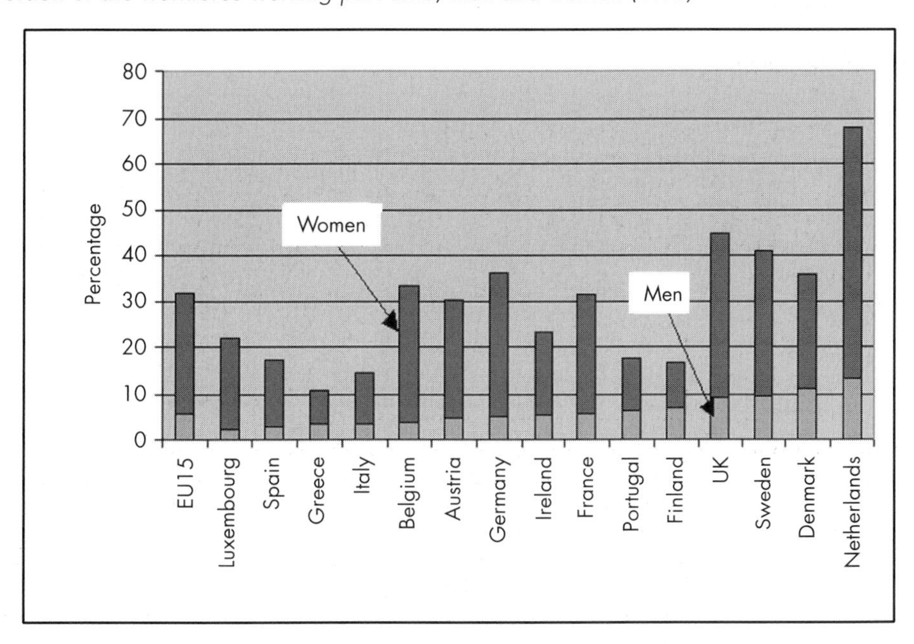

Source: Adapted from *Employment in Europe 1999*, European Commission

Figure 6.3.14 Breakdown of countries' population by age categories (%) (1998)

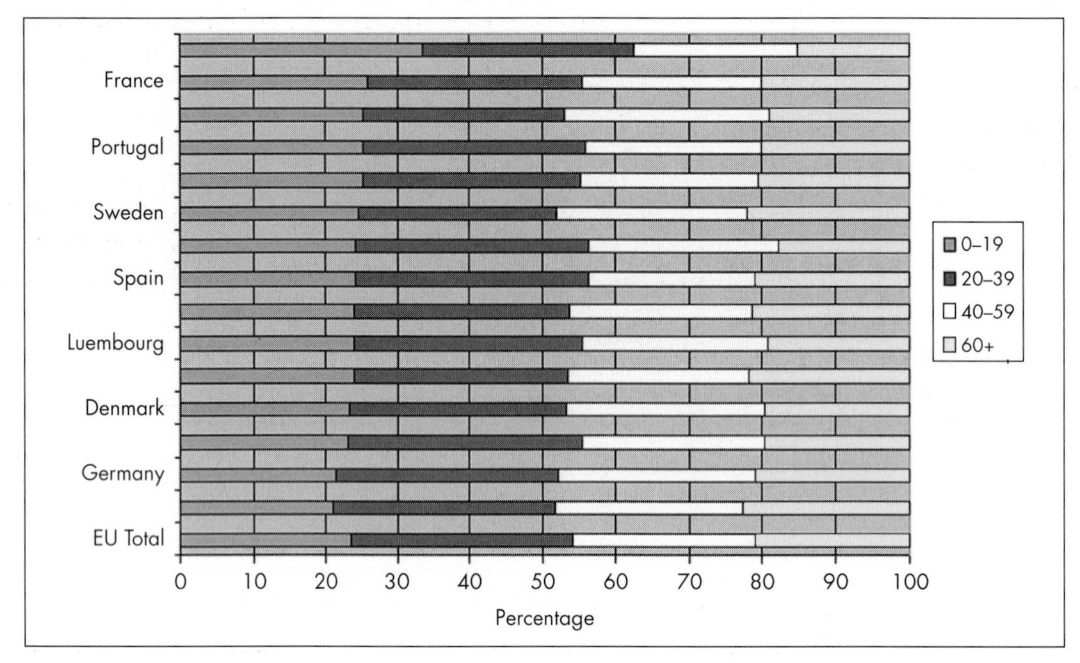

Source: Adapted from Eurostat

with children at school and running a household. In countries like Greece, Spain, Italy and Portugal, where there is less part-time work for women, full-time work is often in the family business and many men and women are self-employed.

Population profiles

The structure of the population also affects markets and the types of products that are likely to be bought. Figure 6.3.14 shows the age breakdown for each country. Where there is a high proportion of people

Figure 6.3.15 Life expectancy for men and women in EU countries (1998)

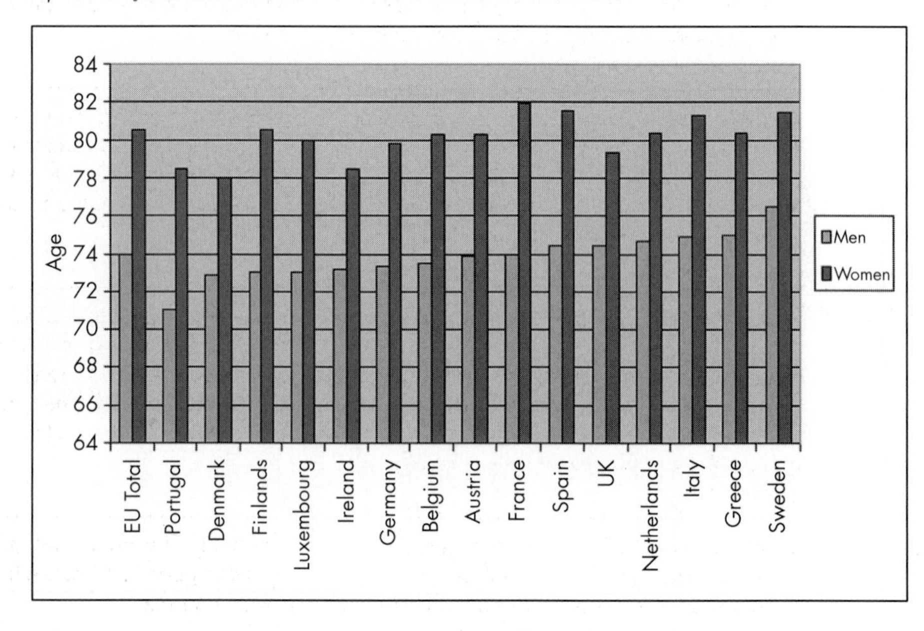

Source: Adapted from Eurostat

below the age of 19, there is likely to be a high demand for educational products, toys, CDs and the wide range of products that appeal to children and teenagers. Where there is a high proportion of people over the age of 60, most will be retired and their priorities will be housing, gardening products, health products and the wide range of goods and services that older people want and need.

Culture, lifestyle, health care provision and diet also affect how long people are likely to live (Figure 6.3.15). In all EU countries women, on average, live longer than men and this affects what provision and products will be needed for the elderly because there are many more older women than men.

In the UK, on average, women live about five years longer than men but in Finland women outlast men by seven and a half years and, in France, this is nearly eight years.

Other differences

There are many other differences and similarities between EU countries and all of them would affect businesses in one way or another. Examples are given in Table 6.3.7.

Table 6.3.7 Differences and how they can affect businesses

	Differences	**How business can be affected**
Diet and eating habits	Many foods are now sold across the EU but countries also have their favourites. Working hours also affect when and what people eat.	The UK sells pigeons, snails and horsemeat to meet demand from the French. Where families have both parents at work convenience foods are becoming more popular.
Sport and recreation	Some sports and recreations have now spread across the EU, such as football, golf, the cinema and discos. Others are still very nationalistic, such as bull fighting in Spain, cross-country skiing in Finland and the bars and ceilidhs of Ireland.	Some leisure and recreation products can be made and sold to any country in the EU. Others must meet the specialist needs of individual countries and even individual regions.
Taxes and the cost of living	Taxation as a percentage of GDP is as high as 54 per cent in Sweden and 53 per cent in Denmark and as low as 36 per cent in Spain and the UK, but the state provides more in Sweden and Denmark than in Spain and the UK.	Where the state controls expenditure, it is important to gain government contracts. Where taxes are relatively low individuals and businesses will make the buying decisions.
Size of agricultural holdings	In Greece the average size of farms is only 4.5 hectares (ha) and, in Italy, it is only 5.9 ha. At the other extreme, the UK has holdings of 70.1 ha., the largest in the EU. France (38.5), Denmark (39.6) and Luxembourg (39.9) also have relatively large holdings.	Businesses supplying, tractors, fertilisers, seeds, etc., need to know what how the requirement for their products will change from country to country, e.g. Greek farmers may need much smaller and cheaper tractors.
Transport conditions	The UK has a rather overcrowded road network and a fairly slow rail network. France and Germany have relatively clear motorways and high speed trains.	The quality of transport will affect the cost of supplying goods and hence the price at which they can be sold.

UNIT 6

End of Unit Assignment

For this unit, you will need to investigate the impact of the EU on a UK business which is already trading in a number of EU countries, or has the potential to do this. Much of the data that you will need to collect will come from general sources, such as textbooks, government or EU publications, the internet, etc., but some will need to come from the chosen business. It is, therefore, important that you have good access to the business or very good details about what the business does in the UK and the EU and how it does this. You will need to know the following facts about your chosen business:

1 What products it produces (this will include services) and what products, if any, it sells in the EU

2 Which countries it sells in

3 Some history of when the business started sales in the UK and the EU and how these have grown

4 What the business's policies and objectives are for sales in the EU

5 What strategies it uses, or could use, to sell its products in the EU – pricing, promotion, distribution, etc.

It would be possible to cover some of the bullet points in the Assessment Evidence grid simply by referring to the basic facts and theories from the textbook. For other bullet points, and to meet the general points listed at the top of the grid, it is necessary to relate the facts and theories to your chosen business. The best way of researching and writing this assignment is to combine the two approaches and apply the facts and theories to your chosen business as you write about them. That is the approach taken below.

For E1 and E2

For E1 and E2, you are expected to give a brief summary of two theories:

- Competitive advantage
- Economies of scale

You will also need to give the main details of the most important EU Acts that relate to these theories and to the creation of a free market in the EU:

- The Treaty of Rome (1957)
- The Single European Act (1986)
- The Treaty on European Union (1992) – Maastricht Treaty

You will need to explain how the developments in the EU have led to a greater opportunity for free trade, the benefits of comparative advantage and economies of scale. You must also outline any problems and threats that the development of the EU has created. These benefits and threats need to be considered in general terms *and* with specific reference to your chosen business. There are also other important acts and regulations that affect free trade and these might also be considered.

For E3

For E3, you need to produce a brief description of the size and main characteristics of the market that your chosen business is operating in the EU. You should produce figures to show the size and nature of the market. You should include these details:

- The size of the market that the business is already in
- The potential size of the EU market, and figures for new countries that might be joining
- A map showing the location of the current and future EU countries and, if possible, details of where the main markets are
- Some details of basic facts about different EU countries and the EU as a whole. Include these details:
  - Population figures, numbers, density, age, location, etc.
  - GDP totals, GDP/head, distribution of income, etc.

- Standard of living including GDP/head but also other measure such as the number of cars, telephones, hospital beds, etc., per 1000 people
- The relative development of the economy

These factors will all create potential opportunities and threats for your chosen business and you should comment on how each of these factors is likely to affect your business as you write about each factor. You should also consider the threats created by EU businesses selling their products in the UK and competing directly with your chosen business.

For E4, C1 and A1

You should now consider all of the sections dealt with above and recommend how your chosen business should react so as to take advantage of the opportunities available from being a member of the EU and what actions it should take to deal with the potential threats (**E4**). As you do this, you should justify these recommendations; for example, if you had suggested expanding into Spain and Portugal, or lowering the price so as to keep the markets your business has in France, you must explain why this is the best action. This justification will allow you to gain **C1**.

Any action that you recommend is likely to require some change in strategy by the business. You need to explain what change in strategy is needed (and hence you will need first to outline the current strategy) and explain what effects this will have on the way that the business operates. For example, if the business currently sells only into Germany and Austria using distributors and you recommend that it will sell into France, Spain and Portugal with its own retail outlets, the strategy will become one of direct selling and the business will have to stock and run shops abroad with its own staff (trained in foreign languages, cultural practices, etc.) or staff recruited from the home countries (and trained to sell in the way that the UK business expects).

Developing new strategies and procedures is challenging, which is why this is graded at **A1**.

For E5

There are many EU policies that affect UK businesses. To fully meet the requirements of **E5**, you should look at a range of these policies, including economic, social, regional and environmental. In particular, you should consider the impact of these policies:

- Monetary policy but, in particular, the introduction of the single currency
- Competition policy
- Social policy including the requirements of the Social Chapter

You will need to describe the main features of each of these policies and the effects that they are having on UK business in general, and on your chosen business in particular. You should consider both positive and negative effects of these policies.

For E6, C2 and A1

For these, you must consider the effects of the policies on your chosen business and recommend how the business should react. Your recommendations must ensure that the business remains competitive. Some reactions, such as introducing the minimum wage must be obeyed because they are the law but, to ensure that the business remains competitive, you might suggest that it concentrates on improving the quality of the products so that customers will buy them, even if prices have to rise to cover the minimum wage.

A basic statement of how the business should react to each of the major policy measures will gain **E6**. Explaining why your recommendations will work and justifying why they are the best for the business will gain **C2**. For this section, you should also consider how these changes will affect motivation in the business.

To gain **A1** you will need to explain how the business will have to change its basic strategies and explain what effects this will have on the way that the business operates. For example, how will the business improve the quality of its products and if this, and the minimum wage, causes and increase in price, how will it persuade its customers to continue buying the products?

For E7

For this, you need to outline basic cultural differences and similarities between countries. You should then explain how it is possible to group countries together because of the similarities, and how this makes marketing in the EU easier. Differences and similarities could be considered in terms of these factors:

- The different economic factors that affect the people, e.g., their levels of income
- The demographic factors, e.g., the age, family size, whether they live in cities or the country
- The common lifestyles and buying behaviour, e.g., whether men and women both work, to what age students remain at school or college, whether shops close at lunchtime, whether people buy fast food and convenience foods or cook full meals for the family, their main sporting activities, and how they spend their evenings
- The way that different countries carry out their business, e.g., whether goods sold direct or through retailers, whether businesses are small family businesses or large national businesses, whether management in the businesses is formal or informal

There have been many studies on Europe, which have considered common characteristics in different countries and you need to consider some of these in your write up. Here are two examples of such studies:

- Ronan and Shenkar
- Hoefstede

Reference to some of these can be found on the internet, for example at www.mv.helsinki.fi/home/kiriakos/text.htm

For E8, C3 & A1

For these, you will need to recommend how your business should deal with the differences that are found in different parts of the EU. In some cases, the need to make changes is obvious. Details about the product will need to be written in the target language, prices may need to be adjusted to cater for people with higher and lower incomes. Other changes may be less obvious. Do different countries think about colours in a different way and will certain advertisements offend certain cultures?

For **E8**, you will need to state which features of your business's products will need to be changed and which can be kept the same. You should consider a range of features:

- The quality of the product
- The price of the product
- How it will be promoted
- How it will be sold, direct, through retailers, etc.
- What name should be used and how the customers are likely to react to the name
- Whether a different marketing mix will be needed for each country, whether countries can be grouped together with the same mix or whether one mix could be used for all EU countries

For **C3**, you will need to justify the changes you are suggesting or, where you have recommended no changes, justify why that is the best approach. It is likely that you will suggest that some features need changing and that others do not. Where features do need changing, this will require a new strategy for the business and new practices. Justifying the new strategy and explaining how that will lead to a new way of marketing, etc. will meet the requirements of **A1**.

For E9, C4 and A2

Your investigation should be well planned, well researched and well presented. To gain the final bullets in each column of the Assessment Evidence grid, you will need to give a detailed list of all of the sources of information you have used (**E9**). You should provide a full list in a bibliography at the end of your work. You should also indicate in the text what your source of information is as you write about it. This can be done by putting a reference to the source next to what you have written – this should done with tables of data, quotations, etc. – or by using footnotes.

When you present your findings, you should present them using a well set out format with headings, paragraphs, sensible font sizes, etc., but also using diagrams, maps, tables, graphs, etc. as appropriate. Making the presentation look professional is why this skill will be awarded **C4**.

It is very important, if you are going to cover all the research and writing up required, that you plan all parts of your work carefully, from choosing the right business and collecting all the data to writing it up accurately and presenting it well. For **A2**, you will need to evaluate how well you carried out your assignment and this should include answers to the following kinds of question:

- How was the business chosen? Was it the right business? How reliable was the data that business provided? Was any data withheld and how did that affect what you could write about? Would a different business have provided better data?
- What sources of information were used for the basic data about the countries? Was the data cross-checked with other sources to ensure that is was accurate? Did it need to be cross-checked?
- Did you adapt any of the data, selecting only part of it, changing the way it was presented, etc? Why did you do this? How did this improve the data?
- How good was your time planning? Could you have made better use of your time and how would that have affected the standard and accuracy of your investigation?

ACKNOWLEDGEMENTS

We are grateful to the following for permission to reproduce copyright material:

- © European Communities, 1995-2001 (olive oil advert, page 21)
- AltaVista (screen shot of web site, page 186)
- Body Shop (logo, page 64)
- BP Amoco plc (advert, page 22)
- Cambridge Technology Partners (advert, page 33)
- Colgate-Palmolive UK Limited (toothpaste slogan "Teeth so healthy they shine" and "Ultra white, ultra fresh", page 73)
- Corel Corporation (screen shot, Bryce, page 179)
- Crown copyright material is reproduced with the permission of the controller of HMSO and the Queen's Crown copyright (DTI 'The Single Market', page 250) printer for Scotland (Figure 2.2.1, page 64; screen shot of HM Treasury web site, page 186)
- Dixons Group plc (screen shot of web site, page 186)
- Glaxo Smith Kline, as owners of Aquafresh, Macleans and Sensodyne (toothpaste slogans "All-in-one protection", "No other anti-bacterial toothpaste cleans better", "Clinically proven relief from pain of sensitive teeth" and "Effective treatment for the pain of sensitive teeth", page 73)
- Guardian Newpapers Ltd (advert, page 20; an extract adapted from "Any bombs, knives, Pepsi?" by Vivek Chaudhary published in *The Guardian* 18 September 2000 © The Guardian 2000, page 34)
- Independent Newspapers UK Limited (extract adapted from "Cereal killer: There's a big cat in court as Kellogg sues Exxon" by Leo Lewis published in *The Independent on Sunday* 22 October 2000, page 48)
- Microsoft Corporation (screen shots, pages 165, 168, 170, 171, 172, 173, 176, 177, 178, 179, 181, 184, 188, 189, 190)
- OECD (Figure 6.3.1, page 271)
- Procter & Gamble UK (toothpast slogan "Fights decay, tartar and plaque bacteria that can cause gum problems", page 73)
- Room For Two (logo, page 65)
- Saga (advert, page 20)
- Sainsburys (extract adapted from their website www.sainsbury.co.uk, page 75)
- Tesco Stores Limited (advert, page 58; toothpaste slogan "Toothpaste for a clean sensation", page 73; screen shot of web site, page 191)
- The *Economist* (article, page 22)
- *The Sunday Times* (advert, page 20)
- Vaughan Data Systems (Beetle Reckoning advert, page 86)
- WHSmith plc (customer comment card, page 92)
- Wizcom (advert, page 47)

We are grateful to the following for permission to reproduce copyright photographs:

- Ace Photo Agency (Rome, page 244)
- Greg Evans International (ship, page 75; interview, page 89)
- Paul Mulcahy (shoe, page 65)
- Pictor International/Image State Picture (modem, page 182)
- Rex Features (Pet rock [Al Freni/Timepix], page 54; Sinclair C5, page 55; Figure 4.1.3, page 163; buying wine, page 245)

INDEX